Reading with Lincoln

Reading with
LINCOLN

ROBERT BRAY

Southern Illinois University Press
Carbondale and Edwardsville

13   12   11   10   4   3   2   1

Library of Congress Cataloging-in-Publication Data
Bray, Robert C.
Reading with Lincoln / Robert Bray.
    p. cm.
Includes bibliographical references and index.
ISBN-13: 978-0-8093-2995-3 (cloth : alk. paper)
ISBN-10: 0-8093-2995-6 (cloth : alk. paper)
ISBN-13: 978-0-8093-8589-8 (ebook)
ISBN-10: 0-8093-8589-9 (ebook)
1. Lincoln, Abraham, 1809–1865—Books and reading. 2. Lincoln,
Abraham, 1809–1865—Knowledge and learning. I. Title.
E457.2.B834 2010
973.7092—dc22   2009051430

Printed on recycled paper. ♻
The paper used in this publication meets the minimum re-
quirements of American National Standard for Information
Sciences—Permanence of Paper for Printed Library Materials,
ANSI Z39.48-1992. ∞

To Spen, for The Friendship

Contents

Preface

As I am constituted I don't love to read generally, and as I do not love to read I feel no interest in what is thus read. I don't, & can't, remember such reading. When I have a particular case in hand I have that motive, and feel an interest in the case—feel an interest in ferreting out the questions to the bottom—love to dig up the question by the roots and hold it up and dry it before the fires of the mind.
—Abraham Lincoln, quoted by William H. Herndon, in "Analysis of the Character of Abraham Lincoln"

To a professor of the liberal arts, as I have been for several decades, Abraham Lincoln's splendid self-education presents an occasion for humility. What I have long tried to accomplish with my students—better reading, better thinking, and better writing—he managed by himself, without formal schooling, and became one of the supreme communicators and leaders in United States history. My label for the public Lincoln is "political artist." That is, he used his reading to help him speak and write with greater authority; and this verbal authority allowed him to reach the American people and to lead them through the national crisis of the Civil War.

This study intends, by considering closely those books that Lincoln is known to have "assimilated to his being" (in William H. Herndon's phrase), to explore what their contents and styles contributed to Lincoln's "liberal arts education" and thereby to his political artistry. From boyhood on, Lincoln's habit of reading concentrated a naturally powerful mind; and reading provided models of voice and diction to one who had inborn talent as a storyteller and a near-flawless memory and therefore needed only the stimulus of literary greatness, and emulative practice, to emerge as a great writer himself. When a youth, Lincoln read avidly whatever print came his way. But, as his words in the epigraph indicate, as an adult

Lincoln always read deeply rather than broadly; for a purpose rather than as a cultural habit. "General reading," he admits, "broadens the mind" and makes it "universal." But only specifically motivated reading "makes a precise deep clear mind"—a mind that may come to understand itself and the world outside. From the Bible and Shakespeare to the rude dialect humor of mid-nineteenth-century literary comedians: whenever Lincoln was moved by literature or needed its language for work, he committed his reading to memory and kept it ready for his own use, public or personal.

Reading with Lincoln owes its origin to a sabbatical leave granted by my institution, Illinois Wesleyan University, during which I completed the annotated bibliography "What Abraham Lincoln Read" (published in the *Journal of the Abraham Lincoln Association*, 2007) and began the book; for its completion, I am indebted to the encouragement of friends in the community of Lincoln scholars, especially Michael Burlingame and Douglas L. Wilson, both of whom kindly read drafts of chapters and urged me to persevere with a subject they thought important to Lincoln studies. I thank as well Robert S. Eckley, Guy Fraker, and Jerry Stone, each of whom read and helped me improve subchapters on Lincoln's study of the law and political economy. Finally, Sylvia Frank Rodrigue, executive editor of Southern Illinois University Press, has assisted me greatly in revising and polishing the manuscript into its final form.

1. The Sometime Schoolboy

He was a Constant and I may Say Stubborn reader.
— *Dennis Hanks*, *in* Herndon's Informants

How and when did Abraham Lincoln learn to read and write? Family tradition, as conveyed by Lincoln's cousin-once-removed, Dennis Hanks, gave Nancy Hanks Lincoln the credit for teaching her young son his letters. She also read to him from the Bible. But if she coached her son in his own first reading, this is about as far as her homeschooling could have gone, for she was at best semiliterate (i.e., could read a little but not write).[1] Local Hardin County, Kentucky, folk-memory had the boy and his older sister, Sarah, trudging several miles from their Knob Creek farm to the schoolhouse of one Zachariah Riney, known as "Monk" because of his Roman Catholicism. The Lincolns' attendance lasted no more than two months during the year 1815 and probably less.[2] Hanks also remembered his younger relative's attending school "with his Sister Sally on Knobb Cr in Hardin Co Ky some 3 or 4 weeks when he was 6 or 7 years old."[3] The schoolmaster there was named Caleb Hazel. His qualifications, according to his friend Samuel Haycraft, consisted of "large size & bodily Strength to thrash any boy or youth that came to his School."[4] Whether the boy Lincoln got the taste of the *hazel* switch on his backside is not known (though likely); but, as Hanks recalled, he did get from the imposing Caleb at least some little assistance in "his letters ABC—spelling reading & writing &c." According to Hanks, these few weeks comprised the total of his Kentucky schooling—"all the Education he had in Ky."[5] If we add a single term with Hazel to that with Riney, two months is the maximum of Lincoln's "formal" education in his native state.

He used two spelling textbooks, probably in this order: Thomas Dilworth's *New Guide to the English Tongue* (1740), a British speller that had

been popular in America since well before independence; and Noah Webster's *New American Spelling Book*, widely known as "Old Blueback" from
the color of its paper-covered boards. Webster followed the hugely successful format of Dilworth: both, naturally enough, began with the alphabet
and proceeded through pronunciation, syllables, one-, two-, three-syllable
words, and so on—and columns and columns of such words to say and
spell. Although most of the spellers' pages were taken up by these lists of
words, they contained as well a modest amount of supplementary material: fables with crude woodblock illustrations, "select sentences" in prose
and verse for reading aloud, and (in Dilworth) a short English grammar
in the form of a catechism:

Q: What is Grammar?
A: Grammar is the Science of Letters. . . .[6]

Webster contained a section devoted to rectifying country dialect to a
national (New England) standard: *follow*, not *foller*; *hollow*, not *holler*; and
the like.[7] Common to the spellers was a relentless Christian edification
in the "lessons of easy words, to teach children to read and to know their
duty." Webster was thoroughly Calvinist and evangelical:

Q: *What is a pure heart?*
A: A heart free from all bad desires, and inclined to conform to the divine
will in all things.
Q: *Should a man's intentions as well as his actions be good?*
A: Most certainly. Actions cannot be called *good*, unless they proceed from
good motives.[8]

Much more amiable, however, is the following, nicely balanced eighteenth-century maxim: "Some men read for the purpose of learning to
write; others for the purpose of learning to talk—the former study for the
sake of science; the latter, for the sake of amusement." For young Lincoln,
this was not an either/or but a both/and proposition: very early in his life
he was assiduously acquiring "science" and at the same time learning
how to hold an audience with amusing talk. In a time and place where
books were as rare as specie money, the contents of nothing printed that
he happened to see were lost on him. Psalms in Dilworth, for instance;
starting with "words of one syllable" ("He that fears not God is in the way
to Death") and moving upward in difficulty, we arrive at this: "The Fear
of the Lord is clean, and endureth forever: The Judgments of the Lord are
alway Righteous and True."[9] The King James *altogether* has become *alway*,

but the verse from Psalm 19 that will ring out a half-century later in the Second Inaugural is now early fixed in this young reader's mind.

After the family moved to Spencer County, Indiana, in 1816, Lincoln had the odd chance for a bit more instruction, eventually comprising the scant "one year" total that he admitted in the Scripps autobiography.[10] Nathaniel Grigsby, Lincoln's friend and then his relation by marriage, provided Herndon with this rude description of their even ruder Indiana neighborhood's first schoolhouse, two miles to the south of the Lincoln farm: "The house was built of round logs Just high enough for a man to stand erect under the ruff, the floore was split logs or what we call punchens the chimney was maid of poles and clay the window was constructed by chopping out a part of tow logs and plasing peeases of split bords at proper distence and then we could take our old copy books and grease them and paste them over the windows this give us lite[.]" Not much light, but at least the well-greased and marked copybooks may have kept out most of the bugs. From this humble Indiana beginning, there followed two more schools under two more masters. But wherever Lincoln studied and with whom, Grigsby recalled, "he was always at school early and atentive to his studies he aways was at the head of his cllass he progessed rapedly in all of his studies[.]"[11] These primitive institutions were "blab schools"—where pupils stood and either read aloud from their textbooks, passing them from hand to hand since the books were few in number, or recited in unison, repeating after the master or a lead student. Hardly an environment conducive to learning, we might think, and painful drudgery for the boys and girls; yet Lincoln managed out of his year or less of schooling the abilities of "*readin, writin, and cipherin*' to the Rule of Three,'" as he wrote to his friend Jesse Fell in 1859.[12]

One of the funniest stories Lincoln ever told drew upon his "blab school" days, either as a genuine memory or from having heard someone else relate it. He spun the yarn for Missouri senator John B. Henderson, who was visiting the White House (probably in the early part of 1862). The pupils, as he remembered from so long ago, were standing in a recitation line, doing Bible verses in turn, and one boy was unfortunate enough to draw the tale of the "burning fiery furnace" from the Book of Daniel (chapter 3)—featuring the three faithful Hebrews with hard-to-pronounce names. Well, he "stumbled on Shadrach, floundered on Meshach, and went all. to pieces on Abednego." Which predictably brought him a head cuffing from the schoolmaster; which just as predictably (this is a well-crafted story, after all) left the boy "wailing and blubbering" as the book moved on down the line. He finally quieted down, but just in time to foresee what was inexorably coming back at him: "Then, like a thunder-clap out of the sky, he set up a wail that alarmed the master." What's wrong now, son? Pointing to the inescapable progress of the text, he cried, "Look marster . . . there comes them same three fellers again!" And for his audience of one, Lincoln was able to seal the humor by beckoning Henderson to the window and pointing out three men approaching the White House door: Charles Sumner, Henry Wilson, and Thaddeus Stevens—radical antislavery Republicans who had been hounding the president over emancipation just like "them same three fellers" had returned to vex the little boy.[13]

Most of Lincoln's precocious development as a reader took place outside of school. There were few books to be had, all in private hands (there was as yet no public library in Spencer County),[14] but these few Lincoln evidently pursued doggedly. Among the titles thought to have been of especial importance to him were *Aesop's Fables*, John Bunyan's *Pilgrim's Progress*, Mason Locke Weems's *Life of George Washington*, Daniel Defoe's *Robinson Crusoe*, and *The Arabian Nights*. Standard textbooks included Nicholas Pike's *The Complete New System of Arithmetick* (1804), and Nathan Daboll's *Schoolmaster's Assistant* (1817), also an arithmetic.[15]

Likewise important was a genre of books often known as *preceptors*. Rather than basic "how-to" manuals, these were anthologies of fable, history, essays, and poetry intended to provide *precepts* (i.e., morals) for young readers. But they also offered *examples* of effective ways of expression. Most central to the education of Lincoln were Lindley Murray's *English Reader* (1799), *The Columbian Class Book* (1824), compiled by Abraham T. Lowe, along with the locally printed (and edited?) *Kentucky Preceptor* (1812).

Louis Warren puts Lincoln's study of Murray's *English Reader* in the early adolescent years, perhaps in association with his few months at James Swaney's school. Excepting the Bible and Bunyan, of the dozen or so books Lincoln was definitely known to have read in Indiana, Murray's *English Reader* would have been the easiest to procure. It was immensely, lastingly popular (by 1850 the book had U.S. sales exceeding 6.5 million copies).[16] According to Herndon, Lincoln judged *The English Reader* "the best schoolbook ever put into the hands of an American youth."[17] Clearly, if Lincoln was still praising a textbook he had read decades before, Murray must have made a very deep impression upon him. But why did Lincoln judge it the *best* among the several literacy textbooks he read? As Murray, the "compiler," noted in his preface, "The language of the pieces chosen for this collection, has been carefully regarded. Purity, propriety, perspicuity, and, in many instances, elegance of diction, distinguish them." And all of the readings sustain the objects of the book: "to improve youth in the art of reading; to meliorate their language and sentiments; and to inculcate some of the most important principles of piety and virtue."[18]

This "three-P's" approach—*purity, propriety, and perspicuity*—Murray had taken directly from Hugh Blair's *Lectures on Rhetoric and Belles-Lettres* (1793), for nearly half a century one of the most authoritative and influential texts on the subject.[19] Blair was an eighteenth-century Scottish Protestant clergyman and professor, whose sermons and university lectures were thought in their day to be theologically liberal and philosophical (he knew and corresponded frequently with David Hume). Murray's considerable debt to Blair is fully acknowledged, both in the long introductory essay, "Principles of Good Reading," and in the anthology's many extracts reprinted from Blair's moral and theological writings.

Would Lincoln have read, approvingly, these little homilies (rarely more than two pages long) by a Presbyterian divine? This is an unavoidable question, as Murray includes thirty-six such, out of a total of eighty-one prose pieces, and it is difficult to imagine Lincoln's so liking *The English Reader* without liking Blair. At least to the extent that Blair advanced "golden rule" ethics and was free of evangelical or proselytizing cant (which even then Lincoln ridiculed?), Lincoln would have taken such pieces at face value. Murray evidently regarded Blair as the perfect model of high moral seriousness propelled by a fine, clear style. All the essays were didactic yet never bigoted and for the most part unsullied by self-righteousness.[20] For instance, in an effective two-paragraph essay on forgiveness, Blair begins with a statement that could easily pass for deistic or stoic: "The most plain and natural sentiments of equity concur with divine authority, to enforce the duty of forgiveness." Only the person who has "never in his life done wrong" has the elect status of "remaining inexorable." And there is no such human. We must all "consider forgiveness as a debt we owe to others." Otherwise, under the baleful influence of passionate resentment, the unbreakable cycle of revenge would tear the polis apart and destine both the hater and the hated to unhappiness. Christ's forbearance ought to be our model here, for "revenge dwells in little minds."[21] Here, then, was *reasonable religion.* "Christ" came into the matter not as redeemer but as the ethical teacher (preceptor) known as Jesus.

In a thematically complementary piece, entitled "On the Evils which flow from unrestrained Passions," Blair continued his edification on this subject. "When man revolted from his Maker," he wrote, "his passions rebelled against himself; and, from being originally the ministers of reason, have become the tyrants of the soul." From this rather Miltonic version of the Fall onward, it has been all down-mountain for humankind; passions rule, unless we can train our minds to resist their importunities: "The great object which we ought to propose to ourselves is, to acquire a firm and stedfast mind, which the infatuation of passion shall not seduce, nor its violence shake; which, resting on fixed principles, shall, in the midst of contending emotions, remain free, and master of itself." For Blair—as for the Lincoln of the 1838 Lyceum Address—the "misrule of passion" is the cardinal threat to liberty and happiness: "It is this which poisons the enjoyment of individuals, overturns the order of society, and strews the path of life with so many miseries, as to render it indeed the vale of tears." Having begun orthodoxly, with the Fall as Our Fault, Blair offers *not* the usual evangelical invitation to spiritual cleansing—being born again and baptized—but the regimen of reason: "to acquire a firm and stedfast mind."[22]

Beyond Blair, Lincoln might have objected to a number of the selections in *The English Reader*. While Murray was born in America and, though a Tory forced into exile after the Revolution, always identified himself as such, he included no "American" literary extracts. Except for a very few translations from the classics, all the selections were British, and for the most part either in pietistic or elevated Addisonian prose. The book was too serious for too long: no comic relief in the form of fables or, God forbid, jokes and puns. Samuel Johnson held forth on "Schemes of Life Often Illusory" and "The Vanity of Riches," while Joseph Addison demonstrated the perfection of his *Spectator* style in fourteen pieces (ten of poetry), including "Omniscience and Omnipresence of the Deity" and "On the Immortality of the Soul."

The English Reader's poetry was restricted to middling works of the seventeenth and eighteenth centuries, with occasional bows to Milton and Pope, as the best representatives, respectively, of sublime blank verse and the heroic couplet. The anthology offered no Chaucer or Shakespeare, almost nothing from seventeenth-century lyric poetry. By contrast, James Thomson's mid-eighteenth-century verse was prominently on display (eight selections, mostly from *The Seasons*, as opposed to a single extract from Thomas Gray's "Ode to Adversity"); and but few predawn signs of the radioactive Romantic sunrise that was about to burn new eyes into readers of English poetry—no William Blake, no William Wordsworth, or Samuel Taylor Coleridge, although their earliest work had recently appeared and could have been available to Murray. True, William Cowper, who was well-represented in *The English Reader* (nine selections) is sometimes thought of as a precursor of English Romanticism, and Murray included verse by minor, late-eighteenth-century Scots poets, though Robert Burns, whose work Lincoln would soon come to love, was absent from the anthology.[23]

One of the selections from Cowper *does* stand out from its context. In 1782 he had published a book-length blank-verse poem entitled *The Task*. This was a sentimental combination of personal narrative, ruralism, and sociopolitical commentary: from a deepening sense of disgust with London's moral depravity and what Cowper saw as the British government's rebarbative behavior on most matters foreign and domestic, he, a man of sensibility, retires to the country to enjoy leisure and nature. In this sense, *The Task* resembles an extended pastoral—yet one equally concerned with moral and political reform. Here is the close of a long verse paragraph decrying slavery in the British Empire:

> I had much rather be myself the slave,
> And wear the bonds, than fasten them on him.
> We have no slaves at home—Then why abroad?
> And they themselves once ferried o'er the wave
> That parts us are emancipate and loosed.
> Slaves cannot breathe in England; if their lungs
> Receive our air, that moment they are free;
> They touch our country, and their shackles fall.
> That's noble, and bespeaks a nation proud
> And jealous of the blessing. Spread it then,
> And let it circulate through every vein
> Of all your empire; that, where Britain's power
> Is felt, mankind may feel her mercy too.[24]

Besides possibly being the first blank verse Lincoln had read, he faced here a commanding literary assault *against slavery*. Cowper not only denounced the British slave trade on humanist moral grounds, with no appeal to Christianity; in addition, he called, in ringing verse periods, for an end to racial prejudice against the stolen, maltreated Africans and, indeed, for the entire abolition of slavery across the empire. We may imagine Lincoln at sixteen, looking across the Ohio toward Kentucky or ferrying passengers and provender back and forth from bank to bank, and learning that what was true of Cowper's England—

> if their lungs
> Receive our air, that moment they are free;
> They touch our country, and their shackles fall

—ought to be true as well for Indiana and the Old Northwest, and one day for the nation.

That which Lincoln would have admired in moderation in *The English Reader* he may have found tiresome upon reiteration: moral seriousness as the chief component, but without the balancing spices of style and flavors of humor. Thus it is fair to conclude that, on the grounds of its pedagogical method and—though this is far less certain—its selections, *The English Reader* would not have seemed to Lincoln "the best schoolbook ever put into the hands of an American youth." Yet Murray's introduction, "Observations on the Principles of Good Reading," provides an argument for reading that would have appealed to Lincoln's dual nature as humorist and man of sorrows: "To read with propriety," Murray announces in the opening sentence of the introduction, "is a pleasing and important attainment; productive of improvement both to the understanding and the heart." Even more important, careful reading was the key to effective communication, in speech and writing, "of ideas and feelings."[25]

Murray assumes that such mastery requires development of skill in reading aloud to an audience. The schoolmaster can help, of course, but a pupil such as Lincoln, almost never in school, could use *The English Reader* as a means of self-tutelage. And he probably did just that. The introduction presents nine categories of voice training: "Proper loudness of voice; Distinctness; Slowness; Propriety of pronunciation; Emphasis; Tones; Pauses; and Mode of reading verse."[26] To each of these in turn, Murray accords a clear, commonsense analysis that conveys useful information to a performative reader such as Lincoln would become. If one possessed by nature a high voice, such as Lincoln's "blue-grass tenor," it was important to realize that this "key" (pitch) was a different sort of thing from *loudness*. That is, the higher-pitched voice could project farther without excessive and tiring volume from the speaker's mouth. Whether in the schoolroom or outdoors, before a small group or a vast crowd, the good reader learns to employ no greater level of loudness than will distinctly communicate to the audience. Similarly, careful articulation ("distinctness") empowers even a weak voice to outperform a strong one, since a phrase not clearly enunciated is meaningless, no matter how forcibly projected. Reading too fast or too slow can ruin the effect of the oral interpretation, so "moderation is requisite with regard to the speed of pronouncing," since precipitant speed "confounds all articulation," while "a lifeless drawling . . . must render every such performance insipid and fatiguing." Pronunciation and emphasis are related difficulties: our tongue's markedly accented syllabication requires the student to do dictionary work to discover where the accents properly fall in words; and emphasis must follow accurate pronunciation for multisyllabic words and be used judiciously with others in order to fix the meaning of a sentence. Murray illustrates this point by altering three of the emphases in the opening lines of Milton's *Paradise Lost*:

> Of man's first disobedience, and the fruit
> Of that forbidden tree, whose mortal taste
> Brought death into the world, and all our woe . . .

Emphasize *man's*, *first*, and *death* successively, and the meaning of the lines changes respectively.

This section on emphasis is the longest in the introduction (five pages), showing the eighteenth century's fascination with *italics* as printed cues for emphasizing words, especially in antitheses or balanced syntax ("A *friend* exaggerates a man's *virtue*; an *enemy*, his *crimes*"). This instance of rhetoric and oral interpretation working in synergy made an important lesson. Lincoln's own written and spoken *emphases* were not generally used so nobly. In his earlier Illinois rhetoric (1830s and 1840s), Lincoln was fond of invective and could bother an opponent with all the sorts of bites and stings along the continuum between mildest irony and most vicious sarcasm. Occasionally he did so frequently enough to deserve Murray's monition against "multiplying emphatical words too much." When he struck in print, Lincoln often provided a liberal peppering of italics to guide his audience to a proper "mental hearing" of his words, as in this closing denunciation from his 1837 "First Reply to James Adams": "I have a character to defend as well as Gen. Adams, but I disdain to *whine* about it as he does. It is true I have no children nor *Kitchen boys*; and if I had, I should scorn to lug them in to make affidavits for me."[27] Telling an opponent not to *whine* is familiar enough, but without knowing the specifics of the contention between Lincoln and Adams, the reader is not likely to understand the phrase *Kitchen boys;* yet the contempt is nonetheless conveyed by the italics.[28]

In Murray's view, "there is not an act of the mind, an exertion of the fancy, or an emotion of the heart, which has not its peculiar tone, or note of the voice, by which it is to be expressed; and which is suited exactly to the degree of internal feeling."[29] When reading another author's composition, the trick is to perceive its intended tone and modulate your voice accordingly; with one's own work, the challenge lies more in the writing than the reading: discovering and embodying just the right tone with which to address the subject. Though Murray says almost nothing about the art of writing, he evidently understands its mutually energizing connection with reading. *Tone of voice* is as relevant to *writing style* as to *oral interpretation*. Writers must find a way to *encode* both meaning (semantics and syntax) and music (style and rhetoric), carried as it were in multiplex on the same linguistic wave. And readers must have the equal skill to *decode* the complex whole with as few errors as possible. Having succeeded, they are then free to write, and so the cycle continues. Lincoln learned his letters, learned to read and to perform. At some point in this process, initiated, we are told, by Nancy Hanks Lincoln's teaching her son the alphabet, continuing from simple to complex books read in and out of school, silently in solitude, "publicly" to his peers, he began to write from his reading—a lifelong habit.

In one of his earlier letters to Herndon (December 1865), Dennis Hanks recalled a book that Thomas Lincoln had bought for his son: "the united States Speaker." This was probably *The American Speaker: A Selection of Popular, Parliamentary and Forensic Eloquence; Particularly Calculated for the Seminaries of the United States* (1811).[30] *The American Speaker* is the least interesting of all the readers and preceptors associated with Lincoln's education. Its preface announces that "in popular governments, Eloquence generally leads to eminence"—a maxim the boy would have hoped prophetic in his case—and touts its selections as "of a character ardent and glowing," since, while "nothing ought to be substituted for reason . . . who will deny to this powerful auxiliary of the truth [i.e., declamation] . . . the whole of the impression, it has made[?]"[31] But the volume itself hardly fulfills these expectations, nor does it really seem "calculated for the seminaries of the United States." Instead, it looks very much like an English import with American additions. *The American Speaker* comprises mostly British parliamentary or public speeches from the mid- to late eighteenth century. A few of these are notable, such as Edmund Burke's (especially when he is concerned with the fate of the American colonies), but many others treat subjects a young seminarian in Indiana would neither know nor care about. There is no poetry, no humor, no narrative. Of the speeches, the only *native* ones are short declarations of injustice by purported "Indian Chiefs," of course translated and rhetorized into the "Great Father/Great Spirit" trope that was already becoming so familiar in the way the native American agon with the whites out West was written (by the whites). In addition, the book reprints a number of Washington's addresses to his troops during the Revolution and includes as well the inaugurals of Adams, Jefferson, and Madison. And then there is William Wirt's speech on Aaron Burr and Blennerhassett at Burr's trial for treason. Had he previously heard of this man and his vaulting ambition?

A number of other "preceptors" or "recitation books" have been associated with Lincoln's Indiana self-education. Among these were *The American Preceptor* (1794) and its successor volume, *The Columbian Orator* (1797), both compiled by Connecticut schoolmaster and publisher Caleb Bingham. Both of these volumes were immensely popular from publication until the Civil War. The only testimony that Lincoln knew either came from Dennis Hanks.[32] If Lincoln in his Indiana teens read *The Columbian Orator*, he would have been doing just what Frederick Douglass, as a slave and therefore surreptitiously, would do a decade later in Maryland. From his father, Lincoln stole time for reading; from his master, Douglass did likewise, much as he would later "steal himself." Through persistence and sheer secret will, these two most famous of nineteenth-century American autodidacts, whose destinies would converge during the Civil War, fashioned educations that made both of them superb political communicators. At about the age of thirteen, Douglass recalled, he "had made enough money to buy what was then a very popular school book, viz: *Columbian Orator.* He found it to be "a rich treasure," one of whose entries helped him toward an identity as a man, though still enslaved. This was the short but very pointed piece entitled "Dialogue between a Master and Slave." The slave has twice run away, twice been caught and returned. His master hotly upbraids him after the second time, "charging the slave with ingratitude. . . . [T]he slave rejoins, that he knows how little anything that he can say will avail" and thus stoically submits to his fate. "But the master, 'touched by the slave's answer,' continues the dialogue: Thus invited to the debate, the quondam slave made a spirited defense of himself, and thereafter the whole argument, for and against slavery, was brought out. The master was vanquished at every turn in the argument; and seeing himself to be thus vanquished, he generously and meekly emancipates the slave, with his best wishes for his prosperity."[33]

Looking back, Douglass remembered that the "Dialogue" had helped him imaginatively aspire to his own freedom, in the meantime keeping up his hope. For the first exercise of his newly granted freedom, the *man* speaks truth to the master's power, denouncing the institution of slavery without stint or any trace of deference to his late master.[34] The seething anger behind this "the fire next time" speech is partly explained by the name of its author, John Aikin (1747–1822), an English radical sympathetic with the Jacobins of the French Revolution (and with Tom Paine); and partly because the "Dialogue" had first appeared at the time of the Haitian Revolution, during which the bloody program of self-freed slaves' revenge against owners was being carried out, dramatically and with ultimate success in Saint-Domingue (after 1804 the nation of Haiti)—to the consternation of the entire white Western world, not least in the slaveholding parts of the United States. Douglass, in *My Bondage and My Freedom* (1855), chose not to upset his largely white audience with his own gloss on the manumitted slave's warning. But a warning it surely was, and its point would not have been missed by Lincoln if he actually did read "Dialogue between a Master and a Slave" in *The Columbian Orator.*

Two further anthologies of U.S. origin deserve a closer look: *The Columbian Class Book* and *The Kentucky Preceptor.* The former was the more substantial (350-plus pages) and higher quality collection. Its first publication in 1824 entails that Lincoln would have seen it only in his later teenage years, when his literacy was sufficient to appreciate the *Columbian* on its own, intellectually solid terms. Unusual for its type, the *Columbian,* compiled by A. T. Lowe, M.D., was not nationalistic but rather suggested through its eclectic contents the largeness of the world, omitting the purple prose, patriotic cant, or Christian didactics commonly found in the genre. The book's subtitle indicates a notable departure from previous literary texts: "Consisting of Geographical, Historical, and Biographical Extracts . . . arranged on a plan different from anything before offered to the public . . . particularly designed for the use of schools."

The *Columbian* included, in addition to standard biographies of Washington and Franklin, selections of poetry from Byron (an extract from *The Corsair*), Milton ("Lycidas"), James Thomson, William Cowper, and Edward Young as well as Alexander Pope's "Temple of Fame," a dream vision of the time-and-tide variety: "For fame, impatient of extremes, decays / Not more by envy than by excess of praise."[35] Among the prose pieces were a description of the destruction of Rome from Edward Gibbon's *History of the Decline and Fall of the Roman Empire*, a long narrative of the American Revolution, and Timothy Dwight's romantic evocation of Crawford's Notch in the White Mountains of New Hampshire, that epitome, along with Niagara Falls, of early-nineteenth-century American romantic landscape sublime. Also a modicum of philosophical and scientific readings, always interesting to Lincoln: comparative historical ethnography and geography (from the Ganges River in India, to ancient Egypt, to contemporary American Indians of the Trans-Mississippi West), an account of several famous volcanoes, and a long essay on various types of mines and mining around the world. *The Columbian Class Book* concludes with Oliver Goldsmith's "A Brief View of the Universe," a deistic paean to the wondrous artistry of "our benevolent Father," as revealed by Newtonian astronomical discoveries, but one which yet has a tinge of science fiction about it: "thousands of thousands of suns," their planets "peopled with myriads of beings, formed for endless progression in perfection and felicity!"[36]

All in all, *The Columbian Class Book* would have presented to the young man challenging and fascinating reading. Rather less so, perhaps, *The Kentucky Preceptor*, a copy of which Lincoln borrowed from Josiah Crawford, for his neighborhood a bookish man, from whom he had also borrowed David Ramsay's *Life of George Washington*, only to have it spoiled by rain— costing Lincoln the labor of three days' "pulling fodder" as recompense. That Lincoln showed the temerity to ask to borrow another of Crawford's books indicates his insatiate intellectual hunger. As the compiler of *The Kentucky Preceptor* (known only as "a teacher") expressed in the preface, "The great importance of having proper books put into the hands of the rising generation, at an early period of life, must be sufficiently evident to every reflecting mind"—the sort of generalization Lincoln would prove fond of in his own writing—since "every reflecting mind" knew that the "future prosperity of [the] country" was staked on education. The high moral and patriotic purpose of education meant that the choice of "proper books" for the youth of the American Republic was crucial: only the best authors who have written the best things should be allowed to speak to the nation's coming generation. No romances, no "tales of love," or anything else that might water "the effeminacy of a corrupted nobility." Rather, *The Kentucky Preceptor* would provide heartier fare for all "industrious republicans."[37]

The Kentucky Preceptor was heavy on the didactic and the democratic and, like Murray, unrelievedly humorless. Still, Lincoln found between the cardboard covers of this small-sized, ill-printed book two pieces of writing that would resonate with him all his life: Thomas Jefferson's "First Inaugural Address" and Thomas Gray's "Elegy Written in a Country Churchyard"—the poem from which Lincoln would provide John Locke Scripps an epigraph for his ancestry and upbringing: "The short and simple annals of the poor."[38] This single, dirgelike line of slow-moving iambic pentameter carried a beast of burden's heavy load in Lincoln's memory: what it said was true, and it was sad. Louis A. Warren thought that Lincoln had read *The Kentucky Preceptor* during his "later adolescent years," by which he apparently meant during and after 1824.[39] He would by then have been capable of handling the language of Gray's poem. But would he have understood it? Because of his maturing recognition of his own humble social status, yes. And Jefferson's statement of the American "creed of our political faith" based on equality before the law might have been the foundation of his own "political religion" as preached in the Lyceum Address.[40]

The Kentucky Preceptor contains a number of less important texts that might also have caught Lincoln's attention. Appertaining to his melancholy were these three verses from Ecclesiastes 7:3–5, part of a series of "selected sentences" for emulation in morals and style: "Sorrow is better than laughter; for by the sadness of the countenance the heart is made better. The heart of the wise is in the house of mourning, but the heart of fools is in the house of mirth. It is better to hear the rebuke of the wise, than for a man to hear the song of fools."[41]

More animating was the epigraph on the title page of the volume, from James Thomson's *The Seasons* (1726), "Spring":

> Delightful task! to rear the tender thought,
> To teach the young idea how to shoot,
> To pour the fresh instruction o'er the mind
> To breathe the enlivening spirit, and to fix
> The generous purpose in the glowing breast.

Most interesting of all might have been the two short pieces against slavery: "The Desperate Negro" and "Liberty and Slavery." The first of these is a melodramatic narrative about an African male slave named Quashi who had grown up as his master's playmate and then been made a black driver of blacks when he became an adult. Quashi was a devoted slave, having always paid assiduous attention to his duties: "In short, here was the most delicate, yet most strong, and seemingly indissoluble tie, that could bind master and slave together." The young owner of the plantation was, however, a stickler for discipline and "inexorable" with the slaves when "a fault was committed." In the course of his duties, Quashi made an unnamed mistake and came due for a "cart-whipping." To save "the smoothness of his skin," he hid among his fellows and went always armed with a knife (another transgression) until he might find someone to intercede with his master. But the former playmates, now both in their physical primes, unexpectedly met: there followed a scuffle; Quashi ended up on top, knife poised to strike. After vindicating himself against the charges, he drew "the knife with all his strength across his own throat" and fell dead on his master's bosom, "bathing him in his blood."[42]

The second narrative, "Liberty and Slavery," was a sort of prose poem in which the narrator imagined what it must be like to spend one's life imprisoned in slavery. Though not explicitly racial, or connected to slavery in the United States, the picture was tragic enough. "I sat down close by my table," the narrator recalled, "and, leaning my head upon my hand, I began to figure to myself the miseries of confinement. I was in a right frame for it, and so I gave full scope to my imagination." The phrase "figure to myself" strikingly suggests some of the word-portraits of Lincoln in deep abstraction that have come down to us from his friends (such as Henry C. Whitney's candid courtroom snapshot: "It appeared as if he was pursuing in his mind some specific, sad subject, regularly and systematically through various sinuosities, and his sad face would assume, at times, deeper phases of grief: but no relief came from dark and despairing melancholy, till he was roused by the breaking up of court, when he emerged from his cave of gloom and came back, like one awakened from sleep, to the world in which he lived, again").[43] The first-person voice in "Liberty and Slavery" thought "to begin with the millions of my fellow creatures born to no inheritance but slavery." But such a vast picture would not come into focus, so instead he sketched a single manacled slave, pitifully hopeless in an obscure dungeon, who added, though ultimately pointless the labor, one stick to a pile for each day passed in the wretched sameness of captivity (he had been confined for thirty years). The scene thus imagined proved too moving for its maker: "I saw the iron enter into his soul—I burst into tears.—I could not sustain the picture . . . which my fancy had drawn."[44]

It is quite possible that these two pieces from *The Kentucky Preceptor*, along with the antislavery passage from Cowper's *The Task* in *The English Reader*, were Lincoln's earliest *literary* encounters with slavery. And in the case of "The Desperate Negro," he was probably reading his first story about African chattel slavery in the United States. Though two were of negligible quality as art, all three pieces gave thoroughly negative representations of the institution—no extenuations or apologetics for slavery here. As the preface to *The Kentucky Preceptor* asserts, the mind's *first* is often its "most lasting impression." So if Warren is correct in placing this book among Lincoln's young adult reading, he might well have had Cowper, "The Desperate Negro," and "Liberty and Slavery" firmly in mind before and during his first flatboat trip to New Orleans (December 1828–March 1829). According to Allen Gentry, the other member of the two-man crew, after they had docked and sold their cargo, he and Lincoln walked around the city, happening upon a slave auction, "and Abraham was very angry." Gentry is also reportedly the source of the *first* version of Lincoln's almost scripturally famous declaration—because poetically prophetic out of the mouth of the future martyr—that "if I ever get a chance to hit this thing I'll hit it hard."[45] If this is all a bit too neatly hagiographic, at least the *reading* part helps us understand the truth of the strongly antislavery foundation of Lincoln's character. He had seen it first in Kentucky, though as a small boy. He could see it still looking (or ferrying) across the Ohio from Indiana, though at a distance. Reading and New Orleans brought slavery close to the imagination and to the senses: too close for comfort when Lincoln and Gentry had to fight off a gang of seven slaves trying to rob their boat at "Madame Duchesne's" plantation somewhere "just below Baton Rouge."[46] By the time he turned twenty, while riding upriver on a steamboat back toward home, Lincoln had learned from experience that slavery was real, from reading that it was wrong.

He drank but little, swore not at all, and didn't smoke or chew. He was morally serious and kept to himself, especially when reading or thinking, which was much of the time. Yet on occasion, especially with the boys on Sundays in the woods, he dwelt carelessly in the House of Mirth. As Albert J. Beveridge observed, "he was no prig . . . and had faults extremely human, such as his love for a certain type of anecdote—a taste which he never overcame and the expression of which . . . was so marked a feature of his manhood and so shocking to the eminent men among whom he did his historic work."[47] Beveridge meant here Lincoln's proclivity for telling dirty jokes. Like Warren, he seemed embarrassed that his hero never got over what he obviously considers a bad social habit, but at least he acknowledges the reality of the behavior (Warren would wish it away). Herndon put this dicey aspect of Lincoln biography in perspective: "the truth is he loved a story however extravagant or vulgar, if it had a good point. If it was merely a ribald recital and had no sting at the end, that is, if it exposed no weakness or pointed no moral, he had no use for it."[48] Of barnyard and backwoods humor there was plenty, and it formed a genuine if sub-rosa part of Lincoln's self-education. But where would he have heard or read off-color stories fashioned so as to be "literary" and have the "sting at the end" that Herndon thought essential?

There are no highways in the research odyssey into Lincoln's early life, only twisting game paths often overgrown with the brush of time and obscure in the long sundown of memory. Follow them as best we can, however, and they may lead back to an old settler telling the next generation a story that is then repeated to a third- or fourth-generation inquirer. In 1881, Nathaniel Grigsby, who had talked to Herndon fifteen years previously, told a man named William Fortune a story. Fortune in turn forty years later related it to Albert J. Beveridge: there had been a joke book passed among the boys which he thought was called *The King's Jester*, from which Lincoln used to entertain the boys with ribald stories read out loud. But Fortune could find no such title in any of the great world libraries he consulted. Consulting the noted bibliographer J. Christian Bay of Chicago, Fortune learned that the book in question was probably an eighteenth-century English publication entitled *Quinn's [sic] Jests; or, The Facetious Man's Pocket Companion*, published in London in 1766.[49] Whatever Fortune thought of this book, Beveridge was not amused but scandalized: "The humor is heavy, the so-called jests often indecent and sometimes so filthy that they cannot now [1928] be reproduced."[50] Which leaves us with a tantalizing but censored description of a book Lincoln is said to have read aloud in the company of other young men.

How likely is it that he did? On the doubting side, *Quin's Jests* had at best a modest popularity, judging by the sole English edition of 1766; and it apparently never did have an American edition. Simply, then, on the basis of availability, the presence of *Quin's Jests* in frontier Indiana is unlikely. Adding to this the confusion concerning the actual identity of the volume, we must be skeptical about whether Lincoln ever saw *Quin's Jests*. Nonetheless, on the assumption that he might have, here are just two of the stories from it that *can* now be reproduced without causing readers an averting of the eyes and stopping of the ears.

Mrs. Woffington one night played the character of Sir Harry Wildair to a very full house, and met with great applause. Upon her coming off in the third act, she said to Quin, who was behind the scenes, "Upon my word, I believe all the house *takes* me for a man."

"By G—d, Madam," said he, "I am pretty sure half the house *know* to the contrary."

Quin being greatly teazed in the company of some frisky girls, by a number of frivolous and impertinent questions, was at length asked by one of them, "Whether his mother had *longed* for anything, and if he was *marked*?"

"Yes, Miss," he replied, "my mother had *a very great longing* for what I am pretty much marked with; and what is more, if she had not *longed* for it, perhaps, I should not have been here."[51]

Stories like these seem innocuous enough to contemporary taste. Rather than jokes per se, Quin's "jests, bon-mots, epigrams and repartee" are almost always humorous anecdotes in which Mr. Quin, *bon vivant* and London theatrical familiar, one-ups his antagonist—somewhat in the manner of nineteenth-century American frontier humor, but less crudely. The examples above are typical in length and structure: all are in the third person; many feature Quin himself as the character making the put-down. There is always a *point*, usually made with a *sting*, thus satisfying Herndon's test for a story Lincoln would have told with relish. Wordplay abounds, as in the equivocal punning on *longed* and *marked* in the second example, allowing wit to enliven an otherwise conventionally male-oriented story of penis length and women's sexual desire.

Less salacious and broader in its range of wit is *Joe Miller's Jests; or, The Wit's Vade Mecum*. Though the only evidence we have implies an encounter considerably later than Indiana, *Joe Miller* will be discussed here because of its cognate relation with *Quin's Jests*. True to its subtitle, *Joe Miller's Jests* was indeed a volume to "go with me": a small (9 ×14cm) duodecimo of 144 pages, with even smaller type (6 point) that the would-be "Wit" might pull from his back pocket to regale his fellows with "the most brilliant jests, bons mots, and pleasing short stories in the English language."[52] As with the Quin book, many of the jokes feature the eponymous character either as joker or butt, and many are also too topically English and eighteenth century to be fully appreciated (much less laughed at) by Lincoln's backwoods Americans. A majority of the stories, really little more than quips, are founded on puns but are only mildly sexually suggestive. A pair of *Joe Miller's Jests* are worth quoting that possibly would have been of particular interest to Lincoln. Two of these ridicule church and clergy:

A CHAPEL of a riding house is made,
Thus we once more see Christ in manger laid,
Where still we find the jockey trade supplied,
The laymen bridled, and the clergy ride.

And,

My lord Stangford, who stammer'd very much, was telling a certain bishop
that sat at his table, that Balaam's ass spoke because he was pri—est—Priest-
rid; Sir, said a valet de chambre, who stood behind the chair, my lord would
say . . . No, friend, replied the bishop, Balaam could not speak himself, and
his ass spoke for him.[53]

Both the stanza and the anecdote are about *priest-ridden communities*: the very thing Lincoln would in 1834 lay at the door of the Methodist
circuit-preacher, Peter Cartwright, whom Lincoln accused in print of *riding*
on the backs of the credulous Methodist faithful of central Illinois. Two
small sorties of wit, and not of the finest, perhaps—that's all these are. But
if Lincoln read them, his mind filed them away, and they were thenceforth
available for debate on religio-political matters: especially the funny and
telling image of an established-church priest bestriding the layperson and
spurring him to carry the clergyman hither and yon.

Another reason to take *Joe Miller's Jests* seriously as Lincoln reading, either in boyhood or later, is that a number of anecdotes said by his
acquaintances to have been told by Lincoln originate in editions of this
volume.[54] According to Henry C. Whitney, Lincoln borrowed a copy of *Joe
Miller* from Judge Samuel Treat and quickly made it his own, "narrating
the stories around the circuit, but very much embellished and changed,
evidently by Lincoln himself."[55]

Considering Lincoln's keen appetite for storytelling and the popularity
of jest books in early-nineteenth-century male America,[56] it is quite plausible that Lincoln knew *Quin's Jests* or *Joe Miller's Jests* or both and that he
memorized and retailed their stories from his youth and throughout his
life. Such books were disgraceful if not wholly forbidden territory (read:
male only), which in itself would have made them rare in pioneer Indiana
and rarely attractive to a teen-aged male experiencing his first great hor-
monal flood. In addition, both the possession of such volumes and their
performance by Lincoln would have conferred social distinction (in an
antisocial way) among the group of young men involved, all of whom were
in the midst of the same biological and social rites of passage.

In terms of verbal ability, Lincoln was naturally a leader. As his playfel-
low Nate Grigsby recalled, "when he appeared in Company the boys would
gather & cluster around him to hear him talk. He made fun & cracked his

jokes making all happy, but the jokes & fun were at no mans Expense—He wounded no mans feelings."[57] We know that Lincoln had an uncanny knack for mimicry. And while southern Indiana may not have offered models of spoken London English to imitate, we may safely imagine Lincoln's making something individual out of the rhythms, emphases, and mincing pronunciation of *Quin's Jests*. And, finally, the two joke books would have been fun to read and perform, unlike all the other books that came into Lincoln's hands (possibly excepting *Aesop's Fables*). While their scatological and bawdy humor hardly seems uproarious today, it doubtlessly set the boys in the woods to guffawing and thigh-slapping. And for Lincoln the *language* and the *story structures* of the jest books would have been instructive in attracting and keeping an audience in a culture that was far more oral than literary, where the art of storytelling was politically necessary and the accomplished Man-of-Words a kind of republican prince. But, most of all, Lincoln would have found *Quin* and *Joe Miller* keenly entertaining—their humor a welcome relief from the lugubrious prose of the *English Reader* and *Kentucky Preceptor* and a needed reprieve from the oppressive company of the goddess of Melancholy, who, well before he had reached ripe manhood, "had marked him for her own."[58]

Even a story with a sting is not necessarily a fable, which always points toward the universal in its moral application. "He kept the Bible and Aesop's always within reach," Herndon wrote, "and read them over and over. These two volumes furnished him with the many figures of speech and parables which he used to such happy effect in his later and public utterances."[59] Lincoln and the Bible will be the subject of part of chapter 5 below, but I discuss his assimilation (almost by heart, though probably not all) of *Aesop's Fables* here, since it is one of the formative books (in an important sense a complement to *Quin's Jests*) from which the young Lincoln performed and even *taught*. To quote once more from Herndon's September 1865 interview with Nate Grigsby: "Mr Lincoln was figurative in his Speeches—talks & conversations. He argued much from Analogy and Explained things hard for us to understand by stories—maxims—tales and figures. He would almost always point his lesson or idea by some story that was plain and near as that we might instantly see the force & bearing of what he said—[.]"[60] The fables traditionally associated with Aesop provided a ready reservoir for this sort of teaching and storytelling, as the tale of "The Men and Zeus" so aptly illustrates. Man, complaining to Zeus about how he had granted animals strength, speed, even wings to fly, while leaving humankind "naked," is properly rebuked by his sovereign: "'You have not taken notice of the gift I have granted you. And yet you have the most: for you have got the power of speech, which is mighty with the gods and with men. It is mightier than the powerful, swifter than the fastest.'" And then, recognizing the gift of God, man went on his way, in reverence and gratitude."[61]

We tend to think of *Aesop's Fables* as a children's book, with a variety of cartoon animals interacting in ways that mildly dramatize human foibles. But the collection of Greek-language vignettes that descended through the ancient Hellenistic and Roman worlds differs in two important ways from our modern sense of Aesop (notwithstanding that most of the tales are largely unchanged). First, the worldview of most of the stories is brutally naturalistic, the humor always at some unfortunate's expense, the punishment for poor judgment usually death. None of this is in the least extenuated: one's death, just or unjust, is laughed at by those who survive. In this respect, the classical *Aesop's Fables* represents an often cruel existential struggle rather than a golden-rule ethos. And, second, the reason behind the compendium was to make a sourcebook for speakers and rhetoricians—educated people who wished to get ahead socially or politically and used Aesop to bolster their wit by providing a pointed story for any purpose. Modern classical scholars think of the gathered fables as a joke book, not unlike *Quin's Jests* and occasionally just as salacious (these, needless to say, were not translated and included in most of the British and American versions of Aesop, intended as they were for the polite "amusement and instruction of youth"). At Athenian *symposia* (drinking parties), wits and high-living gentlemen vied to one-up each other, without sparing the invective, as story succeeded story and the evening descended into drunkenness and sometimes debauchery (think of Aristophanes and Socrates in Plato's *Symposium*).[62]

Many early U.S. editions of Aesop, typically reset from English copies and containing the same or new woodcut engravings, one for each tale, were in print and widely distributed from the time of the Revolution and throughout the nineteenth century. The edition that Lincoln most likely read was one of the several printed by R. Aitken, beginning with the "First *American* Edition" (Philadelphia, 1777).[63] Not all the fables printed were Aesop's but included selections from a number of classical and modern European sources. And the "morals of the stories" in these various English and American editions were often far longer than the fables themselves (exactly the opposite proportion from the original), prolix and pompous, fitted to illustrate the mores of eighteenth-century British bourgeois life. So, while the texts of the fables remained more or less constant, the *universality* of the morals turned out to be highly relativized, with few of the Greek original's ethical points surviving, and no context specific to the

American colonies or to the United States. For example, the preface to the Aitken edition quotes Joseph Addison praising Aesop as "the first Pieces of Wit that made their Appearance in the World; and have been still highly valued, not only in Times of the greatest Simplicity, but among the most polite Ages of Mankind." This was all very well for England before 1775, but not at all relevant to the American colonies in revolt. Consider how Addison viewed the "application" of the fable of "The Poor Man and His Lamb": it managed to "convey instruction to the Ear of a King, without offending it, and to bring the Man after God's own heart to a right Sense of his Guilt, and his Duty."[64] Nothing could be less Greek than this! Or less American, whose radicals were offending George III's ear with every new mail received via packet boat from the colonies. Or, one is tempted to say, less like a tall, young republican atheist by the name of Lincoln who was trying on intellectual, political, and social audacity for size.

Lincoln is known to have spoken or written from *Aesop's Fables* three times. In the 1843 "Campaign Circular" he authored for the Whig Party of Illinois, Lincoln, in arguing for "the adoption of the convention system for the nomination of candidates," alluded to "that great fabulist and philosopher, Aesop," and cited the "fable of the bundle of the sticks" to illustrate the necessity of cohering as a group if political success were to be gained. (He also quoted, in support of this rather mundane cause, the words of the Gospel of Mark 3:25 he would make so famous a decade later: "a house divided against itself cannot stand.") Apparently the Illinois Whigs, like the sons of the ploughman in the fable, were "always quarrelling" among themselves, all ambitious for party preferment, and no amount of scolding or pleading by the father could get them to stop. So he thought of this expedient lesson: asking them to bring him "a load of firewood," he bundled several of the loads and gave one apiece to each son. Now break it up for me, he demanded. But they could not, the bundles being too thick. "The ploughman therefore undid the bundles and handed each of his sons a stick at a time," easy to break. The moral? "If you stay bound together," you will be invincible to your enemies; divided, "you will be easy to defeat."[65] As with the Whig Party, so with the American Republic: neither took this very good advice. But the bundle of sticks, *fasces*, appeared on either side of Lincoln's throne in the Daniel French sculpture for the Memorial in Washington.

Early in the secession crisis of 1861, when Lincoln was urged in the name of appeasement to abandon the forts and other federal property in the South, he responded with "The Fable of the Lion and the Woodman," with an appropriate presidential application: "[A] lion was very much in love with a woodman's daughter. The fair maid, afraid to say no, referred him to her father. The lion applied for the girl. The father replied, your teeth are too long. The lion went to a dentist and had them extracted. Returning, he asked for his bride. No, said the woodsman, your claws are too long. Going back to the dentist, he had them drawn. Then, returning to claim his bride, the woodsman, seeing he was disarmed, beat out his brains. 'May it not be so,' said Mr. Lincoln, 'with me, if I give up all that is asked?'"⁶⁶

His most poignant use of Aesop came in mid-1862, as Lincoln considered the emancipation of slaves in the rebellious states. In a letter to the chaplain of the United States Senate, Byron Sunderland, Lincoln pondered the fate of African Americans, free and slave: "As for the negroes, Doctor, and what is to become of them . . . it made me think of a story I read in one of my first books, "Aesop's Fables." It was an old edition, and had curious, rough wood-cuts, one of which showed four white men scrubbing a negro in a potash kettle filled with cold water. The text explained that the men thought that by scrubbing the negro they might make him white. Just about the time they thought they were succeeding, he took cold and died. Now, I am afraid that by the time we get through this war the negro will catch cold and die."⁶⁷

Significantly, Lincoln remembered both the text and its accompanying "curious, rough wood-cut" from the "old edition" read long ago in Indiana. In the equivalent engraving from the 1777 printing, there are only two men washing the man in the tub whom the fable calls "a Blackamoor," with a third bringing in more water.⁶⁸ The fable is just as Lincoln recalled it, but the "application" that follows says nothing about race or racial matters. That the black is a slave, or the slave black, is a matter of indifference to the commentator on the fable. He merely states and then expatiates at length upon the truth that "many People attempt Impossibilities, for want of considering the Nature of Things aright." Thus, "when people learn to dance without Shape and Mien, to sing, or play on Music, without a Voice or an Ear, Painting or Poetry without a Genius, it is attempting to wash the Blackamoor white."⁶⁹ If one is born a "Blockhead," one remains a blockhead forever. This applies to the *owner* of the "Blackamoor." The slave may have been wretchedly used, but he is not the point.

Lincoln might have both agreed and disagreed with his stuffy English tutor's advice to keep in one's place, a place naturally assigned. On the one hand, blacks were black and would always be, though in America they needn't always be slaves. On the other, the white male citizens of the United States already had, as Lincoln believed (and showed in himself), what the black, slave or free, might never obtain: the "right to rise." And there was more to rising than subsistence economics: it meant the freedom to grow and change; blockheads could learn and geniuses might teach. Nature, romantically and organically considered, consisted in how a being realized itself, not where it happened to be placed at birth. And this ought to be true for *every* human being. Hence, what perhaps fascinated Lincoln most about "The Blackamoor" was its appropriateness as a lesson for a nation engulfed in civil war. For the North, the fight for the Union gradually evolved into a fight, deadly in earnest, to free the slaves, which with each battle looked more and more like a kind of brutal scrubbing of the millions of blacks in a giant cauldron of cold blood. They could never be made white, and whites, most of them, didn't want them around as blacks. But Lincoln worried, with reason, that they might collectively "catch cold and die" before they could be made free—the necessary first step towards any meaningful self-realization. And, despite the homeliness of the figure of *catching cold*, that would be tragically unjust. By late 1862, had the Civil War from Lincoln's point of view become a pointless cold-blooded scrubbing? Yes, but also crucial if the slaves were to be freed, and to that extent *whitened*. This was the paradox of his "application" of the fable, and it added a moral complexity to both text and illustration that went well beyond fate or irony toward tragedy. Thus did Lincoln make "The Blackamoor" his own.

Suppose that Mason Locke Weems (1759–1825), after years of itinerant book-peddling up and down the new United States from New York to the Carolinas, had headed his horse-drawn book cart over the Appalachians into Kentucky, ferrying then across the Ohio River to Indiana. Picture Old Parson Weems, long an Episcopal pastor-sans-parish, "with his ruddy visage and the locks that flowed over his clerical cloak . . . bumping along in his Jersey wagon, a portable bookcase behind and a fiddle beside him."[70] Suppose, further, that on the last venture of his life—say, in 1824—this well-known, highly eccentric author of the mythographic *Life of George Washington*, ended up in Gentryville, Indiana. What would he have had to sell to the locals? Besides his own very popular *Washington* and the subsequent *Life of General Francis Marion*, Weems could have offered a short course in classic English poetry: Milton's *Paradise Lost*, Edward Young's *Night Thoughts*, James Thomson's *Seasons*. Aids to Christian devotion: hymnals by Watts, Bunyan's *Pilgrim's Progress*, Richard Baxter's *Saints' Rest*. And for the profane, novels aplenty and the complete writings of Thomas Paine, including the *Age of Reason* (but with the "antidote," Weems insisted, of "Watson's *Apology for the Bible*").[71]

Now Mason Locke Weems, as far as anyone knows, made no such ultramontane journey in the 1820s to southwestern Indiana: but *someone* who sold books did, or came at least to the Lexington, Kentucky, area. It is a remarkable fact that every single title mentioned above occurs on one bibliographer's list or another of those books Lincoln is said to have read, in the 1820s or a little later in Illinois. Whatever his own politics, Weems carried in his wagon what sold: the poison of Paine in his left hand, the "antidote" in his right, and everything else—all those romance novels, practical treatises on "midwifery," and a curious booklet called *Onania*, "which warned the reader against the dangers of masturbation"—piled up on his lap.[72] And, while Weems's stock was far more liberal in thought and broader in scope than that, say, of the Methodist preachers who also were itinerant booksellers, in just this liberality may we take him as typical of his wandering trade.

Weems had become famous in his lifetime for the one book by which he is still known today, *The Life of George Washington*, whose first edition (1800, and essentially a pamphlet of eighty pages) "appeared . . . only a few months after Washington's death at Mount Vernon on December 14, 1799." Over the next decade, the author continued to revise and add to the work, until by 1808 it had reached the form in which Lincoln would have read it: 228 pages, with the full title, *The Life of George Washington; With Curious Anecdotes, Equally Honorable to Himself and Exemplary To His Young Countrymen*, and Weems aggrandizing himself as "Formerly Rector of Mount-Vernon Parish."[73] Modern historiography has been unkind to Weems, and the derision heaped upon fabrications such as the cutting down of the cherry tree need not be rehearsed here. The point for Lincoln's reading is not that he swallowed the hagiography whole, without uncritical rumination, but that he tasted flavors of *real* honesty, fortitude, and that elusive quality known as *leadership* beneath all the saccharine hortative nationalism in Weems's confabulation. In other words, "the father of his country" proved a worthy father, always an important consideration with Lincoln.

The occasion for Lincoln's one public mention of Weems occurred on his meandering journey by train, as president-elect, from Springfield to Washington, D.C., in February 1861. Speaking at Trenton to members of the New Jersey Senate on February 21, Lincoln recalled his childhood reading of *The Life of George Washington*:

> I got hold of a small book, such a one as few of the younger members have ever seen, "Weem's [*sic*] Life of Washington." I remember all the accounts there given of the battle fields and struggles for the liberties of the country, and none fixed themselves upon my imagination so deeply as the struggle here at Trenton, New-Jersey. The crossing of the river; the contest with the Hessians; the great hardships endured at that time, all fixed themselves on my memory more than any single revolutionary event; and you all know, for you have all been boys, how these early impressions last longer than any

others. I recollect thinking then, boy even though I was, that there must
have been something more than common that those men struggled for.

Aware as he was that the "Second American Revolution" was impending
and secession a fact (at the time of the address the Confederacy already
existed), Lincoln looked to the paternal example of Washington, who had
led the American rebels to victory and shepherded the new nation through
a rather sickly infancy. Commencing with a young *boy's* fascinated reading,
Weems's *Washington* had stuck with him—the events far more than the
manner of their narration—and Lincoln now summoned the "Old Testament" of American civil religion to guide him in saving what he oddly
labeled God's "almost chosen people."[74] In especially noticing the Battle
of Trenton as his example of against-the-odds heroism in the service of a
great cause, Lincoln both appealed to the patriotism of Pennsylvania and
New Jersey and underscored the gravity—as he had said ten days before
in his Farewell to Springfield speech—of the task before him "greater than
that which rested upon Washington."[75] At the same time, however, he could
point to Washington's victory as a token of his own possible success in
preserving the Union. And, perhaps most important, he announced to the
country that he intended to act so as to allow the composition of a "New
Testament" for the United States, one that would fairly allow the deletion
of the qualifier "almost."

Given Lincoln's purpose at Trenton, perhaps *any* book of Revolutionary
War derring-do would have served as well as this one. But it was Weems
that he remembered. He may even have recollected the scene much later in
Weems when Washington, who like Lincoln now, was on his way to assume
the presidency of the United States, had been accorded something like a
Roman Triumph when passing through Trenton in 1789.[76] And what else?
Most strikingly, there was a purported dream of Washington's mother concerning the family's "new house" that suddenly caught fire, with the flames
threatening to consume the roof and send the ceiling and walls crashing
down upon her. Husband, family, servants—all were too terrified to fight
the fire; but young George came to the rescue at his mother's beckoning
and managed to extinguish the flames, first by using an *"American gourd,"*
which was but partially effective, and then with a vessel "like a *wooden
shoe*," which was providentially lent by "a venerable old man, with a tall
cap and iron rod in his hand." And this utensil enabled the boy to put out
the fire. Surveying the damage, George said to his mother, "*We can make
a far better roof than this ever was*; a roof of such a *quality*, that, if well *kept
together*, it will last forever; but if you take it apart, you will make the house
ten thousand times worse than it was before." All that was required was

a "better roof" that would ensure that the house of the Republic covered every American head, and good government would *"endure for ever."*[77]

The mature Lincoln was fond of house figures, and one wonders if the teenager in Indiana was acute enough to comprehend Weems's elaborate application of what we might call the Fable of the First National House. Had Lincoln recalled it half as readily as the narrative of crossing of the Delaware and defeating the Hessians, he might have been struck, amused even, to think of Washington's first saving and then planning to re-roof the house. For this was the ideal American architecture Lincoln in the 1850s saw as the "house divided," destined not much longer to stand, or to be replaced by the sinister house of slavery he kept bringing up in the 1858 debates with Douglas: the one which was being built by a conspiracy among "Stephen, Franklin, Roger and James."[78] Washington's new roof was yet to be put on (standing open like the undomed capital in Washington City); Lincoln would have to do the job if the National House were "to endure forever."

Less abstractly, it is quite possible that the boy Lincoln read one of his first presidential speeches in Weems's *Washington*. Weems quotes in full Washington's Farewell Address of 1796, one of the themes of which Lincoln would later dwell upon in the Lyceum Address: the paramount importance to a republic of respect for the law. In his valedictory, Washington wrote with characteristic humility, thanking the people of America for giving him the opportunity to serve them and now to be free at last to retire to his farm at Mount Vernon and finish his days as a gentleman farmer. Were this all, Lincoln would scarcely have bothered to read attentively, since he did not share his forefather's love of rural and agricultural life. But Washington, having earned the right, also *warned* his young country against the evils of foreign alliances, party politics, and, above all, lawlessness: "Here, perhaps, I ought to stop." But he owed it to the nation to continue, and he did continue for many paragraphs on the subject of the sacredness of *union*. What greatness America had achieved and what success the nation might yet have were owing to liberty's balancing principle: the control of human passion. While he hoped "that your union and brotherly affection may be perpetual; that the free constitution . . . may be sacredly maintained," such a future was far from inevitable.[79]

Some fifteen years after first reading these monitory words, Lincoln spoke to the Young Men's Lyceum in Springfield on "The Perpetuation of Our Political Institutions." Having noted a number of recent and particularly heinous instances of vigilante justice, he deplored what he saw as "this mobocratic spirit, which all must admit, is now abroad in the land," and asserted that if not checked it might break down forever "the strongest bulwark of any Government, and particular of those constituted like ours ... I mean the *attachment* of the People."[80] Washington, too, had used this italicized noun in his Farewell Address: he exhorted Americans to "cherish a cordial, habitual, and immoveable attachment" to free government, one sufficiently strong to resist the inevitable and insidious attacks that would attempt to weaken this national *attachment*. Violent passions—religious, politically partisan, sectional, or simply those of power and greed—undermine attachment and threaten the "perpetuation" of the Union. Had Washington been able to observe Lincoln as he was in 1838, he would have deprecated the younger man's party politics, no doubt, but otherwise have seen in him a rare instance of the profoundly principled, constitutionally conservative patriot he had called upon the new generation of American men to become. Near the end of the Farewell, almost as if turning back for a moment on the verge of leaving the public stage forever, Washington, always self-deprecating, remarks that his "counsels" will not "control the usual current of the passions" of his countrymen, now and in the future, nor "prevent our nation from running the course which has hitherto marked the destiny of nations." This reflection is somber, even pessimistic: there is no automatic "American exception" in the course of empires. Yet if one or another in his direct political lineage should obtain "some partial benefit, some occasional good," then might he return to his estate with as much reassurance as a Stoic is allowed, having offered his last, best advice to a new and growing country.[81]

Lincoln in the Lyceum Address did remember and did reiterate Washington's theme, this time employing the rhetoric of religious architecture with which to represent the decaying National House. The old oaks that were the forefathers are storm-fallen and dead: "They *were* the pillars of the temple of liberty; and now, that they have crumbled away, that temple must fall, unless we, their descendants, supply their places with other pillars, hewn from the solid quarry of sober reason." If upon such a lithic basis, "the proud fabric of freedom" might be rebuilt so as to *endure forever* and Washington to rest content in his grave, then "as has been said of the only greater institution, *'the gates of hell shall not prevail against it.'*"[82]

As we have seen, Abraham Lincoln, youth and man, loved stories—loved reading and telling them. Yet he generally did not care for extended narratives. Though he would gladly sit through a third-rate dramatic comedy, or recite poetry by the hour, he famously once said, "I never read an entire novel in my life!"[83] This emphatic disclaimer notwithstanding, students of Lincoln's boyhood have invariably named three longer fictions as important to his reading in Indiana: *The Arabian Nights*, *Pilgrim's Progress*, and *Robinson Crusoe*. At least one of these (*Robinson Crusoe*) is certainly a novel by modern standards of the genre, and the other two, whatever their forms, are decidedly *long*. It is doubtful that the adult Lincoln would have forgotten having read these classic narratives, since he forgot so little. So either the accounts of his childhood reading are mistaken here, or what Lincoln read of Defoe, Bunyan, and *The Arabian Nights* was fragmentary— pieces of the wholes or their abridgement.

The first thing to note concerning *The Arabian Nights* is that it is, of course, a huge *collection* of tales (rather than a novel-like narrative con- tinuum) linked by the framing device of Scheherazade's telling nightly stories, unresolved at dawn, to hold the interest of her restless and bloody- minded husband-king and thereby postpone her morning beheading—as the sultan, shamed and angered by the adultery of his very first wife, had instituted the practice of marrying a virgin every day, deflowering her that same night, and beheading her the next morning, so as never again to be cuckolded. For a thousand and one nights (nearly three years), Scheherazade forestalls her fate by her adroit storytelling, until at last the sultan softens and lets her live. Some of her tales are long, multifaceted picaresques, the telling of which stretches over many nights; others are as short as jokes or parables or anecdotes. But in most instances, Scheherazade deftly leaves her husband hanging, narratively *unfulfilled*, until the follow- ing night, since by the rules between them she may abruptly leave off telling at the first hint of dawn. And if a tale ends before morning, she instantly begins another, allowing no time for the sultan to remember his murder- ous vow. In this rudimentary narrative sense, then, Lincoln could have read and retold at least the shorter stories he liked best from *The Arabian Nights*. This possibility, however, rests on the supposition that he indeed read some version of the "whole" in order to choose some few stories out of the rich collection of hundreds.

The "complete" *Arabian Nights* did not appear in English until after Lincoln's death. This is not to say that earlier editions did not *claim* to be complete: the first American printing came from Philadelphia, dated 1794 (four volumes bound as two, nearly 550 pages), and announced on the title page that it consisted "of one thousand and one stories, told by the Sultaness of the Indies." This was baldly misleading: there were one thousand and one nights but not so many stories. This edition, based upon the pioneering editorial and translating work of the Frenchman Antoine Galland (1646–1715), whose French edition of *Les mille et une nuits* had appeared between 1704 and 1717, became the standard on which English translations were based for more than a century.[84] While one of these large and putatively comprehensive editions *might* have been what Lincoln dipped into now and again, more likely he read some kind of abridgement of *The Arabian Nights*. The only tales that Lincoln's friends and relatives in Indiana recollected by name were those of "Sinabad [*sic*] the Sailor," though Dennis Hanks, who was living with the Lincolns at their Spencer County homestead, allegedly recalled that "'Abe'd lay on his stummick by the fire and read [*The Arabian Nights*] out loud to me 'n' Aunt Sairy, an' we'd laugh when he did. . . . I reckon Abe read the book a dozen times an' knowed them yarns by heart.'"[85] An idiomatic Dennis Hanks story: but there are two serious objections to it. First, even with Lincoln's capacity for memorization, it is hard to credit that he "knowed them yarns by heart," when this would have demanded the recollection at will of anecdotes from among several hundreds of pages of text. Second, the *source* of Hanks' information is a 1908 piece of *fiction* by Eleanor Atkinson entitled *The Boyhood of Lincoln*. Atkinson's fifty-seven-page narrative purports to be the biographical reminiscences of Hanks, but it is clearly fictionalized and offers no sources for what Hanks says in his monologue about the two of them being boys together.

The unreliability of Atkinson as a source casts doubt upon the entire matter of whether Lincoln read any or all of *The Arabian Nights*. But we still have David Turnham's testimony in *Herndon's Informants*. Turnham, a "near neighbor and friend" of Lincoln's in Indiana,[86] specifically names the *book* Lincoln read as "Sinabad the Sailor," which, if an accurate memory, implies that the seven voyages of Sinbad must have been separately published. And so they were. When English or American publishers offered *selections* from the tales, the choices owed everything to the taste of the editors, some of whom were too fastidious to include ribald stories or those that otherwise overrepresented high animal spirits. Since the original mass of tales included the pornographic and the taboo (even to the frank representation of bestiality), many of the stories were ruled out entirely, while others needed expurgation and bowdlerization. But Sinbad's voyages were perfect for a juvenile audience: adventurous and fantastic without much matter—sensuous or religious—to offend the sensibilities of the Christian parents who would be buying the book for their children. The first separate American publication of Sinbad appeared in the same year as the full edition noted above: *The History of Sindbad* [*sic*] *the Sailor: Containing an Account of His Several Surprizing Voyages and Miraculous Voyages* (Boston, 1794; 121 pages).

What Turnham remembered is therefore plausible. And we can try to rehabilitate Hanks-via-Atkinson if we suppose that Lincoln could well have read one or more of Sinbad's tales to Sarah Johnston Lincoln and her cousin—repeated them out loud enough times that the bones of the stories came to belong to the boy, who then became their *teller*, with appropriate fleshing out in succeeding iterations. This would fit the portrait of Lincoln as an emerging "Man-of-Words." When might this have happened? Dennis Hanks left the Lincoln homestead after his marriage in 1821, so this is the upper limiting date. Louis Warren puts the reading of *The Arabian Nights* in 1819, when Lincoln would have been ten years old.[87] Taking this as the early limit, is it reasonable that the boy could handle the prose of Sinbad's voyages to the extent of being able to interpret them orally to the laugh-out-loud amusement of his family? And, if so, what did Lincoln draw from the tales so as to provoke their risibilities?

To the first question, the answer is, yes, he could have: *if* we continue to assert the model of Lincoln as a sort of child prodigy of reading; *or if* the version of Sinbad he used had been "dumbed down" to the extent that *any* ten-year-old boy with a modicum of literacy could read it. Lincoln had already managed Aesop; Sinbad was only just slightly more challenging. The second question requires reading the stories as if looking over Lincoln's shoulder but, at the same time, fudging a bit. Ignoring for a moment the separate 1794 printing of Sinbad's tale and instead opening the most famous of the "complete" *Arabian Nights* in English, the edition by Richard Burton, to the very first page of the first voyage (after the framing matter of the introduction), we encounter Sinbad reminding himself of something Solomon said that his father used to quote from the Book: "'Three things are better than other three; the day of death is better than the day of birth, a live dog is better than a dead lion and the grave is better than want.'"[88] What jumps out from this is its second term: "a live dog is better than a dead lion," which is taken from the lugubrious wisdom of Ecclesiastes 9:4 and which Lincoln employed against Douglas as a lesser but effective figurative weapon in the House Divided speech: "They [Republican supporters of Douglas] remind us that he is a very *great man*, and that the largest of *us* are very small ones. Let this be granted. But 'a *living dog* is better than a *dead lion*.' Judge Douglas, if not a *dead* lion for *this work*, is at least a *caged* and *toothless* one. How can he oppose the advances of slavery? He don't *care* anything about it. His avowed *mission is impressing* the 'public heart' to *care* nothing about it."[89]

The application of this figure is telling on both Douglas the dead or moribund lion and Lincoln the feisty living mutt that would (and eventually did) take his political place in the national crisis over slavery. But there is no necessary connection between the boy's having *perhaps* read it in *The Arabian Nights* and the politically mature man's putting the apothegm into play in 1858. Cause is not the point here. Rather, we may suggest that the youth in Indiana would have been struck by the figure itself, no matter what its source. He may or may not have known that the proverb derived from Ecclesiastes. To be sure, Ecclesiastes may well have figured in the Lincoln family's Bible readings, and with only a little imagination we can see the adolescent boy meeting the "Preacher's" many doleful reiterations of "Vanity of vanities, all is vanity" with a sad nod of his precocious head. For the source of the "living dog, dead lion" saying, the probability lies with family Bible reading, since the 1794 *Sindbad* omits Ecclesiastes 9:4, giving only the third term of the triad: "Death is more tolerable than poverty."[90] When much later the time came to *use* the saying from this scrapbook of human futility, Lincoln had had it in mind from the start: for this occasion, for this effect, launch the wise saying of the dead lion and the living dog, omitting, since the target is Douglas, the first clause of the verse: "For to him that is joined to all the living there is hope."

Biblical quotations or allusions, even Qur'an-derived, were acceptable to the English or American editors of *The Arabian Nights*. On the other hand, they proved quick to elide anything else they found indecorous. Hence the "virgin mares" Sinbad discovers on the island of his shipwreck in the first voyage are described in the Burton translation as being "covered by" fabulous stallions from the sea, engendering thereby foals worth a great deal of money to the local king—"nor is their like to be found on earth's face." In the 1794 version, however, the mares are simply given a good bath in a fresh-water pool, "by virtue of which extraordinary water, they were rendered stronger and more beautiful."[91] Such antiseptic cleansing of the narrative would have been wasted on Lincoln, who like rural boys every-where thought nothing of seeing one animal "cover" another, whether in the wild or in the barnyard. Of more aesthetic moment, though, is that both abridgement and bowdlerization deprive the story of much of its wonder. Not only are the interpolated verses gone, lyric sources of beauty and wisdom that certainly would have made young Lincoln wonder, but also vivid scenes like that of mythic sea-creatures coming out of the ocean once a year to mate with earth-bound horses, resulting in a hardier, more beautiful breed—these replaced by plodding prose and the tepid and fla-vorless euphemism of a "bath."

One wonders how interesting Lincoln could have found this sort of stuff. Hanks, to repeat, was made to insist that he and Sarah Johnston Lincoln had "laugh'd out loud" when Abraham read to them out of *The Arabian Nights*. But, in the seven Sinbad stories at least, there is very little that we might genuinely call funny: no jokes, no pratfalls or tricks, not even much verbal wit—all of which are found abundantly in others among the tales. Rather than these, Sinbad tells the same cyclical tale seven times: restlessness at home, consequently the sea voyage, shipwreck, mighty rage at having left home in the first place, fabulous adventures, and the nigh-miraculous return to Baghdad, with the principal richer than ever bearing treasures and so on that Allah has blessed him with. It is easy enough to imagine Lincoln *enthralling* his audience with descriptions of the island that was a whale, the giant domelike egg of the Roc, the valley of diamonds, and the cannibal giant. To get Dennis and "Aunt Sairy" *laughing*, however, would have required almost over-the-top, exaggerated oral interpretation on Lincoln's part. That is, might he not have *parodied* Sinbad, using his talent for mimicry and impersonation? Imagine him traipsing around the cabin interior like Sinbad with the naked "Old Man of the Sea" bestriding him and forcing him to go "hither and thither" as a beast of burden, "among the trees which bore the best fruit; and if ever I refused . . . he beat me with his feet more grievously than if I had been beaten with whips . . . and he bepissed and conskited my shoulders and back, dismounting not night or day."[92] Sinbad tells it as a severe trial of unremitting misery; but it could be made ridiculously funny by the right actor.

Lincoln took more seriously another, truer account of shipwreck and slavery: James Riley's *An Authentic Narrative of the Loss of the American Brig Commerce* (1817). He mentioned it to John Locke Scripps as one of the books he had read as a boy, and Scripps duly put a reference to Riley's *Narrative* into his 1860 campaign biography.[93] Warren asserts that Lincoln encountered the *Authentic Narrative* "some time after he read Weems's *Washington*," which by his reckoning would put the reading after 1821.[94] Among the small group of boys' books and Christian tracts we have thus far discussed, the *Authentic Narrative* may seem the odd text out, treating as it does nearly contemporary events in a "fact-based" account. But part of the book's popular appeal (approximately one million copies printed between 1817 and 1859)[95] derived from its being an *American* boy's adventure story—fabulous but real—while the sheer number of books distributed meant that the *Authentic Narrative* could be found all over the United States—even in the rural backwaters of southwestern Indiana.

Riley's was the first extended nonfiction narrative (travel and description) that Lincoln had ever read. James Riley had been born in 1777, the fourth child in a large, always poor Connecticut farming family. At the tender age of eight, young James had been leased by his father to work for other farmers in the vicinity. This was much like Tom Lincoln's hiring Abraham out to day, or even boarding, work; and the practice had pretty much the same deleterious effect on both boys' educations. Riley's various farmers put a stop to his basic schooling in order to make him toil the more, scarcely even providing him subsistent food or allowing him sufficient sleep.

Why waste time in school, the more so as it was *their* boughten time? After all, Riley acidly observed, these farmers had "received but a very scanty education themselves, [yet were] conceited, nevertheless, that they were overstocked with learning, as is generally the case with the most ignorant." Small wonder that by the time Riley left home at fifteen to follow the sea (with his parents' reluctant consent), he was thoroughly sick and "tired of hard work on the land."[96] After rising steadily through the ranks of seamen, he became himself a master and supercargo. Thus Riley was a seasoned captain when he set out in 1815 on the ill-fated voyage of the *Commerce*, which was wrecked off the Moroccan coast in August of that year. He and his crew were captured by Arabs and put into slavery (a number of them did not survive the ordeals of climate, deprivation, and forced labor). After finally being ransomed, Riley recuperated in Gibraltar before returning to the United States and settling down to write his harrowing memoir. (Curiously, in 1818 he made a lengthy tour of the "American West"—that is, the present-day Midwest—that might have taken him through Lincoln's Indiana, in the year of his mother's death from the "milk-sick.")[97]

The *Authentic Account* is yet another story built around the ancient plot of *leaving home to become a man*. We have seen it above in the voyages of Sinbad and shall see it again in Daniel Defoe's *Robinson Crusoe*. This constituted an important subject of desire for Lincoln. If James Riley had been eager to leave the farm, he was naturally glad enough to return to America with his hide intact—where, God willing, he planned to remain, though not as an agriculturalist. As with Riley, the lessons were in the leaving: Lincoln's two youthful "voyages by water," down the river ways to New Orleans and back, showed him the greater world, including the exoticism of the Creoles and the horrors of deep South slavery. His first journey, especially, must have been a bittersweet revelation to Lincoln, since he was legally bound to return to his father's house and surrender to Tom Lincoln his entire wages from the trip—unless he chose to do what he desired, that is, to "light out for the territory, ahead of the rest," as another boy, though a fictional one, would do to escape a tyrannical father in *The Adventures of Huckleberry Finn*. But once legally free from Tom Lincoln, the son would never return to the bosom of the family nor, apparently, wish to.

Riley concluded the *Authentic Narrative* with a paean to the free people and government of the new United States, "whose political and moral institutions are in themselves the very best of any that prevail in the civilized portions of the globe." Yet he regretted that there was a shadow over the glorious Republic: "Strange as it must appear to the philanthropist, my proud-spirited and free countrymen still hold a million and a half nearly, of the human species, in the most cruel bonds of slavery." Because of his recent ordeal as a slave (Lincoln, too, though more nearly figuratively, declared, "I used to be a slave"), Riley would thenceforth devote his life "to redeem the enslaved, and to shiver in pieces the rod of oppression." This sounded like abolitionism, but wasn't. Instead, Riley seemed to be dedicating himself to the promotion of gradual and compensated emancipation, which would do justice to southerners' claims to "property" in the slaves and allow time for freed blacks to become "civilized." In a figure that suggested Lincoln's own mature attitude toward slavery, Riley asserted that "a plan should be devised, founded on the firm basis and the eternal principles of justice and humanity . . . as will gradually . . . wither and extirpate the accursed tree of slavery that has been suffered to take such deep root in our otherwise highly favoured soil."[98] That Lincoln thought to mention *An Authentic Narrative* to Scripps in 1860—more than thirty years after he first had read the book—may have been owing to its currency in the political crisis occasioned by the presidential campaign. For *something*, northerners insisted, had to be done about slavery. Captain Riley had died at sea in 1839, but a new edition of the *Authentic Narrative* appeared in 1859, just in time for the presidential campaign, and Lincoln would have been well aware that this by-then classic story remained on the nation's mind. In alluding to Riley, Lincoln was identifying with a fellow "slave" against slavery.

Perhaps the most popular shipwreck tale of all time, Daniel Defoe's *Robinson Crusoe* (1719), has a claim both as the first English novel and as a classic "boy's book." It is probably under this latter aegis that Lincoln read *Robinson Crusoe*. In addition to Dennis and John Hanks (also a first cousin of Nancy Hanks Lincoln), two Indiana friends whose acquaintance we have already made, David Turnham and Nate Grigsby, told Herndon that Lincoln had known the book.[99] These parallel, independent recollections from four informants attest to *Robinson Crusoe*'s popularity and increase the likelihood of Lincoln's having read it. In its "first English novel" dress, *Robinson Crusoe* is long: and we must keep in mind Lincoln's declaration of never having read any novel clear through. But "boy's book" versions were short; so short that they sometimes were mere plot summaries of the original. One of these we could plausibly imagine coming into the boy Lincoln's hands. According to Warren, *Robinson Crusoe* was one of three books that Sarah Bush Johnston Lincoln brought to Spencer County, Indiana, when she married Thomas Lincoln, but although Warren *assumes* a particular edition (London, 1810) as the one Abraham Lincoln read (ca. 1819), he does not give any provenance that might support this claim.[100] Moreover, Warren seems to think that Lincoln read something close to the full text of Defoe's original, replete with heavy if hypocritical Christian moralizing.

But, in fact, most of the late-eighteenth- and early-nineteenth-century American editions of *Robinson Crusoe* were what their editors referred to as "epitomized"—that is, radically abridged—and they typically narrated only Crusoe's time on the island (thus omitting the entire second half of the novel). Such a version is most likely what circulated in Spencer County. For example, one of printer/publisher Isaiah Thomas's earliest "juvenile" editions (Worcester, Mass., 1786) was only thirty-one pages, into which were crammed both the narrative frame and the island saga but also several woodcuts and two tacked-on pieces of edification for youth (the exemplum of "Wat Wilful," a naughty boy who disobeyed his parents' "advice" to stop playing on the windmill and therefore got a humiliating ducking in the mill pond; and a brief catechism in arithmetic for good boys who would advance in the world). And Thomas includes an advertisement: "Note: If you learn this book well, and are good, you can buy a larger and more complete History of Mr. Crusoe, at your friend the Bookseller's, in Worcester, near the Courthouse." Even had Lincoln somehow obtained this "larger" edition, in three volumes, he would still have been looking at less than Defoe's whole narrative ("faithfully abridged" is how the publisher put it).[101]

Two aspects of *Robinson Crusoe*, whether published in great or small format, "epitomized" or taken whole, saved Defoe's narrative from the strictures against fiction reading that were so deeply embedded in English and American Protestant society during the eighteenth and early nineteenth centuries. First, of course, was his disingenuous claim that the story was entirely true; second, that it was morally "improving" to its readers, inculcating among other things the dangers of disobeying one's parents in important life decisions, as in this quatrain at the end of Thomas's 1786 juvenile edition:

'Twas in this ship, which sail'd from Hull,
That Crusoe did embark;
Which did him vex, and much perplex,
And broke his parents heart.[102]

Defoe, the consummate journalist and ambitious businessman, knew his audience: a "true" tale was a *true-seeming* one, and all he as author had to provide in the way of documentation was the fact that one Alexander Selkirk had indeed sailed to the south seas, been shipwrecked, sustained himself on an island, been rescued, and returned to tell his story. From that point on, it mattered little how his own narrative diverged from the source (or whether he used Selkirk as a source at all). Defoe's *true-seeming* story would be acceptable to pious as well as merely curious readers, though even the most literal-minded of these surely came to realize that what they were reading was a new species of literature, soon to be called the *novel* (after its very newness).

The boy Lincoln might have been gladdened at Crusoe's ultimate rescue, having enjoyed more or less his "true" adventures on the island near the mouth of the Orinoco River off present-day Venezuela (and the fanciful region of Sir Walter Raleigh's "El Dorado" in the last years of the sixteenth century). But it is doubtful that he would have agreed with the stern moral lesson that young master Robinson ought never to have left in the first place: for that was what Lincoln would soon want to do himself. Crusoe's distraught father warned his son that going to sea *"would bring you many an aching heart"*; yet the young man's obstinacy put him on "the first ship that sailed from *Hull*" and on into the story as we know it. By the time he returned, many years later, Crusoe's parents were long dead—and the sun-addled adult perversely blamed himself for this ineluctable fact![103]

In hindsight, Crusoe wishes he had stayed home: yet every page of his adventures is energized by his forthright engagement with alien circumstance. Any reader, juvenile or adult, can see that Crusoe's regrets form a sort of obligatory moral disclaimer, while the story itself is full of felt life (and, subtextually, has the whole template of colonial/anticolonial debate within it). Bored in Hull, as in Spencer County; the flight into adventure a flight from the father (though Crusoe's is kind); the greater world requiring leaving home if the boy is to become his own man.

Ironically, a compelling case *for* suddenly, inexplicably, and permanently leaving home appears in the one book, next to the Bible, most likely to be found in even the humblest Protestant Christian homes of nineteenth-century America: John Bunyan's *Pilgrim's Progress* (1678). As in the case of *Robinson Crusoe*, the same four Indiana relatives and acquaintances named above remembered Bunyan's religious allegory as one of the books Lincoln read.[104] Warren believes that *Pilgrim's Progress* formed an important (and quite pleasant) part of his early education and that the book fascinated him from the moment Thomas Lincoln procured a copy for his son, "who was so delighted that 'his eyes sparkled, and that day he could not eat, and that night he could not sleep.'"[105]

That Lincoln would ignore his meals and his bed to read *Pilgrim's Progress* seems to contemporary taste preposterous. Yes, the book was available and had a Christian sanction as a sort of companion to the Bible; yes, he very probably read it, or read *in* it, as he did whatever printed matter came to hand. But with *delight* or with a fascination that would have made Bunyan of lasting importance? One is reminded of Huck Finn's bemusement in Mark Twain's novel upon discovering a copy of *Pilgrim's Progress* in the overwrought parlor of the Grangerford "mansion": when he looked into the book, he discovered it "was about a man who left his wife and family it didn't say why." Not perceiving Bunyan's allegory, or for that matter knowing what allegory was, Huck had no real use for the book—though he "read considerable in it now and then," finding that the "statements was interesting, but tough."[106] As for the fantastic adventures the pilgrim underwent, they were just so much Tom Sawyer stuff and therefore to be avoided if at all possible. Thus responded Huck Finn, a boy at the beginning of adolescence: and would the nine-year-old Lincoln (for that is when Warren believes he read *Pilgrim's Progress*) have managed any better?

To some extent, the answer depends upon whether Lincoln understood how literary allegory worked. If he did, we might compare him in precocity to Jesus in the temple at twelve, instructing the astonished doctors in the finer points of Jewish theology. On the other hand, we can imagine Lincoln as an eager, fast-developing reader whose appetite was insatiable, fed by anything and everything he could lay his hands on. The truth, as usual, is apt to fall in between. Unlike both *The Arabian Nights* and *Robinson Crusoe*, *Pilgrim's Progress* was usually published just as Bunyan wrote it, without abridgement or rewriting for juveniles. It had to be taken whole or skimmed over or dipped into—but always the book was big and perhaps more imposing than inviting. A typical edition of *Pilgrim's Progress*, such as the one Tom Lincoln is said to have provided for Abraham, would have contained not only the narrative proper—the more familiar first part, Christian's fraught journey to the New Jerusalem, along with his wife's pilgrimage in part 2—but also front matter, including a hagiography of Bunyan, the veritable Protestant saint, and Bunyan's prefatory poem entitled "The Author's Apology for His Book." What is more, some editions contained the bonus of woodcut or steel-engraved illustrations, so that the less attentive reader might see rather than have to imagine, for instance, what the giant Apollyon looked like.

"The Author's Apology for His Book" reveals that Bunyan's project began simply so as to keep his hands from being idle, "to divert myself, in doing this, / From worser thoughts, which make me do amiss." Yet once well begun, *Pilgrim's Progress* had seemed to write itself (though the author would not claim inspiration), and its maker had then to decide whether to publish the work. Having asked a number of his more pious churchly friends, he got from some the conventional negative response:

> *But it is feigned.* What of that I trow?
> Some men, by feigned words, as dark as mine,
> Make truth to spangle, and its rays to shine!
> *But they want solidness.* Speak, man, thy mind!
> *They draw the weak; metaphors make us blind.*[107]

This was the heart of the Protestant objection: Bunyan had written fiction; worse, he had veiled it in figures. To the latter, he has a ready reply:

> Were not God's laws,
> His gospel laws, in olden time held forth
> By shadows, types, and metaphors? Yet loath
> Will any sober man be to find fault
> With them, lest he be found for to assault
> The Highest Wisdom.[108]

Apply it broadly, and this may also serve as the justification for the prose fiction he has designed. Since the complete represented action of *Pilgrim's Progress* is overclouded with figure, which is gospel-approved (hence the interlarding of biblical texts throughout), Bunyan regards the whole as likewise sanctioned: a Christian allegory, a heavenly dream-vision whereby the homely and humble individual fights through hard mortal life to salvation. Or, it may be, Lincoln came to Bunyan just for mental relief:

> Wouldst thou divert thyself from melancholy?
> Wouldst thou be pleasant, yet be far from folly?
> Wouldst thou read riddles and their explanation?
> Or else be drowned in thy contemplation?[109]

Bunyan had been so steeped in the tannins of the King James Bible, yet also determined to write in an English idiom appropriate to a wide readership among the faithful, that his prose style is a curious admixture of the high and the colloquial, the one for didactic conviction, the other for storytelling. In *Abraham Lincoln: Biography of a Writer* (2008), Fred Kaplan asserts that *Pilgrim's Progress* "exposed Abraham to elevated writing, the weaving together of sound, rhythm, and imagistic language for special occasions." And collateral with the hortative diction was the pilgrim's exciting story: besides being a tale of home leaving, it was—again to quote Kaplan—"a story of upward mobility."[110]

But the ideology of *Pilgrim's Progress* is unlikely to have engaged Lincoln. To put it plainly, what Bunyan preached was antithetical to everything Lincoln came to believe about the nature and purpose of human life. Consider the following scene near the beginning of the book, where Christian has only just set out on his journey but already has doubts about the "true way." He meets one of Bunyan's many walking concepts, Mr. Worldly Wiseman, and asks him how to be rid of his "burden": fear of the imminent end of the world as foretold in Revelation. Mr. Wiseman, however, takes Christian to mean the weight on the shoulders of everyman, that is, the baggage of ordinary living. He therefore advises Christian to make for "yonder village" called "Morality," where he would find a gentleman named "Legality" to help him; or, if not at home, there was his son, "Civility," who was sure to be of service.

The ostensible application of the allegory here is straightforward: live morally, civilly, and according to the law and your human burdens are bearable. This was Lincoln's "political religion" as declared in the Lyceum Address. Of course, Christianity is missing, but since for Bunyan Christianity is all, and this-worldly life nothing, the pilgrim, tempted by Mr. Worldly Wiseman's really quite benevolent counsel, must immediately be catechized by "Evangelist" in Pauline justification by faith ("Now the just shall live by faith; but if any man draw back, my soul shall have no pleasure in him" [Hebrews 10:38]). And Evangelist follows this up with a denunciation of Worldly Wiseman and all his type: "he savoureth only of the doctrine of this world . . . and . . . because he loveth that doctrine best, for it saveth him best from the Cross; and because he is of this carnal temper." Christian must therefore "abhor" all worldly advice concerning human law and civility, which had set his "feet in the way that leadeth to the ministration of death. . . . [T]here is nothing in all this noise that thou has heard of these sottish men, but a design to beguile thee of thy salvation." And, as if to punctuate the divine truth of Evangelist's monition, "there came words and fire out of the mountain under which poor Christian stood, which made the hair of his flesh stand up."[111]

Bunyan was a radical dissenter from the Church of England. He spent more than a decade in jail as a prisoner of conscience for refusing to cease preaching what he took to be Christian truth (during which time he wrote *Pilgrim's Progress*). It is hardly surprising then that he despised what passed for civil justice in late-seventeenth-century Britain. In having his Christian pilgrim leave his family and flee the wrath to come, he prophesied both ruination for infidel England and imperishable bliss for the Protestant faithful who shall have the fortitude to push through all the way to Paradise. Yet in nineteenth-century America, a new republican democracy with pretty close to full freedom of religion, both constitutionally and in fact, an ideological fixation on the end-time is—and was largely regarded as—perverse. During the course of the Kentucky Revival (ca.1798–1806) thousands had reenacted, night after night, a symbolic psychodrama of apocalypse. But this turned out to be a remaking of the soul in order to live better and more freely in the United States, then and there in a nineteenth century that was dawning so promisingly for the nation. Spun-off millennialist sects that took the signs and tokens of the last days literally (the Shakers earlier in the century, the Millerites of the 1840s, for instance) were ridiculed, shunned, and segregated in wilderness colonies that were usually all but stillborn once the first enthusiasms passed. As Lincoln would soon understand, the problems of living fully and freely were sufficiently challenging without having one's mind deflected into heaven-making. Lincoln *thought* under the aspect of eternity; he *acted* the better to bring the ideal down to earth. If this were not soul tending enough for the evangelical Christians, well, so be it. *Pilgrim's Progress* could not teach him what he needed, and the only thing he had in common with Bunyan's Christian is that they both left home. But instead of fleeing the wrath to come, Lincoln walked the strait path right into it.

2. Young Citizen Lincoln

His mind was full of terrible Enquiry.
—Isaac Cogdal, *in* Herndon's Informants

On the subject of Lincoln's New Salem education in literacy, no text-book has received more frequent or respectful mention than Samuel Kirkham's *English Grammar* (1824). The village's collective memory testified variously that he read it with Ann Rutledge; he tutored in grammar with schoolmaster Mentor Graham, using a borrowed copy; he recited its lessons in "parsing" to friends like William G. Greene and Lynn McNulty ("Nult") Greene; or he walked solitary over the prairies and through the woods around New Salem teaching the volume's contents to himself.[1] Much later, Lincoln certified the story of having studied *a* grammar book to John Locke Scripps, though not naming Kirkham's: "After he was twenty-three, and had separated from his father, he studied English grammar, imperfectly of course, but so as to speak and write as well as he now does." In addition, Lincoln did not correct the paragraph in William Dean Howells's 1860 campaign biography that *did* name Kirkham as the grammar text studied. Finally, William G. Greene related that when he visited the White House sometime during the Civil War, Lincoln introduced him to William H. Seward as "the man who taught him grammar," which Greene denied in embarrassment. But Lincoln insisted: "'Bill, don't you recollect when we stayed in Offut's store in New Salem and you would hold the book and see if I could give the correct definitions and answers to the questions?' 'Yes,' said Greene, 'but that was not teaching you grammar.' 'Well,' responded Lincoln, 'that was all the teaching of grammar I ever had.'"[2]

No two of these several accounts agree on exactly when or with whom Lincoln read Kirkham's—or possibly Lindley Murray's—*Grammar*, nor does anyone mention what it was that he found so compelling between the covers, nor why he embarked on the study in the first place.[3] The New Salem schoolmaster Mentor Graham remembered offering Lincoln this advice, "If you Ever Expect to go before the public in any Capacity I think it the best thing you can do,"[4] which would indicate that Lincoln wanted and perhaps needed to improve his writing and speaking abilities before standing for political office. Ostensibly, the connection between knowing grammar and literacy (or literary) performance seems commonsensical: one learns to say and write "it is he" rather than "it is him," and so forth. Yet this begs the questions of just what it means to master this subject, and how doing so would help a person become a better communicator in the speaker's native tongue. Alone among contemporary Lincoln scholars, Douglas Wilson has taken the matter seriously enough to look at the contents of Kirkham: "Learning formal English grammar from a nineteenth-century textbook, without a qualified teacher, was a truly daunting task, as anyone who picks up a copy of Kirkham's will readily see. Just to take the first step, mastering the technical terminology, was intimidating." And Wilson cites several of these terms in support of his point: "'diphthong,' 'triphthong,' 'primitive word,' and 'derivative word.'"[5]

But isn't this difficulty of the subject more ours than Lincoln's? After all, *we* are the ones who have trouble understanding the early nineteenth century's textbooks; their readers of the day would have found them much less alien in organization and (to use a grammarian's favorite term) syntax. Moreover, William G. Greene remembered Lincoln's having had no difficulty at all with Kirkham, making himself a "good practical grammarian in three weeks—said to me Bill if that is what they call a science I'll subdue another."[6] But these "sciences" would prove more difficult: Lincoln discovered that Euclid's geometry, and trigonometry for surveying, being mathematically grounded, were far more difficult than English grammar. With these disciplines, he began almost at the zero point compared to the advantage that a lifetime's possession of a tongue gave the grammar student. The gist of grammar was mostly learning the names of and the formulas for what Lincoln had long since been *performing*. Like all speakers of English, Lincoln had been mouthing diphthongs (and perhaps the odd "triphthong") almost from the cradle, and for the last decade or so been writing them— all without possessing the notion that the terms denote double and triple vowels, respectively. And, again, to know that the word *man* is the root from which *manful* is compounded is surely more important than the information that the former is called a "primitive," the latter a "derivative" word.[7] Acquiring a specialized vocabulary allows one to appear philosophically competent in a subject. But the mastery of grammar was not very important to Lincoln's *development* as a writer and speaker. Let us see why.

The earliest claim for Lincoln's grammar study is late 1831–early 1832. William G. Greene told Herndon that while he and Lincoln served as clerks at Denton Offutt's New Salem store, Lincoln "commenced his studies. Mr Lincoln studied the grammar & surveying privately in his store—worked it out by himself alone as I recollect it."[8] Nult Greene put the period of study "in the summer after [Lincoln] came home from the Black Hawk War [1832]," while Mentor Graham recalled the time as early to mid-1833.[9]

The first of these (late 1831–early 1832) is the *only* segment of time *before* Lincoln published his first public essay, "Communication to the People of Sangamo County," which appeared in the *Sangamo Journal* (and perhaps as a handbill) on March 15, 1832.[10] For a young man of no formal education and ostensibly small practice in writing, a youth just turned twenty-three and making his debut in the local public prints, the "Communication" is a surprisingly competent exposition of a political agenda. Centering on Lincoln's devotion to "internal improvements," the essay is well organized, focused, detailed; it employs the buoyancy of general wisdom and logic to keep the ballast of practical information afloat; and it tempers the author's presumption in coming before the people with a nice bit of self-deprecation at the end. In other words, the piece, considered as a whole, is rhetorically effective. Was Lincoln the sole author, or did he receive help from his literary betters? One citizen of New Salem later declared Lincoln had sought his assistance as an editorial eye. John McNamar told Herndon that he had "corrected at his request Some of the Grammatical Errors" in the "Communication." And Mentor Graham was said to have been involved too in the fashioning of the campaign statement.[11] As McNamar's letters to Herndon indicate, he wrote well enough to be of some help to Lincoln, if asked, but Graham undercut his own biographers when he recalled to Herndon that Lincoln could already write "distinctly & precisely" by the time he arrived in Illinois.[12]

Lincoln told the New Salem schoolmaster that he had written familiar letters on behalf of some of his illiterate Indiana neighbors. This clearly locates Lincoln's developed literacy *before* New Salem, that is, in his Indiana boyhood and adolescence. We have seen his rapid self-education in Indiana and know from some of his family and friends there that he was often almost as busy writing as he was reading ("he al so rit while very young"). Besides the "friendly, confidential letters," Lincoln penned verse ("always . . . writing Poetry &c. &c."), varieties of prose ("essays on bein cind to animals and crawling insects"), and even kept a sort of commonplace book, since lost ("He had a copy book—a kind of scrap book in which he put down all things and this preserved them").[13]

One of the Lincoln family's near neighbors in Indiana, William Wood, actually remembered Lincoln as a *published author*, having placed in a newspaper (ca. 1827) an article arguing that education "should be fostered all over the Country," the better to sustain "the best form of Government in the world." Wood also told Herndon that he had read this essay, along with another on temperance, thought them better than anything he got from the newspapers he subscribed to, and helped arrange their publication.[14] Assuming Wood's accurate and good-faith recollection, Lincoln had, by his eighteenth year, begun to write seriously on subjects that would continue to interest him: American "political religion" and temperance.

In this context, Albert J. Beveridge makes an important point in his *Abraham Lincoln, 1809–1858*. Noting that from about 1823 on, the Lincoln family owned a copy of Nathan Bailey's *Universal Etymological English Dictionary* (1721), Beveridge observes, "the fact that this dictionary was at hand must be borne in mind while considering the books read by Lincoln during the years that he remained in Indiana." Bailey's monumental dictionary (sometimes said to be superior to Samuel Johnson's later compilation), as Beveridge points out, "included all English words without regard to their vogue or repute."[15] With such a help at hand, Lincoln could push his reading ability far beyond what we today would call his grade level in school. And we may be sure that what helped his reading also helped his writing.

Another Indiana source went so far as to say that Lincoln had treated the dictionary just as he would have any other book: he read it. "He would sit in the twilight and read a dictionary as long as he could see."[16] Two other dictionaries said to have been used by Lincoln merit mention here. Dennis Hanks recalled James Barclay's *Dictionary* (1774) as being among the family's books in Indiana. Though Lincoln in the late 1850s owned a copy of Noah Webster's *An American Dictionary* (1828), we do not know whether he had had access to this powerful tool during the New Salem years.[17] But either dictionary would have been a most useful reference. Barclay contained some meaty front matter, including an English grammar—which would have served as Lincoln's introduction to the discipline well before Kirkham—and a historical outline of ancient and modern history. Noah Webster's long-classic dictionary was an American original of tremendous and lasting importance. It not only included American English words and usages not found in British dictionaries but provided quotations for word meaning arranged chronologically from earliest to most current senses.

New Salem's William G. Greene offered further corroboration of Lincoln's early literary accomplishment in his first letter to Herndon: "he has often shown & read to me his first Composition he prized it highly it was full of witt & I pronounced a good thing. . . . it was personal an old Lady who lived & died in Sangamon but was written long before he came to Ills I think he informed me that he was about fourteen years ould when he wrote it[.]"[18] While this is somewhat garbled (had the "old Lady" been young in Indiana, when Lincoln wrote her story, then an emigrant to Illinois, where she "lived & died"?), the point is clear enough: Lincoln brought at least one manuscript with him to New Salem. Taken together, this evidence presents us with an interpretive crux in our understanding of Lincoln's education in literacy. Either Lincoln's intensive assimilation of Kirkham's *Grammar* in his first months at New Salem materially aided him in composing the "Communication to the People of Sangamo County"—which he was in all likelihood doing concurrently—or he had previously made himself a more-than-competent essayist in the English language.

Lincoln's "Communication" opens with a fifty-six-word, periodic, complex sentence that carries two interrupting elements and a parenthetic subordinate clause between dashes. The burden of this first sentence is to state the occasion of the essay, his candidacy for the state legislature. Then follows the commencement of its main topic: "Time and experience have verified to a demonstration, the public utility of internal improvements."[19] The phrase "verified to a demonstration," one that we may think of as so typical of Lincoln's logic, is probably adapted from Thomas Paine.[20] A thing *demonstrated* is as undeniably true as a sound geometric proof. In *The Age of Reason*, Paine several times uses the phrase "proves to a demonstration." Interestingly, the proposition Lincoln makes is not true, since nothing from the world of experience can be "verified to a demonstration." The sentence is therefore subtly figurative and the more sophisticated for being so. The opening of "Communication" is far too ably constructed to be the work of a novice writer. Nor does a textbook like Kirkham's *Grammar* afford any relevant theory or practice that could have aided Lincoln in composition of this order, but rather a taxonomy of the English language in stultifying detail over more than two hundred pages—stuff Lincoln might easily take in. As for Kirkham's belief that grammar is *necessary*—"without the knowledge and application of grammar rules, it is impossible for anyone to think, speak, read, or write with accuracy"[21]—Lincoln had shown himself more than sufficient in all three areas. After all, how important to the mind, or useful to the pen, is learning to conjugate verbs that have a different ending only in the third person singular of the present tense, or to decline nouns that inflect scarcely at all? Beyond rote practice on naming parts of speech, "parsing" nouns and verbs, and abstracting rules and definitions, Kirkham provides little enough that would be of practical use to the essayist. This "little" occurs in a short section on rhetoric at the end of the book (219–25). "Rhetoric, or the art of persuasion," Kirkham observes, "requires in a writer, the union of good sense, and a lively and chaste imagination."[22]

Leave out the adjective *chaste* and this might stand as a good characterization of Lincoln's style. But how does one learn proper and effective *rhetoric*? According to Kirkham, from studying the principles of grammar, from which it is derived! And the pedagogue proceeds to name the qualities of "chaste" style, sentence structure, and figurative language and to give the commandments for the proper use of each. As pedestrian and prescriptive as Kirkham is here (he repeats the venerable rule, so often ignored to the benefit of good writing, of not ending a sentence with a preposition), from his brief treatment of figures of speech Lincoln may in fact have gleaned a few kernels of literary wisdom, such as this: "Figures of Speech may be described as language which is prompted either by the imagination, or by the passions."[23]

This part of the *Grammar* includes a brief digression on Hugh Blair, whose prominence in Lindley Murray's *English Reader* we saw in chapter 1. Another popular textbook on literacy that Lincoln is said to have read at New Salem was Blair's *Lectures on Rhetoric* (1783).[24] Blair's *Lectures* are not mentioned by any of Herndon's informants, nor in Beveridge's *Abraham Lincoln, 1809–1858*, nor Louis Warren's *Lincoln's Youth*. The single source asserting that Lincoln read Blair is Henry B. Rankin, whose late and uncorroborated testimony on all things Lincolnian is of doubtful veracity.[25] It is only fair to note, however, that Lincoln would have had access to a copy of Blair's *Lectures* when he resided in New Salem. A man named Matthew Rogers, who farmed in the Athens, Illinois, vicinity from the early 1820s, had a personal library notable for that time and place, and Lincoln is said to have borrowed occasionally from it.[26]

Even if he didn't borrow Blair from Rogers, we can positively assert that Lincoln read the Scot, perhaps unwittingly. For Kirkham boldly plagiarized from the *Lectures'* section on figures of speech: much of the *Grammar's* material in this section is nearly identical with Blair's introduction to the "Origin and Nature of Figurative Language"; likewise, Kirkham's definitions of the major types of figures are clearly taken (again, nearly verbatim) from Blair.[27]

In the end, the grammar acolyte from New Salem gained more from reading and making his own the literary snippets that Kirkham chose as instances of figures than from the master's parsing lessons themselves. As Charles Maltby, who observed him many days and nights at the Offut store, recalled, "his correct mastery of the language was acquired more from reading and writing than from study."[28] The incidentals in the textbook contained much of its value to Lincoln. Near the beginning of the volume,

Kirkham extolled the value of grammar study to young students who would rise intellectually, adding, "and should you not aspire at distinction in the republic of letters, this knowledge cannot fail of being serviceable to you, even if you are destined to pass through *the humblest walks of life.*"[29] Well, Lincoln did want distinction, in the "republic of letters" and in the Republic. In his first publication, supporting his first try for public office, he concluded with a declaration that has become well known for its author's frank admission of political ambition and his nearly palpable anticipation of failure: "How far I shall succeed in gratifying this ambition, is yet to be developed. I am young and unknown to many of you. I was born and have ever remained in *the humblest walks of life.*" If this initial trial of political ambition comes up short, why, then, Lincoln can take it: "I have been too familiar with disappointments to be very much chagrined."[30]

Did the young author unconsciously borrow "the humblest walks of life" from Kirkham? The architecture, the engineering of his writing were by the New Salem years well founded; from then on, he looked for content to furnish the building and language for interior decoration. Of the conclusion to the "Communication to the People of Sangamo County," John Nicolay and John Hay observed in *Abraham Lincoln: A History*, "This is almost precisely the style of his later years. The errors of grammar and construction which spring invariably from an effort to avoid redundancy of expression remained with him through life. He seemed to grudge the space required for necessary parts of speech."[31] What these "errors of grammar and construction" may have been, the two former Lincoln secretaries do not note, and none seems evident to this reader. But their larger point is that Lincoln's style was in 1832 and always would be irregular when judged against the norms of his age (which were still based on eighteenth-century models). The study of Samuel Kirkham's *English Grammar*, firmly founded on those norms, neither helped nor hurt him. As an already capable writer, Lincoln was now searching for content (facts, ideas, arguments) and refinements of style (models, striking expression, attunements of voice). And this was why he read and kept on reading. He would always be that "precocious boy obsessed with words," as Douglas L. Wilson has so nicely phrased it.[32] What his seventy-five-year-old stepmother, Sarah Bush Johnston, remembered from the long-gone Indiana years, "He had a copy book—a kind of scrap book in which he put down all things and this preserved them," was now the province of the capacious and well-organized commonplace book of his mind, in which all the things that counted were "preserved" and made ready for utterance.[33]

During the six years that Abraham Lincoln lived in New Salem, Illinois (1831–37), the pioneer village northwest of Springfield never contained more than twenty-five families—a population of a hundred, say—and not long after he moved to Springfield, the place ceased to exist except as a ghost town.[34] Yet somehow, somewhere in New Salem, Lincoln managed to find the books and the literary conversation necessary to stimulate his intellectual development. He was not quite bookless when he arrived in the village in September 1831. According to his New Salem friend Charles Maltby, Lincoln carried a "small collection of books" that included the poetry of "[William] Cowper, [Thomas] Gray and [Robert] Burns."[35] Among the titles he was to borrow in New Salem would be some quite radical treatises that dramatized the destructive power of religious and political autocracy upon even the most sturdily founded states, particularly Edward Gibbon's *The History of the Decline and Fall of the Roman Empire* (1776–87); or sharply questioned the truth of Christianity and the historicity of the Bible, principally Constantin de Volney's *The Ruins* (1791) and Thomas Paine's *The Age of Reason* (1794). All three of these eighteenth-century classics scandalized the Christian community in Europe and America. Merely to *read* them (especially Volney and Paine; Gibbon had a slightly better reputation) was tantamount to religious heterodoxy: but to *speak well* of them privately among friends, let alone in public, branded the reader an "infidel."[36] Nonetheless, New Salem appears to have had a coterie of freethinkers to whom Lincoln was drawn and from whom he drew these and other, less controversial titles to read.Two prominent New Salem names immediately suggest themselves as sources for the forbidden books, if not the infidelism. James Rutledge, a cousin of Ann Rutledge, was "said to have had a library of twenty-five or thirty volumes," while William G. Greene, Lincoln's intimate at New Salem, attended Illinois College (Jacksonville) between 1833 and 1836.[37] In 1865 Greene recalled to William H. Herndon having lent Lincoln "Gibbons histories," at the same time remarking that Lincoln found in New Salem works of the three poets who would always be his favorites: Shakespeare, Burns (*pace* Maltby), and Byron.[38] According to J. Rowan Herndon, William's cousin, Lincoln had been free to borrow whatever anyone had: "He had axcess to any Books that was in and around the town of Salem for all Knew that he was fond of Reading."[39] New Salem had a reading community of men and women (notably Elizabeth Abell and Ann Rutledge),[40] as well as a penchant for serious talk, as indicated by the existence of the "New Salem Debating Society," meetings of which Lincoln began attending as early as the winter of 1831–32. In the words of Benjamin Thomas, the village had a "budding intellectuality."[41]

Robert R. Rutledge, one of Ann's younger siblings, left a remarkable portrait of Lincoln's debating society debut "about the year 1832 or 1833": "As he arose to speak his tall form towered above the little assembly.

Both hands were thrust down deep in the pockets of his pantaloons. A perceptible smile at once lit up the faces of the audience for all anticipated the relation of some humorous story. But he opened up the discussion in splendid style to the infinite astonishment of his friends. As he warmed with his subject his hands would forsake his pockets and would enforce his ideas by awkward gestures; but would very soon seek their easy resting place. He pursued the question with reason and argument so pithy and forcible that all were amazed."[42] Unfortunately, Rutledge, though his account is so carefully composed as to be literary, offers no clue as to what Lincoln's subject was that night "in [the] underground room of a rude log cabin" in the New Salem vicinity.[43]

It was probably too decorous an occasion for a good shot of infidelity from the Young Turk.[44] But infidelity–that is, radical religious skepticism–was what Lincoln was reading and thinking about. How far did he push his radicalism? Did he really "call Christ a bastard"? Did he take the time and trouble to write a "little book on Infidelity"? So deposed more than one of his New Salem and Springfield friends and acquaintances, speaking or writing after Lincoln's death to William H. Herndon of his character and actions as a coming young man in the 1830s. The most important source on Lincoln's early religious opinions was James H. Matheny, a Springfield attorney who had known Lincoln "as Early as 1834–37." Herndon interviewed or requested written recollections from Matheny four times (1865–70) on the subject of Lincoln's religious views.[45] It was Matheny who had heard Lincoln call Christ a bastard; it was he who, after being increasingly importuned by Herndon (*badgered* might be a better word), admitted that Lincoln himself had declared to him the authorship of the "little book on Infidelity." Matheny's frankness would prove courageous, if incautious; for when Herndon's interviews with him became public in Ward Lamon's ghostwritten biography of Lincoln in 1872, he came under considerable pressure from an outraged Springfield Christian community to recant his account of Lincoln's religious infidelity—testimony he had first freely and then reluctantly given to Herndon "as I got it from Lincoln's own mouth," including the bastardry business and an overall position on Christianity that "bordered on absolute Atheism."[46]

Albert J. Beveridge observes judiciously that Lincoln *read in* the works of the French *philosophes* and Paine.[47] It makes sense to include Gibbon's *Decline and Fall* in this "read in" category. When William Greene loaned Lincoln his "copy" of "Gibbons histories," he was handing off a real heavyweight: its typical nineteenth-century American editions were printed in six or eight volumes in large octavo format, running to some three thousand pages.[48] And, of course, Greene's charity in lending this massive work to his friend in no way guarantees that Lincoln read even a single word of it. Yet what one discovers in *Decline and Fall* is a good deal of thought and style that would have proved engaging, instructive, and useful to Lincoln. Where else could he have found such a rich and deep account of classical and premodern European history? Of the tangled skein of Christian theologies during the patristic centuries of the Church? Of the rise and character of Islam? And, perhaps the profoundest matter for reflection, of the nature of empires and the causes of their declines? Propelling this grand saga was Gibbon's accomplished, eighteenth-century English prose, the equal of which Lincoln had hitherto found only in snatches in anthologies.

A persistent but mistaken notion about *Decline and Fall* is that Gibbon blames Christianity for Rome's demise. This judgment often comes from critics who cannot have read the work but are accepting the traditionally unfriendly Christian viewpoint toward it.[49] In fact, *Decline and Fall* argues that several causes, Christianity—or rather the institutionalized Catholic Church—among them but not by itself decisive, ruined the Roman Empire.[50] Gibbon's long narrative and analysis of this millennium-plus decline set a new standard for modern belletristic history because it insisted on treating *all* religions as part of an overarching secular movement of human affairs. A very different approach had been that of the Frenchman Charles Rollin, who wrote nearly half a century before Gibbon and whose *Ancient History* Lincoln supposedly read in an English translation about the same time he was deep in Gibbon (most probably early 1833).[51] For Rollin, the whole point of the past, as far back as records reached (Egypt), was to vindicate the Christian present against claims that the profane eras had been more civilized. While his *Ancient History* is introduced in a manner Gibbon would find familiar—"it highly concerns us to know by what means those [pre-Christian] empires were founded; the steps by which they rose to the exalted pitch of grandeur we so much admire; what it was that constituted their true glory and felicity; and what were the causes of their declension and fall"[52]—in Rollin's narrative such knowledge is elucidated as providential design and the fulfillment of the world through a Judeo-Christian plot and chronology (because Rollin regards Scripture as inspired, the Old Testament is his principal source for ancient historical truth) that culminates in the eighteenth-century Catholic Church and European manifest destiny.

Hence, Gibbon's treasured truths of human nature as observed in political action do not and cannot have their analogue in Rollin, since his is a history of God's plan unfolding, without human free agency. Still, many of his heroic characters (Romans especially) are nicely drawn, showing a nobility they doubly should not have, as pre-Christians and unfree actors.[53] Because Rollin intended his *Ancient History* for use as a textbook by young adult students, he concocted what he called "epitomes" of Greek and Roman authors (short biographies, summations of quality, and quotations from works) and tried to keep erudition to a minimum. "Students," he insisted, "with a very moderate application, may easily go through this course of study in a year, without interrupting their other studies." Yet, of necessity, there is a mountain of information in a treatise that ranges from earliest Egypt to the Roman Republic (in a sense, a complement to Gibbon's fifteen centuries from the birth of Jesus to the dawn of modern Europe). This all adds up to more than fifteen-hundred pages of rather small type. If Lincoln, with his usual systematic dedication, really did go through Rollin in a year, he must have accumulated, or discarded, or ignored an immense amount of information, much of it presented without sufficient stylistic spice to make the dish palatable. But at least Rollin did offer a "sacred history" to set alongside Gibbon's secular one.[54]

For what Lincoln would have seen in Gibbon's huge literary diorama was nothing like sacred history playing out before him, nor so much Christianity's emasculating imperial Roman virtue, as a complex drama of social, political, and economic strife, of human ambition and greed, and, occasionally, of heroism founded on principle. *Decline and Fall* opens with the glorious late summer of the empire, under the Antonines, "the period in the history of the world, during which the condition of the human race was most happy and prosperous." Marcus Aurelius died in 180 c.e., more than a century before the Christianization of the empire under Constantine; yet even during Marcus's golden reign, Gibbon senses anxieties abroad in Rome: "The fatal moment was perhaps approaching, when some licentious youth, or some jealous tyrant, would abuse, to the destruction, that absolute power which [the Antonines] had exerted for the benefit of the people."[55]

Since Augustus, the Roman Republic had been dead in all but name, though that very name was for centuries further employed by the emperors and the senate to invoke past greatness and celebrate present grandeur. Now came the historical test case of an American Republic. Could it survive, blossom, as had Rome, yet endure, as Rome had not? The language, tone, and sense of Gibbon's passage echo Lincoln's worry in the Lyceum Address. He feared that a tyrant, taking advantage of growing disrespect among the people for the rule of law, might soon arise to destabilize the *American Republic*, which had been founded three generations before—hardly a page in terms of Roman history. But the United States had political fathers at least as distinguished as the Antonines and was bidding to become a new empire, ultimately superior to Rome because more lastingly virtuous and free. As did Washington and Gibbon, Lincoln thought that internal decay rather than foreign enemies was most to be feared: "If destruction be our lot, we must ourselves be its author and finisher."[56] For centuries, the health of the Roman body politic was maintained through a civil religion of ancestor worship, with the greatest generals, senators, and especially emperors deified, idolized (literally), and worshipped for their glorious leadership. To say that Lincoln in the Lyceum Address prescribed something similar for the still-young American Republic sounds very strange indeed. But he did; he called for a "political religion" based on the transcendent heroes of the Revolution and their sacrifices: "Let every American, let every lover of liberty, every well wisher to posterity, swear by the blood of the Revolution, never to violate in the least particular, the laws of the country." Respect for the Founding Fathers, the sentiments of the Declaration of Independence, and the law directed by the Constitution should be instituted (established?) as "the *political religion* of the nation; and let the old and the young, the rich and the poor, the grave and the gay, of all sexes and tongues, and colors and conditions, sacrifice unceasingly upon its altars." What is more, the *stories* of the American Revolution ought to form a part of the national scripture: to be "read . . . and recounted, so long as the Bible shall be read."[57]

A falling away from such a covenant presaged the breakdown of "the attachment of the People" to their government, opening a reactionary way for an ambitious and unscrupulous tyrant and, inevitably, national "suicide." Anxiety about the United States' incipient empire was in the air. It is probably not altogether a historical coincidence that, as Lincoln spoke to the Young Men's Lyceum in Springfield at the beginning of 1838, the Anglo-American painter Thomas Cole had recently concluded a tremendously successful public exhibition in New York of his monumental *Course of Empire* series; nor that the most famous poet of the United States, William Cullen Bryant, had, in the summer of 1832, stood transfixed on the prairies of central Illinois, inspiring himself with the fresh southwestern breezes and envisioning the American empire to come in what would be, after "Thanatopsis," his most enduring lyric, "The Prairies" (1832). Many years later, Bryant recalled having met Captain Lincoln marching his company north to meet Black Hawk and his warriors: "a tall, awkward, uncouth lad . . . whose conversation delighted him by its raciness and originality."[58] We cannot confirm that Lincoln read "The Prairies," though he knew "Thanatopsis" by heart and once recited it to his in-laws in Lexington, Kentucky, and was said by his presidential secretary John Hay to have read other Bryant poems.[59] Still, any seasoned traveler across mid-Illinois, a fortiori one with Lincoln's sensibility, would have been struck by this powerful poem of place and progress. "The Prairies," to a modern taste at any rate, feels restlessly anxious about massive emigration's despoliation of nature and the whites' murderous treatment of indigenous peoples, even as it celebrates young America's westering topos.

Cole and Bryant had been the best of friends until the former's premature death in 1848.[60] And on the subject of the "anxiety of empire," they were of one mind. Cole's five huge canvases allegorically represent humanity's cultural evolution: from hunter-gatherer barbarism, through Arcadian pastoralism, to urban "Consummation," "Destruction," and "Desolation" of empire—the Gibbonian archetypal rise and fall of Rome, with prophetic application to the United States. The last three paintings extravagantly show the operation of national suicide: the lust and luxury of "Consummation" illustrates the potentially disastrous consequences of a social cancer that has weakened the polis from within, so that the great city of the painting is helpless against the "barbarians" of "Destruction" who sack and burn the capital of the empire and then abandon it to the same prolonged "Desolation" that Volney's Pilgrim, as we shall see, beheld among the ruins of an ancient empire in Syria—perhaps an age, if not final, at least as long as the prehistorical "Savage State" with which the series and the cycle began.

Bryant's poem, though far less lurid in its imagery and rhetoric, likewise fantasizes destruction: an "empire" of civilized native Americans, the "disciplined and populous race" of the "Mound Builders," had centuries before been overrun and slaughtered by nomadic tribes from the far west of the continent (the "Red Man"), who were then, in turn, being obliterated by advancing armies of white European settlers. Bryant's voice sings the Mound Builders' dirge, philosophical about the past:

All is gone—
All—save the piles of earth that hold their bones—
The platforms where they worshiped unknown gods—
. . . Thus change the forms of being. Thus arise
Races of living things, glorious in strength,
And perish, as the quickening breath of God
Fills them, or is withdrawn.

And he can partly palliate the rapacious behavior of the Anglo-Europeans: the "Red Man" must expect his depredations to come round again and smite him. But what of the future? Will the cycle be unbroken, or will America providentially prove the exception to history's rule? Bryant would have it so, indeed deeply desires that it be the case, but the poem, after an idyllic evocation of the civilization-to-come of yeomen family farms overspreading the "gardens of the desert," ends ambiguously:

All at once
A fresher wind sweeps by, and breaks my dream,
And I am in the wilderness alone.[61]

Would Lincoln have followed the uneasy logic of Bryant's dream of history? Would he have reflected that "The Prairies" has as one of its themes the tragedy of what he, Lincoln, had just been furthering in the Black Hawk War?

When, nearly thirty years later, Lincoln spoke in New York at the Cooper Union (Monday, February 27, 1860), Bryant, as "chairman of the evening," escorted Lincoln to "the speaker's chair." Bryant was by then sixty-five years old, basking in the light of an unofficially conferred poet laureateship, but really much more influential as the Republican editor of the *New York Evening Post*. Lincoln had just turned fifty-one, but was a much younger man than his host in national experience. Bryant apparently worried lest the rude Illinoisan betray the confidence of the speaker selection committee with a too-western, too idiomatic talk. In his introduction of Lincoln, Bryant praised him both as "'the great champion' of the anti-slavery cause in Illinois" and, based on that encounter on the Illinois prairies, as an *Indian fighter*, and then sat down in some trepidation until a very few minutes later, when Lincoln's "masterful" speech put him at ease, even as it excited the audience all the way through to the rousing and now-famous conclusion (in all-capitals in the printed pamphlet): "LET US HAVE FAITH THAT RIGHT MAKES MIGHT."[62]

Early in the pages of the first volume of *Decline and Fall*, Gibbon offers this observation on religion in Roman society at its peak of power: "The various modes of worship, which prevailed in the Roman world, were all considered by the people, as equally true; by the philosopher, as equally false; and by the magistrate, as equally useful."[63] When Lincoln read these lines, he was a young man in his early twenties; recently emerged from "the people," rapidly educating himself as "the philosopher," and destined to be "the magistrate"—after inauguration in 1861 the *chief* magistrate of the United States, to be accused on every side, throughout the four years of civil war, of embodying the very tyrant he had prophesied in the Lyceum Address. It may help here to look at the etymology of the word *tyrant*. Had Lincoln consulted any of the three dictionaries he owned or had access to, he would have understood the word as Gibbon did, in both its main senses: first, simply as an *absolute ruler*, with neither positive nor negative valence attached, though among the predemocracy Greeks goodness was expected to be the tyrant's norm. Arguably, Augustus and the Antonines had also been benevolent tyrants. Holding near-absolute power, they had ruled with subtlety rather than raw force when circumstances permitted. Gibbon's Augustus, for example, had shown himself "sensible that mankind is governed by names; nor was he deceived in his expectation, that the senate and people would submit to slavery, provided they were respectfully assured that they still enjoyed their ancient freedom."[64]

Lincoln's own political acumen eighteen hundred years later was equally effective, though without the inveterate cynicism of the Roman, and enacted on behalf of a much finer object: to convince "the people" to submit to the end of slavery and thereby themselves remain free. In the two passages here quoted, so characteristic of Gibbon's deft mind realized in handsome prose, we see intellectual features Lincoln perhaps already held close by the early 1830s: a reasonable principle of politics, elegantly stated, and ready for practical application. Despite the repeated cries of his critics, he did not rule like the tyrannical Alexander, Caesar, or Napoleon he had warned his audience about in the Lyceum Address. But during the Civil War, Lincoln when necessary *acted as a tyrant* in Gibbon's better sense of the word. Except for having to stand for reelection in 1864 (a major qualification of this point, to be sure!), he was a de facto dictator in the interests of the people of the Union. He wielded a power far greater than any American president had before him. We may with some confidence venture that Gibbon the historian, while a Whig who supported the Crown during the American Revolution, would have ranked Lincoln's Civil War leadership with that of the Antonines (or perhaps with the later and lesser emperors Constantine and Julian) rather than place him in the company of Nero, Commodus, and their sorry kind—tyrants in the second, and more common, meaning of the word, who deserved Booth's "*Sic semper tyrannis!*" far more than his victim did.

Lincoln and Gibbon both clearly saw the dangers to political order from a populist rhetoric aimed at stirring the passions. First, Gibbon: "Every popular government has experienced the effects of rude or artificial eloquence. The coldest nature is animated, the firmest reason is moved, by the rapid communication of the prevailing impulse; and each hearer is affected by his own passions and by those of the surrounding multitude."[65] And now Lincoln, again from the Lyceum Address, remarking on the decisive role popular passion had played in the American Revolution: "By this influence, the jealousy, envy, and avarice, incident to our nature, and so common to a state of peace, prosperity, and conscious strength, were, for the time, in a great measure smothered and rendered inactive; while the deep rooted principles of hate, and the powerful motive of revenge, instead of being turned against each other, were directed exclusively against the British nation."[66]

This is very strong language concerning the darkness of human nature—where are the "better angels"?—and neither man seriously questioned whether there was such a thing or denied that it had its blacker
side. Without such an external enemy and a noble cause for fighting,
Lincoln feared, the rootedness of evil motives would cause citizen to turn
against citizen, with the rule of law the chief casualty of the conflict. Near
the conclusion of volume 1 of *Decline and Fall*, Gibbon delivers another
of his many memorable maxims, or apothegms, concerning politics and
human nature: "The different characters that mark the civilised nations
of the globe may be ascribed to the use and abuse of reason. . . . But the
operation of instinct is more sure and simple than that of reason; it is
much easier to ascertain the appetites of a quadruped than the speculations of a philosopher."[67] Gibbon's sentiment here is perfectly in accord
with Lincoln's perspective on American society in the Lyceum Address,
which stands as a sort of educational valedictory to New Salem and an
announcement to Springfield that he has arrived: the rising lawyer and
politician, to be sure, but as well the intellectual, having graduated with
his self-made baccalaureate.

And Lincoln would surely have agreed with Gibbon that "passion and
ignorance are always despotic."[68] Whether opposing Peter Cartwright or
Stephen A. Douglas, Lincoln relied on two main rhetorical weapons: "cold,
calculating, unimpassioned reason" in argument, as the best preventative
of that very reason's being overthrown by populist passion; and figurative
language, which both warmed the heart and softened the countenance
of "cold reason." These together, deployed ingeniously, gave his political
communications sufficient authority to meet and defeat the most rabid
brands of populist demagoguery and name-calling. From the first election as an Illinois representative to his single term in the U.S. Congress,
Lincoln had undergone a long apprenticeship: in control, in learning to
take his own medicine of "cold, calculating, unimpassioned reason." As
he learned to argue publicly in the mid-1830s, Lincoln first tried whatever
forensic tricks he thought would work, without regard for the humanity
of his opponents or his own dignity. These were the years that constituted
his aggressive "power to hurt": its weapons including biting burlesque and
ad hominem invective against—to name but one of his favorite and easiest
targets—Peter Cartwright in 1834.

By 1838, though he had by no means given over the practice of "skinning"
his opponents with language, Lincoln sought the basis for a new rhetoric
that would enable him to assume a place in the political caravan. At the
time of the Lyceum Address, did he presciently know that America considered as empire would face a crisis over slavery? Lincoln was preparing

himself as a politician in a higher sense than occupying a seat in the lower house of the Illinois legislature. His reading of Gibbon's *Decline and Fall* helped him intellectually in the service of his "peculiar ambition. . . . of being truly esteemed of [his] fellow man."[69] As Edward Gibbon neared the end of his long literary and historical journey in *Decline and Fall*, having reached the dawns, false and true, of the European Renaissance, he set down one of his most thoughtful generalizations about the relationship between gifted individuals and the inertia of the past that first restrains, but ultimately frees them and their societies to make a quantum leap in human development: "Genius may anticipate the season of maturity; but in the education of a people, as in that of an individual, memory must be exercised before the powers of reason and fancy can be expanded: nor may the artist hope to equal or surpass, till he has learned to imitate, the works of his predecessors."[70] Lincoln was well on his way to meeting precisely this challenge of the past; in the 1830s more so as a literary artist than a politician, but by the end of the decade with his vocational goal firmly in mind: an eccentric but heroic union of the two—*the political artist.*

The Ruins; or, Meditation on the Revolutions of Empires (1791), by Constantin-François Chasseboeuf, Comte de Volney, became popular in the United States immediately upon its first appearance in English and remained in print throughout the nineteenth century. Perhaps the most widely read translation was that by the American poet and Jeffersonian Democrat Joel Barlow, who had worked closely with Volney in Paris in order to make a more accurate, idiomatic, and felicitous version of *Ruins* than had yet appeared in the English language. Barlow's edition was published in 1802 and reprinted again and again in the United States. It is his stylish yet quite readable prose that Lincoln most probably read.[71]

The sole informant to Herndon on this matter is Abner Y. Ellis, the strength of whose testimony is somewhat vitiated by ambiguity in his first written statement to Herndon (January 1866). Ellis declared, clearly enough, that Lincoln "once asked Me if I had ever Read Volneys ruins he Said he had." But he gave no year, either for this conversation or the reading itself. In a letter written a month later, apparently at Herndon's prompting, Ellis tried to provide more detail: "it was in the year 1841 the [*sic*] told me that he had been reading—Volney & Tom Pain but when he had read them I do not know the reason [space] I remember the time it was at My House and he Wrote a Deed for me and I have it Now before Me[.]"[72] Based on Ellis's twenty-five year-old recollection, then, sometime before the date in 1841 Lincoln had read *The Ruins*, but we cannot further narrow the range (1831 being the lower limit).

In the four Abner Ellis letters to Herndon in which Volney is mentioned, his work is always linked with that of Thomas Paine. Yet, as we shall see below, the problem with Paine's provenance is exactly the opposite from Volney's: several informants say Lincoln read Paine, and occasionally when, but usually not *what* he read. Here we have positive testimony of the title of the book (indeed, just as *Gibbon* means *Decline and Fall*, to speak of reading *Volney* is a metonomy for reading *The Ruins*), but we do not know when. Beveridge, as previously noted, asserts that when Lincoln was "about twenty-six years of age [he] read in them," which would make the year circa 1835.[73] There is some reason, however, to prefer an earlier period. The key testimony for Lincoln's composition of "the little book on Infidelity" came from Hardin Bale, whom Herndon first interviewed on May 29, 1865. As Bale remembered, "about the year 1834 A Lincoln wrote a work on infidelity, denying the divinity of the Scriptures."[74] As the following analysis hopes to show, it is highly unlikely that Lincoln, if he did write such an essay when Bale said he did, could have accomplished it without having read Volney's *Ruins* and Paine's *Age of Reason*, since these are precisely the two proscribed books whose arguments did the most damage to the Christian biblical, theological, and institutional positions. And, with the addition of Voltaire's *Important Study of the Scriptures*, they form the only anticlerical ammunition that Lincoln would have had at hand.

What Barlow says of Volney's French in *The Ruins* is equally true of his English translation: "The energy and dignity of the author's manner, the unaffected elevation of his stile, the conciseness, perspicuity and simplicity of his diction, are every where suited to his subject; which is solemn, novel, luminous, affecting; a subject perhaps the most universally interesting to the human race that has ever been presented to their contemplation" (vi). The subtitle of *The Ruins*, "Meditation on the Revolutions of Empires," gives an indication of Volney's comprehensive intent. What Gibbon did for Rome, graphing and documenting its long decline and fall, Volney attempts for all Western empires, reduced to a type and without the weighty context of detail and historical process for any in particular. Like Gibbon, Volney insists on seeing history as the result of free human action. His commitment to the French Revolution requires an agency more amenable to humankind's perfectibility than Fate, the Wheel of Fortune, or Divine Providence.

More than half of the first volume of *The Ruins* treats the causes for the rise and fall of secular empires. Among societies, the just and reasonable prospered, but they collapsed when "ignorance and cupidity" gained the ascendant. What may have struck Lincoln about this section of *The Ruins* is an artful if tragic evocation of the failure of humankind to sustain a just polity—whether in the history of an isolated city-state or a vast geographical empire. Facing the beginning "Invocation" page of *The Ruins* is an engraving of the Pilgrim-narrator of the book seated in a reflective pose before the ruins of Palmyra (Syria) in the Valley of the Euphrates. As he gazes upon the melancholy scene, a nearby stray dog hearkens to his voice: "'Here,' said I, 'here once flourished an opulent city; here was the seat of a powerful empire.'" The "Invocation" itself opens with this apostrophe, "Hail, solitary ruins, holy sepulchers, and silent walls!" Somewhere in their archaeological dust lay the secrets of their fall, which to the reflective mind suggests a future antidote to such a fate: "the sacred dogma of Equality" (ix–x). As the day declines, the Pilgrim beholds a scene much like Cole's *Desolation of Empire.* While it "impressed on my mind a religious pensiveness," it also brings despondency: "Ah! Hapless man. . . . a blind fatality sports with thy destinies! A fatal necessity rules with the hand of chance the lot of mortals" (4–5, 13–14).

This lament approaches the Baptist Calvinism that Lincoln struggled with in his deep need, always denied fulfillment, for a positive metaphysics. And so the Pilgrim, as sometimes did Lincoln, sinks into a "profound melancholy" at what appears to be the inevitability of human social failure. But, right on cue, a "Phantom" or "apparition" appears (the first of Volney's personae) to set our desperate Pilgrim straight as to the real causes of *ruination* and point the way toward progressive truth. Instead of vainly blaming Fate or God, humankind must scrutinize itself in the light of reason and learn that it is (and always has been) owing to unbridled *passion* that miserable desolation visits his creations: "it is not hidden in the bosom of God; it dwells within himself, he hears it in his own heart" (19). Moreover, no single human group has ever been more favored by "providence" than another; all prospered—even "infidels"—so long as they "observed the laws of the heavens and of the earth, when they regulated well-planned labours by the order of the seasons" (20). In other words, live according to nature and you will be blessed. There are no angry, vindictive "acts of God," only natural causes and effects, which human reason can, to a degree, comprehend, control, and even fashion to the happiness of society.

To carry his points, Volney's "Phantom" repeatedly asks rhetorical questions. He piles one upon another, using a second to answer or extend the first, and so on, in a crescendo of contempt at humankind's blindness. The loaded word *infidel* is several times reiterated, twice with ironic italics: "And what is that *infidelity* which founded empires by its prudence, defended them by its valour, and strengthened them by its justice. . . . If such be *infidelity*, what then is the *true faith*?" This is a very good question, and one that Lincoln would long ponder. Here, Volney/Barlow offer an epitomizing lesson in effective prose composition: the preliminary cascading rhetorical questions, the emphases, the balanced tricolon of the syntax in the central point, and the final damning question, "what then is the *true faith*?" The Phantom's peroration now quickly follows, and, as translator, Barlow is compelled by Volney's French to produce a grammatical form that by 1802 was already becoming anachronistic in English: the high-formal diction of the "-eth" verb ending. While not something Lincoln would replicate, its quaintness did not stand in the way of a clear understanding of the sense: "those eternal laws, established by God himself. . . . anterior to all codes, to all the prophets," have been defiled, though they may never be overthrown, by "that *passion* which mistaketh, that *ignorance* which observeth not causes, nor looketh to effects" (22).

Though there was incalculably more information in Gibbon, what Volney offered of ancient history was more readily assimilable, because schematized and conformed to the author's thesis. *Decline and Fall* occasionally reveals British parochial sexism and racism, but *The Ruins* sincerely strives to place the whole of humanity, including women, all colors of skin, and all classes, in its purview. The Phantom takes the Pilgrim on a fanciful flight high above the earth, providing a God's-eye view, and points southward toward Africa: in the "ancient kingdom of Ethiopia . . . a people, now forgotten, discovered, while others were yet barbarians, the elements of the arts and sciences; a race of men now rejected from society for their *sable skin and frissled hair*, founded on the study of the laws of nature, those civil and religious systems which still govern the universe" (30–35). Today we term this viewpoint *Afrocentric*, and Volney states it as decisively as anything to be found in *Black Athena*.[75] Within Lincoln's milieu, it would have met with angry incredulity and deemed as radical as "infidelity" itself and even more pernicious to American social order.

One of the chief goals of Enlightenment writers such as Volney and Voltaire—and one they did not consider impossible of achievement—was to be encyclopedic in their scope of knowledge. In volume 1 of *The Ruins*, Volney ranges at will over the entire anthropological record of the human race. Since he is not writing history in Gibbon's sense of the discipline, he can leave most of the contextualization to his footnotes while pursuing a series of general truths. We are animals; we are self-interested; we seek pleasure and avoid pain; the world was not made for us, but simply made; yet nature allows us to live in the world and make the best of it. In other words, we are naturally free, and reason is our means of differentiating good from evil and of seeking the good. Volney, through the Phantom, announces that the true commonwealth consists of all humans sharing the earth, having equal property, and cultivating it for themselves. However, this *physiocratic* dream—in Lincoln's America, the Jeffersonian vision of a nation of prosperous yeoman farmers—could be (and often has been) fatally compromised both by human passion and *accidents of nature*: "the strong . . . arrogating over [the weak] an abusive right of property," and thus "the *slavery of individuals* prepared the slavery of nations." Chattel slavery, to be sure; but also "*paternal despotism*," which "laid the foundation of despotism in government" (44–45, 60, 68–69, 74–75).

When Lincoln remarked, with or without an ironic modulation in his voice, "I used to be a slave," he meant it in this sense of "*paternal despotism*"—at the hand of Tom Lincoln, who had the law on his side until the boy reached his majority—the daily reality of which in his own life made him sympathetic with African slaves in the southern United States and determined politically to kill the institution by containment.[76] Volney's humanistic cardinal sins, cupidity and ignorance, describe all too aptly the character of Tom Lincoln (at least as the son saw the father), and there were many upland southerners like him who saw education as a waste of time and knowledge as nothing more than getting above one's self. But to Abraham Lincoln, *rising* gave life a purpose. It made for a better-realized individual and a healthier social whole.

In his superb self-education, Lincoln certainly accomplished his individual part. But what of the ignorant thousands around him? Could a democratic society cohere if its people refused to learn the first axiom of the grammar of republican rights: that their freedom was predicated upon the freedom of all, yet all were not free? This returns us to the Lyceum Address and Lincoln's fear of the rise of an American tyrant. Volney, with Gibbon perhaps in mind, saw the establishment of tyranny as the outgrowth of civil war: "In fine, among these rivals, one more adroit, or more fortunate, gained the ascendancy, and concentrated all power within himself. By a strange phenomenon, a single individual mastered millions of his equals, against their will or without their consent; and the art of *tyranny* sprung also from *cupidity*" (80). What was behind this "strange phenomenon"? Individual debility played an important part, but psychologically extrapolated into a social disease: "the people, despoiled of their laws, of their usages, and of the government suited to their characters, lost that spirit of personal identification with their government, which had caused their energy" (84–85). The phrase "personal identification with their government" is especially close to Lincoln's way of stating the same thing: "the *attachment* of the People" to their government. And much of this sentence from the Lyceum Address resembles Volney's point: "Thus, then, by the operation of this mobocratic spirit . . . the strongest bulwark of any Government, and particularly of those constituted like ours, may effectually be broken down and destroyed—I mean the *attachment* of the People."[77]

The institutionalization of tyranny and its corrosive rule over time further debase the people and inure them to a yet more dystopian form of government that we would today call *totalitarian*. And all of this has been, Volney insists, retrogressive, a devolution from the human near perfection of living harmoniously in nature: democracy, aristocracy, theocracy, monarchy, and then the deluge (78–79). From its original condition of bliss in the garden, humanity fell into misery, the successive stages of which became worse and worse. Two metaphysical inventions followed: angry gods that had to be appeased at any cost, and an afterlife of punishment and reward—damnation for the ungodly, a return to paradise (the root meaning of which is "walled garden") for the virtuous. Hence *both* politics and religion were consequences of the fall, the products of human self-hatred (91). Nonetheless, the species can and shall break the cycle of rise and fall, consummation and destruction, according Volney—but only after we know what *God* really is can we know, and act, as *we* really are in nature.

One of the most striking scenes in *The Ruins* now follows: the Pilgrim and his mentoring Phantom (or "Genius," as Volney has chosen to rename him) still ride high above the earth, for perspective's sake, and they see in the Middle East what initially appears to be a plague of locusts. But these "insects mimic[ing] battles" are in fact two great armies clashing. As the observers zoom in for a better look, they notice the priests of the contending nations, Russians and Turks, invoking the blessings of the Almighty upon their arms. The Pilgrim puzzles over this: "I was considering the difficulty with which the common Judge could yield to prayers so contradictory." But the Genius reacts in great anger: "sacrilegious prayers, rise not from the earth! and you, oh heavens, reject their homicide vows and impious thanksgivings!" He is outraged at such a "base conception of the most sublime of beings. . . . Ah! now I know the lying spirit of man!" For this is indeed man making God in his own worst self-image (93–94, 100–101).

Lincoln, too, was offended by the Protestant Christian invocation of an angry and vindictive God. As Isaac Cogdal remembered his frequent conversations with Lincoln "on the question of religion in his own office" in Springfield—sometimes with Herndon present as well—Lincoln "did not believe in hell—Eternal punishment as the christians say. . . . He was a Universalist tap root & all in faith and sentiment." God had not bothered to create and people a world in order to condemn it harshly; rather, Lincoln "believed that nations like individuals were punished for their Sins—there [*sic*] violations of fundamental rights—&c[.]"[78] *If* there were a hereafter, all were "saved" within it. This was Universalism. But if not, people and nations nevertheless were obligated—morally and socially—to live well together in mutual respect. This, too, was universalism: that of Volney's

Enlightenment, as refashioned by Lincoln into the "political religion" of the United States. Based on civil rights, it had as well its practical, individual ethic: "when he did good he felt good," and contrariwise.[79]

The doctrine and practice of importuning God for special favors and expecting them to be granted, even when contradictory, Lincoln found metaphysically absurd. During some of the darkest weeks of his first term, late summer of 1862—probably after the defeat at Second Bull Run but before Antietam and the preliminary Emancipation Proclamation—he set down a short, undated prose paragraph that has come to be known as the "Meditation on the Divine Will." Written for no known occasion, apparently addressed to no one but the author himself, a single paragraph of only about one hundred and fifty words: yet it is one of the most intensely reasoned and powerful pieces that Lincoln ever composed.[80] Here are the first four sentences, lineated the better to follow the logical trail:

> The will of God prevails.
> In great contests each party claims to act in accordance with the will of God.
> Both *may* be, and one *must* be wrong.
> God can not be *for*, and *against* the same thing at the same time.[81]

Though the Union and Confederate polities and armies, like Volney's Russians and Turks, assumed God was on their respective sides, one or the other *had* to be mistaken and *both* might very well be. Lincoln was not willing to repeal the law of contradiction, that most fundamental caisson of reason, even for a putatively omniscient and omnipotent godhead. But if God were constrained by Reason, how much less authority did the priests of the contending forces have in proclaiming God's blessing on their bloody endeavors? Had the North's eyes *truly* seen the coming of the Lord? Had the South *genuinely* discovered that slavery was ordained of God? Volney's Genius thought it blasphemous to make such claims. For Lincoln, however, it was more a matter of accepting the paradox of how to further the cosmic cause of what was certainly going to come to pass: "the will of God prevails."

Yet that will may only be guessed at inferentially, not known directly through revelation or personally through feeling. God's judgments, Volney writes, "are manifested [in] the powerful and simple laws of nature and reason: laws of a common and general mover; of a God, impartial and just, who sheds rain on a country, without asking who is it's [*sic*] prophet; who causeth his sun to shine alike on all the races of men, on the *white* as on the *black*, on the Jew, on the Musulman, the Christian and the Idolater" (107-8). It follows that all social and political solutions founded on equality and justice are "of God" and congruent with his will, and in a more immediate sense are created freely through individual and collective human action.

But the historical record of human society is dismal; and in fact the Genius has shown the Pilgrim so many instances of failure that the latter is about to declare for suicide as the best way out. The Genius replies with acerbity: "'Virtue, then, consists in dying!'" There has been human progress, he insists: demonstrably, individuals have "'ameliorated, [so] why shall not the whole mass ameliorate?'" (122). And, since there never was a golden age, we must not pretend that the past is better than the present, and humankind sadly fallen (124). In fashioning this pep talk, Volney has conveniently forgotten his earlier position on the question of development versus degeneracy: that the natural state of humankind *was* better than the historical, and that having forgotten natural law, we have been on a long downhill run. But if he values education as the principal means of liberation, Volney must show human life as progressive (as he does by pointing up the inestimable value to the spread of knowledge that the reinvention of printing in Europe made possible).

Every man is a scientist, and society flourishes: "by the law of sensibility, man as invincibly tends to render himself happy as the flame to mount, the stone to descend, or the water to find its level." The banishment of ignorance is fundamentally ameliorative and instrumental to human happiness. Indeed, the Genius points out (literally, with a nod to the west) that the happiness of the many is emerging dramatically even at that very moment in a nation called France: "a hollow sound already strikes my ear; a cry of liberty, proceeding from far distant shores." A "wholesome inquietude" alarms a "powerful nation." The Pilgrim is not yet convinced, however. Rather apologetically, he *doubts* that the species can ever cure itself of its social diseases. Far from being offended, the Genius responds with a rhetorical question that could almost have formed Lincoln's motto during the New Salem years: "'And what is doubt . . . that it should be a crime?'" (136–37).

The single political revolution that mattered to Abraham Lincoln was the American. He is not known to have read any of the accounts of the French Revolution available to him—notably Thomas Carlyle's (1837)—and mentioned it but once in his writings (in his eulogy of Henry Clay, and there quoting another source).[82] Anything he knew of its cataclysms he garnered from sources like Tom Paine's biography or from Volney. But Volney treats his own nation's revolution, in the hopeful early phase of which *The Ruins* was written, as a philosophical allegory of human progress rather than a complex historical phenomenon. Millions of French laborers complain of working hard, paying taxes, and yet having the products of their toil expropriated. "Who then is the secret enemy that devours us?" The answer is all too clear: a very small minority composed of "priests of every order, of financiers, of nobles, of men in livery, of commanders of armies; in a word, of the civil and military agents of government." To these fortunate few of the "privileged class," the French peasants were de facto slaves. When the people, assembled under the standard of *producers*, attempt to demand their rights from the *consumers*, they are met with a succession of tired reiterations of the sacred social rightness of the *ancien régime*. Among the privileged, the priests are perhaps the worst: they defame reason, "prescribe obedience," and justify suffering as "the business of this world." But the gathered people, for once making common cause and growing every day more confident, slough this off with commonsense arguments ("Peace supposes justice. Obedience implies a knowledge of the law.") and proceed to declare their sovereignty and the right of revolution. The old orders are terrified at this: "We are lost; the multitude are enlightened." To which the people reply: "You are safe; since we are enlightened, we will do no violence; we only claim our rights" (145–53).

At this point in *The Ruins* (volume 2), somewhat abruptly, the subject shifts from political philosophy to theology. The Lawgiver, the latest in Volney's sequence of spokesmen, holds that since there can be but one God *as* god, the creator of the universe, there must of necessity be but one religion. Not surprisingly, the road to religious unity proves a rocky and roundabout detour: a pompous procession of "priests and doctors" marches along, all in smug assurance that each alone possesses the one true faith. The problem with this plurality, the Lawgiver observes, is that "if truth is one, and opinions are various, it is evident that some are in error" (1). But what shall be the standard of discriminating truth from error? Miracles and martyrs are ruled out, since all factions claim to have had plenty of both, in the distant past, but with no living witnesses to testify to their veracity. Nor can martyrdom here and now "prove the truth of our belief"? Not a whit, responds the Lawgiver: "if you die to prove that two and two make four, will your death add any thing to this truth? And if you die to prove they make five, will that make them five?" Even the most resolute of proto-martyrs cannot deny the truth of the Lawgiver's Lincolnian logic and give up their thoughts of self-immolation (5).

The Ruins concludes with an extended and bitter indictment of priest-craft of all kinds, all times, and all peoples. Quite possibly Lincoln may have borrowed from Volney's materials to build his own case against the clerisy of what he called the "priest-ridden" central Illinois community, as expressed in his 1834 handbill attacking Peter Cartwright, or, it may be, in the "little book on Infidelity"—if these two are not in fact at least partly the same text.[83] Volney's final mouthpiece, the "Orator," drives home a truth amply demonstrated by history but always denied by religious partisans and bigots: that humankind has made God in its own image but did not, and could not, make itself. Nature is our author, and nature is the masterwork of an unknown, or at least unattested God. The entire panoply of religions reduce to one "of the errors of the human mind . . . [which], always dreaming of wisdom and happiness, wanders in the labyrinth of illusion and pain" (192–93).

Volney's bill of particulars against the priests of the world contains two charges that will be familiar to anyone who knows the story of Lincoln contra Cartwright: "That they every where avoided the toils of the labourer, the dangers of the soldier, and the disappointments of the merchant." And: "That, under the cloak of poverty, they found every where the secret of procuring wealth and all sorts of enjoyments" (211–12). Here is the cognate language from Lincoln's letter to the *Beardstown Chronicle*, dated November 1, 1834:

> I beleive [*sic*] the people in this country are in some degree priest ridden. I also believe, and if I am not badly mistaken "all informed observers" will concur in the belief that Peter Cartwright bestrides, more than any four men in the northwestern part of the State.
>
> He has one of the largest and best improved farms in Sangamon county, with other property in proportion. And how has he got it? Only by the contributions he has been able to levy upon and collect from a priest ridden church. It will not do to say he has earned it "by the sweat of his brow;" for although he may sometimes labor, all know that he spends the greater part of his time in preaching or electioneering.[84]

In short, such "priests" as Cartwright did no useful work and were little more than hypocrites and material burdens on the community. An *electioneering preacher* ought to have been an oxymoron in the young American Republic: yet the "priest ridden" people of their churches (in this case Methodist) had allowed themselves to be imposed upon both for money and for political support. Volney's Orator frankly lays part of the responsibility upon the people: "Yes, yourselves cause the evils of which you complain; yourselves encourage the tyrants by a base adulation of their power, by an imprudent admiration of their false beneficence, by servility in obedience, by licentiousness in liberty, and by a credulous reception of every imposition" (217).

Lincoln in the mid-1830s was fighting the deeply rooted authority of a host of Cartwrights (and Cartwright's host, his "Methodist militia") in his state and nation. He deplored their interference in civil matters, where, he thought, policies either furthering or based upon religion constitutionally did not belong. Like Volney, he recognized the difficulty of getting at the truth of the human condition through reason—that is, through the application of analysis to the inputs of the senses—especially when the "affections" (the passions) got in the way, which was just about all the time. But to sustain equality and liberty, the hard way was the only way. "To live in harmony and peace," Volney asserts, "we must agree never to decide on such objects [as we cannot bring to knowledge]," of which religion is the paramount. And this means, from the standpoint of a people's constitution, that "all civil effect must be taken away from theological and religious opinions" (226–27). Lincoln agreed. The reading and full assimilation of *The Ruins* had made him a radical democrat and a radical anticleric, at least for the next few years.

When one comes upon the shocking report in *Herndon's Informants* that Lincoln had "called Christ a bastard," the explanation that immediately suggests itself is that Lincoln was indulging in one of the oldest jokes known to Christendom: Joseph cuckolded by the Holy Ghost, the divine father of Jesus, who was thus conceived outside the marriage bed, with the husband of Mary condemned forever to wear the horns despite later being "kicked upstairs" to sainthood by the Catholic Church. Now Lincoln, we know, was manifestly capable of ribaldry. But this cuckolding story, however offensive to Christians, lacked the "sting" that he required in a jest.

Lincoln may have gotten a more mundane version of the tale from a minor work of Voltaire. But his reading of Voltaire, in the New Salem years or later, is suggested by only one contemporary. John Hill, son of the New Salem storekeeper Samuel Hill, mentions Voltaire in the context of the "little book on Infidelity," but somewhat ambiguously: "I heard of my father having morally compelled Mr Lincoln to burn the book, on account of its infamy & pointing to Voltaire, Paine &c."[85] This might mean that Lincoln was warned against publishing his composition because it made (favorable?) use of "Voltaire, Paine &c." Or it might just as well have been a comparison: publish this, Lincoln, and you'll find yourself in the same disrepute as the other infidels. What follows here is therefore highly speculative.

Voltaire was a kind of polymath—historian, poet, playwright, philosopher, and scientist—and an obsessive and efficient writer in every genre. Thus a typical modern edition of Voltaire's works in English runs to forty-two volumes. In the first half of the nineteenth century in America, printings of his works appeared regularly, usually from British plates, and likewise in multivolume editions. But one piece among Voltaire's hundreds of writings was *not* to be found, even in British and American editions of his complete works: *The* [or *An*] *Important Study of the Holy Scriptures*, which contains Voltaire's most comprehensive and strident attack on the historical and theological truth of Christianity.[86] The critical power of the *Important Study* would, of course, be irrelevant if it wasn't available for Lincoln and others to read. But there was an English version available outside the collected works: a magazine called the *Deist*, published in London, in its second volume (1819) carried what was purportedly the first English translation of Voltaire's *Examen Important*.[87]

In this scathing polemic, Lincoln would have found an exposure of the historical and logical inconsistencies and outright contradictions of the Bible, from the Mosaic books through the New Testament. Voltaire was concerned to show that Moses, if he ever existed, had lived long before his "writings" were set down and could not have been their author or even very likely their oral source (chaps. 1–4). This was followed by a critique of Jewish mores and history that sounds anti-Semitic to modern ears, along with a critical survey of the Jewish prophetic tradition (chaps. 5–9). Then, about halfway through the essay (chap. 10), Voltaire related an ancient Hebrew story concerning the paternity of Jesus, the "Toldos Jeschut" (or "Generation of Jesus").[88] In summary, this is the plot: Mirja (Mary), married to Jocanam (Joseph), committed adultery with a Roman soldier named Pander. Jeschut (Jesus) was the resultant offspring, born a bastard; Mirja was disgraced, Jocanam left his home, and Jeschut became an outcast and in turn grew resentful. Refused schooling because of his illegitimacy, Jeschut railed against the priests, calling them "a race of vipers and whitened sepulchers." Finally, quarrelling with Judas over interest on a debt, he was denounced by Judas as a heretic, was convicted, and put to death.[89]

Lincoln once told Herndon that he believed his mother, Nancy Hanks Lincoln, had been born illegitimate, and that he fancied it was from her father (Lincoln's maternal grandfather), "a well-bred Virginia farmer or planter," that he had inherited "his power of analysis, his logic, his mental activity, his ambition, and all the qualities that distinguished him from the other members and descendants of the Hanks family."[90] That was the emotionally positive aspect of the fantasy of illegitimacy: genetically passed traits that, actualized and put to good use, might raise one far above the class born into. The negative and public dimension was obviously the social stigma branding adultery and birth out-of-wedlock on the unfortunate individuals. While Lincoln never indicated to Herndon that he doubted Thomas Lincoln as his biological father (that would have disgraced his mother), several of Herndon's informants from Indiana and Kentucky frankly declared he wasn't, causing the biographer no end of anxiety as he strove to complete his long-aborning book in the late 1880s (ultimately he averred, somewhat vaguely, Lincoln's legitimacy, and that has largely been the conclusion later biographers have accepted).[91] We have seen that Lincoln disliked, if he did not hate, his father, and we can imagine his regarding Tom Lincoln with disgust, wondering how in the world he had come from such an indigent, ignorant, and unsympathetic upland southerner. So much more pleasant to imagine some Tidewater cavalier or cultured great planter.

Throughout much of his life, Lincoln detested and hoped to transcend his "white trash" origins. He perceived himself as socially incompetent in, if not entirely excluded from, polite society. Though he possessed keen ambition along with his fine intellect and physical strength, he often expected to fail in his endeavors. And then there was that "noonday demon" of depression, so emotionally crippling and inextirpable. It is plausible to suppose that in calling "Christ a bastard" Lincoln was both laughing at Voltaire's satire of Christian credulity, as he titillated his New Salem friends with the "Toldos Jeschut" story, and—in anger and sadness—feeling its jabs in his own existence. Voltaire's Jesus was an object of derision and a victim of prejudice, shunned and ultimately doomed. At the same time, he had a chip on his shoulder that got him into trouble. A nobody claiming special powers, this "Jesus outside the Gospels" died ignominiously and all but unknown, without having made anything good happen in the world. Significantly, the theological Jesus of Christianity, the man-god of the canonical Gospels and Pauline writings, would scarcely ever enter into Lincoln's discourse except as a purveyor of figures of speech, the jewels of thought and language that Lincoln deployed so beautifully in his speeches and writings. But not as his personal savior or redeemer: to a mind such as Lincoln's, that was impossible.

That Lincoln read Tom Paine is attested to by Abner Y. Ellis several times in his letters to and interviews with Herndon. But the particular title he mentioned was the patriotic Revolutionary propaganda of *Common Sense* rather than the religiously inflammatory *Age of Reason*.[92] Nonetheless, by the time his biography was published, Herndon had come to think that the latter book was the one that had mattered to Lincoln: "In 1834, while still living in New Salem and before he became a lawyer, he was surrounded by a class of people exceedingly liberal in matters of religion. Volney's *Ruins* and *Payne's Age of Reason* [sic] passed from hand to hand, and furnished food for the evening's discussion in the tavern and village store. Lincoln read both these books and thus assimilated them into his own being." Volney and Paine were the two authors most closely associated in Herndon's mind with the "little book on Infidelity," which he described as "an extended essay—called by many, a book—in which he made an argument against Christianity, striving to prove that the Bible was not inspired, and therefore not God's revelation, and that Jesus Christ was not the son of God."[93] Much of his ammunition he took from *The Age of Reason*.

Paine wrote much of the first part of the book in 1793, at his French residence in St. Denis (near Paris), finishing the manuscript just as the Terror began to descend. He was arrested, with Joel Barlow present, charged as a "dangerous foreigner" born in a country at war with France (England), and imprisoned in the Luxembourg.[94] Despite having shown himself repeatedly a friend of the Revolution, and having defended it in print with *The Rights of Man* (1791–92), Paine now found himself branded as an enemy of what was almost his second adopted nation (after America). Robespierre, whose ill-will was behind the arrest, mistrusted Paine as one of the detested foreign "paid journalists" whom he considered no better than counterrevolutionaries in their reporting of events; nor could Paine be released from prison, (half-hearted) American diplomatic efforts notwithstanding, until well after Robespierre's fall in late July of 1794. In the meantime, Paine watched helplessly as tumbrels of prisoners were hauled off daily to the guillotine. He became gravely ill with some sort of fever, though when he was able to he continued to write, revising and extending *The Age of Reason*.[95] In November 1794, after eleven months' confinement, he was finally freed.

The first edition of the work (in English) appeared in Paris early in 1795, the dedication "To My Fellow-Citizens of the United States of America" bearing the new-style French date of "8th Pluvoise, Second Year of the French Republic"—though the author was the unhappy prisoner of the republic on that very day. Soon the printing presses in England were busy, and although quickly banned in Britain, its publisher tried and punished for its publication, *The Age of Reason* proved to have lasting popularity there.[96] In the United States, the book, like all of Paine's writings, sold well too: widely denounced *The Age of Reason* might be, its author publicly scorned and damned to hell from countless pulpits, it was just as widely read (we have seen that Parson Weems stocked it as a staple).

Paine regarded *The Age of Reason* as an unblinkingly honest treatment of a subject that not many Americans would face with wide-open eyes. "The most formidable weapon against errors of every kind is Reason," he declared in the dedication. "I have never used any other, and I trust I never shall." Moreover, on the first page of the text, he lays his creedal cards on the table: "I believe in one God, and no more; and I hope for happiness beyond this life."[97] Of course, to a logical mind such as Lincoln's, this simple statement absolved Paine from the charge of atheism. Yet his theological enemies only paid attention to what he did *not* believe in—precisely that which they so adamantly *did*. Denying no human being the right to religious opinion, Paine, like Volney, reserved the god-given right to reject any and all religions that did not meet reasonable standards in their truth-claims. Whether it was Islam, Judaism, or Christianity, he discarded their revelations as against reason, making him to many millions in the Middle East, Europe, and the United States an *infidel*. This label Paine, again like Volney, flatly refused "Infidelity does not consist in believing, or disbelieving," he wrote, but rather "in professing to believe what [one] does not believe" (232).

What, then, were Paine's *reasonable standards* for religious truth-claims? Though he doubted, he did not deny that God might reveal himself to a human being. But he insisted that revelation either to a single person only or as reported by a third party constituted inadmissible evidence in the court of reason. Personal revelation is valid to that human being alone; reported revelation is merely hearsay. We are not obligated to believe anything not communicated to ourselves individually; nor should we be so credulous as to credit what someone else says that God said to him. Thus, though God may have provided "Ten Commandments" to Moses, whatever reason there is to believe in them derives solely from an individual human mind's acceptance of what "any man qualified to be a lawgiver, or a legislator, could produce himself, without recourse to supernatural revelation" (233).

Paine's position here is commensurate both with Lincoln's mode of philosophical inquiry and his legal training. When, in September 1862, a delegation of two preachers, representing a meeting in Chicago that had declared for universal and immediate emancipation of slaves, called on Lincoln at the White House, he countered their stated belief that emancipation was the revealed will of God with this memorable response:

> I am approached with the most opposite opinions and advice, and that by religious men, who are equally certain that they represent the Divine Will. I am sure either the one or the other class is mistaken in that belief, and perhaps in some respects both. I hope it will not be irreverent for me to say that if it is probable that God would reveal his will to others, on a point so connected with my duty, it might be supposed that he would reveal it directly to me; for, unless I am more deceived in myself than I often am, it is my earnest desire to know the will of Providence in this matter. *And if I can learn what it is I will do it!* These are not, however, the days of miracles, and I suppose it will be granted that I am not to expect a direct revelation. I must study the plain physical facts of the case, ascertain what is possible and learn what appears to be wise and right.[98]

That is to say, he must think about it: not be blinded by revelatory light, not even pray, but simply, humanly, think about problems like emancipation.

Lincoln's logic in this passage is impeccable, recalling as it does that of the "Meditation on the Divine Will" (briefly discussed above, and which may have been written in preparation for this meeting), and his language speaks to the preachers on their own ground as well as reason's.[99] That "these are not . . . the days of miracles" is sound Christian doctrine: revelation is closed, so the admittedly crucial matter of divining the divine will is far more difficult—if not impossible—in this postrevelation age. Lincoln serves as the elected leader of a republic in the crisis of civil war; he must think and ultimately act according to his sworn duty. He cannot make Union policy on the hearsay evidence that God has spoken to someone else, even if the alleged audience for the divine is comprised of self-anointed apostles. Nor does he hold any expectation that God will speak privately and personally to him. He must find his way himself, thoughtfully. Those two representatives of the cloth may have left the White House dissatisfied both with the president and his argument, but Lincoln, as so often happened with his importuners, covertly was far ahead of them in having thought through the policy he intended: for some weeks, he had had in a drawer of his desk a draft of the preliminary Emancipation Proclamation, which he would make public less than two weeks after this meeting with the pair of preachers.

The Age of Reason takes deadly aim at Christian credulity. While no crime, as Paine says, credulity functions negatively as a barrier to human happiness. Paine's attack employs direct factual and textual analysis of Scripture rather than the sarcastic hauteur of Voltaire or the far-ranging anthropology of Volney. The story of Jesus's nativity comes under scrutiny as it had in Voltaire's *Important Study*, yet Paine's concern is not with the old Hebrew "Toldos Jeschut" but the scandalously low provenance of the original story out of which myth was confabulated. He first objects on the grounds of hearsay: since, according to Gospel accounts, Joseph told the world that an angel told him that God had impregnated his wife, and then many decades later some *fourth party* wrote the tale down from an oral source who was not Joseph himself, it amounts to no more than "hearsay upon hearsay." Such pseudobiography is ultimately Jesus's fault (and Paine admired the historical Jesus as "a virtuous and amiable man" whose ethical talents were extorted and transmogrified by the Church's desire for "power and revenue"—compare Volney's *cupidity*). Jesus wrote nothing. Others, long after the events, began to claim his life and work for their institution, fashioning out of oral tradition and their imaginations the collective book known as the New Testament. It was the fledgling Christian Church that required a supernatural resurrection to make a theological bookend with Jesus's supernatural conception and birth. Hence, more mythologizing and "wretched contrivance" on the part of early Christian writers—palpably fraudulent to the reasonable eye of history (234–36).

Despite the problematic documentary record, Paine was comfortable with a "historical Jesus." And he regarded the fictionalized Gospels and Christian theology not as objects for ridicule but with a regret approaching pity. The Christian doctrines of the Fall of Man and humankind's redemption through the atonement of Jesus's bitter and violent death struck him as particularly sad. Still, Paine recognized the perversity under which humans often labored: "The more unnatural anything is, the more is it capable of becoming the object of dismal admiration" (239). This pessimistic outbreak distances Paine from Volney's staunch belief in human progress and perfectibility. And, indeed, nearing the end of an eventful and hopeful life, writing just as the French Revolution turned terribly for the worse, he may well have felt that he belonged in Gibbon's company—and Lincoln's, ca. 1835—rather than among the Enlightenment's optimists. He saw that a cure for this social disease of religious "dismal admiration" would require a reeducation in and through nature, using the Book of Nature rather than the Gospels as inerrant text. If only we would discern that "a fair creation [was] prepared to receive us the instant we were born—a world furnished to our hands that cost us nothing." That power which lighted the sun, causes the rain to fall, and "fill[s] the earth with abundance" has done so for us and speaks to us in the various languages of nature. In the end, however, it may be too late to start over, as implied by this last of a series of rhetorical questions: "Or is the gloomy pride of man become so intolerable that nothing can flatter it but a sacrifice of the Creator?" (239).

Lincoln's skepticism concerning the Bible's inspiration has its most likely source in *The Age of Reason*. Paine, in pointing out that the books of the Christian canon—written years after the events they describe purportedly took place—were determined by the voting of Church delegates at a synod held that long again after the writing, effectively shows that the Bible stands *unrevealed*, its many authors *uninspired*. Men made these choices, and some of the choices were absurd. Here Paine modulates from his pathetic into a somewhat sardonic voice, as if he were a lawyer making a cross-examination or a debater summarizing the argument in a case. Of the Old Testament's accounts of the Israelites in books such as Kings and Chronicles, he concludes, "When we read the obscene stories, the voluptuous debaucheries, the cruel and torturous executions, the unrelenting vindictiveness with which more than half the Bible is filled, it would be more consistent that we called it the word of a demon than the word of God. It is a history of wickedness, that has served to corrupt and brutalize mankind; and, for my own part, I sincerely detest it, as I detest everything that is cruel" (242).

These plainspoken words are powerful and read sincerely. Lincoln would have noticed. And more attentively, perhaps, to Paine's relentless logic of cause and effect. No person had made himself or herself; nor could our fathers themselves; and so it goes and goes, on back to a "first cause" at the beginning of creation (252–53). Through the rhetorical/logical device of an infinite regress, Paine states the first principle of Deism and the first argument in its favor. Both point to a creator God metaphysically placed at the center of the universe and infinitely remote from the mundane concerns of his/its human creation. Neither personal, nor immanently present in the Christian sense, the Deistic God is simply *there*, but unavailable to us. Except, perhaps, in the hieroglyphics of Nature and her magnificent Book. And from its pages, he quotes Joseph Addison's loose verse paraphrase of the Nineteenth Psalm (the ninth verse of which Lincoln would use in the Second Inaugural). From watching the great wheel of the heavens from day to night to day, the psalmist comes to a deistic conclusion: sun, moon, planets, stars, though without "real voice, nor sound" (that is, unprovidentially), speak to us by the example of their existence:

> In reason's ear they all rejoice,
> And utter forth a glorious voice;
> Forever singing as they shine,
> THE HAND THAT MADE US IS DIVINE. (253)

In contemplating this physical immensity of the created universe and its supernal beauty, Paine is properly humble as a man and *as a knower*. To know the cosmos is all but humanly impossible; to know God *is* impossible. Paine's *gnosis* is science; he is *agnostic* concerning God. This philosophical garment fit the young man Lincoln. Paine more than once refers to geometry and mathematics as the grammar of God. Alluding again to Psalm 19 as a "theological oration," he declares that its "internal evidence . . . proves to a demonstration that the study and contemplation of the works of creation, and of the power and wisdom of God . . . make a great part of the religious devotion of the times in which they were written; and it was this devotional study and contemplation that led to the discovery of principles upon which what are now called sciences are established" (255). Lincoln may have warmed to Paine's prose here, since it affirms (originates?) his thoughts about the necessary role of reason in finding out knowledge of creation—imperfectly, he would agree, but resulting in real knowledge. Is this not what Lincoln means when he announces that "all creation is a mine, and every man, a miner"? This oddly figurative opening sentence of his 1858 "First Lecture on Discoveries and Inventions" is followed by a paragraph that cements his philosophical ties with Paine.

Nature is knowable, and humankind is so constituted as to need, and to be able, to know it: "The whole earth, and all *within* it, *upon* it, and *round about* it, including *himself*, in his physical, moral, and intellectual nature, and his susceptabilities [*sic*], are the infinitely various 'leads' from which man, from the first, was to dig out his destiny."[100]

By "leads" Lincoln means *lodes*: veins of valuable ore running through ordinary rock, the figure illustrating the inexhaustibly rich *mother-lode* of God-given nature through which we may "dig our destiny." *The Age of Reason* has a brief gloss on the Book of Job, which Paine puts to work in support of his Deism. Lincoln knew Job well, and Job 28 (spoken wholly by the *character* Job) is an extended metaphor of the source of wisdom. "Surely there is a vein for the silver, and a place for gold where they fine it." And so it goes throughout nature, places for everything and everything in them, whether hidden or open. But where is wisdom to be discovered? Not, as Paine (or the Lincoln of "Discoveries and Inventions") would have it, in the science of mining or the science of humankind, not even in the natural beauty of the valleys or the sublimity of the mountains. Rather, "the fear of the Lord, that is wisdom; and to depart from evil is understanding." We recognize Job 28:28 as the text alluded to in the "Proclamation of a National Fast Day," issued on August 12, 1861. It was to be a day of "public humiliation" whereby the citizens of the country, at least those in the North, feeling "the hand of God in this terrible visitation," would cry *mea culpa* and petition God for a return to peace and prosperity, not omitting a prayer for divine blessing of the Union war effort! All this to be done "in the full conviction that the fear of the Lord is the beginning of wisdom."[101]

Such was the official proclamation from the president, fashioned in language and replete with sentiments designed to satisfy even the most rigorous keepers of the Old Testament–like covenant that they believed God had made with his new chosen people: the Lord righteously angry with America over unnamed sins ("our own faults and crimes as a nation") and the people admitting that his punishment of inflicting upon the nation the Civil War was "most justly deserved." If Lincoln were *also* speaking personally here, then he truly had moved a considerable distance from his philosophical position in the mid-1830s—ideologically, as far as Washington was from Illinois. And on the long journey had apparently left Tom Paine, though not the Book of Job, far behind. Lincoln the universal miner had long striven to follow the "infinitely various 'leads'" to knowledge and self-realization; he had thought the earth a fair field and open, intelligible, and fulfilling. Now God, as to Job "out of a whirlwind," was saying: you know nothing about it at all. And Job could only answer, abjectly, "Wherefore I abhor myself, and repent in dust and ashes" (Job 42:6).

But, speculation on his late theology aside, Lincoln at twenty-five had learned at least one practical science that was based on irrefutable demonstrations: surveying. Paine alludes to Euclid, whose proofs in plane geometry Lincoln would soon master. The *Elements of Geometry,* he says, deserves the world's praise as "a book of self-evident demonstration, entirely independent of its author and of everything relating to time, place and circumstance" (290). Euclid employed a way of reasoning that reached truth and pointed toward God. He had done so both for the glory of that deistic divinity and for the benefit of humanity, since his "QEDs" had any number of useful applications. And it followed, Paine continued, that what we can know of the physical universe (a great deal) is based on mathematical structures, just as thinking and language are on logical forms—all God-given and naturally available (290). Applied science, he insists, is made up of "image[s] of principle[s]," taking a rather Platonic view of the ontology of this matter: "All the properties of a triangle exist independently of the figure, and existed before any triangle was drawn or thought of by man." We *discover* triangles from their principles; we *invent* devices such as quadrants and protractors from the achieved knowledge. "The man who proportions the several parts of a mill uses the same scientific principles as if he had the power of constructing a universe" (256–59). What is more, the man who understands the generation of trigonometric functions from triangles will be well on his way to becoming a good surveyor.

At last, then, to the question of whether there ever existed a "little book on Infidelity." As we have seen, several of Herndon's informants declared that Lincoln wrote such an essay, and Herndon himself credited their views. Several generations of later biographers have either uncritically followed Herndon or remained silent, from a general skepticism of Herndon's claims or a lack of interest in the story. Recent historians and critics who have examined the subject seriously, and they are few, have been divided. Douglas Wilson, who has made the most probing study, thinks the composition of the "little book" probable, calling the evidence "very strong."[102] Stewart Winger, on the contrary, is skeptical about Lincoln's having taken his own religious skepticism to this radical degree, allowing only that "it may be true that Lincoln wrote a more radically Painite and 'infidel' book."[103] In fact, no one knows the truth of the matter, nor is ever likely to. The point of any analysis must therefore be hypothetically reconstructive: what might the "little book" have looked like had Abraham Lincoln actually written it?

By the mid-1830s, Lincoln was fully capable of composing what Herndon judged to have been "an extended essay—called by many, a book," attacking Christianity from historical and critical perspectives.[104] As previously discussed, his March 1832 "Communication to the People of Sangamo County" reveals a more than sufficient command of English grammar and rhetoric for its occasion. And he had acquired, through his reading, the weaponry and ammunition with which critically to assault biblical Christianity in its most vulnerable aspects—historical errors and inconsistencies and internal textual deformations. What he assimilated from Volney, Voltaire, and Paine provided the matter; while the eighteenth-century prose artistry of Gibbon, Volney (Barlow), and Paine offered a wealth of compositional models and examples by which Lincoln could refine his style. All told, he had plenty to say on the topic and the means to say it effectively.

What remained was the authorial decision of how far and how hard to push his criticism of Christianity. When Lincoln could speak openly of religion among his New Salem friends, he was, as James H. Matheny put it, "enthusiastic in his infidelity." And, we may assume, Lincoln spoke and wrote sincerely, rather than shockingly just for the sake of shocking. However, since even the comparatively freethinking friends to whom he showed the manuscript *were* shocked by it, Lincoln must have gone "whole hog" in the essay:

• He "call[ed] Christ a bastard" (Matheny). As discussed above, this would entail more than the joke concerning the cuckolding of Joseph, the "Toldos Jeschut" story as related by Voltaire in the *Important Study*: Mirja (Mary) committing adultery with the soldier called Pander, and Jesus, the child of their coupling, being scorned by the world because of his bastardy. This historical "truth" would have effectively discountenanced any claim to divinity made by Christians on behalf of Jesus.

• He "den[ied] the divinity of the Scriptures" (Hardin Bale); and "attacked the Bible & New Testament on two grounds—1st From the inherent or apparent contradiction under its lids & 2dly From the grounds of Reason" (Matheny).[105] This testimony indicates that Lincoln may have closely followed the forensic tactics of Voltaire in the *Important Study* and Paine in *The Age of Reason*: that is, in the former, a close examination of biblical texts in order to show "reasonable doubt" about scriptural veracity; and, in the latter, an exposure of inconsistencies intended to cause the formal collapse into incoherence of the text in question. This was an analytical method sure to appeal to the young lawyer-in-the-making. Always the reasonable standard for judging the truth of *testimony*—for that is what "Moses, Joshua, and Samuel" claim to be offering the world—is that it be "probable and credible," which assertions of *revelations* or *miracles* clearly are not.[106]

• He attacked the institution of the Christian Church and the *contemporary* Protestant clerisy on the grounds of hypocritical behavior and political meddling: "Lincoln once rote an Artical against Peter Cartwrgh which was a good one. . . . you may Bet it used the old man very Ruff it was a hard one" (Caleb Carman).[107] The letter and handbill contra Cartwright, as discussed above, was full of no-holds-barred invective centering on the misery of a "priest-ridden" people that were shamefully being abused by their preachers, Cartwright in particular, who got rich through monies "lev[ied] upon and collect[ed] from a priest ridden church." Lincoln's models here were surely Volney in *The Ruins* and, once again, Voltaire. His denunciation of Cartwright *as a churchman* is as close as Lincoln ever got to Voltaire's cry of "*ecrasez l'infame!*" The assumption here is that this open letter was part of, or at least derived from, the "little book."

• He put believing Christians into a dilemma concerning the Scriptures: "Intense thought with him was the rule and not as with most of us the exception" (Joshua Speed).[108] Near the end of *The Age of Reason*, Paine offers the following summation to what he trusts is the jury of reasonable people in the world: "The evidence I have produced to prove [the Old and New Testaments] forgeries is extracted from the books themselves, and acts as a two-edged sword, either way. If the evidence be denied, the authenticity of the scriptures is denied with it, for it is a scripture evidence; and if the evidence be admitted the authenticity of the books is disproved. The contradictory impossibilities contained in the case of a man who swears *for* and *against*. Either evidence convicts him of perjury, and equally destroys reputation" (368). Now and again in his speeches and writings, from private memoranda to legal opinions to public and political occasions, Lincoln chose the *dilemma* as perhaps the most powerful way of pinning an opponent's argument down. Whether resembling Paine's formal logical dilemma or a more colloquial variety of "either/or," the effect in argument is usually devastating: "damned if you do, and damned if you don't." Thus, in the conclusion to the *Beardstown Chronicle* "skinning" of Cartwright, Lincoln delivers one of his best informal dilemmalike skewerings: held up to ridicule for requiring "two sets of opinions, one for his religious, and one for his political friends," Cartwright's "feverish brain" is sorely pressed to "plat them together smoothly." The preacher either had said he *didn't* or he *did* want "Methodist teachers" for Illinois's public schools. Or he hypocritically said both out of his Januslike double face. Any "intelligent stranger," Lincoln says mockingly, would have a tough time determining whether Cartwright "is greater fool or knave; although he may readily see that he has but few rivals in either capacity."[109] Lincoln's name-calling and frontier burlesque here stood on a hardwood floor of logic, so that the ad hominem attack, and the facts most open to challenge, had a tendency to stick on the target. It was unfair, this "power to hurt," but it worked. Peter

Cartwright may have been the "little book's" chief instance of the dangers of allowing communities to become "priest-ridden."

• "He was full of natural religion" (Leonard Swett): one last iteration of Paine's principal theme can stand for Lincoln's "natural religion": "We can know God only through his works. We cannot have a conception of any one attribute but by following some principle that leads to it. We have only a confused idea of his powers if we have not the means of comprehending something of its immensity. We can have no idea of his wisdom but by knowing the order and manner in which it acts. The principles of science lead to this knowledge; for the Creator of man is the Creator of science; and it is through that medium that man can see God, as it were, face to face" (376). After the heat of denunciation, exposure of intellectual fraud, and ad hominem invective cooled, this was what dominated the mind of Lincoln. Swett was writing to Herndon about the Lincoln he had long known *and the Lincoln he knew at the end*—unchanged in philosophical fundamentals. To Herndon's question of whether Lincoln the president had adopted a different religious viewpoint, Swett simply answered, "I think not."[110]

From ingredients such as these would the hypothetical "little book on Infidelity" have been composed. Its length, as Isaac Cogdal told Herndon,[111] could have been "a letter, pamphlet—book or what not," but let's guess that the manuscript when set in type would have made a pamphlet: an extended essay rather than a proper book, yet probably the longest piece of writing Lincoln had thus far attempted. A possible structure for the "little book" suggests itself: beginning with a critical analysis of Christianity's historical and textual problems, moving to a polemical section on antidemocratic dangers of modern Protestant evangelicalism in the United States (especially concerning certain preachers active "round about Springfield"), and, having shown what a pernicious religion Christianity was, concluding with an affirmation of Deism as the positive religion of Nature, Reason, and the American Republic.

When might he have written it, and under what circumstances? James H. Matheny believed that Lincoln composed the "little book" while still a resident of New Salem, "about the year 1834 or 1835," while Hardin Bale remembered the year as "about 1834." Take this range of 1834–35 as probable, and three points stand out: (1) The composition would have commenced during or shortly after Lincoln's reading of Gibbon, Voltaire, Volney, and Paine; (2) Lincoln, while serving as postmaster, had run for, been elected to, and was serving his first term in the Illinois legislature; and (3) he was in love with Ann Rutledge, who would die on August 25, 1835, plummeting him into the deepest despondency he had yet known in his life.

As has often been noted, the New Salem postmastership hardly demanded much time or energy, and Lincoln, when he was not surveying or attending the legislature, seems to have mostly sat and read or kept store for Samuel Hill. But he might just as naturally have been writing, since the post office was located at the back of the Hill store, with business for neither requiring anything more of Lincoln than rising from his desk now and then during opening hours.[112] On the other hand, the two- to three-month winter session of the General Assembly in Vandalia broke the rhythm of Lincoln's village life. Did the new representative from Sangamon work on the "little book" during his first sojourn in the capital? It brings a slight intellectual frisson to think that, as he journeyed by stagecoach to his freshman term (November 28–29, 1834), Lincoln might have carried in his luggage the manuscript of a work-in-progress which, had its contents become known to his fellow legislators, would surely have provoked their universal outrage and perhaps ended his political career before it began.

Most imponderable of all, how did Lincoln's romance with Ann Rutledge relate to the writing of the "little book"? If he loved her as ardently as some of his New Salem friends and neighbors later declared, and if she was like William G. Greene described her ("her intellect was quick—Sharp—deep & philosophic as well as brilliant"),[113] Lincoln would almost certainly have shared his radical ideas with her. Possibly more: Ann Rutledge might even have contributed to Lincoln's thinking—if only as a critic of his infidelity. Supposing that something like this kind of collaboration actually transpired between them, Ann Rutledge would then have to be seen as a person very different from the womanly norms of her day and unrecognizable in the egregiously sentimental portrait of her that has come down to us in popular fiction.[114] Of course, to those historians and biographers, Benjamin Thomas and James G. Randall preeminently, who discount the entire Rutledge-Lincoln romance as New Salem folklore, it matters not a whit whether Ann was a blushing Christian paragon or Abe's intended radical helpmeet, since what he became owed nothing to her. Perhaps Edgar Lee Masters struck the right balance between Sweet Ann and Sister Rutledge in his well-known *Spoon River Anthology* autoepitaph, the last two lines of which are: "Bloom forever, O Republic,/ From the dust of my bosom!"

A fantasy: Having written his antichristian treatise, Abraham Lincoln like most authors wished to publish it. He wanted an audience; he wanted recognition. Sam Hill and some unnamed others insisted he shouldn't. They convinced Lincoln that publication would kill his political chances. Or Lincoln was not persuaded and still wished to publish, politics be damned. The book was true. So they said, if you don't know what's good for you, we do. Burn the wretched thing. No. Then we shall. Give it here. Then Hill "snatched the manuscript from his hands and thrust it into the stove." "It was in the winter time, as tradition says it was done in fathers store, while there was a fire in the stove, & that there it was burned. . . ."[115]

3. Tragicomic Melancholy

Do you recollect Mr Lincoln's favorite pece of Poetry
"Oh Why Should the Spirit of Mortal be proud."
　　　　　　　—*Abner Y. Ellis, in* Herndon's Informants

Two presidents have their literary work represented, a single poem each, in the canon of nineteenth-century American poetry (John Quincy Adams is the other one). Lincoln's offering is "My Childhood-Home I See Again," a ninety-six-line lyric in ballad stanzas, written in 1846.[1] His having been president of the United States, and a particularly important president at that, opened the gates of Parnassus to him. "My Childhood-Home" could hardly compete at face value with, say, Walt Whitman and Emily Dickinson in the race for "laurels of laureate" in the Republic of Letters. But allow Lincoln his leg up: as a poet, he was no doubt a better president than they would have been. He loved poetry; he wrote poetry. Poems formed his favored reading, and the man who could say of William Knox's third-rate dirge "Mortality" (also known as "Oh why should the spirit of mortal be proud"), "I would give all I am worth, and go into debt, to be able to write so fine a piece," is a man infatuated with poetry and what it can do with human emotions.[2] Yet allusions to the work of poets Lincoln is said to have loved best, Robert Burns and Lord Byron, are missing from his speeches and writings (in the *Collected Works*, Burns's name is mentioned only three times, Byron's not at all). True, these two poets were unserviceable to political addresses or formal state occasions. But why are they likewise missing from Lincoln's private correspondence? And why, for that matter, does he so rarely refer to *any* poet, no matter what his mode of writing or his audience? Here is a deep irony, if not a paradox: apparently the *use* of the English language that meant most to Lincoln was not *useful* to him in his own political life.

The list of major early-nineteenth-century poets whose works have *not* been associated with him is extraordinary: William Blake, William Wordsworth, Samuel Taylor Coleridge, John Keats, Percy Bysshe Shelley, and Alfred Tennyson.[3] These are the Romantic and post-Romantic giants whom we today think of as defining the period and preparing the way for modern English and American poetry. But Lincoln evidently read none of their poems. To their philosophical, lyrical, and intensely figurative and imagistic poetry of *transcendence*, he preferred the dramatic, the humorous, and, it must be said, the earthy, singing sentimentality of poets like Thomas Moore. Byron, Burns, Moore—their verse affected his naturally melancholy sensibility, both deepening his depressive moods and lifting those moods toward cathartic light through song and verbal humor. Poetry moved this self-proclaimed disciple of the dispassionate profoundly; yet its power over him was of the kind that Lincoln, especially in his mature years, would rarely admit even to friends, let alone celebrate publicly. On occasion, however, he would *perform* poetry, as he did other sorts of texts. Sometimes in high drama, sometimes in parody, sometimes both with the same poem, the performance habit was one he developed in childhood and sustained throughout his life.

> Two early verse fragments to begin with:
> Abraham Lincoln his hand and pen
> he will be good but God knows When

and,

> Time What an emty vaper tis
> and days how swift they are
> swift as an indian arr[ow]
> fly on like a shooting star
> the present moment Just is here
> then slides away in h[as]te
> that we can never say they['re ours]
> but [only say] th[ey]'re past.[4]

Taken from the boy Lincoln's arithmetic notebook, where he set them down amid a profusion of numbers, neither of these is original: the first is said to have been a "family tradition" going back to one or another of the many Mordecai Lincolns in the lineage; the other is a version of the first two stanzas of an Isaac Watts hymn, "The Shortness of Life and the Goodness of God." Appropriately for a copybook, Lincoln was *copying*, from which practice he would learn to *imitate*. That he would be good, though God alone knew the date of his election, and that time was an empty vapor indeed received confirmation in his mind and emotions again and again. Loved ones died around him, uncertain of heaven, and the poetry he saw as a child sang the graveyard far more often than the joys of the hearthside.

The Kentucky Preceptor (1806, 1812) presented Lincoln with the first great English poem he would "assimilate to his being," in Herndon's memorable phrase: Thomas Gray's "Elegy Written in a Country Churchyard" (1751). So famous was this poem in its time and beyond that it became the very type of "graveyard school" poetry, so familiar in its diction and lugubrious plaint as to invite untoward amusement today. But to the adolescent Lincoln, the poem might have provoked a deep seriousness consonant with the poem's elegiac form and tone. Here is the first stanza:

> The Curfew tolls the knell of parting day,
>   The lowing herd wind slowly o'er the lea,
> The plowman homeward plods his weary way,
>   And leaves the world to darkness and to me.[5]

Unlike Milton's "Lycidas" a century before, while the poem has some of the surface features of the pastoral elegy ("The lowing herd wind slowly o'er the lea"; the rural setting and the meditation upon death), the conventional shepherd is here a "plowman," nor does the speaker of the poem brood on any hero's death but commemorates an entire population of the "unhonour'd Dead." There is no agonized grieving, no "whys" thrown at heaven. The poem's subject rides on a carrier wave of threnodic music. Fame, memory, time, and their opposites: unrealized ambition, eradicated lives, the timeless grave.

When Lincoln told John L. Scripps, the Chicago journalist who was preparing a campaign biography for the 1860 election, that there was nothing to his early life but what Gray had sung as "The short and simple annals of the poor," he epitomized his family and social background in a single, memorable line of elegiac poetry. Its stately rhythms lent a tragic dignity to humble origins such as Lincoln's.[6] As he had walked the game paths and primitive wagon roads of southwestern Indiana, from pockets of rural squalor to hamlets hardly better, or perhaps sat writing under a shade tree in some small cemetery in his Pigeon Creek neighborhood (Gray's title tells us that the "Elegy" was *written* right there in the churchyard), Lincoln would have felt the full weight of the poem's dim prospect as applied to the likes of himself. If potential greatness lay buried there, so did early evil interdicted by death. Here is the entire stanza (lines 29–32) from which the Scripps line comes:

Let not Ambition mock their useful toil,
    Their homely joys, and destiny obscure;
Nor grandeur hear with a disdainful smile
    The short and simple annals of the poor.

Two poems from Lincoln's early reading especially continued the always-equivocal topic of fame begun in Gray's "Elegy": "Lycidas" and "The Temple of Fame." With "Lycidas," it is fair to say, young reader Lincoln would have struggled. The conventions and artifices of pastoral elegy he might have found baffling, its archaic diction unfamiliar and the poem so classically allusive as to require either textual notes or a reference on Greek mythology, neither of which, we may assume, Lincoln had to hand as he read. But we can well imagine him working at the poem stubbornly, just to show himself that he *could* read it and derive some benefit from his trouble. "Lycidas" sings a beautiful lament over the death of *one dear friend.* Yet this is far from all. Milton, unlike Gray in the "Elegy," cannot let his dear Lycidas, who died before his time in a shipwreck, go to his rest without first prophesying the fall of the corrupt high clergy of the Church of England and then holding forth a (somewhat veiled) prospect of Christian eternity for the departed—these themes in addition to the expected course of lyric grieving that moves from shock to acceptance.

In a headnote to the poem, Milton mentions a second motive for "Lycidas," which "by occasion foretells the ruin of our corrupted Clergy, then in their height." Now this is a most difficult thing to achieve within the Arcadian context of a classical pastoral! One wonders whether a reader like Lincoln, inclined as he was to anticlericalism, would have discerned Milton's critical intent as artfully disguised in the following lines:

The hungry sheep look up and are not fed,
But swoln with wind, and the rank mist they draw,
Rot inwardly, and foul contagion spread:
Besides what the grim wolf with privy paw
Dayly devours apace, and little sed,
But that two-handed engine at the dore
Stands ready to smite once and smite no more.[7]

Written nearly a century after "Lycidas," Alexander Pope's "Temple of Fame" is a dream-vision allegory of more than five hundred lines in the poet's characteristic heroic couplets. Significantly, the moral attitude toward the subject, Fame, is far from settled at the outset. It may be attainable or not; it may be worth attaining or not; it may endure or not. The dream alone will tell. One balmy spring morning, the voice of the poem falls asleep and is vouchsafed a dream of "a glorious Pile,"

> Whose tow'ring Summit ambient Clouds conceal'd.
> High on a Rock of Ice the Structure lay,
> Steep its Ascent, and slipp'ry was the Way.

This "stupendous" Temple squares the circle, four "brazen Gates" surrounding its mighty dome. The western portico represents the heroes of classical Greece, while the "Eastern Front" celebrates the images of Zoroaster, Confucius, and others. Southward is Egypt, with its "long Majestic Race / of . . . Priests," and to the north, a "*Gothic* Structure" shows the bloody and "barb'rous Pride" of the uncivilized tribes with their Druids and Bards.[8]

> To this temple come the many who would be famous:
> Millions of suppliant Crowds the Shrine attend,
> And all Degrees before the Goddess bend;
> The Poor, the Rich, the Valiant, and the Sage,
> And boasting Youth, and Narrative old Age.
> Their Pleas were diff'rent, their Request the same;
> For Good and Bad alike are fond of Fame.

After a lengthy evocation of the court of the goddess, "The Temple of Fame" ends with the poet's firm resolution: "Unblemish'd let me live, or die unknown, / Oh grant an honest Fame, or grant me none!"[9]

Did Lincoln, like the young Alexander Pope, take the moral to heart? In the 1832 "Communication," he concluded, "Every man is said to have his peculiar ambition. Whether it be true or not, I can say for one that I have no other so great as that of being truly esteemed by my fellow men, by rendering myself worthy of their esteem. How far I shall succeed in gratifying this ambition, is yet to be developed."[10] Lincoln implies that, unlike the fictional "tyrant" who would be conjured six years later in the Lyceum Address, he could never woo fame by acting infamously. Let him rather live unblemished *and* die unknown, like the dead in Gray's "Elegy."

In these three poems, two elegies and a dream-vision, the topic of fame, or perhaps we might better say fame forestalled, is either the main poetic preoccupation or an important one. In Gray's "Elegy," the putative "mute inglorious Milton" is kept from expression by his peasant class. The fate of an early death denies the chance for fame to Lycidas. And the dreamer of "The Temple of Fame" awakens to the home truth that pursuing fame may be a damning waste of time. One suspects that Lincoln listened and learned. But of the three poems, he may only have "assimilated" (in Herndon's sense) Gray's "Elegy," which made itself fully manifest to him as a poem singing the sad truths he was daily learning in his own rural Indiana life. If the other two pieces meant less to him, because further *from* him, they were nonetheless cognate in representing in more sophisticated language and form what the "Elegy Written in a Country Churchyard" communicated to him so deeply: what to make of an expressive life. "Art thou, fond Youth, a candidate for Praise?"

Robert Burns was a "Ploughman" in the same way that Abraham Lincoln was a "Railsplitter": from economic necessity. Both men did agricultural labor when they had to for subsistence, and did it well enough, but escaped into books, thought, and writing at every opportunity. Nor were Burns and Lincoln sprung as poets from the soil. Both were mostly autodidacts, and each diligently studied his native tongue (Burns had two) to remarkable effect. Burns's self-education also derived from grammars and preceptors, to classical and Augustan literary models, and finally to the late-eighteenth-century reemergence of Scots dialect poetry and song. And, of course, the culturally obligatory homiletics of an ultra-Calvinist cast. There were for Burns even an abortive few weeks of studying the mathematics of surveying![11] The point of education, if one were needed for two such hungry minds, was to let them get off the farm and into a craft more congenial to their talents and temperaments: fashioning the language to move and convince an audience, Lincoln as a lawyer and politician, Burns as a public poet, both with liberty ever in mind.

Their parallel successes have been treated as sentimental sagas of the triumph of will over adversity, as in this passage from David J. Harkness and R. Gerald McMurtry's *Lincoln's Favorite Poets* (1959): "Abraham Lincoln and Robert Burns, honest and plain men of the people, stand today as the best-loved American and the best-loved Scotsman. The Lincoln log cabin in Kentucky and the Burns cottage in Ayrshire are shrines visited each year by countless admirers of these great figures. Born to poverty and obscurity, rising to heights of fame and popularity through long years of hard work, their lives present an interesting parallel. It is appropriate that Abe Lincoln should have found a kindred spirit in Bobby Burns, who spoke to his heart of the innermost yearnings, disappointments, and sorrows which both had experienced through similar backgrounds."[12] Honesty and hard work we may freely grant to both, but if modern biography has shown us anything new about Lincoln and Burns, it is that they were *not* "plain men of the people." Rather, their psychological distance from class-ridden injustice and poor-white (peasant) plodding provided them the necessary perspective to write and speak compassionately yet pointedly about human rights.

Harkness and McMurtry assert that "Next to Shakespeare, Burns was Lincoln's favorite of all the poets." This reflects Lincoln biographers' near consensus over almost a century and a half.[13] Some who knew Lincoln in New Salem and Springfield remembered Lincoln's *preferring* Burns to Shakespeare, while others have testified to his ability to quote Burns at will (and at length, though William G. Greene's claim that Lincoln "knew all of Burns by heart" is exaggerated).[14] Isaac Newton Arnold, who became acquainted with Lincoln in the 1840s, even recalled that Lincoln had a "lecture . . . upon Burns full of favorite quotations and sound criticisms."[15] One assumes that Arnold here means that Lincoln *wrote* such a lecture. Were this true, and were it extant, the essay would be invaluable, as a rare example of Lincoln's written literary criticism.

Douglas L. Wilson, in *Honor's Voice*, asserts that Lincoln came to relish Burns's poetry while still in Indiana: "By the time he arrived in New Salem his strong partiality for Burns was very evident." We can assent to at least part of this. Lincoln's fellow store-clerk in New Salem, Charles Maltby, remembered in 1884 that among the titles in the small cache of books Lincoln brought with him when he first came to the village was the poetry of Burns.[16] And in 1888 Noah Brooks, an acquaintance from the mid-1850s in Illinois, and later an intimate at the White House, published a biography of Lincoln (intended for a high-school audience) in which he mentioned that Lincoln, while living in Indiana, had borrowed a copy of "Burns's *Poems*, a thick and chunky volume, as he afterward described it, bound in leather and printed in very small type. This book he kept long enough to commit to memory almost all its contents."[17] Again, that phenomenal memory! Even though Brooks does not cite sources in this biography, the implication is clear: Lincoln himself had related to him the story of the borrowed Burns. And the closest student of Burns's influence on Lincoln, Ferenc Morton Szasz, accepts that Lincoln came to Burns while living in Indiana, through that "thick and chunky" edition of his poems.[18] In any case, abundant informant evidence exists of this "strong partiality for Burns," whether newly formed or brought with him to Illinois, among the New Salem and Springfield residents who spoke or wrote to Herndon on the matter. No fewer than nine of Herndon's informants recalled Burns as a part of Lincoln's reading, and several of these made Burns an important part.

Here a semilegendary New Salem name must enter this book: Jack Kelso. He really did live in New Salem, even held property. He walked the muddy street of the village, ate, drank, voted, and presumably paid his taxes. The *legendary* aspect of Kelso's life, however, is what was remembered long after he left the place (and Lincoln's life) for good. To many of his neighbors,

Kelso had been an eccentric and an outsider. Uninterested in "the right to rise," he spent his days hunting and fishing, wandering in the woods, and generally not giving a damn.[19] Married but without children, eschewing farming or store-keeping or anything else that looked like regular business, Kelso, as the collective town-memory would have it, often lolled on the banks of the Sangamon fishing, while reading and talking Burns and Shakespeare with Abraham Lincoln. Was this sheer laziness, not to say vagrancy ("no visible means of support"), or a nobly Thoreauvian self-sufficiency? History can't tell us. As Wilson points out, even the assiduous nose of Herndon was unable to sniff out much at all of Kelso's short time in New Salem, though later, in the 1920s, a local historian named Thomas P. Reep, relying on "unspecified traditional sources," assembled a portrait: Kelso was "one of those peculiar, impractical geniuses—well educated, a lover of nature, with the soul of a poet and all of a poet's impracticability, and who could 'recite Shakespeare and Burns by the hour.'"[20]

Edgar Lee Masters, the author of *Spoon River Anthology*, had grown up in the vicinity of New Salem (long after the townsite had been abandoned) and heard in his boyhood the same sort of "traditional sources"—no more than stories passed along generationally—that Reep was using. In 1928, Masters published a book-length dramatic poem, *Jack Kelso*, that attempted to extrapolate a life for its eponymous protagonist from the several years he had spent at New Salem. As so often proved true of Masters's heroes, mature male life turned out to be a succession of painful failures. But the life of a young adult in the "garden" around the village could be much more pleasant and fulfilling: Wordsworthian "spots of time" might become manifest to the "man of sensibility" who took his book up on a hill to sit under a generous shade tree and read, think, look at the landscape, and daydream. Masters makes the relationship between Kelso and Lincoln one of lover and beloved, not in the physical but the spiritual sense: a friendship of inner-life affinities, a Whitmanlike camaraderie, doomed to separation. Here are lines from Lincoln's act 2 farewell, as he prepares to leave New Salem for Springfield:

> Sorrow comes in my heart. The plaint
> Of something is crying in my ears,
> Like whippoorwills, or autumn sighs
> For thinking of these happy years
> I've lived here in New Salem. Jack,
> This evening ends it, I realize,
> This evening ends it. From what track
> Shall I upon these years look back?
> No one will ever know what you

Have been to me, and how you brought
Books to me for my growing thought.Jack Kelso! What a friend! How true,
How ever even tempered, kind. . . . [21]

If Kelso really did tutor Lincoln in Burns, he would have been inculcating what passed, in 1830 as in 1790, for radicalism. But what about religious "infidelity"? According to James H. Matheny, "Burns helped Lincoln to be an infidel . . . at least he found in Burns a like thinker and feeler."[22] But Lincoln historian Allen C. Guelzo, in *Abraham Lincoln: Redeemer President* (1999) asserted the opposite, insisting that it was Lincoln's predisposition to religious doubt that led him to the poetry: "This skeptical disillusion was what made Lincoln such an admirer of Burns."[23] Burns's gadfly-biting poetry, on the matter of Christianity, hardly compared with the sustained cannon fire of Paine, Voltaire, and Volney. Burns meant music and freedom to Lincoln—not freedom in the abstract but behavioral (including, and perhaps most important, sexual behavior). His connection with Burns in the early 1830s was performative and emulative, and he may well have had an important role model in Jack Kelso.[24] What New Salem recalled of Kelso's character, education, and, for lack of a better word, "lifestyle," make his position of bosom friend and teacher plausible. After all, both men had plenty of free time to wonder as they wandered. Nonetheless, we must keep in mind that, as far as Lincoln's remembered utterances and extant writings are concerned, *no such person as Jack Kelso ever existed.*

Whether Lincoln brought Burns with him to New Salem or savored the poetry from Kelso's or another's copy, it was the same Robert Burns he read. Typically, American editions comprised the Scots dialect verse (generally accompanied by a glossary), the mixed and the wholly English verse, and the songs and their tunes. The poems were often preceded by the poet's biography. For example, the two-volume Philadelphia edition of 1804 contained a fifty-page essay full of details and incidents of Burns's life, some of it taken from his autobiographical letters. Thus, it is very likely that Lincoln knew both the poems and the sad story of the poet.

If Burns the man and the poet meant to Lincoln more than tragicomic excursions in wenching, carousing, and the singing of songs, we must assume that he knew many others beyond the dozen poems remembered by name in *Herndon's Informants*. Of these, six are songs (in the sense of having their musical tunes printed with them), four are lyric (including one dramatic monologue), and two are narrative tales. Of the songs, little need be said. Lincoln enjoyed hearing Burns's and others' songs sung, the more maudlin the better, but he himself was no singer.[25] That leaves six, narratives and lyrics, that demand more attention—and we must add one, to make seven, since Lincoln himself quoted from "Address to the Deil" in his 1837 "Second Reply to James Adams."[26]

By *lyric* we here mean not the great Romantic ode of interior sensibility but shorter poems on ethical or political themes. "Is There for Honest Poverty" is one of Burns's most famous lyrics, known everywhere as "A man's a man for a' that." This poem has several marks of Lincoln's self-identification: obscure social origins, the poverty of a peasant, the sense of inferior rank, arbitrarily determined; but, by the same token, honesty, natural nobility, and the promise of a new day of universal brotherhood dawning. Burns's deft use of "for a' that," both as a refrain and within the verses (thirty times in five eight-line stanzas!), scornfully tosses "a' that" into the "scrap-heap of history." The poem concludes:

> Then let us pray that come it may,
>   As come it will for a' that,
> That Sense and Worth, o'er a' the earth
>   Shall bear the gree, and a' that.
> For a' that, and a' that,
>   Its comin yet for a' that,
> That Man to Man the warld o'er,
>   Shall brothers be for a' that.[27]

As a very late poem (1795) from the premature sunset of a too-short life, "A Man's a Man for a' That" is a testament to Burns's secular humanity, his hope that the liberalism he lived and sang for would one day triumph over the two-headed tyrant of Scotch church and state (no wonder Byron loved him and his poetry and made much of his own "half-Scotch" lineage!). Like Burns's speaker in "hoddin grey" (homespun), Lincoln wore his ill-fitting jeans for longer than he liked and was ridiculed for it; but he traded on his honesty:

> Gie fools their silks, and knaves their wine. . . .
> The honest man, though e'er sae poor,
> Is king o' men for a' that.

The earlier "Epistle to a Young Friend" (1786) offers the poet's avuncular advice to one like a nephew just setting forth: "Perhaps it may turn out a Sang; / Perhaps turn out a Sermon."[28] Since this is one of Burns's poems Lincoln was said to have known by heart, we should be curious to discover what he liked so much about it.[29] Right off, Uncle Rab observes, the younger man will "find mankind an unco squad, / And muckle they may grieve ye." Not that all men are villains:

But Och, mankind are unco weak,
    An little to be trusted;
If *Self* the wavering balance shake,
    It's rarely right adjusted.

The Scots word *unco* is one of Burns's favorite adjectives, usually meaning *strange*, sometimes *very*, and here probably both at once. So the honest man must make his wary way through life, as in stanza 5, speaking frankly only to a "bosom crony," and otherwise,

Conceal yoursel as weel's ye can
    Frae critical dissection;
But keek thro' ev'ry other man,
    Wi' sharpen'd, sly inspection.

In stanza 7, the poet's voice allows that, when gathering "gear" (wealth), one may proceed "by ev'ry wile, / That's justify'd by Honor," not to pile it up or for social show but simply to sustain one's independence. And that upper-cased noun of character, so important (as Wilson has shown) to Lincoln's positive self-image, occurs again in the very next stanza, which asserts the superiority of the inner light over churchly religion:

The *fear o' Hell*'s a hangman's whip,
    To haud the wretch in order;
But where ye feel your *Honor* grip,
    Let that ay be your border:
It's slightest touches, instant pause—
    Debar a' side-pretences;
And resolutely keep it's laws,
    Uncaring consequences.[30]

Burns could be as hard on the established Presbyterian Church of Scotland as it was on him (he was publicly branded as a "fornicator" by his local kirk). Still, two of his most telling poems on the subject of religion indict not the church but churchgoers for their hypocrisy and mendacity: "Address to the Unco Guid" and "Holy Willie's Prayer." Who are the "Unco Guid"? This time it's *strangely* rather than *very*. The full title adds "or the Rigidly Righteous," and the poem carries an epigraph from *Ecclesiastes* nicely versified by Burns, containing these lines: "*The* Rigid Righteous *is a fool,/ The* Rigid Wise *anither*." These "strangely good" folk, then, are the poem's objects of ridicule. Not that they sin less: they just hide better! Be it debauchery or drinking, the "unco guid" either do it in secret or else want to, terribly, in particular the women:

Ye high, exalted, virtuous Dames,
    Ty'd up in godly laces,
Before ye gie poor *Frailty* names,
    Suppose a change of cases;
A dear-lov'd lad, convenience snug,
    A treacherous inclination—
But, let me whisper I' your lug,
    Ye're aiblins nae temptation.

"Perhaps no temptation" to "Rantin Rab," hitting the ladies where it hurt most, in their *amour propre*. Leave it to God, the poem concludes: "'tis *He* alone / Decidedly can try us," since for humans "What's *done* we partly may compute, / But know not what's *resisted*."[31] The moral is clear: mind your own business and down with the self-righteousness of denouncing others. You know but half the *what* and none of the *why* of "your Neebours' fauts and folly!" As Ferenc Szasz has observed, "Address to the Unco Guid" "can be read as a plea for simple charity" that would keenly appeal to Lincoln.[32]

Robert Burns, like Poe after him, was calumniated as a drunkard: in both men's cases, some of their enemies falsely named alcoholism as the cause of death. Lincoln, as is well known, was a near teetotaler all his life, but it is fair to say he despised sanctimony on the issue more than dram drinking itself. On Washington's birthday, February 22, 1842, he delivered an address to the Washington Temperance Society at the Second Presbyterian Church in Springfield, Illinois. The Washingtonians, as they were known, formed a different and more effective temperance organization than had previously been active in the United States. Composed mainly of reformed drunks, its approach to the problem had much in common with today's Alcoholics Anonymous: recognizing alcoholism as a disease caused by what Lincoln called "burning appetites" in the sufferers, and dealing with it through a compassionate program of disciplined support from a community of people who had fought the same malaise. On this occasion, then, Lincoln was speaking to what must have been largely a sympathetic audience. Yet he was as plainspokenly subversive as Burns. He accused the self-righteous of America, and by implication the good bourgeois of Springfield, of what we would now term "blaming the victim." At the outset of his speech, he named the classes of men who had adopted the wrong strategy toward drunkenness: "Preachers, Lawyers, and hired agents," all of whom have held morally aloof from the "mass of mankind" to whom indeed they ought to have been ministering. The result of "too much denunciation against dram sellers and dram drinkers," Lincoln pointed out, was counter-denunciation from the offended parties: "It is not in the nature of man to be driven to any thing; still less to be driven about that which is exclusively his own business."[33]

A great poet or rhetorician can often better his or her antagonists by imitating them. Lincoln's most audacious move in the Temperance Address was to preach evangelical, biblical Christianity to the very people who thought themselves so righteously superior to the fallen-down drunks they were spurning socially or even routinely running out of town after a night in the tank to sober up. There isn't sufficient space to analyze his smooth effrontery in accomplishing this, but readers of the opening paragraph of the speech, with its mock-heroic tone, will quickly get the idea.[34] Suffice to say that Lincoln treats the reformed drunkard like the Christian sinner who is "born again" and runs shouting his salvation among his friends and family—or even in the face of his persecutors. What divine or deacon or churchly matron could object to this reclamation of another poor lost sheep into the Master's fold? Lincoln's call for charity was thrown right back at those who, like Burns's "unco guid," bought their respectability through ostensible holiness. Again like Burns, Lincoln had grown up in a whiskey-drinking culture that both honored and damned the stuff (see Burns's poem "Scotch Drink"). In Scotland, as in Kentucky, Indiana, and Illinois, it had not been a question of "the *use* of a *bad thing* but . . . the *abuse* of a *very good thing*." Such abuse constituted not a moral failing but at worst a "hereditary disease" and at best a habit hard to break. The "grace" to reform is God's grace. For the Washingtonians, there is no unpardonable sin: "As in Christianity it is taught, so in this *they* teach, that 'While the lamp holds out to burn, / The vilest sinner may return.'"[35]

The theology of Lincoln's temperance reform is most interesting. Rather than the Calvinism that he shared with Burns (as something to be opposed and got beyond; as something both faced the bigotry of daily in their respective communities), Lincoln here preached not election and the "unconditional perseverance of the [relatively few] saints," but Arminianism, that is, God's grace freely available to all who seek it. This put him, ironically and no doubt temporarily, in the camp of his old antagonist, the Methodist preacher Peter Cartwright. Lincoln deployed the same triumphalist language that nineteenth-century western camp-meeting revivalists used to trumpet their dramatic success in saving souls, with greater yet to come:

> To these *new champions*, and this *new* system of tactics, our late success is mainly owing; and to *them* we must chiefly look for the final consummation. The ball is now rolling gloriously on, and none are so able as *they* to increase its speed, and its bulk—to add to its momentum, and its magnitude. Even though unlearned in letters, for this task, none others are so well educated.

To fit them for this work, they have been taught in the true school. *They* have been in *that* gulf, from which they would teach others the means of escape. *They* have passed that prison wall, which others have long declared impassable; and who that has not, shall dare to weigh opinions with *them*, as to the mode of passing.[36]

In other words, like the freshman evangelist on the circuit, when all else fails, *tell your story* (and all else *will* fail): only he who has "passed that prison wall" really understands what the imprisonment is like and how to escape it. That was what Cartwright's elders had told him and what he told his several generations of acolytes in Methodism. Yet Lincoln accomplished all this without *himself* being identified with *any* Christian denomination, Presbyterian, Baptist, or Methodist (four years later, in the congressional campaign against Cartwright, he would declare, "That I am not a member of any Christian Church, is true").[37] But that he could wear the preacher's collar when he wished, and outperform the best of them, bothered some of the good citizens of Springfield. As Lincoln's audience exited the church that February day, Herndon overheard some self-righteous muttering: "It's a shame that he should be permitted to abuse us so in the house of the Lord."[38]

Those who harrumphed at Lincoln's speech claimed righteousness for themselves and their kith alone: they were the self-elected elect in just the sense Lincoln repudiated. In "Holy Willie's Prayer," Burns, in what biographer Maurice Lindsay has judged "one of the finest satires in any European tongue," used the form of the self-indicting dramatic monologue to compose "an ageless indictment of cringing, unctuous hypocrisy."[39] The poem is based on a church controversy in Burns's parish of Mauchline. Yet, like Dickens, he could educe the universal from the local. "Holy Willie," "a rather oldish bachelor Elder," has on the day of the poem lost a church trial in which he had brought charges of immorality against another. That evening, he kneels in devotion to his "auld licht" Calvinist God:

O Thou that in the heaves does dwell!
Wha, as it please best thysel,
Sends ane to heaven and ten to hell,
    A' for thy glory!
And no for ony gude or ill
    They've done before thee.
I bless and praise thy matchless might,
When thousands thou has left in night,
That I am here before thy sight,
    For gifts and grace,

A burning and a shining light
    To a' this place.

Of course, Willie esteems himself elected and as such a *saint* on earth who will be eternally in heaven. Yet the part of him that is still *man* (when "Vile Self gets in") suffers the temptations of the flesh:

O Lord—yestreen—thou kens—wi' Meg—
Thy pardon I sincerely beg!
O may't ne'er be a living plague,
    To my dishonour!
And I'll ne'er lift a lawless leg
    Again upon her.—

Perhaps his lust—"this fleshly thorn"—and its expense in fornication were tests of this Lord's servant, "Lest he o'er proud and high should turn, / That he's sae gifted." If so, Holy Willie can stand the pain until it's lifted![40]

The accounts of the flesh settled, he can turn to his church adversaries. Note the deft manner in which Burns has Willie move, without irony except to author and reader, from religious beneficence in the first half of this stanza, to pure malevolence in the second:

Lord bless thy Chosen in this place,
For here thou has a chosen race:
But God, confound their stubborn face,
    And blast their name,
Wha bring thy rulers to disgrace
    And open shame.

And the poem's penultimate stanza rings out like the violent words of one of the Psalmists: O Lord, smite thine enemies, and give no quarter ("and dinna spare!"). Willie's last supplication, however, is reserved for his craven self:

But Lord, remember me and mine
Wi' mercies temporal and divine!
That I for grace and gear may shine,
    Excell'd by nane!

By the time Willie twice exults with "Amen!" he has so fully eviscerated his own moral being that the poet need add nothing to the lesson (nor could he do so adroitly, given the dramatic monologue form). But Scots has a word for the effect of what has just taken place, though not explicitly drawn by Burns: a *skailing*, which is a kind of *taking apart* of the despised subject, not unrelated to the upland southern tradition of *skinning*, when, as Lincoln did to Jesse B. Thomas in 1840, an opponent is verbally flayed alive in the imitated voice and gestures of the victim. Herndon tells us that Thomas was reduced to tears by Lincoln's perfect (but sarcastic) mimicry, just as any village candidate for the role of "Holy Willie" might well have skulked off to nurse his resentment whenever forced to hear someone in the community reciting parts of Burns's poem (and we are told that it circulated freely among the Mauchline folk).[41] Lincoln, less artfully and perhaps less fairly, skinned, while Burns so blithely skailed. Lincoln later apologized, as he should have; Burns didn't, as he shouldn't.

Two narrative poems are among Burns's most famous and both attested as Lincoln favorites: "Tam O'Shanter" (1791) and "Cotter's Saturday Night" (1786). The former, in rollicking four-beat iambic couplets, is a rousing tale of a (supposed) supernatural encounter. The eponymous protagonist may or may not have had his innings with a hoard of "beldams" who pursue him late one night as he rides home from the tavern after a bout of serious wenching, dancing, and drinking. Tam, astride his fast gray mare Meg just manages to escape capture (and damnation) at the hands of an old "carlin" (witch), but his horse has her tail snatched off. "And left poor Maggie scarce a stump." But for the evidence of the tailless nag, it might all have been Tam's drunken hallucination.[42]

"The Cotter's Saturday Night," by contrast, is a sentimental evocation of peasant domestic bliss that eschews Tam's animal spirits for a claustrophobic scene of impoverished but loving "family values" with which the kirk could find no fault—the very thing Tam kept trying to escape. The poem does not *sound* like something Lincoln could read with a straight face, though he seems to have known it well. Yet there was frequently a sentimentalizing tendency in Lincoln's appreciation of poetry that balanced his predilection for satire and even bawdy. He would have recognized in "Cotter's Saturday Night" an idealized, even fantasized, version of his Kentucky/Indiana family life, and one can easily imagine his performing the poem the more feelingly for its being unrealistic. A *cotter*, of course, was a tenant farmer, the head-of-household in a rented cottage, whose almost insupportable labors on a niggardly land only paused at the end of Saturday's toil, with the Sabbath to follow. Burns heads his poem with the same quatrain from Gray's "Elegy" quoted above, ending with the line that Lincoln made the more famous by quoting it to Scripps and could recite well before he had read the Scots poet: "The short and simple annals of the poor."

Ironically, the Cambridge don's elegy reaches further into the real and anonymous life of the peasant farmer than does the "ploughman's" attempt at celebration of the humbly heroic, which comes off in its worst sections as forced and false. When Burns praises the flowering of young love in such circumstances, he freely idealizes: "O happy love! Where love like this is found! / O heart-felt raptures! bliss beyond compare!" A virgin ploughman meets a virgin milkmaid and heaven-on-earth ensues. The cotters' paterfamilias—an hour before in the fields and little different from his beasts of burden—is during supper the august head-of-table and afterwards a domestic *priest* (the "*Saint*, the *Father*, the *Husband*")—leading the family's Bible studies and devotions. His earnest prayers and his rapt congregation put established religion to shame, with its "pomp of *method*, and of *art*," and we are instructed to believe that not only is the cottage the true church but the true Scottish nation:

> From Scenes like these, old Scotia's grandeur springs,
>   That makes her lov'd at home, rever'd abroad:
> Princes and lords are but the breath of kings,
>   "An honest man's the noble work of God."

In short, "the *Cottage* leaves the *Palace* far behind."[43]

Two features of the cultural context in New Salem and Springfield (ca. 1820–44) may be pertinent to Lincoln's *oral/aural* mastery of Burns. First, the *Scot's dialect*. According to Milton Hay, who became acquainted with Lincoln soon after the latter moved to Springfield in 1837, "He had acquired the Scotch accent, and could render Burns perfectly."[44] How might this have occurred? A glossary aids meaning but not pronunciation. Significantly, there *were* a few Scots voices in the Sangamon at this time in the guise of poetasters. Literary scholar John E. Hallwas has identified a canon of poems written and published in the 1820s and 1830s by a Springfield-area writer known only as "H." Among "H's" productions were two satires in passable Burnsian dialect, "Hame's the Best Place A'ter A'" and "Cauld Comfort," both published in the *Sangamo Journal* in December 1831.[45] Whoever "H." may have been, he was superbly literate. Besides Scots, he knew French and Italian and peppered his poems with allusions that demonstrate a classical education and more—there are references to Hindu scripture and Norse mythology. Hallwas determined that "H." was of "Scottish descent" and had left England, probably in the early part of the nineteenth century, in search of "liberty."[46] How he ended up in Springfield, Illinois, remained a mystery, but "H." lived and wrote there for more than two decades, the self-styled "Bard of the Sangamon."

As with Lincoln's own "Suicide's Soliloquy," the *Journal* printed the occasional effusions of local poets, who vied with one another for such laurels as the just-post-frontier community could offer. "H." led the way, publishing seventy-one poems in the *Journal* between late 1831 and the spring of 1846. Both in quantity and quality, he might condescend in print to his lesser brethren, whom he called "the small beer poets,"

. . . your poetasters mad,
Who snort like calves that feel the gad;
And mounted on their own tame juckus,
Think all the while they stride Pegassus.[47]

"H." even had a letter-writing critic, "Scrutator" ("one who scrutinizes"), to whom he responded in a witty Byronic defense called "Bards and Reviewers" that opens "*Scruter, Scrutator, Scru*—which is't / That you subscribe your classic fist?" Critics like Scrutator were full of pretense, while others who tried the lyre were nothing but "small beer poets," unworthy of appearing in the same column with "H."[48]

Was Lincoln such a critic, or perhaps one of the "small beer poets"? Clearly, he was writing poetry during his New Salem sojourn and increasingly in Springfield after 1837. We also know that the editor of the *Sangamo Journal*, Simeon Francis, opened the paper's columns to Lincoln for his political satire and partisan speeches. As New Salem postmaster from 1833 to 1836, Lincoln would have seen and read copies of the *Journal* not long after they were published (as he read every other newspaper that passed through his hands). He would thus have recognized in "H." a poet of ability and sense, better than himself if less gifted than Burns, against whose standard for effective topical and satirical verse he might measure himself and from whom he could learn. Did Lincoln, like "H.," join in the poetic competition to immortalize the quasi-farcical trip of the steamboat *Talisman* up the Sangamon to Springfield and back down again, grounding for a while on the New Salem milldam? Herndon remembered that "numerous" were the poems from ambitious pens on this great event in the *Journal*; and when Paul M. Angle edited *Herndon's Lincoln* (1930), he inserted a dozen lines from H.'s entry to illustrate the point that local poets were on the job, which we here reduce to a quatrain's worth:

Jabez's gude liquors went off slick,
Some for the cash, but most on tick;
The small-beer poets made a show,
And their small whistles loud did blow.[49]

"H." was very much alive—indeed, was Springfield's chief Parnassian—during Lincoln's first decade in the vicinity. From his reading of Burns, Lincoln knew what superlative Scots poetry consisted of; from scanning the large folio, small-print pages of the *Sangamo Journal* for the frequent contributions of "H.," he would have realized how Burns might be successfully imitated. But how he, as a writer and performer of Scots verse, learned *to say the Scots language correctly*, we have yet to comprehend. Doing so is hardly intuitive, as many speakers of English attempting Burns aloud have discovered to their embarrassment. Lincoln had to have heard the poetry recited, more than once, and then practiced it himself—with a coach?

Consider again those whiled-away hours with Jack Kelso, indoors and out. "Kelso" is a Scotch name (the locality of Roxburghshire), and though it is not known whether he or his parents or grandparents were the immigrants, it is plausible to suppose that the Kelso family in Adair County, Kentucky, sustained the linguistic tie with the Old Country, so that when Jack Kelso came to New Salem in 1831, he brought with him his decent education *and* the Scots language.[50] If Kelso and Lincoln were in fact close friends for several years, sharing a passion for poetry, we may reasonably venture that the Scotsman who could "recite Shakespeare and Burns by the hour" may well have taught Lincoln how to do the same, especially with the latter poet's rich and unfamiliar dialect.

Finally, we cannot do justice to the topic of Lincoln and Burns without emphasizing the animal spirits of Burns's poetry, in and out of the canon. Lincoln read and recited from Burns a sexually warm, a *creatural* poetry that was all but proscribed in polite American society—that is, for Lincoln, among the Whiggish aristocracy of Springfield—and patently unpublishable, if not unwriteable, in the nation's fledgling literature. High-spirited lines of a sexually suggestive nature, howsoever satirical in intent, like those from "Holy Willie's Prayer" quoted above ("I'll ne'er lift a lawless leg / Again upon her") were beyond the American polite poetic pale, at least until Walt Whitman's *Leaves of Grass* (1855). We will see this clearly in Fitz-Greene Halleck's tribute poem to Burns, from the reading of which we should not know that Burns was a *funny* poet who *had fun* in his life and art. Burns, in Halleck's view, was all earnest poverty and downtrodden Scotch nationalism, tragically misunderstood by the very people he was attempting to sing. True enough, but not all the truth. Just as Lincoln liked telling dirty jokes, he enjoyed the oral interpretation of vivacious, sometimes salacious, poetry; it is not surprising that Burns's inimitable Scots humor, embodied in an exotic *other* English, became a specialty for Lincoln the entertainer. Whether beguiled by women or bedeviled by political opponents, he could add Burns's Scots wit to his own—as he did in the 1837 newspaper controversy with James Adams, that devil of a widow-harasser whom Lincoln disarmed with a single line from Burns's "Address to the Deil." Here is the way Lincoln put it near the end of his "Second Reply to James Adams": "Adams himself is prowling about, and as Burns says of the devil, *'For prey, a' holes and corners tryin,'* and in one instance goes so far as to take an old acquaintance of mine several steps from a crowd, and apparently weighed down with the importance of his business, gravely and solemnly asks him if *'he ever heard Lincoln say he was Deist.'*"[51] Just like the devil, in Kilmarnock as in Springfield. Both Burns and Lincoln beat the devil by pinning him with the evil eye of satire. Perhaps the one *was* a radical, the other a Deist, and therefore both "infidels" according to prevailing orthodoxy. But let the devil try to tell and make it stick:

An' now, auld *Cloots*, I ken ye're thinkan
A certain *Bardie*'s rantin, drinkin,
Some luckless hour will send him linkan,
    To your black pit;
But faith! he'll turn a corner jinkan,
    An' cheat you yet.[52]

George Gordon, Lord Byron, has come down, by tradition and testimony, as the other of Lincoln's two favorite poets. As William G. Greene told Herndon, "Burns & Byron were his favorite books" during the New Salem years, and his particular Springfield friend Joshua Speed also recalled Byron, as did James H. Matheny.[53] Once the names of Byron and Lincoln are conjoined, it seems natural to imagine affinities of character between the younger reader and Byron's poetic persona. By the mid-1820s his popularity meant that volumes of Byron were *relatively* easy to obtain, and of course "everybody" (i.e., the young, male and female) was reading him. What is more, Byron's poetry was racy, the poet raffish. In Byron's work, Lincoln found a poetry of radical transgression that was yet dressed in the respectability of English aristocracy: if a "gentleman" had written *Childe Harold's Pilgrimage*, it must ultimately be acceptable reading, despite all the subversion of the very mode of life it was passing as (a sort of social transvestism). How deep this subversion plumbed may not have been known to Lincoln, as it was not to many of Byron's English readers: Byron was a bisexual whose predilection was homosexual. He often loved boys and young men and indulged his homosexuality when he thought he could get away with it. Sodomy constituted a capital crime in England, and from the late eighteenth century well into the early nineteenth, the law was apt to be enforced. At Harrow and then at Cambridge, he had some protection as a member of a secret confraternity of "Methodistes" (as they facetiously codenamed themselves). But in his short life after his college years, Byron was forced to behave more carefully and masked (masqueraded?) his real sexual proclivity behind multiple affairs with women, and even marriage, as well as with heroic yet always doomed male-female romances in the poetry.[54]

In his penetrating book about Lincoln's self-education in New Salem and Springfield, *Honor's Voice*, Douglas L. Wilson has suggested another intriguing link between Byron and Lincoln: that the latter, despite his stated disgust with the genre of biography, read Thomas Moore's *Letters and Journals of Lord Byron with Notices of His Life* (1830), sometime fairly soon after its appearance in an American edition in 1831–32. Wilson associates Moore's discussion of one of Byron's near duels with the preposterous Lincoln–James Shields affair of 1842, where Shields had called Lincoln out over some newspaper ridicule and the challenged chose "cavalry broadswords of the largest size" as the weapons to be employed. (The opponents got as far as Alton, whence they intended to row out to an island in the Mississippi owned by the State of Missouri—dueling being illegal in Illinois—before both parties came to their senses and cancelled the whole thing.) In addition, in the context of Lincoln's marriage to Mary Todd (November 4, 1842), Wilson speculates that Lincoln, when a boy asked him on his wedding day where he was going all dressed up, may have had Byron in mind when he answered, "To hell, I reckon." Byron had said of the unfinished *Don Juan*, "I had not quite fixed whether to make him end in Hell, or in an unhappy marriage, not knowing which would be the severest."[55] These two connections of the poet's life with the politician's are important, if for no other reason than that they are unique. In most other cases, Burns always excepted, Lincoln read and absorbed the *poetry* but was indifferent to (or ignorant of) the poet. Yet to a great extent, such identification was inevitable with Bryon, whose huge reputation preceded even his poetry and whose identity readers were ready and all too willing to assume was one with the autobiographical presence in his poems.

Wilson does not discuss the homosexual subtext in Byron's life and poetry. Probably he thought it irrelevant to Lincoln. And it is true that Moore's *Life* is scrupulously silent about what Moore knew to be true about his subject, only calling Byron's Cambridge love affairs "romantic friendships" rather than the life-altering, true-love experiences they really were. Lincoln, on the evidence, was probably not bisexual, despite a vigorous attempt to persuade the world to the contrary in C. A. Tripp's *Intimate World of Abraham Lincoln* (2005—and how odd that Byron isn't even mentioned in this book!). As Joshua Wolf Shenk has pointed out, "the question, as it has been recently framed, of whether Lincoln was homosexual would make a good topic for a high school debating society, because it will admit of no proof in either direction."[56] Yet it may not be amiss to say that Lincoln learned a good deal about sex, love, and friendship—their unpredictability and volatility in particular—from his reading of Byron and may have been a little shocked to recognize a version of his private self-image in the Byronic hero. When he began to worry about the destructive force of the *passions*, it was with good reason: sometimes he felt them coursing untrammeled in himself.[57]

Lincoln's first real knowledge of Byron's poetry had come in the late 1820s, from the *Columbian Class Book* studied in Indiana: "Nisus and Euryalus" (1807, an episode "paraphrased" in heroic couplets from Virgil's *Aeneid*) and a short selection from *The Corsair* (1814). Byron wrote "Nisus and Euryalus" while at Cambridge, a time of intense homoeroticism, so it is not surprising that from the wide range of classical literature available to translate, he chose the tale of a Trojan man and boy, warriors both and very much in love. Nisus is the seasoned soldier, "Well skilled in fight the quivering lance to wield"; Euryalus his constant companion, whose "beardless bloom yet graced the gallant boy," with "A soul heroic as his form was fair."[58] *The Corsair*, a more developed narrative at nearly seven hundred lines, is more characteristically Byronic in its invention and versification:

> Slight are the outward signs of evil thought,
> Within—within—'t was there the spirit wrought!
> Love shows all changes—Hate, Ambition, Guile,
> Betray no further than the bitter smile.[59]

We know that Lincoln somewhat later (probably in New Salem) read *The Corsair* entire and that the poem stayed in his mind all his life, to the extent that he was said to have known "several pages" of it by heart.[60]

Byron's poetry often dramatizes the *passion* of its Byronic hero—a passion that, however intellectualized or repressed by *reason*, ultimately ruled his personality and was the cause of his outsized actions. The hero's passion is both bodily and mental suffering, his reason the ruling power of mind that is threatened to be overset. Lincoln worried about this in himself and may have fantasized Byron's strong, silent, benevolently tyrannical hero as that rare individual of genius that he, Lincoln, both feared and desired he might become. The protagonist of *The Corsair*, Conrad, is an absolutist chief of an outlaw cause, piracy. Here is how Byron characterizes Conrad at the outset of the poem: reserved to the point of being antisocial; temperate among the riotous drunkenness of his men; eats but indifferently, content with a "hermit's board." Yet "His mind seems nourish'd by that abstinence," and as he commands, so his men obey: "That man of loneliness and mystery,— / Scarce seen to smile and seldom heard to sigh." His pirate companions know him not, save as their commander, who without apology orders them to rob and murder and die. "What should it be that thus their faith can bind? / The power of Thought—the magic of the Mind!"[61] Conrad, however, had not been born aloof and evil by nature: in youth,

> His soul was changed . . .
> Warp'd by the world in Disappointment's school,
> In words too wise, in conduct *there* a fool.

Resentment of his social ostracism made him "Fear'd, shunn'd, belied, ere youth had lost her force, / He hated man too much to feel remorse," even believing "the voice of wrath a sacred call / To pay the injuries of some on all."[62] One quality only softened his demeanor: love of a beautiful woman (Medora), fully requited. It would be too tedious here to rehearse the entire plot of *The Corsair*. Suffice to say that Medora dies of heartbreak when Conrad fails to return on schedule from what he intends as his last escapade. In his overmastering grief, his mind and self-control leave him, and he drops from sight (a suicide?). "His heart was form'd for softness, warp'd to wrong; / Betray'd too early, and beguiled too long." His one love, an antidote to early pain, was like a flower sheltered in dark shade; then "The thunder came," whose bolt blasted both her and him, leaving only "shiver'd fragments on the barren ground. With the death of Ann Rutledge, Lincoln apparently suffered Conrad's fictive bereavement: the stoic, the keen and entirely secular mind, was all unmanned:

> The proud, the wayward, who have fix'd below
> Their joy and find this earth enough for woe,
> Lose in that one their all—perchance a mite—
> But who in patience parts with all delight?[63]

Lincoln's best friend in Springfield, Joshua Speed, told Herndon he thought Lincoln had not "ever read much of Byron previous to my acquaintance." James Matheny, another Springfield friend, recalled that Lincoln "loved Byron's Don Juan—Darkness The Hosts of Sanacherib Child Harold."[64] By the mid-1850s, if we credit his fellow circuit-lawyer Henry C. Whitney, Lincoln was treating Byron's poems as old friends. One day in 1854, while visiting Whitney at his law office in West Urbana, Illinois, Lincoln casually went to a bookcase and "took down a well-worn copy of Byron and, readily turning to the third canto of Childe Harold, read aloud from the 34th verse, commencing: 'There is a very life in our despair,' etc. to and including the 45th verse. . . . This poetry was very familiar to him evidently; he looked specifically for, and found it with no hesitation, and read it with a fluency that indicated that he had read oftentimes before."[65] During his many years on the circuit, Lincoln carried Byron with him in his mind, and it only needed an occasion, such as seeing a "well-worn copy" on someone's bookshelf, to set him reading or reciting a favorite poem or passage.

The Bride of Abydos (1813), named by Speed as among Byron's longer poems that Lincoln read, carries the subtitle "A Turkish Tale" and takes as its epigraph this quatrain from Burns:

Had we never loved sae kindly,
Had we never loved sae blindly,
Never met or never parted,
We had ne'er been broken-hearted.

The Bride is similar to *The Corsair* in its highly melodramatic sentiments, its outlaw protagonist (though in the service of a "higher law"—Byron's anarchic notion of justice) and the tragic outcome of its love affair. Both poems feature the opposition or outright revolt of a younger, purer man against entrenched and tyrannical male power—a theme, as we have seen, that was always of interest to Lincoln. In *The Bride* the hero is Selim, who has been raised cruelly by "old Giaffar," a Turkish pasha who has led Selim to believe that he is nothing but a dependent orphan, the illegitimate "son of a slave"—whose mother was a despised Greek and a Christian besides— making him therefore worthless in his "father's" eyes except as a eunuchlike hanger-on at court. But Selim eventually discovers that Giaffar is actually his usurping uncle, who had murdered his brother, Abdallah, Selim's real and royal father, and claimed absolute rule over their joint kingdom. Since learning the truth, Selim has continued his ostensibly effete existence at the Divan, while secretly plotting palace revolution, supported by a loyal force of the disenfranchised.[66]

But love becomes the fatal complication. Giaffar's daughter, the lovely and nubile Zuleika, is to be married off to a sultan, against her will. She loves her "brother" Selim as only a "sister" can, and he feels the same. When he discovers the truth about his lineage, he continues to love Zuleika, now as a lover would, and when he reveals all to her (they are "only" cousins!), she too professes her undying romantic love for him. Henceforth, Selim declares, "Not blind to fate, I see, where'er I rove, / Unnumber'd perils,— but one only love!"[67] As they are about to embark on their escape from Giaffar, they see approaching torches and hear his marching minions. Selim's loyal band is too far from shore to aid him, so he turns to face his fate (as Zuleika hides). He fights valiantly, dispatching foe after foe but giving ground against their numbers. Finally, having fought clear, standing where shore and sea met, he turns for one last glimpse of Zuleika, only to be shot down by Giaffar.

Selim's death must necessarily cause Zuleika's, for this is the calculus of all such tales:

He was thy hope—thy joy—thy love—thy all—
And that last thought on him thou couldst not save
Sufficed to kill;
Burst forth in one wild cry—and all was still.

And the poem concludes with a graveyard retrospect more virtuosic even than Byron's usual graceful facility. Amid a grove of sad cypresses, a "single rose" blooms undyingly, though "the slightest gale / Might whirl the leaves on high," and winter storms blast the spot: "in vain— / To-morrow sees it bloom again!"[68] Lincoln could imagine himself as the Byronic lover and outsider. He could thrill under the poem's rhythmic cadences, as he would have thrilled others in its recitation. In addition, there was the deep, imaginative appeal of Byronic freedom, a radically existential, almost asocial condition.

The poem that made Byron an overnight sensation in England—and some months later in America—was *Childe Harold's Pilgrimage*, the first two cantos of which were published in 1812. Lincoln seems to have known the book-length poem in its full four-canto version (1818). While it is intriguing to think that he may have encountered *Childe Harold* in Indiana, or later in New Salem, most of the evidence of *Herndon's Informants* suggests a Springfield, or post-1837, time frame. It would follow, then, that Byron's two greatest poems, *Childe Harold* and *Don Juan* (1819–24), first found their way into Lincoln's hands in 1837 or not long after—when he was nearing thirty years of age. On the other hand, William G. Greene clearly stated that Lincoln read and admired Byron in New Salem. This *might* mean only a few scattered poems, but it is much more likely to have been a volume of Byron's complete works. On balance, we may say that Lincoln, before he moved to Springfield and became fast friends with Joshua Speed, had had at least the *opportunity* to read Byron through.

As readers and critics have often noted, the first two cantos of *Childe Harold's Pilgrimage* represent Byron the novice poet, the last two, Byron the master. While this may be a little too pat, there is a marked difference between the two parts of the poem, separated as they are by half a decade of practice and polish of the poet's art. The vehicle of the Spenserian stanza, employed throughout, with very occasional interpolated verses in other forms, served Byron well, and its music would have appealed to Lincoln: eight lines of iambic pentameter capped by a ninth that is an Alexandrine of six iambic beats, the whole rhyming (more or less) *ababbcbcc*.

In *Honor's Voice*, Douglas L. Wilson noticed that one of these early stanzas (the eighth) was consonant with what Lincoln had in the late 1830s told one of his "political associates," Robert L. Wilson, "about his own secret sadness": "Although he appeared to enjoy life rapturously, Still he was the victim of terrible melancholy. He Sought company, and indulged in fun and hilarity without restraint, or Stint of time Still when by himself, he told me that he was so overcome with mental depression, that he never dare carry a pocket knife."[69] For comparison of character and sentiment, here is the stanza Wilson quotes from canto 1 of *Childe Harold*:

> Yet oft-times in his maddest mirthful mood
> Strange pangs would flash along Childe Harold's brow,
> As if the memory of some daily feud
> Or disappointed passion lurk'd below:
> But this none knew, nor haply cared to know;
> For his was not that open, artless soul
> That feels relief by bidding sorrow flow,
> Nor sought he friend to counsel or condole,
> Whate'er his grief mote be which he could not control.[70]

Juxtaposed, the texts might be delineating one and the same persona. As the intellectually curious boy Lincoln grew into the reasoning man—also, however, the "man of sensibility"—he moved in his reading, and we may assume in his thought, from a standpoint of "I'd like to be like that" to "That's like me." Odd as it may sound, given their utterly different social statuses, there is a circumstantial parallel biography of Byron and Lincoln as boys and young men. Besides their disposition to depression, both were precocious as readers and then writers; were hypersensitive; had superb memories for literary language; considered themselves social outsiders because "deformed" (Byron's lameness, Lincoln's height, ungainliness, and "ugly" face); could seem almost sociopathically shy, only to break out into unwonted mirth; were kind to animals to the extent of refusing to hunt; given to melancholy and total self-absorption; passionately engaged with and loyal to a few special friends only; magnetically drawn to but wary of women; quick to resent perceived slights; and, most of all, keen to repay all such tenfold in satirical language.

Byron became *Lord* Byron when he reached twenty-one in 1809: at the time, he was just seeing into print his first satire, *English Bards and Scotch Reviewers*, his vigorous rejoinder to criticism of his recently published maiden book of lyrics, *Hours of Idleness* (1807, but containing several poems from the privately printed *Fugitive Pieces*, 1806). Compare this bardic outsetting with Lincoln's. If *Herndon's Lincoln* is accurate, Lincoln wrote and recited a poem at his sister Sarah's 1826 wedding to Aaron Grigsby, scion of the "first family" of the neighborhood. This was "Adam and Eve's Wedding Song," in eight ballad stanzas. While Herndon thought the production "tiresome doggerel . . . full of painful rhymes," it evidently went down well enough on the occasion. But when Sarah died in childbirth not two years later, Lincoln was disturbed not only at the death of his sister but at something he found amiss in the way her husband had treated her during their brief marriage. Perhaps he had been covertly warning Grigsby about spousal abuse in the sixth stanza of the "Wedding Song":

> The woman was not taken
>   From Adam's feet we see,
> So he must not abuse her,
>   The meaning seems to be.[71]

Following Sarah's death, and after not being invited to another Grigsby wedding, he took on the clan not with a violent vendetta but through an acid pen. The mock-scriptural prose satire Herndon entitled "The First Chronicles of Reuben" was the result: "rude and coarse, they served the purpose designed by their author of bringing public ridicule on the heads of his victims." Moreover, Lincoln apparently arranged for the *plot* of the "Chronicles"—two Grigsby brothers marrying two young women on the same day, returning to their father's house to spend the first night, and being somehow put to bed each with the other's spouse—really to be enacted during the wedding festivities at which he was not welcome. From afar, he had concocted and played the puppet strings of an elaborate practical joke at the Grigsby's infare. As for the text of the "Chronicles," according to Herndon it was copied and circulated freely in the Gentryville, Indiana, area and taken with good humor by everyone but the butts, Reuben and Charles Grigsby, who, reverting to upland southerner type, vowed bloody revenge on the perpetrator. But Lincoln wasn't quite finished with the Grigsby sons. He now scribbled a verse attack on brother William, implying if not outright homosexuality, at least debility with women:

> For Reuben and Charles have married two girls,
> But Billy has married a boy.
> The girls he had tried on every side,
> But none could he get to agree;
> All was in vain, he went home again,
> And since that he's been married to Natty.
> So Billy and Natty agreed very well,
> And mamma's well pleased with the match.[72]

Maybe it was high time for Lincoln to leave Indiana, as it was for Byron to leave England! Both young men had discovered their "power to hurt" through literary language during their late adolescence, which is also when they first deployed the gift—which must have seemed heady magic—were socially chastised for it, and struck back again and harder. Of course, when Lincoln was satirizing the Grigsbys, he had no audience beyond his neighborhood and little idea of Byron's poetry, except for that extract from

The Corsair and "The Destruction of Sennacherib." Even less was he aware of Byron's scandalous life. But later, through Moore's biography, Lincoln likely did come to know it. Moore interspersed several hundred of Byron's letters and extracts from his journals within his highly circumstantial, chronological account of the "Noble Poet's" life. As one might expect, Byron had been a brilliant and revealing correspondent, whether on subjects of business or love, physical training or protracted debauchery, literature or horseflesh. Lincoln could never before have encountered such an interesting personality turned inside-out for open viewing. And while Moore's *Life* told the truth about Byron's sexuality only *slant*, to use Emily Dickinson's adjective—some of Byron's frankest journals, which Moore knew, had been destroyed, and others he quoted from, if at all, rather gingerly—it was much more direct in representing the poet's almost unrelieved agony of social, political, and literary conflicts. And what Byron became was fathered by the child he had been. Of that period, 1807–8, during which Byron was reacting against his critics at the *Edinburgh Review*, Moore writes: "The misanthropic mood of mind into which he had fallen . . . from disappointed affections and thwarted hopes, made the office of satirist but too congenial and welcome to his spirit. Yet it is evident that this bitterness existed far more in his fancy than in his heart; and that the sort of relief he now found in making war upon the world arose much less from the indiscriminate wounds he dealt around, than from the new sense of power he became conscious of in dealing them, and by which he more than recovered his former station in his own self esteem.[73]

Lincoln and Byron: the power to hurt through language as a means of "self esteem"; this passage describes Lincoln pretty well at age twenty—or for that matter at thirty-plus. By the time he read Moore's *Life*, he was just beginning to obtain perspective on his own youth and on the now-dead Byron's: "I'd like to be like him" was becoming "That man was like me."

Lincoln in his youth and young adulthood was haunted by three women's deaths—those of his mother, his sister, and Ann Rutledge, occurring (respectively) in his ninth, nineteenth, and twenty-sixth years. Any responsibility he may have thought he had for their dying was a perversion of conscience: that they were gone because they had been *his*, had loved *him*, and been loved in return. But Calvinist gloom, a morbidly sensitive mind, and the "doctrine of necessity" have badly damaged many gifted personalities, Lincoln's included; and the counterforce to these, the worth and end of loving and living here and now was of little consolation; for those he loved were *dead*. No one loved him. So was living well even possible for such as Lincoln? He might observe to Herndon that his "religion" amounted to knowing he was "doing good" because such acts made him *feel* good. But that begged the question of why it was then that he so often and for so long *felt* so bad! Was he not committed logically to the conclusion that he was somehow *doing bad*? His sense of sexual identity, its concomitant needs, may have been key here.

When Herndon frankly declared that "Mr. Lincoln had a strong, if not terrible passion for women," to the degree that "he could hardly keep his hands off a woman," he hastened to add that despite his strong urges, Lincoln "lived a pure and virtuous life."[74] If both parts of Herndon's statement were true, this would have taken some doing on Lincoln's part. Byron, under peril of life or at least personal liberty, had to keep his homosexuality, his own "terrible passion," a secret. But with women he could and did both enact his desires (even feigned desires) and audaciously write a notorious life into popular poetry. The first of these modes of psychological release was prohibited to Lincoln as one who lived "a pure and virtuous life." Poetry was possible: he could write it and people might read it. Yet the budding poet within Lincoln's personality could neither speak freely of what he felt nor expect a sympathetic audience for his frankness, however he might try to transform emotion into verse. Intellectualizing his unhappiness, living with it stoically—these he could manage.

Two other motives of mental anguish afflicted Lincoln: social hopelessness and a mind that thought obsessively. In the summer of 1838, Lincoln wrote a poem called "The Suicide's Soliloquy" which was published anonymously in the *Sangamo Journal*.[75] In this thirty-six-line ballad, the persona, in the woods near the Sangamon River and about to do away with himself, leaves behind a sort of suicide note in verse (a rather unconvincing dramatic situation, since he has to describe his self-death even as he accomplishes it—what does he put down first, the pen or the knife?), which is found "sometime" later next to his bones. The speaker is so miserable that he will risk (indeed, accept) hell as the price of relief from psychic trauma:

> Hell! What is hell to one like me
> > Who pleasures never knew;
> By *friends* consigned to misery,
> > By *hope* deserted too?

Because he has been "dam'd on earth," hell has for him no terrors: at least there the "frightful screams, and piercing pains, / Will help me to *forget*." This is another of Lincoln's challenges to orthodox Protestant morality: a Dantesque endless season in hell as preferable to this *eternal moment* of overwhelming emotional distress: anything, even death, so long as it "ease me of *this* power *to think*."

Of this poem and its author's psyche at around age thirty, Joshua Wolf Shenk (*Lincoln's Melancholy*, 2005) has acutely observed that Lincoln "often evinced both the pain of a sufferer from depression and the curiosity of an observer. He articulated a sense of himself as degraded and humiliated, but also, somehow, special and grand."[76] The type of person Shenk here characterizes is the artist: one who can *make* something out of the phenomenology of depression, even if it is a short ballad representing suicide. Byron, too, was curious about all nature. One of his special studies was the psychology of the artist. He would have agreed with Lincoln that there's hell enough on earth for the sensitive artist, who is bound to be misunderstood and abused while he lives and condemned to feel it keenly. This *was* a depressing sentence of death-in-life. Byron concluded his early poem "Euthanasia" (1812) with advice to any who might wish to be his soul mates:

> Count o'er the joys thine hours have seen,
>> Count o'er thy days from anguish free,
> And know, whatever thou hast been,
>> 'Tis something better not to be.[77]

Two other poems by Byron are particularly pertinent to Lincoln's melancholy and his persona of the Man of Sorrows. "Darkness" (1816) is an apocalypse of doom that startlingly calls to the imagination Goya's near-contemporary *Head of a Dog*, the most famous of his "Black Paintings." The opening line of "Darkness" is a declarative sentence: "I had a dream, which was not all a dream." That is, the doleful end of human civilization, here prophesied, is already present in its outline of fatal necessity. The poem uses blank verse, uncharacteristic of Byron, and the frequently enjambed lines roll like a landslide down a mountain. Manichean dark has won the final battle:

> The bright sun was extinguish'd, and the stars
> Did wander darkling in the eternal space,
> Rayless and pathless, and the icy earth
> Swung blind and blackening in the moonless air;
> Morn came and went—and came, and brought no day.[78]

The remnants of humanity burn everything—forests, their own dwellings—in desperate attempts to restore light to the world. In a hideous antitype of Adam and Eve in the Garden, the last surviving humans manage to light a last feeble fire, but when this suddenly allows them to see one another clearly—their skeletal dehumanization—they "shriek'd,/ and died—/ Even of their mutual hideousness they died."[79]

Lincoln's friend-cum-bulldog-bodyguard, Ward Hill Lamon, remembered that he (Lincoln) admired Byron's "The Dream" (1816)—a kind of

companion piece to "Darkness"—and would sometimes recite its opening lines:

> Our life is twofold: Sleep hath its own world,
> A boundary between the things misnamed
> Death and existence: Sleep hath its own world,
> And a wide realm of wild reality,
> And dreams in their development have breath,
> And tears, and tortures, and the touch of joy;
> They leave a weight upon our waking thoughts,
> They take a weight from off our waking toils,
> They do divide our being. . . .

With "The Dream" in mind, Wilson observes:

> From his arrival in Springfield in 1837, and possibly sometime before, Lin-
> coln's divided nature began to make itself evident. His melancholy became
> more visible and presumably more pronounced, but he continued to be a
> conspicuous source of hilarity and conviviality among his acquaintances.
> . . . With the exception of [Joshua] Speed, Lincoln seems to have become
> increasingly less open and less intimate with his friends and more and more
> reserved in personal matters. That these developments should coincide
> with his attraction for Byron is hardly surprising, for part of the appeal of
> Byron's poetry is its alternation of dark, brooding, melancholic moods and
> stinging and sometimes hilarious satire.[80]

To this convincing characterization of Lincoln in his late twenties and
the affinities with Byron, there is little to add. But we can say something
about the poem itself. "The Dream," also written in blank verse, is (at
206 lines) more than twice as long as "Darkness." What the speaker has
dreamed is a theme and variations on the love triangle: boy loves girl,
who loves another, who doesn't love her as much. The boy's unhappiness
in love causes him to leave on his own Childe's pilgrimage, whereby he
becomes a man. She, the beloved, grows into ripe womanhood, marries the
man of her dreams, yet grows increasingly unhappy. Finally, our pilgrim/
knight-errant returns; but not to her: there will be no happy ending to "The
Dream." Each episodic variation in the poem carries the leading line, "A
change came o'er the spirit of my dream," and each change more deeply
involves the two principals in "sickness of the soul."

The last pair of variations sums up the fates of this man and woman
who were *not* made for each other, yet somehow should have been. Here
we are at variance with Wilson's and Shenk's application of the poem to

Lincoln's psyche. Both interpreters quote the following lines from section 7 of "The Dream":

> And this the world calls frenzy; but the wise
> Have a far deeper madness, and the glance
> Of melancholy is a fearful gift;
> What is it but the telescope of truth,
> Which strips the distance of its fantasies,
> And brings life near in utter nakedness,
> Making the cold reality too real?

Not to say that Lincoln would have disputed the truth of these sentiments: "the glance of melancholy" was a "fearful gift" indeed. But the lines are about the *Lady-love*, not about the long disappointed man. For she has gone mad. In the lines just preceding the quoted passage, we learn that

> . . . her mind
> Had wandered from its dwelling, and her eyes
> They had not their own lustre, but the look
> Which is not of the earth; she was become
> The queen of a fantastic realm.

The other's destiny is grim but heroic: like the fabled king Mithradates, who took a little of every sort of poison to make himself immune, the "Wanderer" consumed the harshest of life's slings and arrows, all the dishes of Pain he was served, until they acted upon him as "a kind of nutriment." Thus was he mystically empowered to befriend mountains, hold dialogs "with the stars / And the quick Spirit of the Universe":

> . . . and they did teach
> To him the magic of their mysteries;
> To him the book of Night was open'd wide,
> And voices from the deep abyss reveal'd
> A marvel and a secret—Be it so.[81]

A dark but powerful accommodation with emotional pain. And to make it clear that Byron and his dreamer hold that the Wanderer has, though perversely, won through to a kind of gnosis, the end frame of "The Dream" declares that though both woman and man ended in misery, she alone ended in madness—no longer knew herself and therefore could not know the world.

Would not Lincoln have agreed that insanity was worse than the "fearful gift"? When he composed the poem known as "My Childhood-Home

I See Again" (1846) after revisiting his old Indiana neighborhood in the autumn of 1844, Lincoln attempted to come to terms with the power of memory to recreate the past in a surreal palette of emotional color. In the first "canto" of the ballad, the poet's voice surveys the present landscape through the imaginative lens of the past, feels the presence and hears the music of mortality:

> I hear the lone survivors tell
>> How nought from death could save,
> Till every sound appears a knell,
>> And every spot a grave.

Such intimations of mortality are necessary to human self-understanding; however emotionalized, they are *of reason*. Not so the spectre of madness in "canto" 2: the boy Lincoln had known as Matthew Gentry—"Once of genius bright,— / A fortune-favored child"—has unaccountably been reduced to a "howling crazy man," shackled to protect himself and the community. Now the returning native son remembers Matthew's night song of madness, "plaintive" and "mournful":

> I've heard it oft, as if I dreamed,
>> Far-distant, sweet, and lone;
> The funeral dirge it ever seemed
>> Of reason dead and gone.

Many nights, the poet confesses, he had stolen away from home "to drink it's [*sic*] strains," when "Air held his breath; the trees all still / Seemed sorr'wing angels round."[82] It was eerily beautiful, Poelike music to the boy Lincoln. Though produced by fearful madness, and unknown as music to its producer, Lincoln could feel its beauty—yet only because *he* had kept his reason, dressed as blackly as it often was in melancholy garb. Did he thus come to see that the *gift* could help him defeat the *fear*?

With poems like *Childe Harold's Pilgrimage* and *Don Juan*, we can play the game of biblical divination: open the book, point blindly to the text, and there will likely appear some sad truth of what Byron called man's "immedicable soul." The third canto of *Childe Harold* was written "in exile" (as were "Darkness" and "The Dream") and published in 1816, following Byron's failed marriage and social banishment from England. A series of its early stanzas comprise a moving meditation on youth's folly and age's wisdom. Advising himself to "think less wildly" than formerly, he laments that his boyish brain had been "awhirling gulf of phantasy and flame," while an untamed heart poisoned his "springs of life." But change had come to him: now he had the "strength to bear what time cannot abate / And feed on bitter fruits without accusing Fate."[83]

Byron's political radicalism recalls that of Volney, though Byron did not believe in the perfectibility of the individual or society. Like Volney's pilgrim in *The Ruins*, the voice of *Childe Harold* sits in somber reflection amid the ruins of Athens ("a nation's sepulchre"), lamenting the vicissitudes of time:

> Even gods must yield, religions take their turn;
> 'Twas Jove's, 'tis Mahomet's, and other creeds
> Will rise with other years, till man shall learn
> Vainly his incense soars, his victim bleeds,—
> Poor child of Doubt and Death, whose hope is built on reeds.

Greece has fallen very far from its classical greatness, fallen as a nation into subjection, but it cannot be redeemed or renewed by any appeal to religion, including the unmentioned Christianity. Leaning against "the marble column's yet unshaken base"—once more the image from Cole's "Desolation of Empire" springs to mind—even his poetic fancy fails him: "It may not be: nor ev'n can Fancy's eye / Restore what Time hath labour'd to deface."[84]

Let us return to that scene in Henry C. Whitney's office in 1854. Lincoln, with apparent nonchalance, took down a copy of Byron's works from the shelf and "readily turning to the third canto of Childe Harold, read aloud from the 34th verse [stanza] . . . to and including the 45th verse." Here is stanza 45:

> He who ascends to mountain-tops, shall find
> The loftiest peaks most wrapt in clouds and snow;
> He who surpasses or subdues mankind,
> Must look down on the hate of those below.
> Though high *above* the sun of glory glow,
> And far *beneath* the earth and ocean spread,
> *Round* him are icy rocks, and loudly blow
> Contending tempests on his naked head,
> And thus rewards the toils which to those summits led.

Whitney was content to quote stanza 45, to remark that Lincoln read it "sadly and earnestly, if, not, indeed, reverently," and leave it at that.[85] But as Wilson has pointed out, the entire sequence of stanzas concerns Napoleon's greatness and his tragic flaw. In Wilson's view, Byron came to recognize that his hero Napoleon's "virtues are his faults . . . [implying] that what brought him up also brought him down." Wilson also convincingly links this part of *Childe Harold* to Lincoln's Lyceum Address of 1838, noting the reference there to Alexander, Caesar, and Napoleon as transcendently ambitious leaders who would never be satisfied by less than the political *all*. Here is the fuller passage from which Wilson excerpts: "Towering genius disdains a beaten path. It seeks regions hitherto unexplored. It sees *no distinction* in adding story to story, upon the monuments of fame, erected to the memory of others. It *denies* that it is glory enough to serve under any chief. It *scorns* to tread in the footsteps of *any* predecessor, however illustrious. It thirsts and burns for distinction; and, if possible, it will have it, whether at the expense of emancipating slaves, or enslaving freemen."[86] Whether speaking of himself, pointing to a rival such as Stephen A. Douglas, or characterizing an archetype, this is Lincoln at his most Byronic: the absolute value to be most feared or most cherished is the great person's *liberty*, and *equality* is to the *"family of the lion, or the tribe of the eagle"* an obvious and undesirable absurdity. Napoleon's tyrannical extremity, at least for Byron, was preferable to the French Revolution's radical leveling. And for Lincoln?

The satire of *Don Juan*, both broadly on human nature and at times damningly topical, aimed at the social and political hypocrisy that Byron believed had infected his native England more deeply than ever before in its history. He would ridicule what his class of Englishman did but hid; he would with unflinching verbal wit score his fellow romantics' bland retreat from the revolutionary aesthetics of their early work; but most of all he would tell the truth about sexual politics, however its revelation might redound against him. Perhaps from his residency in Italy, his learning of Italian, and the careful reading of its poets, Byron chose the *ottava rima* as his stanza, adapting it to English accentuation by employing ten-, eleven-, or twelve-syllable iambic lines, the number of stresses and syllables varying with the comic rhyme. As in this sharply funny attack on his bête noire among rival English poets, Robert Southey:

> Bob Southey! You're a poet—Poet-laureate,
>   And representative of all the race,
> Although 'tis true that you turn'd out a Tory at
>   Last,—yours has lately been a common case;
> And now, my Epic Renegade! what are ye at?
>   With all the Lakers, in and out of place?
> A nest of tuneful persons, to my eye
>   Like "four and twenty Blackbirds in a pye."[87]

We *note* that pronouncing "poet" as *pote* we retrieve the pentameter and heighten the humor; but this is hardly necessary, since the feminine rhymes *laureate*, *Tory at*, and *are ye at* do their dirty work, no matter how we pronounce the word for what "Bob Southey" is.

Lincoln, as already noted, most probably read *Don Juan* when he lived in Springfield. Two features of the poem would have caught and held the adult Lincoln's attention: the poem's "power to hurt" through the pitiless ridicule of an opponent in perfectly apt comic language; and, in addition, the potential force of the poem in political debate and discourse. It was the wit that cut, in prose or verse, and Lincoln's wit was often Byronic. He saved his "most unkindest," as did Byron, for the hypocrisy of political turncoats or those who attacked him personally. When *both* conditions obtained, he was especially fierce. His famous denunciation of George Forquer in 1835, as told by Joshua Speed, provides a definitive instance of Lincoln's skill in this rather cruel game of thrust-and-cut. Forquer, who had had one of the new-fangled lightning rods installed to guard his house, had heard Lincoln speak at the Springfield courthouse and spontaneously rose to reply, being convinced that "this young man will have to be taken down." Forquer then proceeded, "in a vein of irony, sarcasm, and wit, to ridicule Lincoln in every way he could." Standing not over ten feet away, Lincoln, arms folded, listened and burned. When Forquer finished, Lincoln retaliated. As Speed recalled, he ended his rebuttal to Forquer's reply with the following peroration: "The gentleman commenced his speech by saying that this young man would have to be taken down . . . I am not so young in years as I am in the tricks and trades of a politician; but live long, or die young, I would rather die now, than, like the gentleman change my politics, and simultaneous with the change, receive an office worth three thousand dollars a year, and then have to erect a lightning-rod over my house, to protect a guilty conscience from an offended God."[88]

As Wilson has pointed out, on another occasion, and much more gently, Lincoln probed an opponent's weakness by making him seem an "absentee politician," rarely ever home with his constituents. He did so by assembling a pastiche from the opening stanzas of Byron's *Lara* (1814), a narrative poem of the same family as *The Corsair*. Long missing and thought dead, out of nowhere comes the eponymous hero home. The prodigal is welcomed heartily: "There be bright faces in the busy hall, / Bowls on the board, and banners on the wall." *Why* he had suddenly appeared they do not know, but that made the return that much more marvelous:

> He, their unhoped, but unforgotten lord
> . . . They more might marvel, when the greetings o'er,
> Not that he came, but why he came not before.[89]

The astonished crowd might not know, but Lincoln did: "their lord," in this case a hometown boy long gone but now back as a Democratic presidential elector in the campaign of 1840, came "home" that day out of political expediency and no other motive. Did Lincoln read from the borrowed book, or recite from memory? If the latter, did he expect his audience to know Byron's *Lara* well enough to get the joke? In any case, wouldn't it have been fascinating to hear Lincoln, casual before the crowd in his dungarees, delivering comic oral interpretation of these lines—heroic, not ironic, in Byron's original—now put into a sarcastic key and to some extent disarming his "faultlessly dressed" foe even before the fight has been fairly launched?[90]

Wilson has noted a remarkable aspect of this story: Lincoln's careful preparation for the event to unfold as it did. According to Wilson's source, Gibson William Harris, Lincoln, after arriving in Albion, Illinois, where the political debate was to occur, "appeared at the log schoolhouse . . . seeking to borrow a copy of Byron's works." One suspects that Lincoln must have wanted to double-check his memory before going into combat. But if this reminiscence is true, he clearly had formulated his tactics beforehand, while traveling down to Albion, it may be, and needed only a peek at *Lara* to make sure he had the poetry right. But that is the only doubtful part of this otherwise delicious story. Would a "log schoolhouse" in a tiny southern Illinois town, in 1840, really have had a copy of Bryon to lend?

Recall Herndon: "Mr. Lincoln had a strong, if not terrible passion for women." Compare this judgment from contemporary Lincoln scholar Michael Burlingame's *The Inner World of Abraham Lincoln*: "Abraham Lincoln did not like women."[91] These two statements seem incompatible on their face. But are they? The sense that women unfairly belittle a man can produce a rebounding resentment, one which, however, does nothing to lessen and may even heighten his sexual need: and the greater the need, the more keenly resented is the rejection. And round and round the dispiriting game would go: "He could hardly keep his hands off a woman." So it was also with Byron. We might even have added *not liking women* to the catalogue of shared characteristics above. By the time of *Don Juan*, Byron had formed his mature view of sexual politics. Women were the seducers; women were the traducers. Byron himself could claim, against his perceived reputation, that he had never seduced a single woman—though he had made love to them innumerably. This, whether in poetry or life, was a radically unacceptable truth to many of his readers, particularly to those same women who had all but swooned over *Childe Harold's* chaster and more conventional representation of romance. In *Don Juan's* opening canto, the young Don is seduced by the older (and married) Donna Julia. The process is elaborate, step-by-step, and finally to the youth, irresistible. On the fateful June day, the two spend the evening hours in a garden. As the moon rises, so does Donna Julia's confidence: she touches, blushes, reaches, embraces, and then it's the moment of truth (falsehood):

> And Julia's voice was lost, except in sighs,
>> Until too late for useful conversation;
> The tears were gushing from her gentle eyes,
>> I wish indeed they had not had occasion,
> But who, alas! can love, and then be wise?
>> Not that remorse did not oppose temptation;
> A little still she strove, and much repented,
>> And whispering "I will ne'er consent"—consented.[92]

The art is to make the seduced (Don Juan) feel like the seducer, and Julia is as artful as the "best" of her sex.

In his long and unfinished (though often consummated) adventures, Don Juan becomes inveigled with several different woman. All, save one (a nymphet princess on an island where he is a castaway), are less innocent sexually than he is. Most are sexual predators with sufficient power to bend the hidalgo to their will. True, he becomes less resisting as he himself is corrupted, but after all, who could say no to Empress Catherine the Great of Russia and expect to live! As he awkwardly and ambivalently courted first Mary Owens and then Mary Todd, Lincoln might have found both amusement and instruction in *Don Juan's* wealth of "laughing tears" on the subject of love. After hemming and hawing for several months in 1836–37, in a halting courtship carried on mostly by correspondence, Lincoln dumped Mary Owens (or, it may be, shrewdly forced her to dump him). He then in an ungentlemanly but quite Byronic way satirized her in a letter to *another woman* (Mrs. Eliza Browning). Byron often used this tactic in his letters to vent his spleen over the failures of discarded lovers (and wife!), the notion being that the second woman would not only better understand the sexual politics involved—men in general were such dunderheads in these matters—but appreciate more his biting characterizations of another of their sex. As his "third parties," Byron typically chose older women, married women, or indeed women with whom he had been romantically involved (or still was: his half-sister, Augusta Leigh, for instance). With them he could share frank information of the *liaisons dangereuses* sort, further enlivened with witty language-play about the ongoing game of love.

Lincoln had little of Byron's sexual experience nor much of his effrontery, so his "affair of the heart" with Mary Owens ended as partly a joke on himself; to preserve his "honor," and half against his inclinations, he finally proposed, she said "no," and he was "mortified." But there was also now a lingering resentment. His having been refused required some emotional recompense, and language was as usual his best means of payback. Hence this put-down, which has become a famous example of Lincoln the unkind:

> [W]e had an interview, and although I had seen her before, she did not look as my immagination [sic] had pictured her. I knew she was oversized, but she now appeared a fair match for Falstaff; I knew she was called an "old maid," and I felt no doubt of the truth of at least half of the appelation [sic]; but now, when I beheld her, I could not for my life avoid thinking of my mother; and this, not from withered features, for her skin was too full of fat to permit its contracting to wrinkles; but from her want of teeth, weather-beaten appearance in general, and from a kind of notion that ran in my head, that *nothing* could have commenced at the size of infancy, and reached her present bulk in less than thirtyfive [sic] or forty years; and, in short, I was not at all pleased with her.[93]

This is a caricature. And while all caricatures are unfair, Lincoln's is deliberately vicious. As Douglas Wilson has shown in detail, the historical Mary Owens was quite different in appearance. First of all, she was almost exactly Lincoln's age in 1836: twenty-eight. So if she had already lost her teeth, she was unfortunate indeed; if she reminded Lincoln of his mother, this was *his* punitive "immagination" at work. Moreover, New Salem remembered Owens as a tall, broad-boned woman—about five feet seven, weighing perhaps one hundred and sixty pounds: hardly Falstaffian girth or a size likely to make for rolls of fat on her face.[94]

While Wilson also points out that Lincoln may have been writing an "April Fool's" letter, in the spirit of entertainment, and that Mrs. Browning shared the correspondence with her husband, both having a good laugh, one gets a strong sense of Lincoln's pet over having been refused by Mary Owens. This single sentence is telling: "I knew she was called an 'old maid,' and I felt no doubt of the truth of at least half of the appelation." One may read this as an insinuation that Miss Owens may not have been a *maid*. Lincoln suggests the worst thing that could be said of a woman in his milieu and seems delighted to do so!

Beyond sexual politics, in the end what meant most to Lincoln in his twenties and early thirties were the very things that Byron addressed in *Don Juan*. Liberty's struggle against tyranny, free thought over convention and authority, and, perhaps most of all, the eternal war against human hypocrisy in all its manifestations. We may guess that if Lincoln read the following stanza from Canto 10, he delighted both in the sense and the sound:

> Oh for a *forty-parson-power* to chant
> Thy praise, Hypocrisy! Oh for a hymn

Loud as the virtues thou dost loudly vaunt,
   Not practise! Oh for trumps of cherubim!
Or the ear-trumpet of my good old aunt,
   Who, though her spectacles at last grew dim,
Drew quiet consolation through its hint,
   When she no more could read the pious print.

"Forty-parson-power" and the poet's old aunt's ear-trumpet: these were the sort of down-home figures Lincoln loved and learned to use so effectively in his speeches and writings. When Byron wrote like this, he wasn't some etiolated English aristocrat wandering dissolute over Europe: he was, beneath the skin, a kindred spirit, a brother-poet, and someone else who had the "fearful gift."

Decidedly minor poets, British and American, sometimes caught Lincoln's fancy. Lincoln bibliographer M. L. Houser listed Englishwoman Eliza Cook's *Poems* (1838) as one of the books in Lincoln's personal library. Cook's best-known poem was a morbid lyric of domestic sentiment entitled "The Old Arm-Chair," the burthen of which is a woman's nostalgia for the chair in which her mother sat day after day, over a lifetime, until she passed away:

Years roll'd on; but the last one sped—
My idol was shatter'd; my earth-star fled;
I learnt how much the heart can bear,
When I saw her die in that old Arm-Chair.[95]

"Angel Mother" notwithstanding, it is difficult to imagine Lincoln warming to this lugubrious poem. Supposing he knew "The Old Arm-Chair" at all, it may have been in song form, set to music in 1840 by Henry Russell and achieving quite an American popularity. Sung, "The Old-Arm Chair" might achieve a sincere sadness that the meretricious verse lacks.

Another poet who is mostly forgotten today but was a stylish New York tastemaker in his own time, Nathaniel Parker Willis, also managed to get a poem into Lincoln's head, where it resided as a small part of the man's formidable "data base." Willis resided in Washington during part of the Civil War, where he became acquainted with Francis B. Carpenter and the president and Mrs. Lincoln. According to Carpenter—who was in residence at the White House while painting his masterpiece, *The First Reading of the Emancipation Proclamation*—Willis told him "that he was taken quite by surprise, on a certain occasion when he was riding with the President and Mrs. Lincoln, by Mr. Lincoln, of his own accord, referring to, and quoting several lines from his poem entitled 'Parrhasius.'"[96] The title sounds like a throat-clearing, but the poem is in fact a workmanlike narrative-plus-peroration. It is based on the quasi-mythic story of the title character, Parrhasius, an Athenian painter in the era of Alexander the Great, who buys an elderly slave from among the prisoners of Alexander's latest campaign, takes him home, and tortures him to death—all the better to get just the right gestures of intolerable pain for the "Prometheus" he is ready to paint. He has this "right" as a gifted artist exalted over the common herd—something like a Nietzschean *superman.* Thus summarized, "Parrhasius" would not appear to be poetic fare for Lincoln. But the "peroration" that ends the poem would have interested him: it is a censorious reflection on "unrein'd ambition" and the Macbethlike cruelty it occasions. Despite history's repeated lessons, the voice despairs, humankind will not be cautioned; ambition, at least for the genius, is irresistible and alone will "balk not the soul" and fulfill us: though the "beaker" be of "bitterness," yet will it be *full.*

> And from Love's very bosom, and from Gain,
> Or Folly, or a Friend, or from Repose—
> From all but keen Ambition—will the soul
> Snatch the first moment of forgetfulness
> To wander like a restless child away.[97]

Was it with such a span of lines from "Parrhasius" that Lincoln flattered the vanity of N. P. Willis on that day they rode out together in Washington, D.C.?

One more name in Lincoln's compendium of lesser poets. In April of 1860, he had been reading a volume of poetry by Fitz-Greene Halleck, the gift of a Chicago newspaper editor named James G. Wilson. Halleck had been a popular and esteemed American poet of the first half of the nineteenth century, whose popularity had waned by the time Lincoln discovered him. Halleck's most famous collection was *Alnwick Castle, with Other Poems* (1827), which established his high-brow literary credentials. As Lincoln told Wilson in a thank-you note, "Many a month has passed since I have met with anything more admirable than his beautiful lines on Burns," and he also found something to admire in "Marco Bozzaris," a pro-Greek nationalistic poem, part narrative and part lyric, about that people's struggle for independence from Turkey, as embodied in the heroic fight-to-the-death of one of Greece's heroes.[98] Thus in Halleck's slender volume, Lincoln found poetic tributes to both Burns and, indirectly, Byron. But to a later ear, the poems fail to stir. "Marco Bozzaris" seems impersonal and sententious, while that to Burns is slack and insipid:

And Burns—though brief the race he ran,
  Though rough and dark the path he trod,
Lived—died—in form and soul a Man,
  The image of his God.[99]

This is the sort of form-letter epitaph poem that might be predicated of anyone (and representing *no one*, certainly not the huge personality of Robert Burns!).

Halleck said of himself as a poet, "I rhyme for smiles and not for tears," though no such emerge from the two poems quoted. While Lincoln may simply have been being polite in his thanks to Wilson, and we would today likely judge Halleck a versifier at best, his work appears in the same *Library of America* anthology that includes Lincoln's "My Childhood-Home I See Again." Halleck in 1860 would have been deemed vastly the more accomplished poet of the two (assuming that the world had known of Lincoln's versifying), with which verdict Lincoln would have concurred. A story from the Civil War and White House years confirms Halleck's status as a favorite poet of the president. One evening late in June 1862, Orville Hickman Browning, a good friend and at the time senator from Illinois, joined Lincoln for a social hour at the Soldiers' Home. As they sat on the porch steps, Lincoln "took from his pocket a copy of Hallack's [*sic*] poems, and read to me about a dozen stanzas concluding the poem of Fanny. The song at the end of the poem he read with great pathos, pausing to comment upon them, and then laughed immoderately at the ludicrous conclusion."[100] A fascinating detail of this story is Lincoln's pulling the volume of Halleck out of his pocket: the poet and his poems were important enough to be a *vade mecum*.

At over a thousand lines, "Fanny" (1819) is Halleck's longest poem. It is a topical satire of upper-class life in New York City early in the nineteenth century. So dense are Halleck's New York allusions that "Fanny" has to be read with notes to be well understood. Yet the comic versification succeeds to amuse despite the many obscure local references. The narrative pretext of the poem shows a middling businessman and his daughter on the rise in the city. The more money he makes, the more inflated become their combined socioeconomic pretensions, until the inevitable collapse leaves them worse off than they were before their rapid ascent: mansionless, friendless, and instantly anonymous to those who had courted and touted them so recently. Halleck's voice makes fun of Fanny and Father right through their rise and fall, but his satire, though witty enough, lacks the Byronic bite. His two principals are simply fools, neither to be pitied or detested. And the audience of "Fanny" may follow along without much concern for anything other than the music and wit of the poem.

Browning's "about a dozen stanzas" near the end of "Fanny" would have Lincoln commencing reading at stanza 157:

> I hate your tragedies, both long and short ones
>> (Except Tom Thumb, and Juan's Pantomime);
> And stories woven of sorrows and misfortunes
>> Are bad enough in prose, and worse in rhyme.

Then follows the dénouement of the rise-and-fall story—a little sad, to be sure, but nothing extraordinary as such things go. Fanny mostly stays at home in their much-reduced lodgings. With nothing else to do, Father takes evening walks,

> Along Broadway, scene of past joys and evils;
>> He felt that withering bitterness of soul,
> Quaintly denominated the "blue devils";
>> And thought of Bonaparte and Belisarius,
> Pompey, and Colonel Burr, and Caius Marius.[101]

In those fresh salad days not so long ago, Father had esteemed himself a lover of nature and something of a poet. Now on one particular stroll he put a shilling into a telescope to look at Jupiter, whereupon "Sounds as of far-off bells came on his ears— / He fancied 'twas the music of the spheres." But "He was mistaken, it was no such thing, / 'Twas Yankee Doodle played by Scudder's band." Which trick of perception sent him home, composing as he went the "Song" with which "Fanny" concludes. Three eight-line stanzas sing the beautiful music of youth: "When life is but an April day / Of sunshine and of showers." And three deplore the disillusionment of age: "To-day the forest-leaves are green, / They'll wither on the morrow." Taken as *almost* a whole, "Song" appears to be a serious lyric on the topic of transience, the metaphor of the lost mariner, and in appropriate poetic diction. We are free to imagine Lincoln striking a pose on the porch of the Soldiers' Home, where we hear him reading to Browning with soulful gravity, glossing the deep sentiments as he passed them on—until he reaches the final stanza, here given in full:

> The moonlight music of the waves
>> In storms is heard no more,
> When the living lightning mocks the wreck
>> At midnight on the shore;
> And the mariner's song of home has ceased,
>> His corse is on the sea——
> And music ceases when it rains
>> In Scudder's balcony.

And then Lincoln "laughed immoderately at the ludicrous conclusion." Do we?

Browning also recorded Lincoln's affection for another contemporary satirical poet, the Englishman Thomas Hood (1799–1845), who, like Halleck, alternated between pathos and the comic in his poems. On a previous evening that same year (Friday, April 25, 1862), Browning had called at the White House and found the President "alone and complaining of head ache." They soon began talking about poetry, each man quoting "a few lines from Hood." Lincoln then wanted to know whether Browning remembered "The Haunted House" (1844). Browning answered that he had never read it, at which Lincoln sent for the volume and read the entire poem aloud, "pausing occasionally to comment on passages" he thought "particularly felicitous."[102]

"The Haunted House," as its title suggests, is a ghost story, a sort of "Poe-light" treatment of a crime-cursed house and family fallen into ruin. Hood's treatment of the subject is thick with Gothic atmosphere yet lacks the sense of imminent, unbearable horror that Poe managed better than anyone else. The opening stanza is remarkably similar to that of Byron's "Darkness:"

> Some dreams we have are nothing else but dreams,
> Unnatural, and full of contradictions;
> Yet others of our most romantic schemes
> Are something more than fictions.[103]

Both poets and poems locate the blackness within the dreaming self, which designs "something more than fictions" in its half-conscious workings. Or, as Lincoln himself wrote in the second stanza of "My Childhood-Home I See Again,"

> O memory! thou mid-way world
>   'Twixt Earth and Paradise,
> Where things decayed, and loved-ones lost
>   In dreamy shadows rise.[104]

Hood's voice (or dreamer) speaks initially in the first person plural: *we* all of us have such "romantic schemes" gone wrong, which leave the *house* a moldering shell outside, tenantless within. Had there been a death in the family?

> O, very gloomy is the House of Woe,
> Where tears are falling while the bell is knelling,
> With all the dark solemnities which show
> That Death is in the dwelling.
> O very, very dreary is the room
> Where Love, domestic Love, no longer nestles,

But smitten by the common stroke of doom,
The Corse lies on the trestles![105]

Despite Lincoln's rare gift as an oral interpreter of poetry, in this instance he may not have been performing so much as seeking catharsis. William Wallace Lincoln, his beloved "Willie," had died only two months previously, and to its remaining occupants the White House felt haunted.

More typical of Hood is the whimsy of one of the other two poems Browning heard on this occasion, "The Lost Heir." It begins as a lurid mock-ballad of a London tragedy: a child's disappearance and his distraught mother's frantic search for him:

One day, as I was going by
That part of Holborn christened High,
I heard a loud and sudden cry,
That chill'd my very blood.

But when the goodwife calms down sufficiently to speak clearly of her problem, it is in the demotic speech of a breathlessly long line: "'Lawk help me, I don't known where to look, or to run, if I only knew which way—.'" And on she goes for many lines, drawing a crowd at her performance and not letting anybody get a word in edgewise with her catalog of horrors her little boy may be suffering at the hands of a criminal city: "'Or may be he's stole by some chimbly sweeping wretch, to stick fast in narrow flues and what not.'" Finally she notices her vagrant "Billy" pretty near at hand, in no trouble whatsoever, which changes her worry to wrath:

"Why, there he is, Punch and Judy hunting, the young wretch,
                                   it's that Billy sartin as sin!
But let me get him home, with a good grip of his hair, and I'm blest if he shall
                                   have a whole bone in his skin![106]

The poem is replete with mildly Dickensian humor and London's local color. Hood, after all, was also a graphic artist, and often did pen-and-ink caricatures to accompany his comic verse. These "queer little conceits" of Hood's, as John Hay called them, Lincoln liked as much as his verse. Hay remembered a midnight scene late in April 1864, in which the president wandered into the secretaries' "office laughing, with a little volume of Hood's works in his hand to show Nicolay & me the little Caricature 'An unfortunate Bee-ing.'"[107]

But Hood's most effective poems were his moral satires. The best-known example is his long (almost 2,400 lines) narrative-cum-commentary upon avarice, "Miss Kilmansegg and Her Precious Leg" (1840). Noah Brooks, a journalist whom Lincoln befriended and who became a familiar visitor at the White House, remembered that among Hood's works Lincoln "liked best the last part of 'Miss Kilmansegg.'"[108] Without knowing exactly how much of the poem Brooks meant by this statement, it is difficult to deduce where the end of the poem begins. Miss K's Midas-like father had from the cradle smothered his daughter in gold and all things gilded. She knew no world outside the gleam, and even her first misfortune—of only two in a life—seemed to turn out golden: thrown by her thoroughbred horse named "Banker," she suffered a compound fracture of her right femur, which meant, given the surgery of the time, an amputation—alas! But no! She would bear the pain and hide the shame in the glow of a solid gold leg, which, when crafted and fitted and worn into society became the cynosure of all eyes—the women's for envy, the men's for soldered lust and cupidity.

However ridiculous this sounds, Hood brings it off with éclat. The showing of a bit of "precious leg" led to her second, and fatal, misfortune. When she and her leg "come out" at a fancy-dress ball, Miss K. is noticed by a French count, who proceeds to woo her and win her in marriage. But the count proves a dissolute wastrel. He rapidly spends down her fortune in drunken gambling and ignores the marriage bed and his wife in favor of whoring all over town. At last, realizing that the count will stop at nothing short of her complete ruination, the countess calls her lawyers together and has them draw up an unbreakable will, assuring that the leg and she shall go to the grave and remain there attached forever! Not to be denied, not his pound of flesh but several pounds of gold, the count—and now is the point, we may guess, at which Lincoln might have begun reciting to Brooks—steals upon her one night as she sleeps, takes the leg from under her pillow and with it beats the countess's brains out. To the stolid common sense of the coroner's jury, the verdict is obvious: suicide—"because her own leg had killed her!" Hood tacks on a two-stanza moral to the story, the first of which, ringing with Anglo-Saxon cadences, will have to stand for both:

> Gold! Gold! Gold! Gold!
> Bright and yellow, hard and cold,
> Molten, graven, hammer'd and roll'd;
> Heavy to get, and light to hold;
> Hoarded, barter'd, bought, and sold,
> Stolen, borrow'd, squander'd, doled:
> Spurn'd by the young, but gugg'd by the old
> To the very verge of the churchyard mould.[109]

Lincoln always seemed to relish these satires of unworthy rise and justified fall, comically related in verse—a sort of devilish inversion of the later Horatio Alger novels. Herndon tells us that Lincoln *heard*, if he did not read, William A. Butler's *Nothing to Wear* (1857), an immensely popular light satire on social-climbing New York ladies (in this case one "Miss Flora McFlimsey"). "Sometime in 1857," Herndon recalled, "a lady reader or elocutionist" came to town, and he and Lincoln attended her lecture. On the bill was a section from *Nothing to Wear*. "In the midst of one stanza, in which no effort is made to say anything Particularly amusing, and during the reading of which the audience manifested the most respectful silence and attention, some one in the rear seats burst out into a loud, coarse laugh—a sudden and explosive guffaw. It startled the speaker and audience, and kindled a storm of unsuppressed laughter and applause. Everyone looked back to ascertain the cause of the demonstration, and was greatly surprised to find that it was Mr. Lincoln."[110] How to explain Lincoln's outburst? Herndon speculated that Lincoln had had something other than the performance on his mind, lost in one of his reveries. After all, he notes, no one else was laughing at the time. He may be exactly right. But, on the other hand, Lincoln would likely have intently listened and watched such an actress on stage, and his risibilities need not have manifested themselves at precisely the time a humorous passage was given out by the elocutionist. Instead, he may have turned over some of *Nothing to Wear's* lines in his head until they suddenly and uncontrollably forced a public laugh. Here are the verses stipulating Miss Flora's terms for marital engagement to the beau on whom, from many candidates, she has conferred this distinct honor:

> You know I'm to polka as much as I please,
> And flirt when I like—now stop, don't you speak—
> And you must not come here more than twice in the week,
> Or talk to me either at party or ball,
> But always be ready to come when I call . . .

In short, "this is the sort of engagement, you see, / Which is binding on you but not binding on me." Shortly thereafter, poor "Harry" is summarily *disengaged* by Miss Flora for suggesting that, with her closets and closets full of dresses, she surely doesn't require another to wear to the "Stuckups" party on the morrow.[111] Herndon labeled Lincoln "mortified" by his social pratfall at the reading, but the laughter may have originated in someone's "comic" comportment years before during his own *engagements*.

In his later Springfield and presidential years, Lincoln is thought to have expanded his reading of American poetry, approaching at last the "classic" New England poets who set the highbrow standards for national verse.

Among the major names in this group were Oliver Wendell Holmes, James Russell Lowell, John Greenleaf Whittier, and Henry Wadsworth Longfellow. The difficulty, however, is that, with the exception of Holmes (who will be discussed separately below), evidence pointing to particular poems is pretty thin. For Lowell, we have a single report of Lincoln's interest in and enjoyment of *The Biglow Papers* (1848, with another series in newspaper form during the Civil War). Noah Brooks asserted that Lincoln knew Lowell "only . . . as 'Hosea Biglow,' every one of whose effusions he knew"—and some by heart.[112] This is convincing enough, but we may add to it the fact that *The Biglow Papers* featured Lincoln's brand of American humor: social and political satire—the first series of which incessantly criticized the Mexican War—spiced up in comic Yankee dialect. But what of Lowell's "serious" poetry—the volume of lyrics, odes, Arthurian romances, and so on? No evidence anywhere suggests that Lincoln knew any of this. As for Whittier, we have one general statement from his secretary John Hay: "He read Bryant and Whittier with appreciation."[113]

With Longfellow, the case is more complicated. Various authorities insist on the provenance of one Longfellow poem or another, from the shortest lyrics to the longest narratives, but unfortunately these authorities do not always agree: Noah Brooks, for instance, affirmed that "Longfellow's 'Psalm of Life' and 'Birds of Killingworth' were the only productions of that author he ever mentioned with praise" (suggesting that Lincoln *dispraised* some of the rest of Longfellow); while John G. Nicolay, chief among his secretaries, recalled a scene in which Lincoln was left weeping over Nicolay's recitation of lines from "The Building of the Ship"—the metaphor of the foundering Ship of State in the earlier part of the Civil War proving too much for its captain.[114] Beyond these three poems, nothing by Longfellow can be convincingly connected to Lincoln.

"The Psalm of Life" (1838) is Longfellow's most famous short lyric. Many people who recognize its opening stanza might not know the rest of the poem nor even the author's name:

> Tell me not, in mournful numbers,
>   Life is but an empty dream!
> For the soul is dead that slumbers,
>   And things are not what they seem.[115]

Why Lincoln would like a lyric that begins this way is hardly self-evident. From boyhood he had so often been afflicted with what we might call the "futiles" that he had in a sense sung to himself a line related to Longfellow's warning, "Life is but an empty dream": "Time what an empty vaper 'tis." Yet as a young adult he fought hard and long against this sense of futility. We can better understand an affinity with the sincere "ought to" of "A Psalm of Life" by setting it in the context of two other poems on life's purpose and death's prospect that Lincoln greatly admired. One sang, in effect, why bother? the other, don't worry: William Knox's "Mortality" and William Cullen Bryant's "Thanatopsis." The "Psalm's" voice imperatively warns us *not* to deny life's meaningfulness in "mournful numbers"—that is, in dirgelike meter. But this is just what Lincoln's favorite poem, William Knox's "Mortality" (1828), *does do*: "Oh! why should the spirit of mortal be proud?" Knox's voice asks rhetorically, and then proceeds in fourteen four-line stanzas to overdetermine the answer: the spirit of mortal shouldn't be proud, and life *is* but an empty dream. Knox's lines are typically of eleven syllables (occasionally augmented to twelve or even thirteen), commencing with an iamb and followed by three anapests (the stanzas rhyming *aabb*, etc.). Tied to the thoroughly mournful sense of the poem, the rhythm beats out like muffled drums at a state funeral: "The hand of the King, that the scepter hath borne" (da-DUM, da da DUM, da da DUM, da da DUM). Douglas L. Wilson, who has done the most complete and convincing study of Lincoln's admiration for "Mortality," offers this summary of the poem's "argument": "Intended by the poet as a recapitulation of the third chapter of Job and the first chapter of Ecclesiastes, its Old Testament fatalism is unremitting and notably unrelieved by an suggestion of an afterlife. The fate of man—low or high, young or old—is that of the leaves: both 'shall moulder to dust.' Man's joys and his grief, his love and his scorn, are all mere repetitions of those of his forebears and come to nothing. The predominant fact of life is death. Pride in so transient a thing as mortality is obviously misplaced."[116]

To set against Knox, Lincoln encountered the mild, stoic naturalism of William Cullen Bryant's "Thanatopsis," arguably the best-known single lyric poem of antebellum America. Bryant had composed it while a teenager, and its publication in 1817 made the young poet's reputation. From our perspective, the popularity and nineteenth-century staying power of "Thanatopsis" may appear unaccountable. The poem is completely unchristian in its "view" of death, frankly declaring that our end, like our beginning, is entirely natural. What is more, death is final. The only afterlife we might be a part of is the organic but figurative one of "ashes to ashes." Such a view would be celebrated by Walt Whitman more than a generation later, but in 1817 America the message was new and quite against the Christian grain. The orthodox view of death pictured a frightful prospect of eternal judgment, too often dire, should the dying, as was likely, be of the unelect (Calvinism) or the unregenerate (Evangelicalism). To Bryant's patient, old-sounding voice, however, death was neither to be desired nor avoided but *lived*. For one about to be bereaved, if not for the one dying, the tonic was to

> Go forth, under the open sky, and list
> To Nature's teachings, while from all around—
> Comes a still voice—Yet a few days, and thee
> The all-beholding sun shall see no more. . . .

Nature's voice murmurs the truth of life's transience in a mildly melancholy key, it is true, but a *pleasing melancholy*. Death is a good thing because a natural thing. In its closing lines, "Thanatopsis" bids the reader

> . . . approach thy grave,
> Like one who wraps the drapery of his couch
> About him, and lies down to pleasant dreams.[117]

This from a teenager! The entire poem reads and feels similarly: the measured blank-verse consolation for an elder dying, sung by a precocious youth who has yet to live.

The account of Lincoln's reading Bryant and "Thanatopsis" comes from William H. Townsend in *Lincoln and the Bluegrass* (1955). In the autumn of 1847, on the way to Washington, D.C., the new Whig congressman Lincoln and his family stopped for an extended visit with Mary Todd's parents and other relatives in Lexington, Kentucky. Not surprisingly, Lincoln was drawn to the substantial family library. One set of books interested him so keenly that he not only read but (according to Townsend) penciled in marginalia as he turned pages. These were the *Elegant Extracts* from English belles lettres in six volumes, including "Thanatopsis," which he read and "committed . . . to memory" and then formally recited to the assembled Todds.[118]

By contrast with both "Mortality" and "Thanatopsis," Longfellow's "Psalm of Life" is imbued with the early-Victorian gospel of striving in the face of doubt—perfectly warranted if, indeed, "things are not what they seem." Life does often appear blank and black as the death with which it closes, and there may well be nothing beyond the grave, but for Longfellow this was an existential challenge to best the Grim Reaper through an energetic, creative teleology of *action*:

> Not enjoyment, and not sorrow,
>   Is our destined end or way;
> But to act, that each to-morrow
>   Find us farther than today.[119]

Idealistic advice for a "hypochondriac," and we may be sure Longfellow and Lincoln both tried and failed to follow it.

As president, in the midst of the Civil War, Lincoln had the authority both to propose and dispose—in other words, *to act*—and in so doing he was transcending the past and creating the American future. If his reading of Longfellow occurred mainly at this time, he might have welcomed these lines in a fashion he could not have as a youth:

> Lives of great men all remind us
>   We can make our lives sublime,
> And, departing, leave behind us
>   Footprints on the sands of time.

Verses on the legacy of greatness, apparently without a hint of irony attached (the "sands of time" are notoriously impermanent). So, Mr. President, "be up and doing," ready "for any fate." But, most of all, in the face of *events* that control, "learn to labor and to wait"—despite what happens to footprints in the sand.

Longfellow's "The Building of the Ship" (1849) is a patriotic oration with both lyric and dramatic elements. Yet everything in the poem submits to the rhetorical and allegorical architecture: this is a *real* ship abuilding, and it is also the United States Ship of State. The *Master* shipwright instructs his apprentices:

> Choose the timbers with greatest care;
> Of all that is unsound beware;
> For only what is sound and strong
> To this vessel shall belong.
> Cedar of Maine and Georgia pine
> Here together shall combine.
> A goodly frame, and a goodly fame,
> And the UNION be her name![120]

Lincoln, the curious inquirer into how all things worked, and especially timber-framed structures serving to house the Republic, would have been satisfied with Longfellow's account of the framing of the ship in the yard. As he read, he could watch the poet watching:

> Day by day the vessel grew,
> With timbers fashioned strong and true,
> Stemson and keelson and sternson-knee,
> Till, framed with perfect symmetry,
> A skeleton ship rose up to view!
> And around the bows and along the side
> The heavy hammers and mallets plied,

Till after many a week, at length,
Wonderful for form and strength,
Sublime in its enormous bulk,
Loomed aloft the shadowy hulk!

Finished and launched, the *Union* had been built to sail forever.

Thou, too, sail on, O Ship of State!
Sail on, O UNION, strong and great!
Humanity with all its fears,
With all the hopes of future years,
Is hanging breathless on thy fate.

An insupportable burden for the best-built, even the *Providentially* built ship? It is interesting to note that Longfellow finished and launched "The Building of the Ship" in 1848 and 1849, respectively: written near the end of the Mexican War, so deeply unpopular in New England (during which time Lincoln was in Congress), published the year before the "Great Compromise of 1850," one of the provisions of which, the Fugitive Slave law, was considered in Longfellow's region no compromise but bald appeasement of the South. It would be rough seas for the *Union* over the following decade. It was early in the Civil War that Lincoln stood in the White House weeping over John Nicolay's recitation of Longfellow's closing lines:

Sail on, nor fear to breast the sea!
Our hearts, our hopes, are all with thee;
Our hearts, our hopes, our prayers, our tears,
Our faith triumphant o'er our fears,
Are all with thee,—are all with thee!

Here the *Union* was, fighting against the *Lee* shore, in shoal water, and likely to founder. Lincoln may have been crying for the *reality* of the ship's danger, and for the always hopeful beauty of the poet's American *allegory*.

Another patriotic poem that reportedly made President Lincoln choke up was Oliver Wendell Holmes's "Lexington" (1836), a commemorative hymn to the first dead soldiers of the American Revolution. Noah Brooks wrote that Lincoln read the poem to him, faltering at the lines that begin the final stanza: "Green be the graves where her martyrs are lying! / Shroudless and tombless they sunk to their rest." "You read it," Lincoln whispered. "I can't."[121] Given Lincoln's genuine suffering over the casualty reports he was daily receiving during the "second American Revolution," this sensitive response to Holmes's "Lexington" is fully credible.

But was Holmes a major poet in Lincoln's eyes? Surprisingly, that is the collective claim of several students and scholars, who list no fewer than fifteen of his individual poems—more than for any other poet—as having been read by Lincoln. Among these, his favorite Holmes poem was "The Last Leaf" (1831), which several of Lincoln's acquaintances remembered his fondness for. The *locus classicus* among these accounts is found in painter Francis Carpenter's *Six Months at the White House*. On the evening of March 25, 1864, Carpenter had a tête-à-tête with Lincoln in the president's study. After some desultory conversation and reading from Shakespeare, Lincoln turned to one of his favorite poetic subjects: the mysterious authorship of "Oh Why Should the Spirit of Mortal Be Proud?" ("Mortality"—apparently he still did not know the name William Knox). By an association of ideas, Lincoln then juxtaposed "Mortality" to "some quaint, queer verses, written, I think, by Oliver Wendell Holmes, entitled 'The Last Leaf.'" And he proceeded to recite the fourth stanza of the poem:

> The mossy marbles rest
> On the lips that he has pressed
>   In their bloom;
> And the names he loved to hear
> Have been carved for many a year
>   On the tomb.[122]

Then came the now famous, emphatic critical opinion: "For pure pathos, in my judgment, there is nothing finer than those six lines in the English language!"[123]

If by *pathos*, Lincoln meant evoked feelings of sympathy and sorrow, we can agree that Holmes's stanza has something of that effect. The difficulty is with the comparative *nothing finer*. Does he mean in all of the poetry and prose of the English language over the centuries? Not to deprecate Lincoln's taste—he was entitled to like what he liked—but this judgment reveals much about what he *hadn't* read. From lyric poetry, he was content with the verge of sentimentality, which so often in nineteenth-century America displaced the genuinely tragic. Had Lincoln known Wordsworth, Keats, and Shelley, he probably would not have esteemed Holmes's lines so highly. And he might have aimed higher in his own poetry. For in poems like "The Last Leaf," Lincoln was seeing his own writerly predilections. It is a striking coincidence that both Holmes and Edgar Allan Poe shared Lincoln's year of birth (and Longfellow and Whittier were born in 1807): these *poets*, Lincoln included, were of a *new* generation. They saw the passing of the *greatest* generation, the Revolutionary, and strove to make a national literature from that complex of cultural memory. Holmes composed "The

Last Leaf" the same year Lincoln came to New Salem and himself became a serious writer: two talented young men using the past as present matter for their young nation's literary future.

The old gentleman observed by the voice of Holmes's poem is sometimes identified as Major Thomas Melville (Herman Melville's grandfather), reputed to have been one of the "Indians" who threw the shipload of tea into Boston Harbor. Seen sixty years later, in his eighties, this "last leaf" of the Revolutionary oak "totters o'er the ground / With his cane," still wearing his ancient, three-cornered hat and "queer" breeches. The young watcher of this living archeological specimen must needs "grin" at the scene; but not in any disrespectful way, nor noticed by the object, who is oblivious of the present. All this may have been "subtextual" for Lincoln. For if he did not infer that this "last leaf" had been a conspirator at the Boston Tea Party (the hat is the only *textual* clue, though Holmes included an explanatory note in some later editions), then the *pathetic* lines were to him what mattered in the poem. Though first published in a small magazine in 1831, "The Last Leaf" came to wide notice when included in Holmes's first collection, the *Poems* of 1836. Most likely, this is where Lincoln encountered it, very possibly at the time he was thinking of the lament for the Fathers whose passing he would lament in the Lyceum Address.

Not until 1916 did someone suggest that Abraham Lincoln had read Walt Whitman's *Leaves of Grass* (1855). Henry B. Rankin, in *Personal Recollections of Abraham Lincoln*, claimed that in the late 1850s he had interned in Springfield as a law apprentice with the firm of Lincoln and Herndon, that Herndon had brought a copy of *Leaves of Grass* to the office, occasioning discussions "hot and extreme . . . concerning its poetic merit" between Herndon and the law students, and that after a time Lincoln had become markedly interested in the book. Rankin further asserted that on a certain day Lincoln "took up *Leaves of Grass* for his first reading of it" in front of the others, who watched him as he read to himself for "half an hour or more," when, "to our general surprise," Lincoln returned to the beginning of the book and "began to read aloud. Other office work was discontinued by us all while he read with sympathetic emphasis verse after verse. His rendering revealed a charm of new life in Whitman's versification. Save for a few comments on some broad allusions that Lincoln suggested could have been veiled, or left out, he commended the new poet's verses for their virility, freshness, unconventional sentiments, and unique forms of expression, and claimed that Whitman gave promise of a new school of poetry." Moreover, Rankin insisted, Lincoln "time and again" returned to *Leaves of Grass* and soon knew it so well, appreciated it so much, that he "foretold correctly the place the future would assign to Whitman's poems," and that his initial volume would be succeeded "by other and greater work." This rush of memory had come forcibly to Rankin's mind nearly a decade later, after the assassination, when he read Whitman's "immortal elegy, 'O Captain! My Captain!'"[124]

This is a dramatic scene that, if verified, would significantly alter our view of what Lincoln valued in poetry. And Rankin would deserve credit for bringing these two supremely great democrats together in a consummation long and devoutly wished for. But, unfortunately, his account is most likely an entire fabrication. As the redoubtable Lincoln scholar William E. Barton remarked in his *Abraham Lincoln and Walt Whitman* (1928), "It is unfortunate, if this story came so vividly to Mr. Rankin's recollection in 1865, that he waited more than half a century before telling it."[125] Waited, that is, until most were dead who could call him a liar—and especially William H. Herndon. While it is true that Herndon owned a copy of *Leaves of Grass* (probably the 1856 second edition), he never indicated that Lincoln knew of the book, much less read it. Such an omission is quite telling, since Herndon generally recalled the specifics of Lincoln's reading when he had knowledge of it. Barton further noted that by the late 1850s Herndon "was watching" his law partner's political rise "with Boswellian interest, taking notes on his sayings and doings, and preserving his memorabilia for subsequent use." Would he therefore not have had something to say, in his private jottings if not in the 1889 biography, about Lincoln's engagement with *Leaves of Grass*?

Thus did William E. Barton bury Henry B. Rankin. But he has not stayed buried. In *Lincoln and Whitman: Parallel Lives in Civil War Washington* (2004), Daniel Mark Epstein disinterred the old prevaricator's corpse and attempted to restore some credibility to his law-office story. According to Epstein, the year was 1857, and the young law clerks, following Herndon's lead, had been reading the first reviews—extravagant in their praise or dismissal—of *Leaves of Grass*. And when Herndon turned up one day with a copy, they all fell to with appetites whetted by the sensationalism now associated with Whitman.[126] As to Lincoln's entering the picture, Epstein silently fictionalized the scene, going so far as to put specific passages in the mouth of the reader (in this case, lines 6–15 of "Song of Myself"):

> The light of afternoon streamed through the office windows, gilding the dust motes.
>
>> Houses and rooms are full of perfumes—the shelves are crowded with perfumes,
>> I breathe the fragrance myself, and know it and like it,
>> The distillation would intoxicate me also, but I shall not let it.[127]

Epstein justified his acceptance of Rankin's account by criticizing "Reverend" Barton, whom he labeled a "rival biographer" who had written a "popular" book on Lincoln and Whitman. Since Barton was said to have had a "hostile spirit toward Whitman," it followed that he would do everything in his power to discountenance Rankin.[128] But this won't do. First of all, Henry B. Rankin was *not* a biographer but a memoirist touting his alleged connections with Lincoln; second, William E. Barton was, and remains, a Lincoln scholar of good repute, several of whose many books on Lincoln continue to be of use today (*The Paternity of Lincoln* [1920], to name one of the best). That he may not have valued *Whitman* to the extent that the poet's biographers desired is not a criticism of his work on *Lincoln*—unless one chooses to monger motives: Barton's alleged "hostile spirit toward Whitman," Epstein asserts, compelled him to dissociate the poet from the president, in the process violating the prime directive of scholarship!

If the thesis that Lincoln read Whitman were merely a matter for bibliographers to quarrel over, we could stop worrying about the truth of Rankin's 1857 tableau vivant and enjoy Epstein's evocation. But *Lincoln and Whitman* stakes a good deal on its historicity. The book's overarching claim is that Lincoln's encounter with *Leaves of Grass* profoundly affected his literary style: "Whether Lincoln read all 384 pages of the book is uncertain. But the poetry of Whitman Lincoln did read left its mark upon him in 1857. In that transitional year a change came over Lincoln. The change is evident in his speeches, an alteration in idiom that has never been thoroughly explained. Lincoln's early successes in debating, in the courtroom and 'on the stump' . . . resulted from his spellbinding powers as a storyteller and his mastery of logical demonstration and analysis." But he was not yet a poet: "It would take a touch of the poet to move Abraham Lincoln's oratory from the cold light of rhetoric into the warm iridescence of dramatic literature."[129] And, Epstein insisted, this is what Walt Whitman accorded him, the idiomatic, poetic license to speak prophetically in the House Divided speech and beyond. Just how this influence discharged electrically from the personality and text of Whitman into the high-capacitance vessel of Lincoln is suggested, more than argued, throughout the rest of Epstein's book.

His is a huge claim—that Lincoln became the literary master he manifestly was in the late 1850s and 1860s—because *Leaves of Grass* taught him a new voice, perhaps even a new perspective on American democracy, the implication being that Lincoln would not and perhaps could not have gotten there otherwise. It is well beyond our scope here to evaluate this hypothesis in full. Epstein's method is to juxtapose extracts from Whitman's and Lincoln's writings (he lineates the latter so they appear like the former's free verse) and then either draw points from the parallels or let them speak how they will for themselves. Epstein is a shrewd reader: his points of textual analysis are often well made and well taken. Yet they are not an *argument* for the influence of Whitman upon Lincoln but rather an *association* of the utterances of two literary geniuses who were often of one mind on the nature and future of democracy and the American Republic. When Lincoln, on September 30, 1859, announced to an audience of Wisconsin farm families, "Every blade of grass is a study," he said something strikingly like Whitman's voice at the outset of "Song of Myself": "I lean and loafe at my ease, observing a spear of summer grass."[130] For both men, to observe was to think about, and by 1860 both had been doing so for decades, often called lazy and no-account for not tending to business. So far, so much alike. But were they thinking the same things? Whitman saw in the blade of grass the Emersonian all-in-small and mystified it to the metaphysical end of the universe. Lincoln saw agronomy and other sciences and refused to push material knowledge toward a transcendence he did not philosophically credit. This is not so much to criticize Epstein as to assert that the differences between the men's philosophies are as important as their affinities concerning democracy. Perhaps, to conclude, *Lincoln and Whitman* is truer to its subtitle, "Parallel Lives," than to its thesis. For as the country land-surveyor and master of Euclid might have said, if lives are truly parallel they do not meet in this vale of tears, only at infinity. Both Whitman and Lincoln would have been content to leave it at that.

John Todd Stuart, Lincoln's political mentor and first law partner, remembered that the still-young lawyer had "carried Poe around on the Circuit—read and loved the Raven—repeated it over & over."[131] Edgar Allan Poe's most famous (and most parodied) poem first appeared in a book publication in 1845, as the title poem of a volume entitled *The Raven and Other Poems*—probably the one Lincoln took with him and apparently too often forced upon the captive audience of lawyers (at least for Stuart's taste). As generations of high-school students have learned, "The Raven" is difficult to recite straight-faced. It invites, almost compels, parody, such as the one called "The Pole-cat," which Lincoln read in an Illinois newspaper in 1846.[132] We can imagine Lincoln, looking rather an American Gothic figure himself, squeezing all the horror out of Poe's music until it alchemically turned into mock horror and the refrain of desolate "nevermores" over the vanished "Lenore" produced laughter instead of tears.

Yet we may be mistaken about this, deceived by time and taste. What today looks irresistibly inviting as an object of satire, Poe's mid-nineteenth-century audience could and did read as a solemn, even heartrending lyric of love, loss, and death. Parodies notwithstanding, "The Raven" at its appearance was by many esteemed Poe's finest poem, and we may be sure that this high valuation did not derive from its being funny!

For Lincoln the reader and performer of poetry, we are tempted to invent a portmanteau word, *gloomour*, silly as it sounds, to suggest his tightly wound emotional helix of gloom and humor and the remarkable way in which the one could instantly transform into the other, and neither exist without its double. And in this *duplicity* lay entwined the near-contradictory potential energy to laugh and weep in a single moment, and to make others follow his lead. Reading privately, Lincoln could give way to the powerful negative charge of tragic melancholy. Reading aloud to an audience, his electricity might flow toward the positive pole of the comic (remembering that even the voice in "The Raven" is beguiled by the bird into smiling—very evanescently!) and the cathartic *discharge* of emotion. But neither could be wholly present or wholly absent, while together they made tragicomic melancholy.

4. Necessity and Invention

There are no accidents in my philosophy.
—*Abraham Lincoln, in* Herndon's Lincoln

In the congressional race of 1846, when partisans of the Democratic candidate and militant Methodist preacher Peter Cartwright accused Abraham Lincoln of "infidelity"—a renewal of whisperings about his New Salem and early Springfield freethinking radicalism—and Democrats pushed him hard on the issue, Lincoln late in the campaign issued a handbill in which he cleverly defused the charges without actually denying them.[1] We need here be concerned only with a single phrase from Lincoln's defense: the "Doctrine of Necessity." He defined this as the human mind's being "impelled to action, or held in rest by some power, over which the mind itself has no control." Because Lincoln went on to associate the Doctrine of Necessity with "several of the Christian denominations" and then declared that he had "left off" holding such a view for "more than five years," scholars have generally assumed that he was speaking of his boyhood Baptist Calvinism having, as it were, hung over into his mature years.[2] And this may very well be true: God's eternal decrees, the universe's *i*'s dotted and its *t*'s crossed even before Creation. Historian Allen Guelzo argues in "Abraham Lincoln and the Doctrine of Necessity" that the Calvinism of the Lincoln family's Baptist subdenominations in Kentucky and Indiana was unrelentingly doctrinal about predestination and election.[3] As a generalization, this is reasonable, though there is room for some nuance among modes of Baptist theology. While the boy Lincoln did not follow his parents in joining the church, he could not have escaped Calvinism's midnight moon shadow, further obscuring a temperament already predisposed to melancholy. The Calvinism of frontier Baptist sects—whether "Regular," "Separate," or "Primitive" (or "Hard-Shell")—might be variously mild or severe, depending on the preacher's and congregation's attention to the letter of the theological law, yet ever present in one version or another. The Lincolns had come from Kentucky as Separate Baptists (no written creed) but eventually associated with the Regular Baptist (formal creed) Little Pigeon Church in Indiana, after these Separate and Regular branches had declared for union. The Little Pigeon articles of faith unsurprisingly included the key predestinarian tenet: "we believe in Election by grace given in Christ Jesus Before the world began & that God Cawls regenerates & Sanctifies all who are made meat for Glory by his special grace."[4] That Calvinism made bitter-tasting food for thought to the young Lincoln is altogether likely. And for historian Stewart Winger, some variant of theological determinism remained with Lincoln throughout his life, a more profound influence than humanistic or scientific accounts of free will or its absence in human affairs.[5] Arguably, however, Calvinism was the beginning rather than the end of his thinking about determinism.

Guelzo asserts a later intellectual source in the utilitarianism of Jeremy Bentham and John Stuart Mill, though Lincoln is not known to have read Bentham and seems only to have dabbled in Mill.[6] The balance, then, would seem to teeter toward the theological end of the beam. There is, however, another possible source, a philosophical one, for the Doctrine of Necessity: David Hume's *Inquiry concerning Human Understanding* (1748). The exact phrase in just the sense Lincoln uses it occurs several times in the *Inquiry* (and occasionally elsewhere in seventeenth- and eighteenth-century philosophy). Here is the classic Humean formulation of the Doctrine of Necessity: "It is universally allowed, that matter, in all its operations, is actuated by a necessary force, and that every natural effect is so precisely determined by the energy of its cause, that no other effect, in such particular circumstances, could possibly have resulted from it."[7]

William Herndon recalled that one day Lincoln had remarked to him, "There are no accidents in my philosophy. Every effect must have its cause. The past is the cause of the present, and the present will be the cause of the future. All these are links in the endless chain stretching from the finite to the infinite."[8] This viewpoint corresponds closely to that of Hume by way of John Locke and Thomas Hobbes. While Lincoln might have come to his deterministic metaphysical view either on his own, or from somewhere else in his desultory reading, it is worth our trouble to propose, hypothetically, the influence of Hume. At a minimum, the congruence of their philosophical positions is remarkable, as indicated by another passage from Hume's *Inquiry concerning Human Understanding*: "nothing exists without a cause of its existence . . . chance, when strictly examined, is a mere negative word, and means not any real power which has any where a being in nature."[9]

What is the likelihood of Lincoln's having read Hume? Our single authority, as it so often proves, is Herndon himself. In a letter to Francis E. Abbott, Herndon mentions having loaned Lincoln books by a number of authors, including Ralph Waldo Emerson and Hume.[10] When this may have occurred, and whether Lincoln actually read Hume at that unspecified time, Herndon does not say, though we may reasonably include it within the span of years of their law partnership, 1844–60. More speculatively, we can suppose that Lincoln might have encountered and read Hume well before he knew Herndon—perhaps as early as his reading of the other radical and skeptical writers during his residence in New Salem. In this context, Hume's two ultraskeptical essays on religion, *The Natural History of Religion* (1757) and *Dialogues concerning Natural Religion* (1779), would certainly have fueled the young man's antichristian ardor had he encountered them at the same time he was reading Voltaire, Volney, and Paine. Besides Herndon's assertion, the argument for Hume's influence on Lincoln's philosophy rests upon the affinity of ideas, as well as the not inconsiderable fact that Hume was a master of English prose style: clear and direct and concerned with communicating his ideas to readers baffled by and excluded from the hermetic mysteries of obscurantist metaphysicians. Lincoln would have understood his commonsense arguments, admired his style, and delighted in his plainspokenness.

Herndon, who was a thoroughgoing Transcendentalist of the Theodore Parker stripe—he read and corresponded with Parker in the 1850s, all the while attempting to interest his partner in Parker's writings—thought that Lincoln had no head for metaphysics. In an oft-quoted passage from his biography, Herndon declared that "[by] reason of his practical turn of mind Mr. Lincoln never speculated any more in the scientific and philosophical than he did in the financial world. He never undertook to fathom the intricacies of psychology and metaphysics." In one sense, Herndon saw Lincoln accurately here. For Herndon's—like Parker's and Emerson's—Transcendentalism rested upon yet another reinvention of Platonic idealism. That humankind essentially *were* souls, that God was the "Oversoul," and that the intuitive communion between the two actuated an "innate" sense of Right, Beauty, Perfection, and Duty—all this and more constituted the metaphysics of Transcendentalism, which exalted intuition and imagination over Lockean perception and experience. Lincoln appeared to want none of this. "Investigation into first causes," Herndon noted with just a shade of complaint, "abstruse mental phenomena, the science of being, he brushed aside as trash—mere scientific absurdities."[11] Though a radical dissenter from orthodox Christian theology, Parker was a Unitarian minister in good standing, and Herndon, while antagonistic toward establishment

(Protestant Evangelical) Christianity, wished to uphold at least a universal beneficent force that humans could commune with or "participate in," as the Platonists would have it—which is another way of saying that Herndon found little incentive to cleave *to* the philosophy of David Hume, a philosophy that had neatly cleaved *off*, as with Occam's razor, all the fat and gristle of idealism. Lincoln, to the contrary, for the most part lived and thought as a materialist: the radical outcome of Hume's arguments in *An Inquiry concerning Human Understanding*.

Thus, in a more strictly philosophical sense, Herndon was mistaken. Lincoln's preoccupation with physical cause and effect was just as metaphysical an inquiry as any brand of Platonism. Metaphysics is the philosophical account of reality. As Hume insisted and Lincoln agreed, metaphysics need not and ought not be therefore abstruse. "Obscurity, in the profound and abstract philosophy, is . . . the inevitable source of uncertainty and error. Here, indeed, lies the justest and most plausible objection against a considerable part of metaphysics, that they are not properly a science"—arising instead from a human vanity that deliberately mystifies the ordinary knower and leads him into the "entangling brambles" of superstition.[12] Metaphysics properly belongs to the genre of knowledge Hume calls "matters of fact" rather than to "relations of ideas," the truths of mathematics and geometry. Since all matters of fact are "founded on the relation of *Cause and Effect*," metaphysics comprises the intellectual search for ultimate cause, though for Hume such an inquiry was doomed to defeat: "These ultimate springs and principles are totally shut up from human curiosity. . . . the observation of human blindness and weakness is the result of all philosophy, and meets us, at every turn, in spite of our endeavours to elude or avoid it."[13]

Such radical skepticism about human knowing is what Immanuel Kant and the post-Kantian Transcendentalists sought to refute, inventing along the way what we call Romantic Idealism—which, according to Stewart Winger, Lincoln encountered in his reading of articles in the *Whig Review* in the mid-1840s. Winger argues that through such journalism Lincoln was introduced to the Romantic doctrine of the primacy of the imagination, that exalted organ of the mind by which humans might both *understand* through reason and *create* the world imaginatively.[14] This is intriguing: on the one hand, the imagination was always claimed as a surpassing power of human genius—which Lincoln certainly admired in Byron—capable of transforming any apparently predestined status quo, which his own ambition urged him to do. But, to reiterate, Lincoln's love of poetry rarely extended to the reading or reciting of Romantic lyrics—no Wordsworth, for example, and thus no familiarity with the famous formula in "Tintern Abbey" that reality was "what we half perceive / And what create."

So, even allowing for an inoculation of 1840s Whiggish Romanticism and the sort of Protestantism that went along with it, Lincoln mostly remained with Hume on the matter of the human futility in seeking ultimate knowledge. This was Lincoln the scientist. Yet when it came to politics and what he took to be the needs of the United States, he moved, as had the Founders, to posit something transcendental, something a priori and not subject to alteration over time: that was human rights, which cannot be shown to obtain according to Hume's analysis of matters of fact apprehended through experience. For rights to exist behind the scrim of conventional or traditional mores required a transcendental assumption, which Lincoln seemed eager to make, pleasing his partner Herndon and, indirectly, Theodore Parker. Nevertheless, concerning the motives of the human heart, Lincoln proved a stolidly Humean epistemologist. Rights may have been "endowed" to humankind by whatever creative force had caused the universe, applicable in the aggregate; but the individual animals of our species, in possession of rights or not, were subject to the same natural laws as any other thing composed of matter and energy. Herndon remembered that Lincoln always denied that humans possessed altruism or freedom of will: "The great leading law of human nature is motive. He reasoned all disinterested action out of my mind. I used to hold that an action could be pure, disinterested, and wholly free from selfishness; but he divested me of that delusion. His idea was that all human actions were caused by motives, and that at the bottom of these motives was self. He defied me to act without motive and unselfishly; and when I did the act and told him of it, he analyzed and sifted it to the last grain. After he had concluded, I could not avoid the admission that he had demonstrated the absolute selfishness of the entire act."[15]

And the branching, indefinitely long path of causation, retraced by the scientist, was to Lincoln precisely this sort of a search for the first cause of things: an Aristotelian quest in which the inquirer might find *nothing personal* at the goal—no available godhead, no bliss, no redemption; but *nothing more original* either—the existential, metaphysical end of the Prime Mover Unmoved. What Hume saw, and Lincoln sensed, was that the human mind could backtrack causation, just as far as one's life and intelligence would permit, and with luck and pluck get within range of the elusive first cause. What it could not accomplish, however, was the return mental journey carrying the boon of predictive power from the hard-won backwards knowledge, still less any sure knowledge of the first cause's persistence into the present.[16] That which had caused the universe would not necessarily cause its future—at least not in such a way as to allow human intelligence to say with authority what that future will be. Yes, the past had fomented the present through its complex of causes; and the present likewise shall compel the future. But we (absolutely?) could not know from past causation what future effects would be. Inquiry was a one-way street. Back from effect, but not forward from cause. After all, the sun might *not* rise tomorrow. And, as in physics, so in ethics.

Or was it? The Doctrine of Necessity ultimately made God, not humankind, responsible for all causes and effects in the universe, whether good or evil. Hume thought this preposterous: "Ignorance or impotence may be pleaded for so limited a creature as man; but those imperfections have no place in our Creator."[17] Since some human acts *are* criminal, and God *is* perfect, the age-old problem of evil is left a mystery. "To reconcile the indifference and contingency of human actions with prescience," Hume continues, "or to defend absolute decrees, and yet free the Deity from being the author of sin, has been found hitherto to exceed all the power of philosophy." Hume's advice, then: we must leave "a scene so full of obscurities and perplexities, return, with suitable modesty, to [philosophy's] true and proper province, the examination of common life."[18] To which retreat, we may hope, Lincoln offered his benedictory "amen." Hume the philosopher in this case lived a vital life in the mundane realm of being, while Lincoln the politician was obliged to accept the course of common life as *real*.

Immediately following the *Inquiry* in the sort of edition Lincoln would probably have read is Hume's *A Dissertation on the Passions* (1757). This was a subject of long and intense interest to Lincoln, who always wished to know what constituted the relationships between emotion and reason, both philosophically and in terms of the emerging science of psychology. Adapting the principle of *association of ideas* from the *Inquiry*, Hume asserts that "all *resembling* impressions are connected together; and no sooner one arises than the rest naturally follow. Grief and disappointment give rise to anger, anger to envy, envy to malice, and malice to grief again."[19] Still, the passions are a product of nature. Hume's theory of morals, therefore, must hold that all our emotions, resulting as they do from "impressions" (from, that is, sensory perception), play—or may be made to play under reason's tutelage—a positive part in human individual thought and social actions. Both from within ourselves, and from those who watch us and judge our actions, we receive cues that make us feel "pain or pleasure," the indicators of blame or praise by which we comport ourselves and are made relatively satisfied or dissatisfied with our lives.[20] Hume's position here is strikingly akin to what Lincoln once said about his own religious impressions. One day somewhere in Illinois he had happened upon a "class meeting," where he heard an old-timer testify that "when he did good, he felt good, when he did bad, he felt bad. That, says Lincoln, is my religion."[21] Of course, the equation between good doing and good feeling is common and obvious enough that Lincoln might have picked it up anywhere or simply endorsed it as what he considered a *necessary connection*, universally felt, between modes of action and passion. The old-timer at the class meeting had got it right and without wasting words. But its very simplicity was Hume's point: he had attempted to abstract an ethical theory from natural processes and ordinary human behavior. And this intellectual approach, generally, was Lincoln's too. His so-called religion was in reality his *ethics*: transactions among human beings that please us when we pay what we owe to the being of others and displease us when we cheat them of that debt.

As for the faculty of reason in humankind, Hume neither reified it as did the Transcendentalists nor quite allowed it sovereignty in the person. "What is commonly, in a popular sense, called reason," he wrote, " . . . is nothing but a general and a calm passion, which takes a comprehensive and distant view of its object, and actuates the will, without exciting any sensible emotion."[22] Odd as this may seem as a characterization—negative only, "reasonable" being what we are when we do not feel—it is cognate with Lincoln's view that only when passion's troubled waters are well-oiled can a person live with himself and thereby for others. Perspective—Hume's "distant view of [passion's] object"—is another name for Lincoln's celebrated ability to think things through, for the most part unimpeded by emotional noise. For Hume, "*strength of mind* implies the prevalence of the calm passions above the violent," though, he judiciously adds, "there is no person so constantly possessed of this virtue, as never, on any occasion, to yield to the solicitation of violent affection and desire."[23] This Lincoln well knew, from too painful experience. Supposing that he agreed with Hume's conclusion in the *Dissertation on the Passions*, namely, that "in the production and conduct of the passions, there is a certain regular mechanism, which is susceptible of as accurate a disquisition, as the laws of motion . . . or any part of natural philosophy,"[24] it would not have followed in his mind that anyone could explain what this *mechanism* was. "Susceptible of disquisition," yes; known, no.

From the first 1860 presidential campaign biographies on, it has been a commonplace in accounts of Lincoln's life that the young man in New Salem had had a notion to become a lawyer as early as 1831–32, but soon gave it over, not commencing any serious study for the profession until after his first election to the Illinois state legislature in 1834 (he received his law license on September 9, 1836).[25] The source for this two-stage preparation was Lincoln himself. In the Scripps autobiography of 1860, Lincoln recalled that he had "thought of trying to study law—rather thought he could not succeed at that without a better education."[26] This suggestive recollection may imply that during the 1832–34 interim Lincoln had worked to get that better education before once more picking up perhaps the one law textbook he had all along possessed: *Blackstone's Commentaries on the Laws of England* (1765–69). From this we can posit that in 1831–32 Lincoln read *some* of Blackstone, perhaps the lengthy introductory chapter on the nature and history of the English law, suspended his reading, and then returned to the *Commentaries* in 1834. A number of New Salemites recalled that Lincoln was first seen reading the *Commentaries* over the fall and winter of 1831–32.[27] Well into the twentieth century, a story persisted that, while working at the grocery with William F. Berry, Lincoln had found his copy at the bottom of a barrel of truck bought cheaply of someone on his way out of New Salem.[28] This appears to be a fabrication. Better evidence suggests that Lincoln purchased his set of Blackstone at a sheriff's sale in Springfield at some unspecified time fairly soon after his arrival, or perhaps obtained a copy from some local justice of the peace.[29] But it is the *what* rather than the *when* or *from whom* that is important here. Lincoln, from reasons of poverty, at that time had few books he could call his own. As we have seen, he borrowed freely from the meager personal libraries of his neighbors. That he would actually *pay* for a book indicates its high reputation even in a tiny, frontierlike Illinois village. Somehow, he seems to have known how respected Blackstone was among the small class of better-educated westerners—the more so among the region's attorneys and politicians. Presumably, the *Commentaries* were the first law volumes Lincoln ever owned, and, like all other books he came across at this still callow and intellectually hungry period of his life, we would expect him determinedly to read what he had found. Which some of his New Salem cohorts insisted he did with a vengeance: Isaac Cogdal, a farmer and stonemason, told Herndon that "the first book I ever Saw in L's hand was Blackstone—in 1832," and "He was then reading Blackstone—read hard—day & night—terribly hard."[30] And when in 1834 Lincoln took up law studies in earnest, he worked himself mentally to the bone, studying to the extent that some of his friends thought his health would break under the strain, added to the anxieties of his debts and the illness and death of Ann Rutledge in August 1835, and apparently it did.[31] In any case, most of the surviving reports show us a young Abraham Lincoln who was by the end of 1834 working harder intellectually than he ever had before, determined to become a lawyer.

And that meant, so he thought, mastering Blackstone's *Commentaries*. Purportedly, Lincoln averred in 1860 that the reading and study of Blackstone had had a major impact upon him. According to one source, Lincoln went so far as to declare that he had "never read anything which so profoundly interested and thrilled" him as those two volumes, adding, "never in my whole life was my mind so thoroughly absorbed. I read until I devoured them."[32] Moreover, Lincoln, when a mature member of the bar, twice recommended Blackstone in letters to would-be lawyers; in the second instance he wrote, "Begin with Blackstone's Commentaries, and after reading it through, say twice, take up Chitty's Pleading, Greenleaf's Evidence, & Story's Equity &c. in succession."[33] Clearly, to Lincoln's way of thinking, Blackstone was the foundation of legal self-education.

Let us briefly consider the steep and rugged slope that Lincoln would have had to climb in order to conquer Mt. Blackstone. The 1832 New York edition under discussion here would have been typical of what Lincoln read: four books bound in two volumes, nearly 1,700 pages of text (10-point type) and notes (8-point), with these notes, added to by later authorities, taking up at least as much space as Blackstone's original.[34] A formidable read, then, for anyone. But this high peak would not have daunted the ambitious and strong-legged climber was already reading Gibbon's *Decline and Fall* at the time he came upon Blackstone!

While there is no doubt that Blackstone was both popular and important to the training of antebellum American lawyers, it is curious nonetheless that a book so utterly English in its purview and application should be a requisite for the training of the bar of a republican democracy. Partly this was owing to Blackstone's lucid, deep, and comprehensive presentation of the English Common Law, much of which had relevance to American custom and legal practice, dating from the colonial era; most important, the grand guarantee of *habeas corpus*, "a natural inherent right" and the guarantor of English liberty. It was "doctrine coeval with the first rudiments of the English constitution" and had proved sturdy ("though sometimes a little impaired by the ferocity of the times, and the occasional despotism of jealous or usurping princes") ever since "established on the firmest basis by the provisions of *magna carta*" (2:1:107). If this were the first Lincoln had heard of the majesty of habeas corpus in protecting natural rights, it was a lesson he needed to learn, since, as president, he would temporarily suspend habeas corpus in order to uphold it in the long run.

Though they may not read as such today, the *Commentaries* were intended for a lay audience. Their author had originally given the material as lectures at Oxford—where gentlemen were made, not lawyers. Blackstone considered the law a necessary subject for liberal learning, what an aristocratic Englishman ought perforce to know about the law of a kingdom he would in due course help to govern. By ironic extension, one might see young American "gentlemen," in and out of school, encountering in Blackstone a prospect of the law as civilization, as immemorial custom grown from first principles, now in the United States more freely and widely applied. Thus, as Blackstone wrote in his preface, he who first learns the *letter* of the law "has begun at the wrong place." Without first principles, "the least variation from established precedents will totally distract and bewilder him." Besides, what gentleman, titled or natural, would "submit to the drudgery of servitude and the manual labor of copying the trash of an office?" (1:1:18–19).

So Lincoln, who hated all modes of drudgery, followed Blackstone along the right way of learning—the spirit of the law first. The introduction to the *Commentaries* is an eighty-six-page treatise on the immemorial basis of English law, which Blackstone believed to be grounded in *natural law* as laid down by a Supreme Being, the God of both nature and revelation. To this extent, Blackstone aligns his thought with Church of England orthodoxy. But in no fundamental way does he require any further Christian theology, since the Common Law derives from the singular revelation of the Scriptures and, more important, from nature's laws understood and modified according to traditional usage over the centuries. The law is therefore secular, instituted "that man should pursue his own true and substantial happiness" (1:1:25, 27, 88–92). Following John Locke, Blackstone places the rights of persons—life, liberty, and property—before the social contract, which is itself based on the half-grudging acceptance of the human necessity of getting along with one another so as to be able to exercise those rights and save the tribe from anarchy. This required a *"political union; by the consent of all persons to submit their own private wills to the will of one man, or one or more assemblies of men"* (1:1:35). And, over the centuries, the organic Common Law gradually became the unwritten but plenipotent means of upholding and improving the freedom God and nature had endowed Englishmen with. Americans too? Yes, and more so than any citizen of England might imagine! Coming as he was to revere the Declaration of Independence, Lincoln would readily have seconded Blackstone's foundation of the law in natural rights—without the institution of monarchy, of course. Rights were universal, governments relative. The Revolution had asserted to England and the world that a republic was a far better form of social contract through which to sustain and nurture the rights of humankind.

Lincoln could assimilate Blackstone's introduction because he already knew what the "learned commentator" was talking about. But the succeeding 1,600-plus pages of the *Commentaries* were another matter. When he resumed the ascent of Mt. Blackstone in 1834, he had no tutor. It was all private reading, studying, and thinking. By then, Lincoln was far too old for grammar school; the new college over in Jacksonville was too rich for his blood; and, besides the schoolmaster Mentor Graham, there was no coterie of friends with whom to share the agonies and joys of an education got from a few books (yet every one important) with only scattered opportunities to read them.

Despite such difficulties, by late 1834 Lincoln had built from his other reading a substantial base camp from which to launch his assault on the summit. Over the past two years, he had realized something important about himself: he could compete in his milieu politically; he was headed to the state legislature in Vandalia, the New Salem area's newly elected representative in the lower house. With this success, his aspiration to the law may well have increased dramatically and seemed to him not only possible but just a matter of will and effort and time.

The image of Lincoln besting Blackstone is immensely appealing. We can see him, as Herndon did, alone, outdoors, and at all hours, peering at the small type of the *Commentaries*, climbing mentally from foothold to foothold, and coaxing from the text the forms and the lingo that would at last make him an Illinois lawyer. Day and night, indoors or out, in all weathers—Abraham Lincoln carried the volume around the New Salem vicinity and rarely stopped reading it.[35] The book was an obsession with him. But that does not mean he *assimilated* the whole of the *Commentaries* in Herndon's sense. Rather, the truth is probably that Lincoln read what he could read in Blackstone and passed over the rest. For the volumes presented reading challenges to Lincoln that he frankly could not have met, however hard he tried. This is literally true. Open either volume to any page: the Latin passages from Roman legal authorities, frequent and substantial, are not translated, nor likewise the many Latin legal terms. What is more, the *Commentaries* contain more than a few citations in "law French," the language and substance of which had entered and dominated English law for a time after the Norman Conquest. Little of this would Lincoln have been able to make out. A few of the Latin terms he might have known from his playing at law in Bowling Green's justice of the peace court ("He figured conspicuously as a pettifogger before the justice of the peace").[36] And context, of course, could help, as we shall see in the example below—but only a bit. Without a pocket dictionary and a glossary of legal terms—and there is no evidence that he possessed either at the time he read Blackstone[37]—Lincoln's only recourse would have been to skip over the Latin and French and press on with the English.

Even the mother tongue might prove difficult because of the feudal basis of English Common Law. Blackstone typically begins a subject with a definition, clear enough, then follows on with numerous glosses, including Medieval case law, until the reader feels, as Lincoln very well may have, like he is slogging across a wide prairie slough without landmarks of home. And then there are the notes. By time of the eighteenth London edition (1832), the footnotes to Blackstone comprised several generations of commentaries on the *Commentaries* by subsequent English legal authorities, along with the very occasional remark from an American lawyer. These copious notes, interlarded with centuries of precedents, it is worth repeating, make the *Commentaries* about again as long as Blackstone's original text. Thus the book as a whole became like a palimpsest of a millennium of English Common Law—to an American reader in 1834, more a paleographic discovery than an up-to-date textbook.

Beneath the jargon and verbiage, however, was a story: how Englishmen over the centuries established and proved their rights before the law. The indistinct outline of such a buried narrative would have appealed to Lincoln and spurred him patiently to dig it up. A single example both of the pains and rewards of mining Blackstone will have to suffice. It pertains to land tenure. In the antebellum United States, and more particularly in the Old Northwest, where much of the territory, and later states, was public domain, possession of land in "fee simple"—that is, land bought with cash or on terms from the government, or from someone who had got in ahead and made a claim—was very common. Such land was paid for and held without conditions—no mortgage, no strings. Like any immigrant to the American frontier, Lincoln would have grown up hearing conversations about the basics of land tenure and later, as a surveyor, came to know the "metes and bounds" of land description.

Here is Blackstone's exegesis of this familiar legal term, beginning with its definition: "Tenant in fee-simple . . . is he that hath lands, tenements, or heriditaments, to hold to him and his heirs for ever; generally, absolutely, and simply" (but notice the word *tenant*). To this is opposed holding land in *allodium*, or "property in its highest degree," which the owner "hath *absolutum et directum dominium*"—that is, the land is his own *demesne*, or domain. But in England, "this allodial property no subject has [since] all the lands in England are holden . . . of the king" (1:2:81).

From the word-thickets of Blackstone's explanation, a *story* strives to emerge: in England, only the king owns land absolutely, and tenancy in fee-simple remains a form of feudal service to a lord or series of lords. The vaunted English liberty of property (as of person) was conditional on being the king's subject. In the United States, deliberately and emphatically, land held in fee simple had been freed from all such feudal associations, save the vestiges of customary legal language. Hence any American with the means could do what no Englishman ever could: have his fee-simple holdings treated in justice as allodial: by which the common man became, in the eyes of the law, as good as a king. Our humble citizen of the Republic might, in other words, *disenthrall* himself. Lincoln used this powerful Medieval verb just once, in his annual message to Congress, December 1, 1862. In the last sentence of the penultimate paragraph, he wrote: "As our case is new, so we must think anew, and act anew. We must disenthrall ourselves, and then we shall save our country." The final paragraph of this address has become much better known, with its admonition that begins, "Fellow-citizens, *we* cannot escape history."[38] Curiously, however, in transforming *fee-simple* possession into *allodial*, many American citizens had effectively *disenthralled* themselves and escaped the long feudal history of slavery and dispossession.

The most important fruit of Lincoln's reading of the *Commentaries* surely consisted of coming to know something of the history and philosophy of English law. As a practicing attorney for nearly twenty-five years, Lincoln would cite Blackstone in only three of his cases. How-to information he got from textbook sources such as Chitty's *Practical Treatise on Pleading*, or Greenleaf's *Treatise on the Law of Evidence*.[39] But he took Blackstone's measure nonetheless and could show the little New Salem world what he was made of, what he would become: a lawyer and a gentleman. People who walk around reading books are at least in part attitudinizing—Lincoln not excepted. As would be the case with the proofs in Euclid's geometry, Lincoln "read hard—day & night—terribly hard" in order to prove he could do a mighty thing, gaining confidence in his intellectual powers, along with a certain notoriety among his neighbors. One of them, Russell "Squire" Godbey, told Herndon that "the first time I Ever Saw him with a law book in his hands he was Sitting astraddle of Jake Bails woodpile in New Salem—Said to him—'Abe—what are you Studying' 'Studying law'—replied Abe. 'Great God Almighty' Said Godbey."[40] The good squire couldn't understand such business: he knew of no "Mt. Blackstone" in the vicinity of New Salem.

William E. Barton, in *The Soul of Abraham Lincoln* (1920), and, much more recently, Wayne C. Temple, in *From Skeptic to Prophet* (1995), both reached the conclusion that Lincoln, sometime between 1849 and 1850, read at least parts of James Smith's *The Christian's Defence* (1843). What makes their opinions especially important is that, perhaps unique among the students of Lincoln's religion who mention *The Christian's Defence*, Barton and Temple took the trouble to examine the book. Barton declared that Lincoln first encountered and began reading Smith's volume during a visit to his in-laws in Lexington in "the spring of the year 1850," following the death of his young son, Eddie; then in Springfield soon afterward, he obtained a copy, probably from the author himself, and finished reading the book.[41] Temple agreed that Lincoln discovered Smith in Lexington while staying at the Todd mansion, but he dated the trip to October of 1849; and he, too, was confident that Lincoln later read the rest of the book right through (probably before Eddie's death in February 1850, but possibly in the grim period just after).[42]

Both scholars, moreover, accepted that Lincoln came to know and trust Smith and his theology in Springfield. Temple believed that "this learned minister's hard logic seem[ed] to have impressed him greatly"—to the extent that Lincoln "pondered *The Christian's Defence* very minutely," just as a lawyer might do with an opposing counsel's argument. In addition, Temple noted, Robert Todd Lincoln much later remembered seeing a copy of the book on the shelves at the family home.[43] For his part, Barton referred to Smith as Lincoln's pastor, though of course Lincoln never did join Smith's First Presbyterian or any other church. In addition, Barton affirmed that there was more than sufficient second- and third-hand testimony to support his conclusion that Lincoln read and approved of *The Christian's Defence*: "That Mr. Lincoln was impressed by the book is as certain as human testimony can make it." In his final judgment of Smith's work and its influence on Lincoln, Barton insisted that "the more carefully these lectures are examined, the more probable does it appear that in form and method they would have been likely to make, what they appear to have made, a very strong impression upon Abraham Lincoln."[44]

To one who has read the book closely and all the way through, the claims of Barton and Temple seem untenable. James Smith's *The Christian's Defence* is a great white elephant of a book—in its size, readability, and popularity (little in its day, none at all now). Published in Cincinnati in 1843, its two-volumes-in-one add up to a galumphing 700 pages, the text in small type, the frequent footnotes even smaller.[45] Smith compiled the *Defence* out of his notes from a protracted debate that, according to Temple, had gone on for eighteen nights![46] Smith had squared off with the "infidel" C. G. Olmsted in Columbus, Mississippi, in the spring of 1841 and then compounded *The Christian's Defence* for publication. Lacking more bibliographic data, the best guess is that the book had a small printing, which according to Barton, had been completely presubscribed, therefore denying *The Christian's Defence* any general distribution.[47] It has never been reprinted, and copies, scarce by the time Smith came to Springfield in 1849, are extremely rare today.[48]

In his attempt to prove the truth of the Old and New Testaments, Smith almost literally "threw the book" at his opponents, who were Deists, skeptics, atheists—in other words, infidels of every stripe. *The Christian's Defence* is a miscellaneous compendium of tactics, weapons, and ammunition by which those who were *already* Christian could first defend themselves against the calumnies of nonbelievers and then go on the offensive and send the unregenerate straight to debaters' hell. As his title page indicates, Smith employs as collateral for his argument "copious extracts from learned authors." These sometimes run for pages at a time, making it unclear just who is speaking, or even what the original point of a given passage is. To these sources he adds what seem like innumerable biblical citations and authorial glosses on them. Although Smith sets forth an overall plan for *The Christian's Defence* (he would state all the objections to the revealed truth of the Bible, then meet and defeat them, as he had Olmsted in their late agon in Mississippi), the text in fact reads eccentrically, as if the author had written down whatever occurred to him and afterwards did little revision. Despite Smith's device of heading each chapter with a précis of the problem or problems at issue and then attempting their solution in the main body of the text, the book just seems steadily to accumulate material. Thus it can strike one as more a pedantic parade of learning or a miscellany of preacherly notions or simply a sustained rant against infidelism, than a *systematic* defense of the Protestant Christian religion or a manual for confounding skeptics. After nearly seven-hundred pages of this, *The Christian's Defence* will have exhausted its audience, as Smith's relentless viva voce version had evidently done to his victim in debate.

My own reading of *The Christian's Defence* contravenes some of the chief qualities that Barton and Temple found in the book: its order and system. The other principal reason they advanced for Lincoln's having admired *The Christian's Defence* is the author's strength of mind: Smith wrote, Barton declared, "with logical acumen and force of reason."[49] This claim of logic as a cardinal feature of the prose—and one that would undoubtedly have appealed to Lincoln—must, however, be tested against the actual arguments in the book.

In the preface to *The Christian's Defence*, Smith admitted that as a young man—say, about Lincoln's age in his first New Salem years—he had himself been an infidel: "In early life [I] was a Deist, from principle. Led astray by the sophisms of Volney and Paine, without demanding proofs or seeking for objections, [I] jumped at the conclusion that Religion was a fraud contrived to govern mankind" (1:x). So he and Lincoln had commenced their spiritual journeys from very similar skeptical starting points. Having subsequently seen the light, however, Smith became a Christian, a Presbyterian minister, and an active apologist for the church. And Lincoln? Well, it was Smith's self-appointed task to bring all such stubborn, hard-thinking infidels around to the Gospel Truth. His approach in *The Christian's Defence* followed two lines, not always well-defined or integrated: an "important examination" of the New and Old Testament Scriptures, which activity Smith was confident would prove their historical and literal accuracy; and a characterization of the human being that would, while demonstrating Smith's own fund of liberal learning, convince his readers of our superiority to all other worldly creation. In other words, Smith would offer us his apologetic interpretations of both the Book of Nature and the Book of Revelation.

On the subject of natural history, Smith can be risible, as when he invidiously compares the brute sensibility of animals to human beings' higher one: "The body of the animal is either covered with scales or feathers, with fur, wool, or bristles," which, Smith somehow concludes "approach more or less nearly to the nature of vegetables." Thus a hairy black bear, for instance, is deprived "of the more tender and delicate sensation" that a man is accorded through his bald skin. To be fair, Smith does attempt to differentiate between humans and animals by the more conventional appeal to our higher intelligence: "The animal possesses a *sentient life,* man an *intelligent nature*" (1:7–8). But we are the crown of creation, Smith asserts, because our "intelligent nature" is god-given: the brain is not the mind, and the mind is not the soul (though included in it).

How do we know this? Smith dares any "materialist" to show that the brain and the mind are one entity. He takes the Cartesian position that we only know matter because we can think about it through the mind, the epiphenomenon of which is consciousness. "The existence and operations of the mind, account for all the phenomena which mind is supposed to exhibit; but the existence and action of matter, cannot account for one of the phenomena of mind." Whether this was in fact the state of psychology in 1843 is of secondary importance to Smith's strong antiempiricism. Because science *had not* shown a brain-mind identity up to then, Smith concludes that it *could not* and that the soul-mind view is, to his satisfaction, established (1:11–12). The logician in Lincoln would have criticized the argument here; Lincoln the empiricist would have rejected Smith's conclusion.

Because Smith, like Lincoln, requires a cause for every effect, lest the universe be unintelligible, he must ultimately recognize a First Cause. In Lincoln's terms, that is, Smith must accept the Doctrine of Necessity. But this is too much like Deism, too close to unreconstructed Calvinism, and it denies free human agency apart from God-as-cause. So Smith moves from what is a perfectly logical retracing of the chain of effect and cause back to the universe's origin into the miraculous world of Revelation: God later changing his mind, and the Bible as the record of the changes.

Thus committed to viewing the Bible as the revealed world of God (though a literalist only when it suits him), Smith declares, this time against

Tom Paine, that Moses really did write the Pentateuch, contemporary with its events, and that the Jewish captivity narratives, the books of the kings and prophets, and so on can, on archaeological and historical grounds, be taken as true (1:195–200). And this is at least arguable. But Smith's defense of biblical miracles would have received a severe cross-examination from reader and lawyer Lincoln. Miracles such as the parting of the Red Sea, Smith insists, *must* be accepted as of and from God. Why? Because repeated attempts by infidels to naturalize events like these have failed: with no detectable natural cause, then, the sea must there and then have split as the Bible, the word of God, says it did. Once again, the fact that an event has not been explained scientifically becomes the principle that it cannot be. More damningly, Lincoln would surely have noted two further and related flaws in Smith's position. First, the assumption of what is to be shown, namely the actuality of the phenomenon (sea parting to allow the good guys through); and, second, its notorious circularity, often present in *The Christian's Defence* but never acknowledged by Smith (1:270–80).

Perhaps more nearly convincing are Smith's arguments concerning the historical accuracy of the New Testament, which he insists meets all the tests of literary authenticity: written *by* named authors, *about* an actually existent subject, *at* (or near) the time of the events, and *consistent* with other contemporary sources. While yet prone to debater's hyperbole ("That Jesus Christ flourished in Judea during the Augustan Age, and that the writers of the New Testament were his contemporaries, are facts much better supported and authenticated than that there lived such men as Cyrus, Alexander, and Julius Caesar" [2:4]), Smith, as a seminary-trained Presbyterian minister, is on solider ground with the "historical Jesus" than with pseudoscientific explanations of Hebrew mythology, such as the notion that God *could* have stopped the earth's rotation, holding back the sunset and moonrise, to allow Joshua's slaughter of the Gibeonites (Joshua 10:12). According to Smith's authorities, to do so safely would have required only about eighteen minutes of the Great Engineer's time (1:305)! In assuming that the Gospels are eyewitness accounts of Jesus's life and ministry, Smith gives them primary-source authenticity. This appears reasonable enough on its face and may well reflect the paleographic understanding of the New Testament among Christian clerics and scholars during the first half of the nineteenth century. But it is far from being "abundantly proved," as Smith insists, that "all these books were written by the persons to whom they are ascribed, and published soon after the introduction of Christianity into the world" (2:126). Moreover, the Gospel authors and the Apostles had been men whose "faith in Christ was the result of rational conviction, not upon internal persuasion alone, but in the irrefragable evidence of clear and stupendous miracles" (2:133). But, in the end, what was this "irrefragable evidence"? Once more, the circle closes: it was that the Evangelists (or their later amanuenses) saw and felt the miracles of Jesus as irresistible and set them down as true.

Now and again in *The Christian's Defence*, Smith's authorial persona—when he checks himself from ad hominem abuse of his opponents—is that of the disinterested scholar sustaining a Christianized version of the classic "argument from design." He borrowed it from William Paley's *Natural Theology* (1802), a treatise Lincoln also knew of and may have read (probably he was familiar with the arch-metaphor of the Divine Watchmaker and his Watch that figuratively constituted the universe).[50] For liberal Protestants—and Smith would have regarded himself as such—the argument from design kept God in the Big Picture, though barely discernible behind the opaque mask of a deistic Divine Author. But Lincoln knew from his radical readings that there was a chasmal distance between a Prime Mover, forever unmoved after he designed and wound the clock and set it ticking, and the triune Christian God, with Jesus Christ ever immanent in the world to offer personal salvation, to suspend time, space, and cause, and to judge us, to our eternal bliss or pain. Such a cosmic gap would, for Lincoln, be unbridgeable. In his twenties in New Salem, he had scoffed at it; nearly forty years old when he ostensibly read *The Christian's Defence*, he may by then have moved toward a deterministic Deism. But there is nothing in his intellect, no record in his words or actions, of any affinity for Christian theology. And this is just what lurks behind Smith's claim to reason and liberalism in his book: an orthodox commitment to Protestant Evangelicalism, with its emphases on revelation and conversion and eternity. Hundreds of pages of purported facts and arguments give place to the mystical doctrine of revelation and regeneration as the sole means to truth: "Let it not be supposed . . . that the author would disparage the internal evidences of the truth of Revelation. They form a most important branch of the argument, but which can be properly appreciated, only by the regenerated Christian, who, by the teachings of the Spirit, has been brought to a knowledge of God, and his attributes, and without which teachings man can have no better knowledge of the moral character of the invisible God, than the man who is born blind can have of the colors of the rainbow" (1:3 n.).

The Bible is the revealed word of God and yet can only be truly known a posteriori to evangelical regeneration, to which state one had been led by the revealed word of God . . . and so on, to complete and reinscribe the circle. In such an affirmation of evangelicalism, Smith necessarily denies the adequacy of commonsense reasoning to ascertain all the historically and scientifically contingent truths he otherwise cites and touts in *The Christian's Defence*. Furthermore, if the matter needs repeating, the conversion model of knowing what can be known of God was for Abraham Lincoln—whether in the 1830s or 1850s—intellectually and emotionally unacceptable. That one's natural gift of reason had first to be overthrown in order to be allowed to operate within the narrow confines of a faith-based religion would have appeared to him as sufficient grounds for dismissal of the book and author that said so.

In the pre-Darwinian 1840s and 1850s, Lincoln became, in Herndon's words, "a warm advocate of the new doctrine" that would soon be known as evolution. Herndon further remembered "[a] gentleman of Springfield gave him a book called, I believe 'Vestiges of Creation,' which interested him so much that he read it through."[51] Because the first American edition of *Vestiges of Creation*, one of the most important treatises on evolution before Darwin's *Origin of Species*, appeared in the first part of 1845, that year may serve as the early limit for Lincoln's reading. Originally published anonymously in London in 1844, the book—eventually identified as the work of Englishman Robert Chambers—was not a static text. Rather, as it went through several editions in the years following publication, Chambers corrected errors of fact brought to his attention by scientists and gave his critics space to reply to his arguments.[52] Hence during the remainder of the 1840s and well into the 1850s, *Vestiges* became a progressively refined argument, which means that if Lincoln looked at a later edition, he would have had more (and better) matter to digest. At the same time, however, Chambers's overall position on evolution remained the same: a near-atheistic account of the development of a universe that was composed of matter and structured by natural law.

The author of *Vestiges*, trained as a journalist, wrote clearly and engagingly for a popular audience. And he knew his science. Between the covers, Lincoln would have found the most up-to-date account of physical science available to a lay reader of the time. The subjects ranged from Laplace's nebular theory of cosmology and Newtonian astrophysics, through geology, paleontology, biology, and chemistry, to psychology and what today we would call the neuroscientific "brain-mind hypothesis." Through all of this material ran Chambers's thesis of progressive development. He held that the universe, as the mid-nineteenth-century observed it, had come about through aeons of movement from simple to complex—as had all biological life, including *homo sapiens*. Nothing was excused from this law of progress; nothing, not even humankind, was exceptional. Occasionally, Chambers would lighten the naturalism and determinism of his view with a bow toward the "Great Being" that had made all this possible. He was willing to credit a Designer, even a Grand Design. But that work was long ago done. The Author of the universe he removed to the dark, cold place of a Prime Mover Unmoved. No room for a personal god in Chambers's system, then, and not one reference to Jesus or Christianity. Lincoln, even in his radical years in New Salem, had not previously read a book so comprehensive in its view of science, so logical in theorizing its subject.

Here is an example from *Vestiges* concerning the human mind that would have sat the long-limbed, recumbent reader Lincoln up straight: "Where our perceptive faculties are baffled, we dream; where they compass their object, we inquire after cause. Such is the law of our minds, which cannot have been bestowed upon us without being designed for a good end. And, indeed, it is by experience placed beyond all doubt, that to yield to this impulse is to use a direct means of improving our condition on earth, and to advance the scale of moral as well as intellectual being."[53] Inquiring after cause was one of Lincoln's cardinal mental habits, and dreaming when his "perceptive faculties" were baffled was another. Ultimately, the human mind derived from some sort of cosmic super-intelligence. But Chambers argues, and Lincoln would have agreed, that the laws governing cause and effect were "but as expressions of Will and Power," and not so much the human's will and power as the originator's (10). Here, then, was a scientific accounting for fate and destiny, though one that seemed to deny human agency. As with Hume and Calvinism, Chambers described a deterministic universe.

Yet the metaphysical implications of *Vestiges* are less important than the close analysis Chambers makes of scientific evidence, especially as found in the earth's fossil record. That these material "vestiges" point to organic development over hundreds of millions of years is today taken as a matter of course. But in 1844 to disregard the Mosaic creation story as mere myth showed daring. "It is now time to say," Chambers wrote, "that from an early portion of the sedimentary rock series to its close, the mineral masses are found to enclose remains of the organic beings . . . which flourished upon earth during the time when the various strata were forming" (31). In an imaginative flight of fancy, Chambers asks us to look back with our eyes to a time (the Oolitic Period) when there were no eyes. A dynamic natural paradise would have appeared, "spread out . . . during whole millenniums" waiting for beings such as humans to evolve: "the stream flowing and glittering in the sun, but not to cheer the eye of man; the whole jocund earth spread out in unenjoyed beauty, as yet unwitting of the glory and the gloom which human impulses were to bring upon it" (89).

The Creator of this "jocund earth" had worked through natural law, also his creation; so must humans do if we wish to comprehend creation and our place within it. While "the ignorant believe the very hand of Deity" is to be found everywhere and always in the world, and the learned theists speak of "creative fiats," "interferences," and "interpositions of creative energy" (for all of which read *revelation*), science has had the cumulative effect of showing (probabilistically) that, marvelous as nature is, it did not come about through the marvelous but "*in the manner of natural law*" (113, 115). Here Lincoln might have noted with appreciation Chambers's use of Occam's razor to account for the geological facts of the earth's history: "Let us remember that, in such speculations, the explanation which is most simple, and which makes the least demand upon the puerile emotion of wonder, is always, other things being equal, the most acceptable." And this simplest explanation for organic nature was Progressive Development (155, 179).

Chambers's scientific account of creation sternly put the biblical version on report. In this connection, it is worth reiterating that Lincoln, child and adult, would have encountered an entrenched Christian viewpoint at every turn in his life. For example, a highly esteemed Methodist preacher, Peter Akers, whom Lincoln probably heard preaching at a Springfield-area camp meeting in 1837—a sermon in which Akers prophesied a great national upheaval over slavery, which reportedly moved Lincoln greatly—spent decades of his life preparing a meticulous dissertation on biblical chronology. It would be the only book Akers published (1855), and it was hermetically sealed against any oxidation by facts known to natural philosophers.[54]

Chambers's notion of progressive development ineluctably took him down the dark cul-de-sac of racialist ethnography. *Vestiges* featured the "Caucasian race" as the most highly evolved branch of the human family, with, predictably, Africans the least so (261, 266). It is easy now to see the obvious error, confusing or conflating biological with cultural evolution, science with ideology. But whether such a view directly influenced Lincoln's rare declarations of white superiority is doubtful: he did not think deeply on the matter, most often (as in the concessions on racial hierarchy in the debates with Douglas) going along with conventional white opinion that pale skin alone was sufficient to give whites the supervening place in American society.[55] But Lincoln did not go so far as Chambers. Blacks were not *by nature* inferior, simply by circumstance; whites believed they deserved to be ahead of blacks because modern historical events had made them so, and they desired to maintain this status quo.

Natural rights were a different matter. Both Chambers and Lincoln accepted that these were fundamental to the definition of *homo sapiens*. One of the aspects of *Vestiges* that may have focused Lincoln's attention is its treatment of the philosophy of mind. Chambers argued that the human mind, as everything else, grew from a natural base (i.e., not out of or in conjunction with a soul). In his estimation, the mind ought to be viewed as the highest known attainment of organization, the genuine "crown of creation" that elevated humans above the "lower animals" and necessitated a polity founded in natural rights. At the same time, and inconsistently, Chambers wanted to leave room for what he called "an immortal spirit" (286–87). In the larger context of *Vestiges*, this was probably a sop to prevailing theism, for only a few pages later Chambers reiterates his materialist (naturalist) stance: "The difference between mind in the lower animals and in man is a difference in degree only; it is not a specific difference." Furthermore, consciousness itself had arisen out of a "necessary relation" between sense data (perception) and the processing of such information by the brain (292, 294–96). As a whole, then, *Vestiges* proposed a view of both the universe and humankind that was philosophically monist and scientifically naturalist.

Lincoln would have agreed—as regards physics, chemistry, and so on. But what of human ethics, especially the "problem of evil"? Chambers had an answer, and we may say, a *Lincolnian* answer: his Designer/Creator had endowed *homo sapiens*, through evolution, with the faculties of hope and reason with which to master the difficulties of existence. In this view, the problem of evil became not what to do with "fallen" human nature but rather how to employ reason to subdue and order the passions. If human beings acted evilly, it was due to having habituated themselves to desire, this owing in turn to poor self-rule and its attendant arrested development. Our habits indicated our free will: we could choose to improve or go to the devil. Good or evil turned out to be a matter of deliberation. Reasonable action would lead to the one, passionate indulgence to the other. Over time, Chambers rather optimistically ventured, the *tendency* would be toward the good. How could a disciple of progressive development not be a meliorist?

The personal war of conscience with desire; the political war of reason with passion: Lincoln fought both. As the melancholy fatalist, he might well have shaken his head at Chambers's belief in a hopeful outcome for humankind. Yet he was also reading, or soon would be, similar views even more optimistically expressed in the works of William Ellery Channing and Theodore Parker. Both of these American Unitarian clergymen grounded their thought in Transcendentalism rather than natural science. But if science *and* religion agreed on the progressive human prospect, so much the better. This was something a good man would like to believe. As ever the case with him, though, Lincoln looked for matter his mind could use in his political artistry rather than a systematic philosophy. *Vestiges* proffered arguments from the Book of Nature, and to the extent he found these clear and convincing he would have filed them away for future reference.

Chambers ended *Vestiges* with a similar chiliastic vision of consummating human progress. He held that the blood-blotted copybook of the human past actually boded well: "I conceive the *possible development* of higher types of humanity,—beings less strong in the impulsive parts of our nature . . . more strong in the reasoning and the moral . . . more fitted for the delights of social life, because society will then present less to dread and more to love." Until that great era, however, we should stoically suffer life in this veil of tears and "wait the end with patience and be of good cheer" (322, 324–25). One half of which advice Abraham Lincoln took to heart.

What is *political economy*? According to Francis Wayland, D.D., author of antebellum America's most popular treatment of the subject, "POLITICAL ECONOMY is *the Science of Wealth*"—where by science he means "a systematic arrangement of the laws which God has established . . . of any department of human knowledge," and where wealth is "any object, having the power of gratifying human desire, which is capable of being appropriated." Yet the good doctor of divinity and president of Brown University holds also that "the principles of Political Economy are so closely analogous to those of Moral Philosophy, that almost every question in the one, may be argued on grounds belonging to the other."[56] So Wayland stated in the preface and introduction to *Elements of Political Economy*, first published in 1837 and in print (and often used as a textbook) right through the Civil War. The conjunction of "moral philosophy"—Wayland's academic calling—with an economics of the gratification of desire may seem to us strange, but, insofar as the pursuit of wealth was also the pursuit of happiness, ethics, individual and social, remained at the heart of political economy: goods were Good.

Wayland's *Elements* was a book much to Abraham Lincoln's taste. As Herndon recalled, in an 1886 letter to his co-biographer Jesse Weik, "Lincoln ate up, digested, and assimilated Wayland's little work."[57] As we have seen before, when Herndon uses the verb *assimilated* in connection with Lincoln's reading, even when he employs a metaphor such as eating and digesting, he means *assimilated* in the strongest, most literal sense of the word: a mastery so complete as to make the work in question his own. Herndon adds that Lincoln liked the subject of political economy more generally, having "more or less peeped into" related titles by John Stuart Mill (*Principles of Political Economy*, 1848) and Henry Charles Carey (*Principles of Political Economy*, 1837).[58] Though it is unlikely that Lincoln knew either of these books thoroughly, or others of the kind, Herndon's remark about Lincoln's affinity for political economy must be taken seriously. It derives from the time of the partnership, when he and Lincoln were closest, and when the senior was keeping the junior partner busy with his deepening political interests and activities. Most of all, on the basis of Lincoln's having *assimilated* Wayland, we must look closely and carefully at this work, in hopes of recovering what Lincoln found useful in it.

Basically, political economy consists of nonquantitative economics, built around the familiar nostrum of supply and demand and the problematic relations between capital and labor. Lincoln himself used the term in this manner in his remarks at Indianapolis (September 19, 1859): "There is a difference of opinion among political economists, about the elements of labor in society. Some men say that there is a necessary connection between labor and capital, and this connection draws with it the whole of the labor of the community. They assume that nobody works unless capital incites them to work. They say there are but two ways: the one is to hire men, and to allow them to labor by their own consent; the other is to buy the men and drive them to it, and that is slavery." While *some* political economists—was Lincoln here thinking of George Fitzhugh and his 1854 book, *Sociology for the South*?[59]—asserted that the slave was actually better off than the hired laborer, because his needs were provided for irrespective of his capacity to work, Lincoln emphatically repudiated such a view. For it denied labor any real status in the dialectic with capital and was therefore both unfair to laboring individuals and prevented a healthy economic dynamic from operating in society. If industrious laborers accumulated capital and used it to hire others to labor for them, this was their right.[60]

Here, then, is one statement of Lincoln's "right to rise," which should be accorded all freemen (and all men should be free). Thus labor itself has intrinsic value to, and in, a free society, and this labor theory of value is the foundation of Lincoln's economic thinking. He found its authoritative embodiment in the opening chapter of Wayland's *Elements*: "It is plain, that if a man expend labor in the creation of a value, this labor gives him a right to the exclusive possession of that value." The value added by labor is what makes its produced "objects of desire" exchangeable: since no laborer will be likely to give away this value added, a market economy naturally arises which is based primarily upon supply and demand.[61]

It is fair to say that Lincoln was interested much more in the everyday fact of *labor's value added* than in the theory of a market economy as classically described by Adam Smith in *The Wealth of Nations* (1776). Lincoln disagreed with Wayland's criticism of high tariffs:[62] the tariff might or might not affect wages and productivity one way or the other; author and reader could argue about that, as did the country's political parties, the Whigs being consistently protariff. But that labor both *had* value and *added* value to the economy was an important concept, one that resounded in Lincoln's deepening beliefs in the dignity and autonomy of all individuals.

And he wished to use it as substantiation for the arguments on free and slave labor that he began forcefully making during his September 1859 speaking tour in Ohio, Indiana, and Wisconsin.

If the labor theory of value was correct, Lincoln could confidently use its central principle to criticize slavery and its economy on the grounds of reciprocal unfairness: to the slave, of course, who was systematically deprived of the right to the fruits of his labor, but also to the freeman, who was in another fashion stripped of his labor's intrinsic value by the rigged competition of slavery. Though Wayland has nothing to say about slavery, his glosses on the topic of labor are cognate with Lincoln's: "The universal law of our existence is, 'In the sweat of thy face shalt thou eat thy bread.'"[63] As Wayland saw the human condition, God had endowed human beings with the strong limbs and supple minds to labor, with the desire to do so, and with the rightful expectation of possessing the products of our labor, or bartering them for others more deeply desired. And, since the biblical sentence contains a metonymic phrase for the physical labor of the human body ("sweat of thy face"), it follows that the laborer, before he can own anything else, must own his body. This is the fundamental right of property (human capital) that allows labor to be an extension of ownership (production). And it should, it eventually must, be recognized universally in any society that intends itself to be free.

About two-thirds of the way through his epochal Cooper Union Address (February 27, 1860), Lincoln rhetorically asked this question of the southern people: "And how much would it avail you, if you could, by the use of John Brown, Helper's Book, and the like, break up the Republican organization?" Lincoln answered decisively: "Human action can be modified to some extent, but human nature cannot be changed. There is a judgment and a feeling against slavery in this nation. . . . You cannot destroy that judgment and feeling—that sentiment—by breaking up the political organization which rallies around it."[64] Everyone listening then, and afterwards reading the speech in print, knew the fate of John Brown, lately hung as punishment for the Harper's Ferry raid. But many in Lincoln's audience would also have caught the allusion to "Helper's Book"—which we very likely do not understand today. Why would Lincoln have made a mere book coeval with John Brown in calling down southern (and Democratic) opprobrium on his barely adolescent Republican Party?

The author of the volume at issue was Hinton Rowan Helper; the title was *The Impending Crisis of the South*; and the year of publication, 1857. By the time of Cooper Union, the book had sold more than sixty thousand copies and was touted by its supporters as the most effective antislavery publication since Harriet Beecher Stowe's *Uncle Tom's Cabin* (1852).[65] Indeed, if effectiveness meant reducing its target, the oligarchy of southern slaveholders, to spluttering rage, *The Impending Crisis* might well have been *more* effective than Stowe's novel. And this from a *North Carolinian*; and this from a (self-styled) *political economist*; and this, finally, from a *white supremacist*. While he had no desire to live with free blacks, favoring their complete colonization outside the United States, for the abolition of slavery, Hinton Helper stood as uncompromisingly firm as any New England ultra: he demanded abolition immediately, without compensation to slaveholders, and by force of arms if necessary. Such views put Helper considerably to the left of Lincoln and many members of the Republican Party. These moderates on slavery were by 1860 having a difficult time meeting the southern charge that he (Helper) and they (Lincoln, Seward, et al.) were all tarred with the same Black Republican brush.

Even a cursory look at the text of *The Impending Crisis* will show why many southerners were incensed by the book and some Republicans put on the defensive. As early as 1869, an article in a Washington newspaper asserted that Helper had presented Lincoln with a copy of *The Impending Crisis*, which he had read and to an extent annotated, marking particularly several passages that quoted the Bible against slavery.[66] But the modern bibliographical association of Helper with Lincoln derives from Carl Sandburg in *Abraham Lincoln: The Prairie Years* (1926). It was Sandburg who boosted the book's importance for Lincoln to the first rank of his late-1850s reading. He told the story of Herndon's having brought a copy of *The Impending Crisis* back from his eastern trip in the early months of 1858. According to Sandburg, Lincoln had read and annotated this "sad and terrible book," pondering its abolitionist arguments in preparation for the House Divided speech (June 16, 1858).[67]

Sandburg pictured Lincoln as a somewhat resisting reader: "As he read the book he marked passages he could not say yes to, such as this one: 'Out of our effects you have long since overpaid yourselves for your slaves; and now, sirs, you *must* emancipate them, or we will emancipate them for you.'" Nor could Lincoln endorse Helper's notion that "all proslavery slaveholders" were criminals who deserved the penitentiary. But Helper did influence Lincoln, Sandburg insisted: "Part of his analysis went into his speech so soft, so quiet, beginning, 'If we could first know where we are, and whither we are tending, we could better judge what to do, and how to do it.'"[68] The connection between *The Impending Crisis* and the House Divided speech is unconvincing.[69] Nothing in Lincoln's famous opening connotes Helper's radicalism. At Springfield, on the occasion of his formal nomination as the Republican candidate for the U.S. Senate (June 16, 1858),

Lincoln was, as usual, obsessed with Douglas and far more concerned with defeating his "popular sovereignty" and thereby preventing the extension of slavery into federal territories, than with Helper's militant version of abolitionism—or any other version, for that matter, since "abolitionist" was the last label Lincoln wished to attract to himself.

Lincoln sometimes affected a sense of solidarity with the *people* of the South, if not their politicians. He best stated this in the Peoria speech of October 16, 1854: "I think I have no prejudice against the Southern people. They are just what we would be in their situation. If slavery did not now exist among them, they would not introduce it. If it did now exist amongst us, we should not instantly give it up." He understood the South's predicament partly because he was himself southern. Born in Kentucky, the child of an upland southerner, Lincoln of course lived most of his life north of the Ohio—but always in non-Yankee communities that might have been to a degree antislavery but were otherwise sympathetic to the South from which so many of their people had recently come. In the same section of the Peoria address, Lincoln amplifies the point: "When southern people tell us they are no more responsible for the origin of slavery, than we; I acknowledge the fact. When it is said that the institution exists; and that it is very difficult to get rid of it, in any satisfactory way, I can understand and appreciate the saying. I surely will not blame them for not doing what I should not know how to do myself. If all earthly power were given me, I should not know what to do, as to the existing institution."[70]

Since Helper believed he knew precisely what to do about slavery, and when and how to do it (now and by force), a fitter role for *The Impending Crisis* in Lincoln's political calculus was as an example of dangerous radicalism to be held off: stay to the right of Helper by adhering to the Constitution's silent assent to slavery in the original South; yet make the status quo progressive by insisting that slavery be confined thereto, while northerners patiently awaited its death from lack of new soil and nurture. Helper would have agreed that slavery, without more room, would eventually die. But he was too stirred up to wait indefinitely for the inevitable. Further, Helper was, like some radical Republican senators during and after the Civil War, vindictive toward his home region (self-exiled, he could never return to live there once he published his book). Taken as a whole, then, *The Impending Crisis* would seem to have had no positive value to Lincoln. But it probably was interesting to him. In the first place, Helper wrote effectively—always an attraction for Lincoln. True, he showed at times a tendency to rhetorical self-indulgence, but, as Sandburg rightly noted, Helper assumed a powerful persona as a Jeremiah for the nation (South *and* North). In his righteous indignation against slavery, Helper

could hurl verbal thunderbolts with the loudest of the northern abolitionists and, at least on the page if not in person, he looked his southern
enemies, the slaveocrats, right in the eye, unblinkingly.

Lincoln's association with *The Impending Crisis* is complicated by an
important fact. By mid 1859 a number of Republican leaders had read and
approved of the book; then some of them, led by Horace Greeley, publisher
of the powerful *New York Daily Tribune*, went so far as to endorse the publication of a *second version*—a cheap edition that could be quickly printed
by the thousands and distributed nationally (even in the South, or so Helper
and the missionary Republicans hoped) at a comparatively low cost (sixteen
cents per copy). The new version was entitled *Compendium of the Impending Crisis of the South*; copies began rolling off the presses of New York's
Burdick and Company late in 1859.[71] But what was this compendium, and
how did it differ from its progenitor? Given the standard dictionary sense
of the word, one would expect Helper's *Compendium* to be a briefer treatment of its subject, a sort of digest reduced from *The Impending Crisis*. This,
however, it was not. Basically, the *Compendium* contained all the political
economics of the original (including the statistical tables) and most of the
prose. One new chapter appeared: a long string of antislavery statements
by "living witnesses," mostly northern literati. What was omitted from the
Compendium were a few of Helper's most incendiary indictments of the slaveocrats, along with the elision of the *n* word wherever it had occurred (not
often) and the occasional substitution of a euphemism that a little softened
his contempt for southerners who would not challenge the ruling oligarchy
(one of his favorites, "lickspittle," was refined to "sycophant"—as if this
would ease the damning effect!).[72] The reason for such revisions was simple:
toning down the rhetoric, while insisting on the truth of the evidence and
argument, was intended to make the *Compendium* more acceptable as an
important 1860 Republican presidential campaign document.[73]

If the *Compendium* seemed to some "markedly less radical" than *The
Impending Crisis*, Helper's thought remained unflinchingly abolitionist.[74]
And whoever among the Republican leaders might have thought that the
Compendium would transform both northern fence-sitters and the non-
slaveholders of the South into new Republicans and abolitionists had been
fondly dreaming. While Helper's second try was intended to be less pugna-
cious toward the South, it was nonetheless plenty offensive enough. Even as
copies of the *Compendium* flowed across the northern and western United
States, Helper and the Republicans discovered that the book's mere physical
presence in the South constituted an outrage to the region's sensibilities.
And sometimes an illegal outrage: "In many Southern localities it became
a crime even to possess the book."[75] The problem of Helper's radicalism

was compounded by the declaration of war on the South—and much more than a cultural war—pronounced in *The Impending Crisis*: "Now, sirs, you *must* emancipate [your slaves]—speedily emancipate them, or we will emancipate them for you!"[76] This insurrectionist statement was deleted from the *Compendium* (along with a few others of its ilk), but the damage was done—still doing, actually, since *The Impending Crisis* remained in print during the life of the *Compendium* and for that matter had been read first and probably just as widely as the later volume.

Some southerners not unreasonably believed that Helper, for all his statistics and tables, was simply another rabid abolitionist threatening civil war. A reader today might almost agree: in either format, Helper's book was disturbing. Indeed, no American—and this could have included Lincoln—even needed to open the volume itself: it became a sensation through partisan New York newspaper puffery (*Daily Tribune*) and vitriolic reaction (*Herald*), articles which were republished widely.[77] The Harper's Ferry raid, John Brown's trial, and his execution (on December 2, 1859) had already driven public opinion further from what little was left of common political middle ground. Now followed the dissemination early in 1860 of thousands of copies of the *Compendium*. And, finally, there occurred the protracted crisis of electing a Speaker of the House for the last national congress before secession. This fascinating, suspenseful story is too complex and lengthy to recount here. Suffice to say that the matter had as its root cause the leading Republican candidate's endorsement of *The Impending Crisis*. For John Sherman of Ohio had leant his name to a circular aimed at raising money for the publication of the *Compendium* (without, as it happened, having read *The Impending Crisis*).[78] The Republican Party had more representatives (109), but no majority; the Democrats had elected 101 members, but these were deeply divided into Douglas and Buchanan administration adherents. After many votes over many weeks, Sherman withdrew, his party having proved unable to find him a majority of votes. Thereafter, endorsement of Helper's book(s) became the South's litmus test of whether *any* representative from *any* region or party might sit in the Speaker's chair. In this manner did southern representatives win what turned out to be their last political victory in the Congress of the United States of America.

During the 1840s and 1850s, in or out of politics, Lincoln strove to keep himself informed of southern opinion. Except for his brief but acute observation of southern representatives during his single congressional term, he did so at a distance, through reading newspapers and keeping an ear to the ground. In addition to the *Richmond* (Va.) *Enquirer*, which

Lincoln read regularly, Herndon recalled that the law office subscribed to the *Charleston* (S.C.) *Mercury* and the *Richmond Examiner*, remarking as well that he (Herndon) had "bought a book called 'Sociology,' written by one Fitzhugh, which defended and justified slavery in every conceivable way."[79] This was George Fitzhugh's *Sociology for the South* (1854), a proslavery apology that Helper refuted in *The Impending Crisis*. Whereas Helper called for yeoman southerners to unite with the North against the slave oligarchs, Fitzhugh just oppositely convoked the union of such southern men and their families with their betters—humane, civilized, aristocratic slaveholders (as he saw the patrician class in his home state of Virginia)—in order to vindicate the justice of the slave system against calumnies from the North. Purporting to be a work of political economy, or of that brand-new science, sociology, Fitzhugh's book had practically none of the empirical basis of either discipline. Compared to Helper's *Impending Crisis*, it was propaganda posing as scholarship. *Sociology for the South* mounted a lofty but merely assertive attack on classical capitalist economics, free trade, and social liberty—all of which Fitzhugh blamed for the decline of Western civilization (ever since Greece! but with the noble exception of the 1850s South) and the reduction of society to a portending Hobbesian war of all against all. As a *tour de force*, *Sociology for the South* might have attracted Lincoln's attention. Certainly the book had its moment of national notoriety: upon publication, huzzahs all round "at the south," detestation from northern liberals and abolitionists (William Lloyd Garrison branded the book as "shallow, impudent, and thoroughly satanic").[80] Yet we must remember that, though Herndon put Fitzhugh on the table, we cannot assume Lincoln read him. If he more than paged through *Sociology for the South*, the motive may have been to highlight proslavery points he would have to counter in political debate.

One such point was Fitzhugh's audacious assertion that northern laborers of the 1850s were themselves slaves de facto, since they could not achieve through their paid labor, assuming employment in the first place, even what the average chattel slave in the South "earned" for the duration his or her life: namely, food, clothing, shelter, medical care, retirement, and burial.[81] Fitzhugh, blithely implying that this humanitarian level of care was the norm among slaves and slaveholders, in effect sneered at Lincoln's vaunted "right to rise": it was at best a vapid political promise, at worst a Big Lie—so unlikely was it that any laborer in the North could disengage himself from the capitalist trap of low wages and heartless competition for the raw means of existence. There might be a little *money*, from time to time, but there could never be true *community*—democratic or patrician—in the North. Let the few true masters rule, Fitzhugh urged, and, as in his vision of the South, the multitude of the mastered will soon be much happier, because "free" of the unwinnable game of socioeconomic success. This was the nonsense Helper would confute with his formidable statistics concerning the *actual* southern economy. But more than a bad argument, incredible on its face, Fitzhugh's book may have bothered Lincoln personally. For, of course, in Fitzhugh's utopia, Lincoln would have been one of the mastered many rather than the privileged few—stuck as a lifelong tenant behind on the rent rather than an owner, a journeyman carpenter forever dunning for payment rather than a national messiah; with no right to rise, but mired in his predestined place as an underman. If he read *Sociology for the South*, how he must have hated it!

American Unitarianism, American Transcendentalism, and the "commonsense" mind of Abraham Lincoln might appear to have nothing in common. But Lincoln, through his reading during the latter half of the 1850s, came to know the best of antebellum New England Unitarian religious and social thought. This is convincingly attested by two men who knew him well, William H. Herndon and Jesse Fell. In March 1858, Herndon, returning from an eastern trip loaded with books from New York and Boston, had introduced Lincoln to a range of essays by a favorite author, Theodore Parker, whom he had visited in Boston. At some time previously, while engaged in conversation, Fell had spoken favorably of William Ellery Channing's "Sermons & writings generally." Lincoln was interested. And Fell not long afterward presented his friend with "a copy of Channing's entire works." Subsequently, the two men discussed Channing and Parker, with Fell becoming convinced that Lincoln approved of both.[82]

At the time of Fell's gift of the set, the late William Ellery Channing's collected works (six volumes) were in their fifteenth edition, containing everything he had published from his earliest and most conservative Unitarian sermons to his final thoughts concerning the shadow of slavery on the American Republic.[83] It is likely that Lincoln picked and chose from the groaning board of this intellectual feast. Channing was never narrow; he showed no taint of bigotry on any subject. His test of an extraordinary mind—which he himself brilliantly passed—was its possessing "great ideas" and expressing them well. As a reader and critic, he sought to discover in an author "what thoughts and feelings predominate, stand out most distinctly, and give a hue and impulse to the common actions of his mind."[84]

This statement would have drawn Lincoln in. He, too, thought about thought. He searched for patterns and preoccupations in his mind, often dark ones, where Channing's literary voice sustained an optimism in all mental weathers. But on the matter of moving effectively from thought to action, Channing may have given the inertial Lincoln something new to think about. The preacher's theology was firmly anti-Calvinist: "Man's free activity is as important to religion as God's infinity. . . . We must believe in man's agency as truly as in the Divine."[85] Though less markedly than his contemporary, Ralph Waldo Emerson, and his protégé, Parker, Channing was a Transcendentalist (perhaps the first such Platonic thinker Lincoln had encountered). As such, he concentrated upon the human soul's transactions with the divine: one to One. "We must start in religion from our own souls."[86] Revelation was immanent in the material world, especially in nature, which was, as Henry David Thoreau put it, a "uniform hieroglyphic" of the Ideal. What was revealed to one who looked first and closely at Nature, then inwardly into oneself, was an analogously pervasive divinity within the individual. In social and political life, the outer tokens of the improving soul—or consciousness, or mind—became good, ethical human action out of free human agency.

The first essay in Channing's first volume is a penetrating study of John Milton's mind and character, poetry and prose (1826). If Lincoln read it, he must have come upon Milton's remarks on the sanctity of the genius-writer's call, appropriate to the developing *political artist*: the gift of literary artistry, though "most abuse [it]," is the "power . . . to inbreed and cherish in a great people the seeds of virtue, and public civility." The chosen singer or sayer has the high responsibility of bringing his people back to public virtue, a *religious* duty of utmost import. Speak, Milton enjoins the true poet, of "whatsoever hath passion or admiration in all the changes of fortune from without, or the wily subtleties and refluxes of man's thoughts from within."[87]

Channing opened to Lincoln a serious and liberal imagination deeply engaged with only the most important subjects. He wrote not political polemics or religious apologetics, still less journalism, but *essays* in the traditional humanistic sense of the word. Reading Channing should have constituted for Lincoln a master class in the craft of the long essay and the proper moral use of learning in democratic communication. Naturally, some of these essays would have appealed to him more than others; "The Union" (1829), for example, which is the next-to-last piece of volume 1. Here was a topic, Channing declared, "of transcendent and universal interest." From the mid-1820s to his death, Channing was just as staunch a Unionist as Lincoln would become. He believed and repeatedly wrote that union alone made community and the realization of natural rights practicable, most basically by protecting individuals against harm from others. To this extent, he was pragmatic about keeping the states together. But he also insisted upon the transcendental *ideal* of the American Union, the manifestation of which in actual political and social life needed constantly to be perfected by citizens left free by limited government to find the good in themselves and enact it. While an Emersonian optimist about both individual and social melioration, he could rather grimly predict that disunion, to him a real possibility (with New England leading the withdrawal), would lead to civil war or, worse, a national conflict of all against all—this owing to the tremendous physical and mental energy of the American people, bound by the nuclear force of union, which would explode into anarchy should the center not hold.[88] When he wrote "The Union," Channing had been more worried about *northern* secession, though after the South Carolina nullification crisis of 1832 and the rise of radical abolitionism in New England, he turned his regard southward.

In 1835 Channing published his masterpiece, an extended essay—really a short book like Emerson's *Nature*—simply called *Slavery*. Never himself a radical abolitionist, Channing approached the vexed topic with equanimity and a comprehensive understanding, yet always from the inflexible principle that as a moral wrong slavery could never be a social or political good. His position was very close to Lincoln's as expounded in the late 1850s. Whether Channing therefore influenced Lincoln's thought is an important question, though one difficult to answer definitely. But we may assume that if Lincoln read anything by Channing carefully, it was this important work.

Channing's argument against the peculiar institution is founded on an appeal to human nature as fundamentally rational. "If we cast [reason] down from its supremacy, if we inquire first for our interests, and then for our duties, we shall certainly err. We can never see the right clearly and fully, but by making it our first concern."[89] As early as 1845, Lincoln had begun calling slavery a "moral evil," as he also became preoccupied with "seeing the right," and so he may have felt satisfaction at the famous Unitarian divine's corroboration.[90] But Channing went further. He placed what he considered a rational moral truth—slavery is evil—as the foundation stone of the edifice of argument on slavery. Lincoln, likewise: "If slavery is not wrong, nothing is wrong."[91] Admit this truth, Channing wrote, and the national conversation of what to do about slavery could begin in earnest. Unlike those who deprecated any discussion of slavery as agitation, Channing announced forthrightly that "slavery ought to be discussed"— frankly and fully. But the colloquy should "be done with a deep feeling of responsibility . . . so as not to put in jeopardy the peace of the Slave-holding states" (10). Even this statement of careful conservatism would hardly have appeased some southerners, who wanted no talk of slavery at all and were by the 1830s beginning to move from the traditional disposition of slavery as a "necessary evil" to proclaiming it a "positive good." Lincoln, one senses, would have warmly agreed with Channing and on grounds the long-dead Channing could never have known. For, especially in the wake of the Kansas Nebraska Act and the Dred Scott decision, the North discovered a new urgency to come to grips with slavery once and for all. Discussion of the issue became the more exigent as it became, practicably, less possible.

But *why* is slavery morally wrong? Channing, like Lincoln, asserts a natural rights position based on the "self-evident truths" of the Declaration of Independence. Because he has little biblical or theological baggage to weigh him down (no Sons of Ham nonsense, no Calvinistic determinism, no evangelical notion of postponing liberty until the afterlife), Channing is free to treat natural rights as simply God-given—a priori, self-evident, and without theological strings attached. What is more, rights are the basis for deducing a moral imperative. If "all men are created equal" and endowed with certain "unalienable rights," the crucial question becomes *who or what is a man*? If one is a man, then one has rights. Deny humanity to African slaves or any other dispossessed class and you offend intuition, common sense, and science. But, as Channing observed, this is habitually what thousands of southerners did. Yet, surely, under God, Africans and slaves were men no less than their "owners." Self-evident truths are at heart inarguable, since "an argument is something clearer than the proposition to be sustained"; and anyone who does not immediately apprehend such truths "is hardly to be reached by reasoning" (18). Nonetheless, it was his duty to attempt by moral suasion to change the mind of even the hardest case.

Given that "man has rights by nature," there can be no property in humans. "What rights these are, whether few or many, or whether all men have the same, are questions for future discussion. All that is assumed now is, that every human being has *some* rights." Further, all humans have "Essential Equality" (20–21, 32). By this Channing means that we possess, besides "*some* rights," souls and a moral nature (reason)—cardinal attributes that enable human progress, even human perfectibility. Lincoln, though always dubious about general moral improvement, came down hard for "*some* rights" for slaves, and he preached the right to rise, economically if not morally, as due all persons. But were such rights for Lincoln "natural"? With the Peoria speech of October 16, 1854, Lincoln began what would become his characteristic appeal in political debate with Douglas to the Declaration of Independence as the fundamental statement of American republicanism. He called the Declaration's principle that a government derives its legitimate authority "from the consent of the governed" the "sheet anchor" of that republicanism. And for the first time in his recorded speeches, he applied the consent principle to slaves and slavery. Men and women in bondage could hardly be said to consent to their condition, nor (obviously) were they at all able under slavery to enjoy "life, liberty and the pursuit of happiness:" "Allow ALL the governed a voice in the government, and that, and that only is self-government."[92]

To give Lincoln's "ALL" such a voice would, of course, entail a recognition of rights and seems to imply citizenship and franchise, too—though by no means was Lincoln in 1854, or in the 1858 debates with Douglas, for that matter, really ready to go this far—"*some* rights," but let us postpone their specification until the *first* right, freedom, can be gained. If the words *unalienable* and *natural* mean the same thing, then Lincoln had all he needed from the Declaration, and Channing may not have added anything to his thought on the matter. Still, it is suggestive that Lincoln did not use the phrase "natural rights" until after the limiting year for his reading of Channing (1857). In the first senatorial debate with Douglas, at Ottawa, Illinois, on August 21, 1858, Lincoln proclaimed "that . . . there is no reason in the world why the negro is not entitled to all the natural rights enumerated in the Declaration of Independence." While he conceded that Douglas was right in denying complete equality between blacks and whites, Lincoln insisted that "in the right to eat the bread. . . . which his own hand earns. *he* [the Negro] *is my equal and the equal of Judge Douglas, and the equal of every living man.*"[93]

Enjoying the fruit of one's labor is undoubtedly among Channing's "*some* rights." And here, as does Channing, Lincoln distinguishes *natural* rights from what we now call *civil* rights (e.g., citizenship and franchise). The former are a necessary condition for the latter. They are not conventional, generated, or rescinded by any social compact, but exist prior to society. They may be altered only by the presocial individual who has them. According to Channing, all rights derive consequently from a single Great Right: "As every human being is bound to employ his faculties for his own and others' good, there is an obligation on each to leave all free for the accomplishment of this end" (34–35). Part Christian, part Enlightenment, part Transcendental, and part Kantian: Channing's version of the Categorical Imperative is a moralization, a personalizing of Jeffersonian thought about rights that is appropriate both to American economic individualism and dynamic religion.

As an abrogation of natural rights, Channing believed that slavery was immoral, absolutely. As such it could not be reformed and must be abolished: "An institution so founded in wrong, so imbued with injustice, cannot be made a good. . . . Slavery is thus radically, essentially evil" (98). But how to accomplish abolition? "Since we"—that is, all Americans—"have no [Constitutional] right of interference" (Lincoln's oft-declared position), "to the slave-holder belongs the duty of settling and employing the best method of liberation" (106). To hasten that fortunate time, opponents of slavery should strive to kindle the conscience of the South. The means of abolition would become apparent to those whose spirit to emancipate was so moved. Meanwhile, northern "ultra," or radical, abolitionism must be censured. At worst, its adherents were culpable of employing unlawful means, justified, as they believed, by a noble end. At best, the Union was unsettled because of antislavery agitation (not the same thing as *discussion*). Calls for immediate emancipation, without conditions or recompense to the slave owners; propagandizing among the slaves; even urging slave revolts (though Channing thinks this is a calumny against radical abolitionists, unproved and unlikely)—all such actions he reproves as both wrong and finally counterproductive. Rather, "let the truth, and the whole truth, be spoken without paltering or fear; but so spoken as to convince, not inflame, as to give no alarm to the wise, and no needless exasperation to the selfish and passionate" (129). What was requisite for emancipation was a "fervent zeal, such as will fear no man's power, and shrink before no man's frown, such as will sacrifice life to truth and freedom. But this energy and will ought to be joined with deliberate wisdom and universal charity. It ought to regard the whole, in its strenuous efforts for a part" (130). *Will, wisdom, charity, the whole*—did the politically ambitious and politically engaged Lincoln of the late 1850s see himself believing and acting in Channing's universal terms?

In the 1840s and 1850s, Theodore Parker, through a series of popular but uncompromising and controversial sermons, given mostly in and around Boston, but widely circulated in printed form, thoroughly radicalized Channing's Unitarianism. Parker effectively reduced Jesus from a divinity to a great moral teacher whose messiahship was the reform of civil society through bold, individual initiative founded on Transcendental ideals. The most iconoclastic of these sermons, entitled "The Transient and Permanent in Christianity" (1842), held that whatever value the Christian religion had had, and would continue to have, rested not on the "personal authority of Jesus" but "the immutable truth of the doctrines themselves." Parker thought it "difficult to conceive any reason why moral and religious truths should rest for their truth on the moral authority of their revealer, any more than the truths of science on that of him who makes them known first or most clearly." Christianity's moral principles no more relied on Jesus's having expounded them than those of geometry depended upon Euclid's say-so. "The authority of Jesus, as of all teachers, one would naturally think, must rest on the truth of his words, and not their truth on his authority."[94] And, finally, in the workings of a Transcendental moral system, there was no room for mere theology. All men and all Christian sects during all ages, Parker noted, "were quite as confident as we that their opinion was truth, and their notion was Christianity and the whole thereof." They became persecutors, and they were wrong.[95]

"The Transient and Permanent in Christianity" constituted a manifesto-like break from even the previously most liberal views of Unitarianism. Predictably, Parker's words caused a storm of reaction. He and his views were denounced as heretical from many other Boston pulpits, and calls sounded out loudly for Parker's excommunication. That wasn't possible under Unitarian rules of polity, but Parker could be, and was, shunned and denied preaching rights at many area churches. Channing, for his part, may have been saddened by the apostasy, but he was as always charitable, saying of Parker's sermon, "Let the full heart pour itself forth."[96] A reader today may still feel something of the shock that "The Transient and Permanent in Christianity" produced. Parker told the truth as he saw it, without regard to the sensibilities of his audience—whether the congregation sitting right before him or the thousands who would read his sermons in the newspapers. He named names and looked the named squarely in their eyes. As a Transcendentalist, he fixed upon the Ideal and would not compromise with the mundane. He was a hellfire-and-brimstone preacher without a hell in his credo—only the conscience that suffered for not doing the right—once again, Lincoln's own sort of religion. And he spoke and wrote with a perfervid directness, sometimes subtly seasoned with irony and wit, sometimes with red-pepper sarcasm. "The Transient and Permanent" epitomizes Parker's thought and style: beguilingly radical and readable, sufficiently so to remind Lincoln of his own religious radicalism of the 1830s.

Turning to an essay that Lincoln almost certainly read, "The Effect of Slavery on the American People," which Parker delivered as an Independence Day sermon at the Boston Music Hall on Sunday, July 4, 1858: Herndon recalled that he had presented Lincoln with a copy of this speech, which his partner read, annotating a Parker tricolon that Lincoln would later immortalize in the Gettysburg Address: "Democracy is Direct Self-government, over all the people, for all the people, by all the people."[97] In his well-known and authoritative *Lincoln at Gettysburg* (1992), Garry Wills first noted this famous correspondence of phrase and then posited deeper affinities of thought between Parker and Lincoln: "The real importance of Parker cannot be reduced to a tag, to one phrase in one or another text. There was a much larger consonance of the two men's thinking, certainly in politics and probably in wider areas as well."[98] One of these areas may have been religion, and Wills cites Fell's remark in his 1870 letter to Ward Hill Lamon: "If . . . I was called upon to designate an author whose views most nearly represented Mr. Lincoln's on this subject, I would say that author was Theodore Parker."[99] If Fell and Wills measured Lincoln truly here, it is notable that, since Parker's religion was wholly devoted to seeing the ideal of the Right, and acting upon it, Lincoln's "political religion" was exactly its secular parallel, from the Lyceum Address in 1838 to the contest with Douglas twenty years on.

What else might Lincoln have gleaned from Parker—ideas, arguments, and expressions? The analysis that follows will be limited to the sermons and essays contained in *Additional Speeches, Addresses, and Occasional Sermons*, for that is the sole title we may be confident was on the law office table in March of 1858. Most of the pieces in its two volumes hammer away at the injustice and immorality of slavery and the series of political crises that threatened the Union in the 1850s. Without Parker's title of "Minister of the 28th Congregational Society in Boston" on the title page, one would scarcely know that an *ordained Christian minister* was speaking or writing, rather than a journalist or politician with abolitionist credentials. Rhetorically, Parker gave no quarter to his enemies, nor asked any of them. He had implacably opposed the Fugitive Slave Act (1850), the enforcement of which "legalized kidnapping" in Boston and so infuriated him that he undertook acts of civil disobedience against the rendition of escaped slaves back to the South.[100]

This legislation he considered the most harmful that mendacious northern politicians had allowed to be perpetrated upon America. Parker largely blamed Massachusetts senator Daniel Webster for the law. His presidential ambitions and political expediency in supporting its passage—not a "compromise," as Webster himself (and Lincoln, accepting Henry Clay's position) regarded it, but a pusillanimous perversion of principle for profit, what Parker called "hunkerism"—had resulted in a moral disaster for the nation. After Webster died a disappointed man in 1852, Parker preached a stunning funeral eulogy that did not so much praise as damn its subject, excoriating along the way both the slaveocracy and its complicit New England "hunkers": "Slavery, the most hideous snake which Southern regions breed, with fifteen unequal feet, came crawling North; fold on fold, and ring on ring, and coil on coil, the venomed monster came: then Avarice, the foulest worm which Northern cities gender in their heat, went crawling South; with many a wriggling curl, it wound along its way. At length they met, and, twisting up in their obscene embrace, the twain became one monster, Hunkerism; theme unattempted yet in prose or song: there was no North, no South; they were one poison!"[101] Webster's was, in

Parker's estimation, a Miltonic fall from the highest parapets of justice and liberty. Lesser betrayers, he remarked, New England had certainly endured—most notably, Benedict Arnold and Aaron Burr. But as Daniel Webster was a far greater man than either, so was his fall the more tragic: "He lay there 'not less than archangel ruined,' and enticed the nation in its fall. Shame on us!—all those three are of New England blood! Webster, Arnold, Burr!" Yet Parker professed that he had once loved and honored Webster, "not blindly, but as I loved a great mind, as the defender of the Constitution and the Unalienable Rights of Man."[102] But after 1850, that was all over—and in Webster's death there would be no *nil nisi bonum* (if not good, nothing) on Parker's part: "No living man has done so much to debauch the conscience of the nation. . . . He poisoned the moral wells of society, and men's consciences died of the murrain of beasts, which came because they drank thereat."[103]

Did Lincoln shrink from Parker's harsh judgment of one of his longtime Whig heroes? He had read many of Daniel Webster's speeches in the newspapers, most notably the famous "Second Reply to Hayne" (1830), and had followed Webster's political career throughout the 1830s and 1840s; only Henry Clay of Kentucky, his "beau ideal of a statesman," had been more important as a living model for enlightened Whig politics. Lincoln knew Webster long before he had heard of, let alone read, Theodore Parker. And in the late 1850s, during Lincoln's ascension in the Republican Party, both the thought and character of the Massachusetts senator remained important to him. He quoted a well-known sentence from the peroration of the "Reply to Hayne" as part of the toasting at a Republican banquet in Chicago (December 10, 1856): "Not Union without liberty, nor liberty without Union; but Union and liberty, now and forever, one and inseparable."[104]

Herndon asserted that Lincoln had studied this Webster oration closely enough for its opening to reappear in the House Divided speech, and many Lincoln biographers have followed his lead.[105] But is this rhetorical connection clear? Webster had begun his speech with the figure of a mariner emerging from "thick weather" to take his bearings; likewise, the Senate should "imitate this prudence, and, before we float farther on the waves of this debate, refer to the point from which we departed, that we may at least be able to conjecture where we now are."[106] Compare Lincoln's opening: "If we could first know *where* we are, and *whither* we are tending, we could then better judge *what* to do, and *how* to do it."[107] The correspondence seems tenuous, the less compelling as the subjects of the two orations are quite different: Webster argued against "states' rights" in the matter of nullifying a Federal law duly passed by Congress and signed by the president; Lincoln undertook to make clear the cause of continuing slavery agitation in the nation—it was a disease whose crisis had to be reached and passed. True, both addresses invoked the perpetuation of the American Union as devoutly to be wished, but Lincoln's thrust in the House Divided speech probed the question of whether a Union with nationalized slavery was finally worth preserving.

This is not to say that Herndon was mistaken in claiming Lincoln's close reading of the "Reply to Hayne." We need only notice one other passage to confirm it. Midway in his very long speech, Webster had remarked, in the context of the "origin of this [American] government, [i]t is ... the people's Constitution, the people's government, made for the people, made by the people and answerable to the people."[108] Indelibly familiar! Yet, as will shortly appear, Lincoln had in Parker's writings another possible source for the Gettysburg tricolon.

As Webster had been New England's heroic arch-Whig, so Henry Clay, who died a few months before him, had been the same for the American West. Lincoln's eulogy, delivered on July 6, 1852, in the Hall of Representatives at the capitol in Springfield, Illinois, showed a proper respect for "Harry of the West," though without eloquence. Granted that Parker felt a moral mandate to defend truth against partisan politics, whereas Lincoln had a party stalwart to commemorate, Lincoln's effort—the part not borrowed and read verbatim from a newspaper article—was dull, even perfunctory, especially given the deceased's status in the eulogist's political pantheon. Without criticism of Clay, yet at the same time unconvincing in his praise, Lincoln spoke as if the sun had gone down after a pleasantly temperate and calm day: "But Henry Clay is dead. His long and eventful life is closed. Our country is prosperous and powerful; but could it have been quite all it has been, and is, and is to be, without Henry Clay?"[109] The Compromise of 1850, of which Clay had been the political engineer, had saved the Union. Now all was well. If Lincoln ever really believed his own words, he would be startled out of such political maundering exactly two years later, in mid-1854, when Stephen A. Douglas's Kansas-Nebraska Act "aroused him as he had never been before."[110]

Parker, too. On February 12, 1854, not long after the legislation was introduced in Congress, he gave the first of several addresses on what he saw as this latest and most serious threat—that is, since the Fugitive Slave Law—to the actual liberty of free Americans and the potential liberty of slaves. Lincoln most likely encountered "The Nebraska Question" in *Additional Speeches* in 1858, as he prepared for the senatorial contest against Douglas, though he may have read it earlier in a newspaper.[111]

Much of the matter of "The Nebraska Question" had been on Lincoln's mind since 1854. But, in the interim until 1858, the *Dred Scott* decision had

come down from Roger Taney's Supreme Court, changing the rules concerning the extension of slavery into new American territory (and perhaps
old). *Dred Scott* effectively meant that free Negroes and slaves could not
be citizens of the United States and indeed possessed "no rights that the
white man was obligated to observe." Parker, of course, understood the
amplifying or multiplying power of the complex of democratic perversions
comprised by the Fugitive Slave Act, the Kansas-Nebraska Act, and *Dred
Scott*. In its overview of the history and politics of slavery, "The Nebraska
Question" ranges far beyond its title. Parker denounces Douglas's perfidy
in repealing the Missouri Compromise only as a coda. The rest (the first
sixty-odd pages) comprises an extended disquisition on the moral progress
of Euro-American civilization, which had thrown off, slowly and with
difficulty, three successive modes of tyranny: "Theocracy, Monarchy, Aristocracy." Now Parker's and Lincoln's generation, the descendants of those
who had struggled for liberty, faced the evilest, most tenacious tyranny
of all, a "Despotocracy" not only of the southern slave power but those in
the free states too timorous and Hamlet-like to "take arms against a sea of
troubles and by opposing end them."[112] The annihilation of "despotocracy"
posed for Parker the last and greatest moral and political work for America.
Succeeding, it would bring about the true age of democracy, which Parker
described in the now-famous triad of "government of all, for all, by all."[113]

By the 1850s, Parker had done with preaching moderation or caution
or any sort of gradualism on slavery simply to preserve the Union. To his
mind, the Union was a political convenience, desirable and expedient only
so long as subject to the "higher law" of natural rights, God-given and
inalienable. The pernicious institution of slavery flaunted Parker's higher
law. If the persistence of the American confederation meant continuing to
tolerate enslavement, why, then, as far as he was concerned, the Union *ought*
to dissolve—with the righteous minority of slavery-hating northerners
taking the initiative for divorce. And if the South for her part truly wished
to part with its more civilized and prosperous brother, good riddance! But
Parker did not expect the North to leave: while it kept making money from
southern cotton, there was no "danger of dissolution"![114]

Lincoln wholly disagreed with Parker about the desirability of disunion
on moral grounds. At the same time, however, he found the concept of the
higher law, when applied to the American Union, attractive. This ideal,
inchoate in his younger years, assumed for Lincoln a much greater intellectual and emotional importance in the second half of the 1850s, and from
1854 on Lincoln too was growing impatient with a South so demanding and
intransigent that it would threaten disunion whenever northern opinion
galled or Congress displeased it. Without agreeing either to abolition or

disunion, what Lincoln could take from Parker was a way to depoliticize the slavery issue by raising it to the moral, effectively transcendental, plane where Right and Rights converged.

Unsurprisingly, Parker's odd coinage *despotocracy* appears nowhere in Lincoln's writings, but *despotism* does—seventy-six times in the *Collected Works* from 1852 on.[115] The most famous instance, often quoted, comes from Lincoln's letter to Joshua Speed of August 24, 1855, whose penultimate paragraph concludes: "As a nation, we began by declaring that '*all men are created equal.*' We now practically read it 'all men are created equal, *except negroes.*' When the Know-Nothings get control, it will read 'all men are created equal, except negroes, *and foreigners, and catholics.*' When it comes to this I should prefer emigrating to some country where they make no pretence of loving liberty—to Russia, for instance, where despotism can be taken pure, and without the base alloy of hypocracy [*sic*]."[116] There is a parallel to Lincoln's sentiment in "The Nebraska Question." After a series of firebrand rhetorical queries concerning the justice of Congress's allowing "two hundred squatters"—said to be the whole number of voters in the Kansas Territory—"to establish the worst institution which Spain brought out of the middle ages . . . [and] Russia treads under her feet," Parker avers that if this be just, he might as well "go back and, O, most Imperial Nicholas! let me learn political justice from thee, though last great tyrant of the Western world!"[117]

Each writer used mid-nineteenth-century Russia as the definitive example of a nation oppressed by the tyranny of an absolute despot who kept a large fraction of his people in serfdom—nearly as deplorable a human, sociopolitical condition, Parker implies, as that of the American South with its chattel slavery. Unless Lincoln had read a newspaper or pamphlet version of "The Nebraska Question," this mutual disgust was probably a coincidence, but an intriguing one.

Parker had the genuine radical's proclivity for "conspiracy theories." So, to a degree did Lincoln, although his conspiracies were more rhetorical and forensic exercises than articles of belief. As the American 1850s unfolded, a decade of crescendo, Parker thought he saw evidences North and South of the slave power's secret and ever more insidious conniving. Like Lincoln, Parker believed there might even be a conspiracy to nationalize slavery in the United States: "The South will claim that the master has a right to take his Slaves into a free state. . . . That will restore Slavery to the North and enable the sons of New England to return to their native land with their 'chattels personal.'"[118] When we consider that Parker spoke *before* the Kansas-Nebraska Act was passed in Congress and signed into law, and fully three years *before* the *Dred Scott* decision, his words sound prescient.

In fact, his vividly imagined scenario resembles Lincoln's own conspiracy theory, first publicly outlined in the House Divided speech in Springfield, June 16, 1858. In the wake of *Dred Scott*, Parker's 1854 forebodings must have seemed to Lincoln entirely justified. Lincoln offered his Illinois Republican audience not only his most famous borrowing of biblical metaphor but a quasi-comic parable of the notorious quartet of house-builders ("Stephen [Douglas], Franklin [Pierce], Roger [Taney] and James [Buchanan]"), who had surreptitiously gotten together to erect a new national edifice that would be "thenceforward and forever" slave. "We cannot absolutely *know* that all these exact adaptations are the result of preconcert. But when we see a lot of framed timbers, different portions of which we know have been gotten out at different times and places and by different workmen—Stephen, Franklin, Roger and James, for instance—and when we see these timbers joined together, and see they exactly make the frame of a house or a mill, all the tenons and mortices exactly fitting . . . in *such* a case, we find it impossible to not *believe* that Stephen and Franklin and Roger and James all understood one another from the beginning."[119]

The parallels and cross-currents between the sermons and speeches of Parker and Lincoln suggest that the latter was stimulated by the New England radical's thought. By the time of the House Divided speech, had Lincoln made his way through *Additional Speeches, Addresses, and Occasional Sermons*—about three months between first seeing the volumes and his nomination speech in Springfield? In his "Thoughts on America" (May 31, 1854), Parker had addressed the annual meeting of the Anti-slavery Convention in Boston. Near the end of a long, fiercely indignant indictment of slavery and a tallying of its dire effects on American civilization, he prophesied a national apocalypse soon to come: nothing less than the death and destruction of the United States. Ultimately, "the question is not merely, shall we have Slavery and Freedom, but Slavery OR Freedom. The two cannot long continue side by side."[120] And a little more than a month later, in a sermon called "The Dangers Which Threaten the Rights of Man in America" (July 2, 1854), Parker declaimed that "there can be no national welfare without national Unity of Action," which presupposes a "national Unity of Idea in fundamentals. Without this a nation is a 'house divided against itself'; of course it cannot stand."[121]

Theodore Parker saw the American house fatally divided just as Lincoln did: "a figure without equilibrium," the parts out of balance, the structure doomed without basic rebuilding ("all *one* thing, or *all* the other"). Lincoln, of course, knew and had employed Mark 3:25 before he ever read Parker. He had combined the figure with Aesop's fable of the bundled sticks in the Whig campaign circular of March 1843.[122] Whatever use of the figure he had made previously, in 1858 Lincoln appears to have perceived both the logic and potential rhetorical effect of the "house divided," borrowed and adapted it from Parker, and gone ahead with the speech, against the advice of his political friends (excepting Herndon). In so doing, he made the saying more nearly immortal than had Jesus, at least for Americans: from universally true to powerfully specific when applied to the arch-topic of slavery as alone capable of rending the Union. The difference between the two "preachers," Parker and Lincoln, was that Parker *did* expect the divided house to fall. And, for the sake of natural rights and the Right, the Higher Law, and the realignment of man with Nature with God, he may even have wanted it to.

From Washington, on March 17, 1862, an ex-Methodist, soon-to-be-ex-Unitarian minister by the name of Moncure Daniel Conway, born in Virginia but long living in the North, wrote to his wife, "By the way Mr. Lincoln said the other day that he had got the 'Rejected Stone' by heart. He said he was astonished to learn that its author was really a native of Virginia."[123] As we have frequently observed, when Abraham Lincoln was truly taken with a poem or a story, he could in fact get it by heart, and often did. Yet if Conway's statement about *The Rejected Stone* is even a fraction true, it must have been a peculiar and painful catechism that Lincoln memorized this time. Here he was, scarcely a year in office, the commander-in-chief of a large army daily growing, managing a civil war that had begun badly for the Union, suddenly finding himself alluded to, even directly addressed, in a book by an abolitionist he hadn't heard of before, one who was urging (if not demanding) that in the name of the "Higher Law" the president emancipate the southern slaves and chastising him for being laggard in this matter. Because *The Rejected Stone* was a 131-page book, we may suppose that Lincoln was characteristically funning when he allowed he had gotten the thing "by heart." He more likely meant that he had *taken the book's lesson about emancipation to heart.*

Conway's *The Rejected Stone* had first appeared in October 1861. It was a shocked, grieving reaction on the part of a now-northern abolitionist to the Union defeat at first Bull Run (Manassas). As so many other abolitionists must have done, Conway had assumed that Union arms would prevail over the "rebels" simply because their antislavery cause was just—godly just ("Mine eyes have seen the glory / Of the coming of the Lord," as Julia Ward Howe would write the following year). That quick, decisive victory eluded the northern troops could only mean that God wanted more of the Lincoln administration and the Union army: He wanted emancipation, and He wanted it then and there!

More than forty years later, in his autobiography, Conway recalled that "at that time of agony I received information from Washington that the Republic of Haiti had sent a message to Washington to request permission to send there an ambassador, and that the Secretary of State, after some evasion, had at last answered, 'The fact is, Washington cannot receive a black minister.'" This injustice led to the writing of his book: "Then there arose before me as if in letters of flame:—*The stone which the builders rejected is become the head of the corner.*"[124] Conway's outrage at William Seward's racist policy resulted in the inspired agitprop of *The Rejected Stone.* For even with the slaveocratic South in full rebellion, diplomatic relations with the New World's *second* republic were interdicted because the ambassador would be black! Obviously, to Conway and the abolitionists, the Union needed prodding, continually, to understand that emancipation was both morally right and a "military necessity." This was the burden of Conway's argument—in a style orphic and aphoristic, fabulous, satirical, rife with dire prophecies, and on every page hortatory.

After the modest success of first publication of *The Rejected Stone,* Conway authorized a "second edition" (really a larger second printing with an added preface), which came out in March 1862.[125] The fact of a reprint indicates a continuing interest in the book, including the president's. As the author wrote in the preface to the new printing, "The victories of our arms, still more this noblest victory,—the word 'Emancipation' uttered from the White House,—make the conditions under which the second edition of this work is issued much brighter than those which attended its original publication" (v).

Whether Lincoln read the 1861 or 1862 printings, he found himself arraigned as the leader of a great national hope now malingering. Yet, oddly, as critical as Conway was of Lincoln's inaction on emancipation, he opened *The Rejected Stone* with a paragraph the president could fully agree with: "In the popular mind, the brave sufferings of our past, the fruitions of our present, and the visions of our future, as a people, are baptized and consecrated in the name of UNION. The very word has thus become a talisman, which, because so long supposed to contain all the secret of our national health and wealth, has gained the command of all the living forces of the New World" (vii). The word *talisman* stands out from its context in this overheated prose. Conway appears to imply that what has long brought good fortune may transform into evil if its owner should come to *idolize* it. This implication is made manifest further along in *The Rejected Stone* with respect to the moral and practical short-sightedness of Unionism for its own sake: "The popular mind has been so Union-besotted, that it has gone blindly, deeper and deeper, into the danger it meant to avoid by clinging to the Union. As an ideal, we should have been guided by it to a solid shore: as an idol, we have drifted with it on the breakers" (21). This deft passage, with its juxtaposition of *ideal* and *idol*, might almost have been a direct exhortation to Lincoln, who, some thought, tended to make and worship the latter out of the former. Quoting Cicero: "Who can tell but that the people may come to believe that these stones and pictures are the gods themselves" (19).

In one of *The Rejected Stone's* central points, Conway took a view of the Founders, the Constitution, and the original status of slavery that Lincoln had long held: "It [the Constitution] was the result of certain compromises made by its builders; and freemen had either to endure it as best they could, or, as some of the bravest did, take sides with the stone which the builders rejected" (15). The "rejected stone" itself was Justice, and Liberty meant emancipation for the several millions in the Republic who had for so long been grievously denied it. But Conway also invoked Parker's "higher law" as prior to and above any social contract, even the Constitution of the United States: "In its susceptibility of amendment, the Constitution recognizes the Higher Law,—the only law that never fails to be executed" (17). The advent of civil war, however, made emancipation by amendment a moot gesture, unacknowledged by the states in rebellion and of little practical effect where slavery did not exist and had not existed for many decades.

Conway also held that the Declaration of Independence, Lincoln's own keystone to the arch of the American Republic, the very stone rejected by Douglas and others, was "a study of the millennium; and that does not bloom on the sapling of one revolution, nor of a thousand." The signers of the Declaration "did but make us a saint's day," and making and keeping it holy was the long, hard work of later generations, the latest of which was Conway's and Lincoln's (20). But Conway could not see concerted action even being contemplated, much less put in train. After half a year's sporadic fighting, the North lay irresolute, the South at the ready. This was the fate of a people who denied its god, versus one that had the bejeweled black idol of slavery well in view. Wittily, Conway urged Lincoln to *get off the fence* and commit to the destruction of slavery. Stay there, he cautioned, and you might just be cut in two, "so razor-like" had the top rail become from years of abrasion "on each side" (30–31). Lincoln had, after all, been elected president by "the noblest revolution the world ever saw," and he ought therefore to combine "the weapons of truth" with those of war to assure the elevation of the "rejected stone" to "the head of the corner" (80).

The entirety of chapter 17 of *The Rejected Stone* takes the form of an open letter to President Lincoln. It amplifies the imperative to get off the fence. And then Conway's supplication of Lincoln begins, in a rolling, biting, emotion-accumulating period: "Now, therefore, I sir, the writer of these pages . . ." and concludes many lines later, "do now implore the President . . . to proclaim to the world that this country links its destiny with that of Universal Freedom." In between, Conway, who notes that he had cast his vote for Lincoln, laments the pain and loss of the war, the alienation of the good citizen, and the apparent ascendancy to power of villains and sycophants (95–96). Here indeed was a passage Lincoln might have "got by heart"!

Beyond the preaching and beseeching, which are relentless throughout the chapter, Conway stressed that what was right according to the "higher law" was also constitutionally permitted. "The Constitution and laws, in providing for possible war, do in case of war, at once deliver up the Government to the laws of war." The means to justice were immediately available to Lincoln because of the presidency's war powers. He should not hesitate to use them.

Conway next wields one of Lincoln's favorite logical ploys, the either/ or disjunction, at the presidential fence-sitter: "Either the principle which placed you in office [Freedom], or the Institution which is in deadly grip with it [Slavery], must fall to the ground." He continues, "to preserve the Union merely" was not why he had been elected by the people: "*that* they had under Fillmore and Buchanan and Pierce" and could have continued such preservation by voting in one or another of Lincoln's opponents. This meant that the *people* wanted something *more*, and *better*, than the old Union countenancing slavery. "If Freedom can alone be free by the destruction of slavery," he declares, "you cannot, in honor, flinch from signing the death-warrant of that system" (105–6). *In honor.* So Lincoln was honor-bound both morally and by the contract of his election. He must hearken to that very "honor's voice" he had first read of in Gray's "Elegy" and act according to what was perhaps the leading principle of his character, as Douglas L. Wilson has so persuasively suggested in his study of the ethical formation of the adult Abraham Lincoln in *Honor's Voice*.

The open letter concludes with a strikingly prophetic vision of what rests on Lincoln's choice. Emancipation, and all will be well with the nation, with glorious fame assured to the Great Emancipator. But to refuse the cup? "Woe to him to whom four millions of slaves shall point their shackled hands, and say, 'There is just the one man, whom, out of Earth's millions, God elected as him who should have power to remove our yokes, to raise us from beasts of burden to men; unsealing for us the fountains of affection, hope, aspiration, which the Father has provided as living water for his weary children. He swooned on the great moment" (111). And was cursed by history. Mighty solemn words, unquestionably. But did they, along with the rest of the exhortations of *The Rejected Stone*, actually convince Lincoln either to draft the Emancipation Proclamation or ultimately to make it Union policy?

A skeptic might say that, at most, Conway's charged presentation of the case for emancipation, like Macbeth's phantom dagger, merely marshaled Lincoln the way he was already going. Any determination of the influence of *The Rejected Stone* is made trickier by our not knowing precisely *when* Lincoln read the book. Still, regarding Conway's letter to his wife (March 17, 1862) as firm evidence of the fact and plausible evidence of the time, we can reasonably hold that *The Rejected Stone* had been on Lincoln's mind in the spring and summer of 1862. During this period, the president (1) on July 1, 1862, issued his formal call for "300,000 volunteers"; (2) on July 12 urged politicians from the slaveholding border states to agree to gradual compensated emancipation to be followed by colonization of free blacks; (3) on July 17 rather reluctantly signed the Second Confiscation Act (which had a provision for the eventual emancipation of slaves taken in the course of war); and (4) on July 22 presented the first draft of the Emancipation Proclamation (which he may have begun composing as far back as early June) to his cabinet.[126] The first of these acts certainly indicated Lincoln's desire to prosecute the war more forcefully; the second and third, his willingness to entertain emancipation as a war measure; and the fourth, his decision to make emancipation the order of the commander-in-chief. In the end, *The Rejected Stone's* contribution may perhaps best be seen as an aid to Lincoln as he concentrated his mind on the question of emancipation and came to his decision.

A coda: Moncure Daniel Conway visits the White House, sometime in January 1862. Senator Charles Sumner of Massachusetts—who may have given Lincoln a copy of *The Rejected Stone*—had obtained an appointment for Conway and his friend, William Henry Channing (William Ellery's nephew), and the two young men arrive promptly at 8 A.M.[127] They hoped to urge—what else?—emancipation, but Conway was anxious lest Lincoln might hold against him his animadversions on the recent firing of Gen. John Charles Frémont over the general's order that rebel property in Missouri be confiscated, including any slaves, who would then be de facto free. Conway, at a mass meeting in Cincinnati (October 24, 1861) had fulminated publicly in denunciation of the administration's behavior, which he took as evidence of appeasement of the border states (especially Kentucky and Missouri, which had remained in the Union *with* slavery). Now, not knowing Lincoln, he anticipated equal treatment. But he and Channing were received warmly enough. In the private interview, as they took turns at persuasion, Conway asked a question right out of *The Rejected*

Stone, whether the people "might not look to him as the coming Deliverer of the Nation from its one great evil?" The president temporized. Conway persisted. The president murmured, perhaps at some future time, and so on. Conway made one last attempt. Lincoln put him off with a story. The present political situation reminded him of that thirsty man down-east in Maine who found he could only obtain liquor from a druggist, but he wasn't sick, and so . . .

Before they knew it, Channing and Conway were out the White House front door and back on the streets of Washington, D.C.[128] And the Emancipation Proclamation nestled snugly in the back pocket of Abraham Lincoln's mind.

5. Nothing Equals Macbeth

He read Shakespear every evening—not the Bible.
— *Ninian W. Edwards, in* Herndon's Informants

No literary influences on Abraham Lincoln are invoked more often, or more uncritically, than the poetic dramas of William Shakespeare and the Christian Bible. And in an important sense, both collections of texts were one: Elizabethan and Jacobean in origin, Shakespeare's published plays and the King James Bible. The cadence, figures, fables, semantics, and syntax all belonged to an era of style and sense long over by Lincoln's time of reading, yet both texts were widely, almost universally, read and treasured as anthologies of Western civilization. The Christian Bible was considered timelessly true in Lincoln's America because so generally believed to be the revealed Word of God. Shakespeare, by contrast, was much less well known, though to initiates like Lincoln his works comprised a kind of secular Bible, full of unimpeachable, universal, humanistic wisdom to match the divine—but not for those demanding certainty. Shakespeare's truth was in the dialectic of the dramatic agon; his manifold truths carried by serpentine verse through the labyrinth of plot and character whose heart, if found, beat in the syncopation of "forever questions." In fact Lincoln used these two great sources very differently: the Bible he employed for his *public* utterances, while Shakespeare typically served as the final existential statement of how he, as a private person, saw the human condition. The Bible for the country: Shakespeare for himself. Not that this formula is absolute or may be fairly measured quantitatively: two significant exceptions to the "public" rule will be noted below.

We know that Lincoln "carried a well-worn copy of Shakespeare" and at one trial used Iago's famous lines from *Othello*—"Who steals my purse steals trash," and so on—to win acquittal for two boys who refused to pay a debt when it came due.[1] But the fact remains that despite several allusions to Shakespeare's plays in his *Collected Works*, Lincoln employs only one, *King Lear*, in political argument (a comic remark of the Fool concerning Lear: "He's a shelled pea's cod"),[2] while he employs the Bible in a hortatory context much more freely and frequently. Charles Edward Macartney, in *Lincoln and the Bible* (1949), tallied "seventy-seven quotations from, or references to, the Bible" in the speeches and writings of Abraham Lincoln.[3] Macartney's short book is marred by the illogic of its Christian apologetic thesis (to *allude* to the Bible is hardly the same thing as to accept any theology derived from it). And his count of seventy-seven quotations is highly misleading: though the number might sound large—as if Lincoln were a preacher taking a text every time he spoke publicly—nearly half (34) of Lincoln's biblical references occur in a single work, the first lecture on "Discoveries and Inventions," wherein the author uses the Hebrew Bible as a source for talking about the technical and industrial progress of human civilization (and there is not a jot of religion in the lecture).[4] More generally, we find that when Lincoln employs a biblical story or figure, he often does so either humorously or didactically, without being at all religious in Macartney's conventional Methodist way.

Still, *Lincoln and the Bible* remains a useful source for considering Lincoln's rhetorical tactics in mustering the "Good Book" to advance his own political agenda. Concerning the Lincoln-Douglas debates, Macartney noted that "in 1858 the knowledge of the Bible and the ability to quote it was an effective and popular weapon of the political orator, and no one used that weapon more successfully than Lincoln."[5] While we may reasonably doubt this last assertion, Macartney was right about an 1858 audience's acuity in recognizing even embedded biblical allusion within political speechifying. As a gifted communicator, Lincoln could rely on seasoning his words with timely echoes of or references to the Scriptures in order to connect with *all* of his audience, even when—or perhaps most effectively when—he employed the Christian Scriptures silently. A telling example of this covert deployment of the Bible occurs in the 1838 Lyceum Address. In his opening, Lincoln praises the Founding Founders for their mighty Revolution and the establishment of the American Republic: "Their's [*sic*] was the task (and nobly they performed it)," so enduringly that no European (or other world power) could "by force, take a drink from the Ohio, or make a track on the Blue Ridge, in a trial of a thousand years." This reads—and must have sounded—like nationalistic rodomontade coming from the throat of a young orator of ability, just about to turn twenty-nine years of age and trying his voice not as a state legislator or a political candidate but an intellectual among peers. Lincoln warned his audience, as patriotic

Americans, to fear not invasion but internal devolution: "If destruction be our lot, we must ourselves be its author and finisher. As a nation of freemen, we must live through all time, or die by suicide."[6]

Two aspects of the Lyceum Address have struck critics and biographers, one stylistic and the other topical: the taint of purple in Lincoln's rhetoric and the identity of the great tyrant—some American Caesar or Napoleon—whom Lincoln imagines might one day overthrow a Republic internally weakened by mobocratic behavior. Passionate and irrational retaliatory social behavior (lynching a hapless black or murdering the Illinois abolitionist Elijah Lovejoy) was for Lincoln a potentially fatal falling away from the standard of America's "political religion." Mob rule, generalized across the land, signified a broken covenant. But a covenant that had been autochthonously engendered by *ourselves* for *ourselves*, rather than one made more or less under duress with the Hebrew or Christian God. In this regard, it is striking to know that the phrase "author and finisher" quoted above has its origin in the Christian Bible, Hebrews 12:2: "Looking unto Jesus, the author and finisher of our faith." As both *authors* and *finishers* of our own national faith, Lincoln set responsibility for its perpetuation squarely in the laps of the people, individually and together. Did his silent invocation of "author and finisher," then, resonate with his audience of young men in Springfield, on January 27, 1838? Subtly, it probably did: Lincoln got preacher's points without acting the preacher.[7]

Such covert use of the Bible contrasts with the much more famous "house divided" figure employed twenty years later. In his Springfield speech accepting the Republican nomination for senator, Lincoln undertook his oratorical task *exactly* as a minister before a congregation. After a solemn introduction, Lincoln announced his text: "A house divided against itself cannot stand." In the preceding chapter, we examined the sources that could have suggested to Lincoln the use of this red-letter language of Jesus (Mark 3:25). The point here is that both Lincoln and his audience would readily have known the verse—if not the rather obscure parable in which it occurs—and that its figuration was both logical and prophetic: to remain whole, the Union would have to "become all *one* thing, or *all* the other."[8] Slyly, perhaps, Lincoln did not remind his hearers that these were the Christian God's words. Coming from his unsanctified lips, this would have been inappropriate, if not hypocritical. Lincoln thus successfully enlisted the Christian rhetoric of "a house divided" into the service of his "political religion."

During the early debates with Douglas, the incumbent pummeled Lincoln for having said that the Union, as the divided house, could not "endure, permanently half *slave* and half *free*." Why not? Douglas asked rhetorically; after all, it *had* endured that way since its founding. And Lincoln, Douglas insisted, was demagogically stirring up sectional, if not abolitionist, feeling by declaring otherwise. Lincoln's attempts to meet such criticism were aided by a small forensic trick. During the opening debate (at Ottawa, August 28, 1858), Douglas forcibly asserted that the Founders had known just what they were doing when they framed the Constitution so as (silently) to allow the continuation of slavery in whichever states wished to do so. And ever since, he added, the national union had not only endured, whether as a compromise or a consensus, but prospered, as be believed it would prosper into the future.[9] Lincoln countered by playing what we today would call "the religion card," but humorously, so as to avoid any taint of hypocrisy.

When Lincoln came to the podium, after asking one of his backers to hold his coat while he "stoned Stephen," he threw Douglas's charge back in his face: "Does the Judge say it *can* stand?" If so, then his quarrel was not with Lincoln but with "an authority of a somewhat higher character." This of course brought laughter. And Lincoln astutely followed up his advantage with a version of "but seriously, folks": "I know that the Judge may readily enough agree with me that the maxim which was put forth by the Saviour is true, but he may allege that I misapply it."[10] What Abraham Lincoln says may not be true; what Jesus said is unassailably true, because he is God-in-Christ, the "Saviour" of the fallen human race. According to the 1828 Webster's *American Dictionary of the English Language* (one of the dictionaries Lincoln knew and used), "savior" is "properly applied only to Jesus Christ . . . Geo. Washington may be called the saver, but not the *savior* of his country." There is a touch of effrontery in Lincoln's invocation of "Saviour," for he was never a Christian, nor arguably at this time even a theist (though he may have died as one).[11] Yet he appealed to the reflexive religiosity of his audience: if the *Saviour* said it, it was true; and the application of the "house divided" figure to the Union was thereby biblically sanctioned. Standing or falling, however, what the country demanded in 1858 was a flesh-and-blood Saver to work out in the Republic the ineffable will of the Saviour's Father.

In January 1851, old Tom Lincoln lay dying in his cabin in Coles County, Illinois. After ignoring three letters from family members communicating news of his father's mortal illness, his son finally responded: Abraham Lincoln would not be coming down to Coles, as he was too busy, not to mention that his wife Mary was "sick-abed." But he had some advice for his father: "tell him to remember to call upon, and confide in, our great, and good, and merciful Maker; who will not turn away from him in any extremity.

He notes the fall of a sparrow, and numbers the hairs on our heads; and He will not forget the dying man, who puts his trust in Him."[12] And Lincoln concluded with a line or two of hope that the whole clan would be reunited in heaven. The author of *Lincoln and the Bible*, concerned to make Lincoln a Christian believer (as well as a good son), twice calls this a "beautiful letter." A number of Lincoln's best modern biographers have been far less kind. Albert J. Beveridge detected "among these familiar phrases of unction . . . the life-long antagonism" Lincoln had felt for his father; Benjamin Thomas noted that the letter had an "unconvincing tone" without "even a pretense of affection"; and David Donald, too, found Lincoln's words "unconvincing" as well as "strained," adding that it was "really addressed to his backwoods relatives who thought in the clichés of Primitive Baptists."[13]

None of the three biographers thinks for a moment that Lincoln himself believed the "familiar phrases of unction" he was writing. In fact, the sanctimony of the words reveals Lincoln at his most hypocritical. Every sparrow's fall noticed by God and the numbered hairs of a man's head (Matthew 10:29–31; Luke 12:6–7) are familiar (and harmless) nostrums that could provide a sort of etiolated consolation to a dying man and his family. But the picture of a heavenly family reunion was to Lincoln hardly imaginable. Would the circle be unbroken by and by? Would there be a better home awaiting in the sky? Most probably not, but the sentiment sufficed for a dying father whom the son had never loved.

The popular and eloquent preacher Henry Ward Beecher was for a time in 1862 editor of the *New York Independent*, and a most unfriendly paper to Lincoln it was. Someone having presented him with a clipping collection of Beecher's editorials, Lincoln began looking them over. He became angry, and with reason. The editor had written not only antiadministration polemics—Beecher was perturbed that emancipation had not happened—but personal attacks that wounded Lincoln where he was most vulnerable, his humble social origins and lack of education: "It would be difficult for a man to be born lower than he was. He is an unshapely man. He is a man that bears evidence of not having been educated in schools or in circles of refinement."[14] It may have been at this point in his reading that Lincoln, "dashing the package [of clippings] to the floor . . . exclaimed, 'Is thy servant a *dog*, that he should do this thing?'"[15] A very good question, and had the Reverend Beecher heard it, he would have recognized its source (2 Kings 8:13). Lincoln's hurt and anger were raw in him. For the little fyce that had four years ago yelped at Douglas and nipped at his heels was now president of the United States and commander-in-chief of the Union army. Yet still did he think of himself as some sort of detested yellow dog by comparison with more socially accomplished men.

One of the more problematic biographers of Abraham Lincoln is Henry C. Whitney. Though manifestly a close associate of Lincoln on the Illinois 8th Judicial Circuit between the years of 1854 and 1858, and arguably even Lincoln's friend during that period and the Washington years, Whitney's recollections of the man, written long afterward, have often been taken with a dose of skepticism by Lincoln scholars. Doubts of his veracity have arisen not from Whitney's main work, *Life on the Circuit with Lincoln* (1892), but because of his publication in 1896 of what he claimed to be a verbatim record of Lincoln's "Lost Speech" (delivered in Bloomington, Illinois, on May 29, 1856). The editors of *The Collected Works of Abraham Lincoln* (1952), still the canonical Lincoln, rejected the Whitney text as unreliable if not bogus, and today the scholarly consensus is that, for whatever reason, Whitney fabricated the whole thing.

Nonetheless, some of Whitney's remarks on Lincoln's self-culture merit examination. Consider this passage from *Life on the Circuit with Lincoln*: "His favorite books were the Bible, Shakespeare, Bacon, Burns, Petroleum V. Nasby's letters, Baldwin's Flush Times of Alabama and Recollections of A. Ward, Showman. Was there ever such a curious *mélange* of almost supreme greatness and boyish vacuity as was compressed in this unique, uneven and incomprehensible man?"[16] Here is a very strange list of seven favorite books, one that, if accurate, really is the outward sign of a man whose mind and emotions truly were a "*mélange*." Whitney alone among all informants on Lincoln's reading mentions Francis Bacon, and most of us today would not even have heard of the other three authors and their books and would be puzzled to see the strange names of A(rtemus) Ward and Petroleum V(esuvius) Nasby in the company of Shakespeare!

Oddly, however, from corroborating testimony we know that Nasby *was* a Lincoln favorite, and Ward too. The pen names of David Ross Locke and Charles Farrar Browne, respectively, they were among the most popular "literary comedians" of the Civil War era, writing topical satire from the viewpoint of the everyday American. Lincoln was an avid reader and reciter of both. With Joseph Glover Baldwin's *Flush Times of Alabama and Mississippi* (1853), the case is weaker. But since Baldwin was a recent literary ancestor of both Ward and Nasby, we may plausibly suppose that Lincoln read and appreciated *Flush Times* because of this kinship.

Which leaves the seventh name on Whitney's list: Francis Bacon, the Elizabethan and Jacobean courtier and intellectual whose *Essays* (collected and published in final form in 1625) have become, along with Montaigne's, supreme classics in the genre of the familiar or personal essay. In an 1898 article for the *Arena* magazine, Whitney elaborated on the matter of Lincoln and Bacon: "He once spoke to me in highly eulogistic terms of Bacon, at which I expressed surprise, and ventured to object that he had been accused of receiving bribes." True, Lincoln admitted, but what he took never affected his legal decisions, which were straightforward and just! He admired Bacon, Whitney recalled, "in spite of his flagitiousness."[17] Lincoln apparently knew Bacon's biography, especially the story of his great fall when convicted (not merely accused) of having taken bribes while holding the eminent office of Lord Chancellor in 1621.[18]

The Francis Bacon of the *Essays* is learned to such an extent that Lincoln could not have read him without aids. He would have needed a text like that of "Knight's English Classics" (London, 1840), in which the many Latin quotations are translated (with the original Latin included as footnotes) and the spelling is modernized. Of the fifty-eight pieces comprising the 1625 edition, a majority cover topics of character and conduct and of statecraft. Of the latter, we might well say *princecraft*, since Bacon writes on this subject with a distinctly Machiavellian bent. Many of his essays treat of the power and conduct of "the Prince"—for which topics Lincoln maintained a Byronic fascination—and he would have discovered in Bacon a felicitous, though antique, style and wit, propelled by apt deployment of fable, parable, and maxim—all as seasonings for his benevolent cynicism, or *Realpolitik*.

In the very first of his essays, "Of Truth," Bacon equates honesty with truth in matters of "civil business." But probity, while necessary to both prince and courtier (much more, he thinks, to the latter), is not by itself sufficient: for while "clear and round dealing is the honor of the man's nature," yet "that mixture of falsehood is like alloy in coin of gold and silver, which may make the metal work better, but it embaseth it."[19] To Bacon's mind, this was the way ambitious men were, the way the polite world was. If not himself a cynic, Lincoln as president had to understand those who were, and so became, as Seward famously said, "the best of us." Similarly, in "Of Simulation and Dissimulation," Bacon could have been describing Lincoln the political artist when he wrote, "if a man have that penetration of judgment as he can discern what things are to be laid open, and what to be secreted, and what to be showed at half-lights, and to whom and when . . . to him a habit of dissimulation is a hindrance and a poorness." The moral: do not dissimulate; rather, "set it down, that a habit of secrecy is both politic and moral."[20]

Deliberately or not, President Lincoln comported himself politically according to Bacon's maxim. In managing his cabinet, he often acted as if Bacon were his mentor: "As to secrecy, princes are not bound to communicate all matters with all counselors, but may extract and select; neither is it necessary that he that consulteth what he should do, should declare what he will do." What Bacon called the "unsecreting" of affairs came not from the prince himself but his advisers, any one of whom might be "*full of leaks.*" It followed that "the greatest virtue of a prince is to know his own."[21] And understanding his opponents comes next: "If you would work any man, you must either know his nature and fashions, and so lead him; or his ends, and so persuade him; or his weaknesses and disadvantages, and so awe him." In important matters, a ruler "may not look to sow and reap at once; but must prepare business, and so ripen it by degrees."[22] This describes Lincoln's approach to leadership very well.

Here are the opening words of the essay "Of Great Place": "Men in great place are thrice servants; servants of the sovereign or state; servants of fame; and servants of freedom; so as they have no freedom, neither in their persons, nor in their actions, nor in their times."[23] The sentiment reminds us of Lincoln's remark that he "had not controlled events, but events had controlled" him. The man in great place was never free. For Bacon, it was "the solecism of power" to pursue an end "and yet not endure the means." When we think of Lincoln's agonized introspection about his leadership and its relationship to history, fate, destiny, or God's will (as in the "Meditation on the Divine Will"), we can imagine Bacon's words in the president's mind: "*Remember that thou art a man* and *Remember that thou art a God* or *a representative of God*; the one bridleth their power and the other their will."[24] More generally, with regard to managing people, whether important or importunate, Bacon and Lincoln agreed: "It is a point of cunning. . . . that when you have anything to obtain of present dispatch, you entertain and amuse the party with whom you deal with some other discourse, that he be not too much awake to make objections."[25] Right out of Lincoln's handbook of politesse!

How often did Lincoln get his way or deflect his opposition through the diversion of some "back in Illinois" story, relevant to the business at hand or not! Bacon amplifies his point, almost as if he had the far-future Lincoln in mind: "Some have in readiness so many tales and stories, as there is nothing they would insinuate, but they can wrap it into a tale, which serveth both to keep themselves more in guard, and to make others carry it with more pleasure."[26] Even when Lincoln's auditors knew a story was coming, and that they would be had, the comedy resistlessly played itself out, typically with the audience as butt and the president remaining one-up in the unending political game.

Bacon did not have to face the ethical dilemma of African chattel slavery, which had scarcely begun in British North America by the time of his death. But he did warn his readers of an analogous kind of slavery created by debt. "Of Usury" (by which he means money lent at any interest rather than at exorbitant interest, as in our conventional sense) argues that the debtor, as Bacon knew to his deep chagrin, might easily become indentured to his debts. The immorality, however, lay with the lender: "The usurer breaketh the first law that was made for mankind after the fall, which was, *in the sweat of thy face shalt thou eat thy bread;* not, *in the sweat of another's face.*" Thus was he also the "greatest Sabbath-breaker, because his plough"—accumulating interest—"goeth every Sunday."[27] The usurer hurt himself, his victim, and the commonwealth. To Lincoln, one human's holding another in slavery became the moral equivalent of a usurer's bleeding his debtor: both were thereby robbed of a freedom they were entitled to by nature.

Lincoln often turned to Genesis 3:19 when he wished to illustrate the natural right of all members of humankind to possess the product of their labors.[28] He demonstrated an especially withering anger against southern Christian preachers who defended slavery as "ordained of God." The preacher sits in the shade while his slave "Sambo" works. Is it by "God's will" that the one labors and the other eats the fruits of that labor? The preacher's Bible is silent on the matter, or at most ambiguous. So the preacher/slave owner has the final say: but if he detects that indeed God wishes Sambo to be free, then the preacher will have to go to work for his own bread. Will he then "be actuated by that perfect impartiality, which has ever been considered most favorable to correct decisions?"[29]

Of Bacon's essays on character and conduct, several offer insights relevant both to Lincoln's self-estimation and to the man his friends and acquaintances closely observed but scarcely succeeded in knowing. One of the president's most admirable traits was his forbearance, often shown through a kindred virtue, patience. Though he felt keenly the constant slings and arrows that struck him from the press, from the political opposition, even from his friends, he rarely shot back. As one newspaper reporter noted (in 1862), "'Mr. Lincoln is a *good listener.* He will patiently hear any man, (unless he is reminded of an anecdote, which he at once relates,) and he thus patiently gathers tribute from all, often submitting to severe criticisms from tried friends.'"[30] Lincoln understood that everyone wanted something from him and always from self-interested motives. Thus he would have agreed with Bacon's observation, "why should I be angry with a man for loving himself better than me?" The more serious the wrong, and the greater the power of the prince, the more forbearing he should be: "it is a prince's part to pardon; and Solomon, I am sure, saith, *It is the glory of a man to pass by an offense.*"[31] Who "studieth revenge keeps his own wounds green, which otherwise would heal."[32]

Love, envy, ambition—this trio of related "affections" (passions) Bacon considered the strongest. Love, insists the essayist, great spirits have nothing to do with, since love and wisdom are incommensurable.[33] Envy and ambition, however, are not so easily disposed of; even the wisest of public men suffer from the one because constantly prodded by the other. For more than twenty years, from the late 1830s on, Stephen A. Douglas had been Lincoln's arch-competitor, the person whom he envied most in the area where his ambition pricked the most: politics. "Envy is ever joined"—this from "Of Envy"—"with the comparing of a man's self; and where there is no comparison, no envy."[34]

Near the end of 1856, Lincoln admitted Douglas's superiority: "With *me*, the race of ambition has been a failure—a flat failure; with *him* it has been one of splendid success."[35] Yet in the 1858 campaign for the senate, he hoped to show himself Douglas's equal or perhaps overtop him. Lincoln could not help knowing he was in an invidious position with Douglas. Aside from his own sensitivity to social standing, all he would have had to do was compare his opponent's parades through the congressional districts of Illinois, full of the pomp and circumstance of partying supporters, first-class private railway carriages and cannons to announce his arrival at every stop along the way—compare this with his own humble dress, minimal entourage, and occasional inability even to get a seat on the crowded Illinois Central with its unfriendly conductors. He had revealed this invidiousness in the House Divided speech. Invoking "the Preacher" (Ecclesiastes 9:4), Lincoln declared, "a *living dog* is better than a *dead lion*"—with Douglas the lion that was, if not dead, "caged and toothless," while a high-yapping but determined little fyce named Lincoln nipped around his feet.[36] The outcome of the election indicated that this dog's day hadn't quite come, but the living dog had been heard; and, in fact, the caged and toothless lion would indeed be dead, politically and physically, within two years.

Bacon took for granted that the traits of human character were influenced (if not caused) by the balancing act of the Medieval "four humours." The key to mental health was *balance*. The characteristic of ambition derived from the work of the humor choler, which "maketh men active, earnest, full of alacrity, and stirring." But if blocked, choler "becometh adust [fiery], and thereby malign and venomous." When checked in their careers, however, the ambitious "become secretly discontent . . . which is the worst property in a servant of a prince or state."[37] Were we to substitute *depressed* for *secretly discontent* we would have the "humourous" diagnosis of Lincoln's melancholy. This is not altogether to joke: ambition thwarted can cause anger, and anger self-directed can in turn cause depression: choler (yellow bile) becomes melancholy (black bile).[38]

Several times in this book we have seen Lincoln's fascination with "vaulting ambition." From introspection, he knew its power over the personality; from reading, he recognized the allure of "bestriding" (one of his preferred verbs in this context) the world like a colossus; and from political experience, especially of course the presidency, he concluded, along with Bacon, that the ruler could not *unbridle* ambition and hope successfully to govern over the long term: "He that seeketh to be eminent amongst able men, hath a great task, but that is ever good for the public; but he that plots to be the only figure amongst ciphers is the decay of a whole age."[39] So proved Napoleon and Stephen A. Douglas. But somehow Abraham Lincoln remained "ever good for the public."

While neither physically deformed nor really ugly—as he, joking or serious, sometimes considered himself to be—Lincoln often suffered the contempt of those who thought his ungainly physiognomy betokened a bumpkin within. How wrong they were—Stanton, McClelland, and the rest. In "Of Deformity," Bacon observed that "whosoever hath anything fixed in his person that doth induce contempt, hath also a perpetual spur in himself to rescue and deliver himself from scorn."[40] If applied to Lincoln, Bacon's shrewd perception anticipates, quite remarkably, the diagnoses of modern psychology. According to psychologist G. Stanley Hall, "[Lincoln's] height, long limbs, rough exterior, and frequent feeling of awkwardness must have very early made him realize that to succeed in life he must cultivate intrinsic mental and moral traits, which it is so hard for a handsome man or woman to excel in. Hence he compensated by trying to develop intellectual distinction."[41] The operation of this "perpetual spur" can be seen in Lincoln's deliberate, unstinting self-education. Reading, writing, and speaking gave authority to the political artist; but reading especially also gave pleasure. Lincoln the mature writer would have admired the balanced syntax and the wisdom of this passage from Bacon's "Of Studies": "Studies serve for delight, for ornament, and for ability. Their chief use for delight is in privateness and retiring; for ornament, is in discourse; and for ability, is in the judgment of business. . . . To spend too much time in studies is sloth; to use them too much for ornament is affectation; to make judgment wholly by their rules is the humour of a scholar." And all this is capped with a maxim: "[Studies] perfect nature, and are perfected by experience."[42] One can see this educational "receipt" in Lincoln's political practice: poetry and Shakespeare for private delight; the Bible and rhetorical studies for public speeches and writings; and essays like these by Bacon as a supplement to judgment. Another tricolon fits Lincoln almost uncannily well: "Reading maketh a full man; conference a ready man; and writing an exact man." The younger Lincoln's self-discipline in mastering Euclidean geometry shows that he was of a similar mind to the Elizabethan judge and courtier: "let him study the mathematics; for in demonstrations, if his wit be called away never so little, he must begin again." In sum, "every defect of the mind may have a special receipt" in study—melancholy included.[43]

Abraham Lincoln, the aspiring rookie politician (1832), confessed that his "peculiar ambition" was simply "being truly esteemed of my fellow men, by rendering myself worthy of their esteem."[44] To put this in Baconian terms, by acting honorably Lincoln hoped to gain honor, the achievement of which "is but the revealing of a man's virtue and worth without disadvantage." And heroic honor consists of action in accordance with high ambition—such action as "hath not been attempted before," and done not in pursuit of fame but for meritorious ends.[45] Of Bacon's five "degrees of sovereign honor," the first three are the original founders of states and commonwealths, the lawgivers, and the "*deliverers* or *preservers*."[46] In the Lyceum Address (or "The Perpetuation of Our Political Institutions"), the founder is of course Washington; the lawgiver(s), the makers of the Constitution. But the "deliverer or preserver," the leader that rescues his country from "servitude of strangers or tyrants," who might that be? Such a one qualifies for "an honor . . . which may be ranked amongst the greatest, which happeneth rarely; that is, of such as sacrifice themselves to death or danger for the good of their country."[47]

On Monday, September 22, 1862, Lincoln convened his cabinet at the White House in order to discuss the promulgation of the preliminary Emancipation Proclamation. Ahead of this momentous business, the president read to his captive audience a curious composition entitled "High-Handed Outrage at Utica." It was from the pen of the literary comedian Charles Farrar Browne, better known to his legions of readers as Artemus Ward (according to Carl Sandburg, Browne had recently sent Lincoln a copy of *Artemus Ward: His Book* [1862], which contained "High-Handed Outrage" among its many comic sketches).[48] All but one of the cabinet liked the reading, or pretended to. The exception was Edwin Stanton, "who thought it inappropriately frivolous for such a solemn occasion."[49] Lincoln's affection for low-brow humor from all regions of the United States is well attested. Biographers from J. G. Holland (1865) to Michael Burlingame (2008) have mentioned the story by Artemus Ward at the Emancipation Proclamation cabinet meeting.[50] But alone among them, Carl Sandburg chose to delve into the *why* of Lincoln's demotic taste, to which he devoted several pages—really an interpolated essay in literary criticism—in *Abraham Lincoln: The War Years* (1939) to explore the peculiarities of the genre. "High-Handed Outrage" is in many respects typical. Browne wrote for the *Cleveland Plain Dealer*, couching Ward's dialect "lubrications" as familiar letters to the editor of that important western paper. The sketch Lincoln offered to the cabinet is short (running less than two book-pages). It features the author's trademark phonetic orthography, malapropos word choice, salty idiomatic language, and irreverence toward its subject. Artemus Ward, the traveling circus showman (think P. T. Barnum in small), gives his editor the freshest advice from exotic American locales such as "Utiky, York State." Among the showman's attractions was a wax figure tableau of the Last Supper. All was going well until "a big burly feller" approached the display, grabbed the figure of Judas by the feet, and commenced stomping him. Waxen or not, said the native, "Judas Iscarrot can't show hisself in Utiky with impunerty by a darn site!" What could Ward do but sue him for damages? And the "Joory brawt in a verdick of Arson in the 3d degree."[51]

Lincoln's reading took only a couple of minutes, hardly an imposition even on the dour and self-serious Stanton, while the rest of his cabinet should have enjoyed the brevity of the "Outrage," if nothing else. But why did Lincoln admire this sort of thing, and, as some said, inordinately? First, because Browne and the tribe of literary comedians made him laugh and quite probably right out loud—when, that is, he did not "'preserve his own gravity, though his auditors might be convulsed'"[52]; second, because the dialect and narrative manner were cognate with his own and formed part of his storytelling technique; and third, at least as important, the broad, democratic satire of every kind of American pretence was dear to Lincoln's heart, and an old literary habit of his own, even though as president he mostly bit his tongue rather than say what was on his mind. So he read and quoted the literary comedians instead.

Like many people with a strong sense of humor, Lincoln needed his most when under the greatest stress. His friend, biographer, and Illinois congressman, Isaac N. Arnold, recalled meeting with the president at the White House in the immediate aftermath of the Battle of Fredericksburg (December 13, 1862). Instead of commiserating over the Union defeat, as he expected, Arnold found himself listening to Lincoln reading Ward's sketch on his visit to the Shakers.[53] The congressman was sufficiently shocked to remonstrate: "Mr. President, is it possible that with the whole land bowed in sorrow and covered with a pall in the presence of yesterday's fearful reverse, you can indulge in such levity?" And Carl Sandburg picks up the story from here: "Then . . . the President threw down the Artemus Ward book, tears streamed down his cheeks, his physical frame quivered as he burst forth, 'Mr. Arnold, if I could not get momentary respite from the crushing burden I am constantly carrying, my heart would break!' And with that pent-up cry let out, it came over Arnold that the laughter of Lincoln was a mask."[54]

Or was it genuinely therapeutic? The painter Francis Carpenter thought that Lincoln received from humor "the relief which another man would have found in a glass of wine."[55] The president needed to laugh, and Ward et al. provided the kind of writing that would work its cure on him. They were "the foremost funnymen of the age," Sandburg observes, "important voices of democracy," and they "understood the ways of Lincoln"—adopting him as one of their own.[56] Lincoln, of course, knew all about the vagaries of country juries that delivered verdicts of third-degree arson in cases where there had been no fire, nor for that matter sufficient heat to melt wax. There is also Browne's subtext (really bubbling at or quite near the surface) of religious intolerance as destructive to the Republic, which we know appealed to Lincoln. The true Democrat must be tolerant in all things social and political , while the narrow and ignorant scion of "1 of the first famerlies in Utiky" must be made to appear ridiculous.

Browne himself was a staunch Unionist but not especially friendly to blacks, free or slave. Still, he supported Lincoln politically and was comically sympathetic to Lincoln's plight in defending himself against the plague of office seekers that descended upon him even before his inauguration. Browne's caricature of an Abraham Lincoln helpless before such an assault created a comic type that would be continued and elaborated by other writers (most notably Robert Henry Newell, whose pen name said it all: "Orpheus C. Kerr"). Of all the Artemus Ward vignettes, surely Lincoln would have appreciated most the one about himself, "An Interview with President Lincoln." Purportedly the fruit of a personal call on the president-elect in Springfield—late in 1860 or early in 1861—Browne's Ward's burlesque depiction of Lincoln at bay in his own home is worthy of Mark Twain, who in fact would soon be doing similar comic sketches.

"'I hav no politics,'" Ward announces at the beginning of the piece. "Nary a one." And "there4" he might visit Lincoln's "humstid" with the clearest of consciences: neither offering political advice nor begging for a job for having supported the Republican ticket. "I found the old feller in his parler, surrounded by a perfeck swarm of orfice seekers." Naturally, Lincoln thinks he's just another such, but Artemus quickly disabuses him: "'Mr. Linkin, who do you spect I air?'" As an independent traveling showman, conscious of the duty he owed to circus traditions, office-seeking was far beneath him; he had come simply to pay his respects to the new president.

> "Mr Ward, sit down. I am glad to see you, sir."
> "Repose in Abraham's Buzzum!" sed one of the orfice seekers, his idee bein to git orf a goak [joke] at my expense.
> "Wall," sez I, "ef all you fellers repose in that there Buzzum thare'll be mity poor nussin for sum of you!" whereupon Old Abe buttoned his weskit clear up and blusht like a maidin of sweet 16.

This might have quieted the first lot, but just then a second, and then a third group forced their way into Mr. Lincoln's parlor (where is wife Mary? She would have shown them the door, and quick). "One man from Ohio," Ward remarks, "who had about seven inches of corn whiskey into him, mistook me for Old Abe, and addrest me as 'The Pra-hayrie Flower of the West,'" while another suppliant with a prominently red nose flattered the president-elect as "a seckind Washington & the Pride of the Boundless West." Ward, always the showman and now suddenly a deal maker, proceeds to offer red-nose a "small post-office," but that proud Ohioan, offended, rebukes him: "A patrit is abuv them things, sir!"[57] And so on and on, or "etsettery & sow 4th," as the irrepressible Ward would say (and write). Burlesque, once well launched, can but burlesque its way to an absurd ending. Following a spirited denunciation of the office seekers' venality and impudence, the showman threatens the mass of suitors with an attack from his menagerie (waiting in cages outside) if they won't leave poor Old Abe alone (and note the quotation from *Macbeth*): "'Go home. Stand not upon the order of your goin, but go to onct! Ef in five minits from this time'" sez I, pullin out my new sixteen dollar huntin cased watch, and brandishin it before their eyes—'Ef in a single sole of you remains on these here premises, I'll go out to my cage near by, and let my Boy Constructor loose! & ef he gits among you, you'll think old Solferino has cum again and no mistake!'" Lincoln was grateful: "'How kin I every repay you, Mr. Ward, for your kindness?'" Not, the showman replied, with a job but by "'givin the whole country a good, sound administration. By poerin ile upon the troubled waturs, North and South. By pursooin a patriotic, firm, and just course, and then, if any State wants to secede, let 'em Sesesh!'" The president-elect could not take the last part of this sound advice, but he liked the rest.[58]

On April 6, 1865, very near the end of the war, and his life, Lincoln gave a last recital of Artemus Ward. He and his entourage were encamped at City Point, Virginia, after the president had visited Petersburg and the abandoned Confederate capital of Richmond. While relaxing, we may suppose, in the tent of Col. Theodore S. Bowers, Lincoln read from Browne's sketch, "Cruise of the Polly Ann."[59] Why Lincoln chose this text from all those available in *Artemus Ward: His Book* becomes clear when we note the context. A burlesque of coursing the "high seas" of the "Wabash Canawl" is comically fitting, since young Lincoln had twice been a riverman on flatboats bound for New Orleans but never journeyed beyond fresh water. What is more, the president and his entourage had gently floated down the Potomac aboard the steamer *River Queen* and would very soon steam serenely back up the river to the capital. "Cruise of the Polly Ann" is a raucous send-up of the "two-years-before-the-mast" genre, of the sea-voyage that makes a boy a man, as told from a lately rediscovered diary. The "vyge" took place when Ward had been a young man, in whose "Brite Lexington . . . thar aint no sich word as fale." The running joke of the piece depends for effect upon the comic substitution of canal tow-horses for sails and wind power, muddy water for high seas: "Monday, 2. P.M. Got under wa. Hosses not remarkable frisky at fust. Had to build fires under 'em before they'd start." Once moving, though, they pulled the *Polly Ann* "threw deliteful country. Honist farmers was to work sowin korn, and other projuce in the fields. Sublime scenery. Large red-heded gal reclining on the banks of the Canawl, bathin her feet."[60] All was smooth "sailing" until Wednesday, when Ward "riz early" to find a "hevy sea on, and ship rollin wildly in consekents of pepper-corns having bin fastened to the forrerd hoss's tail. 'Heave two!' roared the capting to the man at the rudder, as the Polly give a friteful toss. I was sick, an sorry I'd cum. 'Heave two!' I hearn him holler agin, and stickin my hed out of the cabin winder, *I hev*."[61]

Except for the "capting's" being beaten to a pulp while drinking ashore at a "grocery," the remainder of the cruise passed peacefully. "Eventually we reached our jerny's end. This was in the days of Old Long Sign, be4 the iron hoss was foaled. This was be4 steambotes was goin round bustin their bilers & sendin peple higher nor a kite. Them was happy days"[62]—for Lincoln on the Mississippi in 1828 and 1831, as on the Wabash Canawl for Artemus Ward: Old Long Sign.

Another humorist whose works Lincoln often returned to was David Ross Locke, who during the Civil War wrote under the outrageous pseudonym of Petroleum Vesuvius Nasby. Like Ward, Nasby spoke in a dialect suggestive of rural southern Ohio and spelled so "fonetickly" as to be nearly unreadable today. But Lincoln, memorizing and reciting, did not so much *read* Nasby as *perform* him. Lincoln blithely inflicted Nasby on members of his cabinet, and once again it was Edwin Stanton who angrily objected, though only when safely out of the presence: "God damn it to hell. Was there ever such nonsense? Here is the fate of the whole republic at stake, and here is the man around whom it all centers, on whom it all depends, turning aside from this monumental issue to read the God damned trash of a silly mountebank!"[63] Clearly, whatever it was in Nasby that his boss relished, the secretary of war did not share the taste.

In the case of the *Nasby Letters*, even more than that of *Artemus Ward: His Book*, Lincoln had good reason to admire Locke's work, which took more artistic risks and therefore, when successful, had the greater satirical impact. For Nasby was a *Democrat*, proslavery, a hater of blacks, and an enemy of the Lincoln administration (in short, he was a "Copperhead"). His first act in print (March 1861) had been to declare the secession from Ohio and the Union of a hamlet named Wingert's Corners, both to show solidarity with their southern brethren and because the people of the village "hez too long submitted to the imperious dictates uv a tyranikle government"—a government that "hez compelled us, yeer after yeer, to pay our share uv the taxes" while ignoring repeated demands that the Corners be made the capital of the state.[64] These were only the leading grievances in a long bill of particulars filed by Nasby as the leader of the populist revolutionaries. Silly enough, we might agree with Stanton. But when in the second letter Nasby commences on the "nigger question," his racism turns out to be as brutal and ignorant as, to use the most infamous example in American literature, Pap Finn's in the Mark Twain novel. Satire depends for its force on an indictment of injustice and hypocrisy that is also funny. First-person self-satire further requires an ironic distance between the "I" of first person and its puppeteer, that is, between Nasby and Locke. Nasby *believes* what he says, however superior the reader may feel about his pig ignorance; and what he believes, to be effective satire, must strike us as simultaneously intolerable and, yes, funny. Appalled laughter, we might call it. Without ironic distance, intended by the writer and perceived by the reader, self-satire fails, and the verdict falls on the author: angry parents demand that school boards forbid the teaching of *Huckleberry Finn* to their children; readers dismiss Locke as a racist.

In "Negro Emigration," Nasby rails against blacks, free or escaped, heading north into Ohio and settling around Wingert's Corners. Why, already fifteen had come into town "and yesterday another arrove." Before long, he fears, all the whites will be out of work and the "poor hows and jail" full to overflowing—with whites. To meet this crisis, Nasby convenes a mass meeting of citizens. They come up with a series of resolutions that are about as nasty (and as Nasby) as one would expect—while rebounding ironically against the paranoiac whites: "Resolved, That this Convenshun, when it hez its feet washed, smells sweeter nor the Afrikin in his normal condition, and is there4 his sooperior."[65] The "Convenshun" concludes with Nasby's call to white vigilantism: cleanse the Corners of blacks, and let any citizens of the Corners who are sympathetic to them beware: "Arouse to wunst! Rally agin Conway! Rally agin Sweet! Rally agin Hegler! Rally agin Hegler's family! Rally agin the porter at the Reed House! Rally agin the cook at the Crook house! Rally agin the nigger widder in Vance's Adishun! Rally agin Missis Umstid! Rally agin Missis Umstid's children by her first husband! Rally agin Missis Umstid's children by her sekkund husband! Rally agin all the rest of Missis Umstid's children! Rally agin the nigger that cum yesterday! Rally agin the saddle-culured girl that yoost 2 be hear! Ameriky for white men."[66]

This tirade has been quoted at length because Lincoln was hugely amused by "Missis Umstid" and her unnumbered children by any number of men. To later readers, Nasby's rants may be boringly unfunny. But could we have witnessed a remarkable scene one evening at the Soldiers' Home in Washington, Lincoln striking an attitude before the fireplace and launching into a recitation of the whole of "Negro Emigration," with particular emphasis on the mock-rallying cry quoted above—then we might have been converted into Nasby fans right there on the spot.[67]

Massachusetts senator Charles Sumner, while himself no reader of what he called this "peculiar literature," understood both its value to the North as satire and its appeal to Lincoln. In an introduction to the 1872 republication of *The Nasby Letters*, Sumner recalled that, "appearing with a certain regularity and enjoying an extensive circulation . . . [the letters] became a constant and welcome ally. Unquestionably they were among the influences and agencies by which disloyalty in all its forms was exposed, and public opinion assured on the right side."[68] According to Sumner, Nasby was Lincoln's favorite among the literary comedians: "He read every letter as it appeared, and kept them all within reach for refreshment." One morning, very late in the president's life (March 18, 1865), Sumner called at the White House on business, in the midst of which Lincoln "broke into quotation from Nasby." But not getting the desired rise from his audience (or as Sumner euphemistically puts it, "finding me less at home with his favorite humorist"), Lincoln said, "'I must initiate you.' Rising from his seat, he opened a desk behind, and, taking from it a pamphlet collection of the letters already published, proceeded to read from it with infinite jest, while his melancholy features grew bright. It was a delight to see him surrender so completely to the fascination. Finding that I listened, he read for more than twenty minutes, and was still proceeding when it occurred to me that there must be many at the door waiting to see him on graver matters. Taking advantage of the pause, I rose, and, thanking him for the lesson of the morning, went away." Sumner, who was leaving what would be his last private interview with the president, also recalled that Lincoln said this about Nasby: "For the genius to write these things I would gladly give up my office."[69] This was cognate with a remark made years earlier concerning the poem "Mortality": it would have been worth everything else to have written it, Lincoln declared. He would have gladly been a poet, or a humorist; but all he turned out to be was America's greatest political artist.

"The President was in an excellent humor," Secretary of the Navy Gideon Welles noted in his diary for June 17, 1863—this because Lincoln was relieved to hear that General Lee and his Confederate army had *not* crossed the Potomac into Pennsylvania (though Lee soon would—the battle of Gettysburg was a day short of two weeks away); and now, Lincoln thought, he could treat with levity the panic that had "alarmed Pennsylvania and the country." To Lincoln, the fight that hadn't occurred "would be a capital joke [for] Orpheus C. Kerr to get hold of." Innocently enough, Montgomery Meigs "inquired who this person was." "'Why,' said the President, 'have you not read those papers? . . . any one who has not read them must be a heathen.'" Lincoln enjoyed Kerr hugely—except when the satirist turned his pen against the president himself. "'Now, the hits that are given to you, Mr. Welles, or to Chase, I can enjoy, but I dare say they may have disgusted you while I was laughing at them. So *vice versa* as regards myself.'"[70]

Orpheus C. Kerr was the clever pen name of Robert Henry Newell, a New York bohemian, journalist, and litterateur, whose humorous dispatches from Washington, D.C., to the *New York Mercury* made him famous as a satirist of the Civil War. Newell wrote a Kerr letter nearly every week for the first two years of the conflict, and these were collected in book form as *The Orpheus C. Kerr Papers*, first and second series (1862, 1863). Newell's ventriloquism through his Orpheus made for a voice far different from that of Browne/Ward and Locke/Nasby. Despite the clownish name, Kerr spoke in a more refined, middle-brow literary way: he commented on the panoply of American commedia dell'arte types: Union officers, fat, drunk, and confused about their duties; terbacker-chewing Confederate bumpkins, clueless about why they were fighting; and bloviating politicians, their squinty, jaundiced eyes always on the main chance. In addition to caricatures of every sort, Newell/Kerr showed a remarkable gift for pastiche and parody: the *Papers* are shot through with poems that gently ridicule the notable poets of the day, from Longfellow and Whittier of New England to N. P. Willis, the "society verse" beau of New York.

As Welles recalled, Lincoln loved this, except when Newell's barbs flew at him. Concerning a Lincoln reading of Kerr, we must always remember the impressive effect he had as an oral interpreter of any text, from the ridiculous to the cosmopolitan. Lincoln, it is worth repeating, was a master mimic. Because nearly every one of Kerr's dispatches to the *New York Mercury* was a send-up of the conduct of the war, Lincoln might read in every one a mild (though sometimes fantastic) satire that nonetheless came from the pen of a patriot. For Newell always wrote as a confirmed Unionist. His prose had an unusual blend of archness, playful language, and sentimentality that would appeal to his northern public, while it disarmed the objections of those he made fun of. In one letter, Kerr is sent to the War Department to recruit Secretary Welles as a stand-in grandmother for a wounded soldier whose last request is to see his old gram. (Welles is reported not to be available: he is too busy inspecting a model of Noah's Ark.) The reader is meant to smile at the vision of Welles with his flowing white beard (Lincoln nicknamed him Neptune) standing uncomfortably at the bedside of the perishing private (though of course he lives: the army doctor, an ex-blacksmith, is prevented from amputating his leg to cure a head cold).[71]

All in good humor, you see, so how could Lincoln avoid his turn to bear the gentle comedy of observations such as these? "When Abe was an infant of sixteen, he split so many rails that his whole county looked like a wholesale lumber yard." "The President wore his coat and whiskers, and bowed to all salutations like a graceful door-hinge."[72] But he might have been "disgusted" at this parody of a presidential address, proffered for a flag raising at the General Post Office: "On this present occasion, I feel that it will not be out of place to make a few remarks which were not applicable at a former period. Yesterday, the flag hung on the staff throughout the Union, and in consequence of the scarcity of a breeze, there was not much wind blowing at the time. On the present happy occasion, however, the presence of numerous zephyrs causes the atmosphere to agitate for our glorious Union, and this flag, which now unfolds itself to the sight, is observed, upon closer inspection, to present a star-spangled appearance."[73]

In this case, Lincoln deserved the ridicule. He had in fact made such a speech on Wednesday, May 22, 1861: "I had not thought to say a word, but it has occurred to me that a few weeks ago the 'Stars and Stripes' hung rather languidly about the staff all over the nation. So, too, with the flag, when it was elevated to its place. At first it hung rather languidly, but the glorious breeze came, and it now floats as it should. . . . And we hope that the same breeze is swelling the glorious flag throughout the whole nation."[74] Fatuous words spoken extempore and better forgotten (note the clank of the repeated "hung rather languidly"). But there they were, mocked in the next Kerr letter in the *New York Mercury*, made to seem ridiculous as well as empty, returning to afflict the one who uttered them as part of an endless round of public appearances in Washington.

During the hottest and most humid months of the capital summers, Lincoln and his family would sometimes retreat to the Soldiers' Home, located on higher and more salubrious ground to the north of the White House. According to Matthew Pinsker in *Lincoln's Sanctuary: Abraham Lincoln and the Soldiers' Home*, sometime in the early fall of 1864, an English visitor named George Borrett called upon Lincoln late one evening at the Soldiers' Home. Though Borrett came without appointment, "a sleepy Lincoln appeared in his slippers and graciously agreed to sit with [Borrett and his company] in the parlor." At length the president "turned the talk to the poetry of Alexander Pope, whom he said he admired greatly," and proceeded to recite from memory the last six lines from the first epistle of the *Essay on Man*:

> All nature is but Art, unknown to thee;
> All Chance, Direction, which thou canst not see;
> All Discord, Harmony, not understood;
> All partial Evil, Universal good:
> And, spite of Pride, in erring Reason's spite,
> One truth is clear, "Whatever is, is right."[75]

To this notorious conclusion, Lincoln said he had a philosophical objection: "if whatever *is* is right, why, then whatever *isn't* must be wrong."[76] While Lincoln did admire the *Essay on Man*, in this instance he not only recited Pope but remembered Orpheus C. Kerr. In a mock-biography of the Italian patriot Garibaldi, datelined Washington, May 7, 1862, Newell had included this aside, apropos of nothing: "Thus the aspect presented by Garibaldi throughout his career, leads our thoughts into all the deep meanderings of the German mind, and teaches us to perceive that 'whatever is, is right,' as whatever is not, is wrong."[77] When it came to jests, ripostes, and stories, Lincoln was both a magpie and a mockingbird.

Finally, we must also highlight Newell/Kerr's superior gift of poetic pastiche—a gift that Lincoln would have very much appreciated. In every fourth letter or so in the first series, the author embeds a poem, either parodying or imitating a well-known American poet or embodying his own answer to his muse. Several of these are quite serious in tone and very effective *as poems*. When, in late April of 1861, disunionists in Maryland murdered a number of Massachusetts volunteers on their way to Washington, Kerr told the story in a striking rewriting of Poe's "The Raven" called "Baltimore." Because of this outrage, the city—the very city of Poe's death—will live in ignominy. Here is the last stanza:

> And the Eagle, never dying, still is trying, still is trying,
> With its wings upon the map to hide a city with its gore;
> But the name is there forever, and it shall be hidden never,
> While the awful brand of murder points the Avenger to its shore;
> While the blood of peaceful brothers God's dread vengeance doth implore,
>   Thou art doomed, O Baltimore![78]

In another poem (published January 30, 1862), the lyre of Orpheus sings a dire warning to the warring factions, North and South. While they are mauling one another in a war of attrition, deep down in Mississippi the slaves are preparing to revolt. Free them, and the cause of the conflict disappears. But not to do so risks disaster for the nation. Late one night in northern Virginia, a lone Union sentry, perhaps not fully awake, is approached by a wraithlike figure of a man, "wrinkled, grim, and old," yet dressed as a soldier who can tell him what, "looking South . . . is hidden from thine eye." It is a bloody slave uprising in which no white will be spared. Because the slaves' cause is just, the fierce, implacable, and sanguinary revolution will be justified:

> And who is it that says so?
> Why, that dress is Putnam's own!
> Soldier, soldier, where art thou?
> Vanished—like a shadow gone!

The ancient shade of Revolutionary War general Rufus Putnam has come from his New England grave to warn all Americans that the war issue is the evil of African slavery and that if the North does not move to emancipation, and immediately, the slaves will free themselves, and violently. As a tagline after the poem, Kerr observes: "the Southern Confederacy may come to that yet . . . if it don't take warning in time from its patron Saint. I refer to Saint Domingo . . . I refer to Saint Domingo."[79]

Whom, after all, was Lincoln seeking to entertain with his readings from Ward, Nasby, and Kerr? Himself, but with an audience. His cabinet, despite grumblings from Stanton, would, by custom and familiarity, indulge this as one of his harmless eccentricities. They knew the stories were coming and reacted politely to a deft oral performance of a type of literature not one of them would have chosen as his own recreational reading. And, beyond the cabinet, every colonel, every courtier, would have responded to the president's literary sallies with appropriate applause. Lincoln knew that on such occasions he had a captive audience. A genteel guest on the trip to City Point, the Marquis de Chambrun, praised Lincoln's interpretation of Shakespeare, both because he, like all educated Europeans, appreciated Shakespeare and was curious or perhaps a little in awe of the president of the United States standing there before him reciting those great speeches from *Macbeth*. But if Chambrun happened to be in the colonel's tent that day at City Point, notwithstanding his command of English, he could have had little understanding of Lincoln's performance of American regional and dialect humor. It all came down to royal prerogative. It pleased Lincoln

to read something from Ward or Nasby or Kerr, trifling or not by the genteel standards of the age; and therefore it must needs please his audience
to listen and appear to laugh, however they might privately deprecate such
tawdry literary taste.

At the back of the 1788 edition of William Scott's *Lessons in Elocution* (first
published in England in 1779), on facing pages, are two speeches from
Shakespeare's *Hamlet* that Lincoln came to know by heart: King Claudius's
"Oh! my offense is rank" (3.3.36–72) on the murder of his brother, Prince
Hamlet's father; and the prince's more famous soliloquy, "To be, or not to
be" (3:1.58–92).[80] As a boy in Indiana, perhaps even before his teens, Lincoln
had had the opportunity to read and study Scott's popular anthology, a volume that Sarah Bush Johnston was said to have brought with her to Indiana
when she married Thomas Lincoln in 1819.[81] While Scott's *Lessons* may or
may not have been the boy Lincoln's first encounter with Shakespeare, it is
a striking coincidence that these two passages from *Hamlet* would figure
publicly in his presidential life more than forty years later.

In 1863 the American Shakespearean actor James H. Hackett made
two sets of appearances at Washington theatres, performing as Falstaff in
Henry IV and *The Merry Wives of Windsor*. President Lincoln, who loved
the theatre, is known to have attended four of these shows—one in March
and three in December.[82] Soon after his March 14 performance, presumably
aware that the president had been in attendance and in an attempt to curry
favor with Lincoln, Hackett sent him a copy of his just-published *Notes
and Comments upon Certain Plays and Actors of Shakespeare*.[83] While it
is doubtful that Lincoln ever got around to reading the book, he did belat-
edly send Hackett a note of thanks for the gift. In his letter, Lincoln rather
unguardedly spoke of his love for but incomplete reading of the plays:
"Some of Shakespeare's plays I have never read; while others I have gone
over perhaps as frequently as any unprofessional reader. Among the latter
are Lear, Richard Third, Henry Eighth, Hamlet, and especially Macbeth.
I think nothing equals Macbeth. It is wonderful. Unlike you gentlemen of
the profession, I think the soliloquy in Hamlet commencing 'O, my offence
is rank' surpasses that commencing 'To be, or not to be.' But pardon this
small attempt at criticism."[84]

This might have been the end of the matter had not Hackett, in an act
of unconscionable self-promotion, printed a broadside of Lincoln's letter
and handed it around. Though the broadside cautioned that it was "not for
publication but for private distribution only," inevitably Lincoln's political
enemies got hold of copies and commenced sneering at the president for
his poor taste in Shakespearean soliloquies.[85] The irony was that Lincoln

had very probably studied the text of *Hamlet* more thoroughly than any of his critics, and his preference for Claudius's speech over Hamlet's resulted from mature critical reflection. The world might not have agreed with him, but no one who knew Lincoln's possessive attitude toward poetry he loved could honestly say that he hadn't thought the matter through. Characteristically, Lincoln responded mildly, even stoically, to Hackett's lese majesty: "My note to you I certainly did not expect to see in print; yet I have not been much shocked by the newspaper comments upon it. Those comments constitute a fair specimen of what has occurred to me through life. I have endured a great deal of ridicule without much malice; and have received a great deal of kindness, not quite free from ridicule. I am used to it."[86] Ridicule with or without malice notwithstanding, Lincoln would hold to his unconventional taste: for he knew what he liked because he liked what he knew.

But why did he prefer Claudius to the Prince? Generations of readers have praised "To be, or not to be" as great dramatic poetry; and the morality of the two speeches is also in favor of the prince: Hamlet, after all, is suffering because he has *not* done murder, his uncle because he has. The obvious reason for Lincoln's preference is that the words of the usurping fratricide somehow meant more to him. But, again, *why*? Since he did not say, any speculation would necessarily require a sound understanding of his psychology—the achievement of which has proved a most difficult matter for Lincoln's legion of biographers. Still, we may risk a few tentative observations. First and foremost, Claudius speaks of his corroding, crippling guilt, a topic always fascinating to Lincoln, whose emotional sensitivity and surpassing imagination enabled him (condemned him?) to envision another's sins and the consequent guilt. Claudius, like Macbeth, murdered his kinsman and his king. Lincoln obviously did no such thing. Claudius, again like Macbeth, writhed in agony over a heinous wrong he could neither accept in himself nor repent of (compare Macbeth's speech uttered *before* the regicide: 1.7.1–28). Lincoln, lacking the sinful act, had no need of repentance. But he felt guilt. For deep and obscure reasons, he seemed to identify with the guilty, especially those who had done their bloody deeds from the prickings of outsized ambition. Both illegitimate Shakespearean kings speak similarly of their suffering, unmitigated because their sins cannot be atoned. Both are aware of ambition as the first cause of their falls.

> [Claudius]
> I am still possessed
> Of those effects for which I did the murder—
> My crown, mine own ambition, and my queen.[87]

[Macbeth]
I have no spur
To prick the sides of my intent, but only
Vaulting ambition, which o'erleaps itself
And falls on th' other.[88]

By these standards, it is fair to say that Prince Hamlet has no ambition; and therefore he is less interesting to Lincoln, who was deeply infected with it. To recall Bacon's warning: ambition is a desire and therefore irrational (though it can be rationalized); and desires will out. All that reason can manage is to make ambition's outcomes less than wholly destructive to the leader whose will-to-power has been loosed upon the commonwealth, which stands to gain so long as its prince's ambition is channeled by his reason and a little checked by the state. Lincoln never committed "patricide" upon the United States of America, as one of the psycho-biographers has charged, but he did feel guilt and responsibility for the unprecedented carnage of the Civil War. His ambition had put him in the presidency, and the result was that hundreds of thousands of young men died. The logic of this connection is fallacious, *post hoc ergo propter hoc*, but that might not have stopped Lincoln's conscience from self-blame. He had had the will; then he got the power; finally, the disasters of war began.

To call Lincoln a good mimic, as we have, is to finally undervalue the quality of his histrionic gift. He was an *impersonator*. And, though he would never say so, with Shakespearean characters he could have competed with the likes of Hackett and other "gentlemen of the profession." Francis Carpenter, the painter who resided in the White House for several months in 1864, while working on his great canvas, *The First Reading of the Emancipation Proclamation*, now and then provided an audience of one for Lincoln's Shakespearean impersonations. Carpenter, in his memoir called *Six Months at the White House* (1866), vividly recalled an extended sitting for the painting on March 2, 1864. "Presently the conversation turned on Shakespeare," and more particularly upon *Hamlet*. Lincoln said: "There is one passage of the play of 'Hamlet' which is very apt to be slurred over by the actor, or omitted altogether, which seems to me the choicest part of the play. It is the soliloquy of the king, after the murder. It always struck me as one of the finest touches of Nature in the world." "Then," Carpenter continues, "throwing himself into the very spirit of the scene, he took up the words:—'O my offence is rank . . .'" Hearing the entire speech recited from memory, and done so powerfully, overwhelmed Carpenter: Lincoln spoke "with a feeling and appreciation unsurpassed by anything I ever witnessed upon the stage."[89] That same evening, Lincoln went to Grover's Theatre to watch Edwin Booth in *Hamlet*.[90]

On another occasion during that winter of 1863–64, Lincoln, accompanied by his journalist-confidant Noah Brooks, went to Ford's Theater—once again to watch Edwin Booth doing Shakespeare.[91] They slipped in through the stage door and entered one of the stage boxes "without being seen by the audience." As Brooks recalled, the two of them took their seats "in a box directly under the one in which he was afterward assassinated," the president being throughout the performance "in a remarkable flow of spirits, and [making] many comical remarks on the progress of the play. From their private vantage they watched Booth (elder brother of John Wilkes Booth) as Shylock in *The Merchant of Venice*. As is well known, this is a Shakespearean drama far too dark to be easily experienced as a "comedy" in the usual sense of the term, though it was so-classified in the First Folio of 1623 and sometimes still is. It is true that for the young Italian romantic couples of *Merchant* the action indeed proves to have been much ado about little—for they triumph over the Jewish usurer and are poised to live happily ever after at the close of the play. But Shylock, rather than getting his comic comeuppance, is tragically reduced and becomes pitiful in the audience's eyes: his large fortune forfeited to the state, his daughter married to a Gentile, and himself forced to convert to Christianity.

As Brooks and Lincoln strolled from the theater afterward, Lincoln observed, "it was a good performance, but I would a thousand times rather read it at home, if it were not for Booth's playing. A farce, or a comedy, is best played; a tragedy is best read at home."[92] The implications of this intriguing statement are clear: Lincoln regarded *The Merchant of Venice* as a tragedy, not a comedy; he believed that tragedies were better experienced in personal space than seen socially; and that theatrical performance could actually diminish the cathartic power of a great tragedy. Such provocative views, if publicly known, might well have brought down on him the same derision as had the public revelation of his predilections in *Hamlet* soliloquies. Fortunately, Brooks was more discrete than had been Hackett: he did not reveal the episode at Ford's until 1877. Yet once again, and strikingly, Lincoln's critical judgment transcended conventional wisdom. That tragedy was "best" when read (or recited) has support in Aristotle's *Poetics*,[93] while his reclassification of *The Merchant of Venice* as a tragedy seems today to be familiar and right. As in politics, so in poetry: Lincoln probed more deeply.

Lincoln's tally of the Shakespearean dramas he had "gone over . . . frequently" is surprisingly short when we think of those long-gone, idyllic days on the banks of the Sangamon, reading Shakespeare and Burns with Jack

Kelso. One or the other, probably Kelso, carried a volume of Shakespeare. But after a while, the twain may have needed no book at all: *reciting* to one another, passage after favorite passage, almost in the manner of a western contest that continued until either Jack or Abe called "hold, enough."[94] Fanciful, certainly, though not impossible if what he wrote to Hackett is true. Lincoln's partial Shakespeare is notable for what is *not* on the list: no romances (what a shame that he did not know *The Tempest!*), and among the comedies only *The Merchant of Venice* and *The Merry Wives of Windsor* (the first a dark comedy and the second a tour-de-force for Falstaff, whom he also liked in *Henry IV*). Evidently Lincoln got all the comedy he needed from the low humor of the literary comedians. That leaves the major tragedies and histories, and what we might term the tragic histories such as *King John* and *Richard II* and *III*. Critic and historian Matthew Pinsker believes that Lincoln's mature preferences in Shakespeare derived largely from his own involvement as leader during a time of revolutionary tumult: "Naturally, many of the Shakespearean plays and passages Lincoln seemed to admire most dwelled on themes of rebellion, usurpation, and ambition run amok. The historical dramas that he quoted from so freely, such as the plays about the House of York and the House of Lancaster, vied for control of the nation. The tragedies he preferred, like *Macbeth* or *Hamlet*, concerned the nature of evil and civil disorder created by disruptions in the succession of kings."[95]

Concerning the history plays, especially all the Henrys, Pinsker is convincing; but the tragedies pose deeper interpretive challenges. What reader, audience member, or critic comes away from an experience with *Macbeth* understanding "the nature of evil"? The gallant and heroic warrior Macbeth, at the outset of the drama a well-regarded man of both bonhomie and arete, rapidly becomes a moral monster, until by act 5 we desire his death *both* for the sake of the kingdom of Scotland and for his own. This is not to isolate and define evil but to wonder at its incomprehensible reality. That evil exists; that Lincoln could mutter to himself, "there but for the grace of God go I"; and that unperceived grace—in Lincoln's theology, the unknowable will of God—might be removed at any moment: these were the solemn affirmations of tragic catharsis: a realm of knowledge more felt than thought.

Lincoln, besides performing, sometimes served as his own dramaturg. On the same occasion that the painter Carpenter heard and was moved by "Oh! my offense is rank," the president followed his recitation with a brief seminar on the proper way to deliver the lines with which *Richard III* opens:

Now is the winter of our discontent
Made glorious summer by this sun of York,
And all the clouds that lowered upon our house
In the deep bosom of the ocean buried. [96]

In Lincoln's view, actors and directors too often "entirely misapprehended" the tenor of these verses: "It is quite common," he instructed Carpenter, "for an actor to come upon the stage, and, in a sophomoric style, to begin with a flourish"—and here he spoke the speech in such a sophomoric way— "Now . . . this is all wrong. Richard, you remember, had been, and was then, plotting the destruction of his brothers, to make room for himself. Outwardly, the most loyal to the newly crowned king, secretly he could scarcely contain his impatience at the obstacles still in the way of his own elevation. He appears upon the stage, just after the crowning of Edward, burning with repressed hate and jealousy. The prologue is the utterance of the most intense bitterness and satire." Having made his director's "note" clear, Lincoln then changed hats and, "unconsciously assuming the character," impersonated from memory the then Duke of Gloucester in his entire forty-line opening soliloquy. Carpenter was awed. The speech was delivered "with a degree of force and power that made it seem like a new creation to me. Though familiar with the passage from boyhood, I can truly say that never til that moment had I fully appreciated its spirit. I could not refrain from laying down my palette and brushes and applauding heartily." In Carpenter's finished painting, the president is seated a little left of center, his right hand on the arm of a chair, looking out of the frame at a slight angle. Was this his attitude during the performance that day? Not being able to bow from such a posture, did Lincoln acknowledge his audience's approval with a nod of the head? In any case, with a quick brushstroke of flattery, the admiring painter told Lincoln that he had missed his calling. Which was just wrong enough "considerably" to amuse the Great Emancipator.[97]

Then, too, he could be part of his own audience and deeply affected. On May 11, 1862, while at Fortress Monroe, Virginia, on military business, Lincoln took a reading break and asked for a copy of Shakespeare. This was supplied by a staff officer, Col. LeGrand B. Cannon, whom the president requested to remain. "He read from MacBeth Lear & finally King John, & in reading the passage where Constance bewails the loss of her child to the King, I noticed that he was deeply move[d], his voice trembled."

And Father Cardinal, I have heard you say
That we shall see and know our friends in heaven.
If that be true, I shall see my boy again.

. . . .

Grief fills the room up of my absent child,
Lies in his bed, walks up and down with me,
Puts on his pretty looks, repeats his words,
Remembers me of all his gracious parts,
Stuffs out his vacant garments with his form;
Then have I reason to be fond of grief.[98]

William Wallace Lincoln had died on February 20, at the age of eleven. "Willie" was perhaps his father's favorite among the four Lincoln sons, and his death after a sudden illness (typhoid?) overwhelmed both the president and Mary Todd Lincoln.[99] Three months later, Lincoln still carried an immense burden of grief, though characteristically hidden. Or for the most part hidden. Colonel Cannon witnessed its power that day at Fortress Monroe, called forth by Lincoln's utterance of Constance's speech: "He said, did you ever dream of a lost friend & feel that you were having a direct communion with that friend & yet a consciousness that it was not a reality? My reply was, yes I think we all may have had such an experience. He replied so do I dream of my Boy Willey. He was utterly overcome. His great frame shook & Bowing down on the table he wept as only such a man in the breaking down of a great sorrow could weep."[100]

Together with the contradictories of fatality and guilt, personal grief and political and military disillusionment forced Lincoln, toward the end of the war and his life, to the brink of a nihilism that not even the joking of the literary comedians could prevent—such humor now tended to exacerbate the tragedy rather than lighten it, much as the punning of the drunken Porter in *Macbeth* only deepens the gloom around the castle. As Carpenter remembered, "During the first week of the battles of the Wilderness [commenced May 4, 1864] he scarcely slept at all." Had he, by some twisted logic in his deep but troubled mind, "murdered sleep"? The editor of the *Philadelphia Press*, John W. Forney, who happened to be present when the president received the first casualty reports from Grant in Virginia, heard him cry mercy: "My God! My God! over 20,000 men killed and wounded in a few days. . . . I cannot bear it! I cannot bear it!"[101] It seems that had Mary Todd Lincoln herself suddenly perished at that moment, Lincoln, like Macbeth, might have blankly said, "she should have died hereafter." He was to that degree distracted. One evening, Forney came to the White House, where he found the president "ghastly pale," with "dark rings under his caverned eyes." Lincoln was reading Shakespeare—*this* Shakespeare:

Tomorrow, and tomorrow, and tomorrow
Creeps in this petty pace from day to day
To the last syllable of recorded time,

And all our yesterdays have lighted fools
The way to dusty death. Out, out, brief candle.
Life's but a walking shadow, a poor player
That struts and frets his hour upon the stage,
And then is heard no more. It is a tale
Told by an idiot, full of sound and fury,
Signifying nothing.[102]

He took this text, he explained to Forney, for *consolation*.

Eleven months later, the war was won for the Union. Lincoln, though vastly relieved, did not necessarily feel better about life in a metaphysical sense. On his last trip into Virginia, to City Point and beyond, into Petersburg and the fallen Confederate capital, Richmond, Lincoln continued to have Shakespeare, and especially *Macbeth*, on his mind. Some lines of the usurping king's, spoken to Lady Macbeth soon after the regicide, kept occurring to Lincoln:

But let the frame of things disjoint, both the worlds suffer,
Ere we will eat our meal in fear, and sleep
In the afflictions of these terrible dreams
That shake us nightly. Better be with the dead,
Whom we to gain our peace have sent to peace,
Than on the torture of the mind to lie
In restless ecstasy. Duncan is in his grave.
After life's fitful fever he sleeps well.
Treason has done his worst. Nor steel nor poison,
Malice domestic, foreign levy, nothing
Can touch him further.[103]

On Sunday, April 9, during the upriver return of the *River Queen* from City Point, the Marquis de Chambrun recalled that during the entire day "the conversation turned on literary subjects," and the president favored the company with readings "for several hours," mostly from Shakespeare, "especially *Macbeth*," and more particularly "the lines after the murder of Duncan, when the new king falls a prey to moral torment." This speech, Chambrun emphasized, was "dramatically dwelt on." "Now and then [Lincoln] paused to expatiate on how exact a picture Shakespeare here gives of a murderer's mind when, the dark deed achieved, its perpetrator already envies his victim's calm sleep. He read the scene over twice.[104] Lincoln possessed the same kind of eidetic imagination as Macbeth: one to which "present fears/ Are less than horrible imaginings." The former were diminished, if not vanished, by April 1865. But "horrible imaginings" ceased only with death—when the imaginer was in his grave, at last sleeping well.

Another passenger on the *River Queen*, Senator Charles Sumner, also listened to Lincoln on that occasion and remembered the president holding "a beautiful quarto Shakespeare in his hands."[105] For what was likely his final reading of Shakespeare, Lincoln possessed a fine copy in a fine binding, a correlative of his rise from circuit lawyer in Illinois, carrying a cheap, worn, dog-eared Shakespeare, to "prince" or "king" or president of the United States, whose last books were gilt, even as the gilded age began.

There was the dream of stumbling upon the lying-in-state before his own funeral. Absurd, since he didn't believe in dreams or premonitions of any sort, except when he did. Yet once dreamt (sometime in the second week of April 1865) this one kept coming back to the dreamer like Banquo's ghost, which would not down. He told Ward Hill Lamon about it and, after prodding, he told Mary: "I kept on until I arrived at the East Room, which I entered. There I met with a sickening surprise. Before me was a catalfalque, on which a corpse wrapped in funeral vestments. Around it were stationed soldiers who were acting as guards; and there was a throng of people, some gazing mournfully upon the corpse, whose face was covered, others weeping pitifully. "Who is dead in the White House?" I demanded of one of the soldiers. "The President," was his answer; "he was killed by an assassin."[106] Mary was deeply troubled. Her husband, while having given credibility to the dream through his need to speak of it, urged her to forget the whole thing—an impossibility for either of them, though she would have years longer to brood on its having come true.

> *For God's sake, let us sit upon the ground,*
> *And tell sad stories of the death of kings—*
> *How some have been depos'd, some slain in war,*
> *Some haunted by the ghosts they have deposed,*
> *Some poisoned by their wives, some sleeping kill'd,*
> *All murthered.*[107]

Appendix

Notes

Index

Appendix: The Books That Abraham Lincoln Read

This list is adapted from "What Abraham Lincoln Read: An Annotated and Evaluative Bibliography," published in the *Journal of the Abraham Lincoln Association* (2007) and available online at the Association's website, www.abrahamlincolnassociation.org. The list includes individual poems but not individual songs. Only those titles that received an "A" (very likely read) or a "B" (somewhat likely read) are included here. The dates represent the year of original publication or first publication in English.

Addison, Joseph. *Cato: A Tragedy* (1713)

Aesop's Fables (1525)

"Am I for Peace? Yes!"

Angell, J. K. *A Treatise on the Limitations of Actions at Law and Suits in Equity and Admiralty* (1846)

Arabian Nights (1706)

Babes in the Wood (1793)

Bacon, Francis. *Essays* (1625)

Bacon, Leonard. *Slavery Discussed in Occasional Essays from 1833–46* (1846)

Bailey, Nathan. *Dictionary of English Etymology* (1721)

Bailey, Philip J. *The Beauties of Festus* (1851)

Baldwin, James G. *Flush Times in Alabama and Mississippi* (1853)

Bancroft, George. *History of the United States* (1834)

———. *The Necessity, the Reality, and the Promise of Progress of the Human Race* (1854, 1855)

"Barbara Allen" (traditional)

Barclay, James. *Dictionary* (1774)

Barrett, Joseph H. *Illustrated Life of Abraham Lincoln* (1860, 1864?)

Bartlett, John R. *Personal Narrative of Explorations and Incidents in Texas, . . .* (1854)

Beecher, Henry Ward. *Editorials* (1861–62)

Bible (King James Version)

Blackstone, William. *Commentaries on the Laws of England* (1765–69)

Blanchard, Amos. *American Military Biography* (1825)

Browne, Charles Farrar. *Artemus Ward: His Book* (1862)

Bryant, William Cullen. *Poems* (1821, 1832)

———. "Thanatopsis" (1817)

Bulwer-Lytton, Edward. *The Lady of Lyons* (1838)

Bunyan, John. *Pilgrim's Progress* (1678)

Burns, Robert. *Poems* (1786)

———. "Address to the Unco Guid"

———. "Auld Lang Syne"

———. "Cotter's Saturday Night"

———. "Epistle to a Young Friend"

———. "Green Grow the Rushes"

———. "A Heart-Warm Fond Adieu"

———. "Holy Willie's Prayer"

———. "John Anderson, My Jo"

———. "Lament for James, Earl of Glencairn"

———. "A Man's a Man for A' That"

———. "Tam O'Shanter"

———. "'Twas Even"

———. "Willie Wastle"

Butler, Joseph. *The Analogy of Religion* (1736)

Butler, Samuel. *Hudibras* (1663)

Butler, William A. *Nothing to Wear* (1857)

Byron, George Gordon, Lord. *Poems* (1815)

———. *Bride of Abydos* (1813)

———. *Childe Harold's Pilgrimage* (1812–18)

———. *Corsair* (1813)

———. "Darkness"

———. "Destruction of Sennacherib"

———. "Devil's Drive"

———. *Don Juan* (1819–24)

———. "The Dream"

———. "The Girl of Cadiz"

———. *Lara* (1814)

———. *Mazeppa* (1819)

———. "Nisus and Euryalus"

Chambers, Robert. *Vestiges of the Natural History of Creation* (1844)

Chandler, Mary G. *Elements of Character* (1854)

Channing, William Ellery. *Works* (1841)

Chitty, Joseph. *A Practical Treatise on Pleading* (1809)

Clay, Henry. *Speeches* (1843)

Conway, Moncure D. *The Rejected Stone* (1861, 1862)

Cowper, William. *The Task* (1785)

———. "Charity"

———. "On the Receipt of My Mother's Picture"

———. "There Is a Fountain Filled with Blood"

Cruden, Alexander. *Concordance to the Holy Scriptures* (1737)

Daboll, Nathan. *The Schoolmaster's Assistant* (1799)

Davies, Charles. *Elements of Surveying* (1830)

Davis, William W. H. *El Gringo; or, New Mexico and Her People* (1857)

Defoe, Daniel. *Robinson Crusoe* (1719)

"The Democratic Battle Hymn" (?)

Dilworth, Thomas. *A New Guide to the English Tongue* (1761)

Dupuy, Starke. *Hymns and Spiritual Songs* (1818)

Elliott, Jonathan. *Journal and Debates of the Federal Constitution* (1836)

Emerson, Ralph Waldo. *Essays: 1st Series* (1841)

———. *Representative Men* (1850)

Emory, W. H. *Reconnaisance in New Mexico and California* (1848)

Euclid. *Geometry* (?)

Everett, Edward. *Address at Gettysburg* (1863)

Fitzhugh, George. *Sociology for the South* (1857)

Flint, Abel. *System of Geometry, Trigonometry and Rectangular Surveying* (1804)

Ford, Thomas. *History of Illinois* (1854)

Frémont, John C. *Fresh Evidence of the Continuance of the Slave Trade* [England] (1824)

———. *Report of the Exploring Expedition to the Rocky Mountains* (1845)

French, Jonathan. *The True Republican* (1841, 1852)

Gibbon, Edward. *History of the Decline and Fall of the Roman Empire* (1776)

Gibson, Robert. *The Theory and Practice of Surveying* (1814)

Giddings, Joshua. *Speeches* (1853, 1854)

Gilman, Charles. *The Illinois Conveyancer* (1846)

Gilmore, J. R. *Among the Pines* (1862)

Gray, Thomas. "Elegy Written in a Country Churchyard" (1751)

Greenleaf, Simon. *A Treatise on the Law of Evidence* (1840)

Grimshaw, William. *A History of the United States* (1814)

Guizot, François P. *Essay on the Character and Influence of Washington* (1840)

Hallam, Henry. *View of the State of Europe in the Middle Ages* (1818)

Halleck, FitzGreene. "Alnwick Castle"

———. "Burns" (1827)

———. "Fanny" (1819, 1821)

———. "Marco Bozzaris"

———. "Red Jacket"

Halleck, H. W. *Military Art and Science* (1846)

Hawes, George W. *Illinois State Gazetteer* (1858)

Helper, Hinton Rowan. *The Impending Crisis of the South* (1857)

Hentz, Caroline Lee. *The Mob-Cap and Other Tales* (1848)

Hesiod. *Georgics* [*Works and Days*], trans. George Chapman (1618)

Hickey, William. *The Constitution of the United States* (1846)

Hill, John. *Opposing Principles of Henry Clay and Abraham Lincoln* (1860)

Hitchcock, Edward. *Religious Truth Illustrated from Science* (1856)

Holland, William M. *The Life and Political Opinions of Martin Van Buren* (1836)

Holmes, Oliver Wendell. *Poems* (1850)

———. "Ballad of the Oysterman"

———. "The Chambered Nautilus"

———. "The Last Leaf"

———. "Lexington"

———. "September Gale"

Homer. *Iliad*, trans. George Chapman (1598–1608)

———. *Odyssey*, trans. George Chapman (1616)

Hood, Thomas. *Poems* (1840)

———. "Faithless Sally Brown"

———. "The Haunted House"

———. "The Lost Heir"

———. "Miss Kilmansegg and Her Golden Leg"

———. "The Spoiled Child" (humorous sketch, 1861)

———. "Up the Rhine"

Horace. *Works of Horace* (1826)

Howells, William Dean. *Lives and Speeches of Abraham Lincoln and Hannibal Hamlin* (1860)

Hume, David. *Essays* (1741? 1758?)

———. *History of England* (1754–62)

Hyde, John. *Mormonism* (1857)

Illinois Revised Laws (1829, 1841–45)

Indiana Revised Statutes (1824)

Jackson, Andrew. *Proclamation against Nullification* (1832)

Jefferson, Thomas. *Works*, vols. 4, 7–9 (1853–54)

———. "First Inaugural Address" (1801)

Kendall, George W. *Narrative of the Texan Santa Fé Expedition* (1844)

Kenney, James. *The Illustrious Stranger* (1824)

Kent, James. *Commentaries on American Law* (1826)

The Kentucky Preceptor (1806)

Kirkham, Samuel. *English Grammar* (1820)

Kirkland, Charles P. *A Letter to the Honorable Benjamin P. Curtis* (1862)

Knox, William. "Mortality" (1824)

Lanman, Charles. *Dictionary of the U. S. Congress* (1859)

The Law of Nature (1796)

Lear, Edward. *A Book of Nonsense* (1856, 1861)

Lempriere, John. *Classical Dictionary* (1788)

Lesage, Alain R. *Gil Blas* (1715–35)

Lincoln, Abraham, and Stephen A. Douglas. *Political Debates* (1860)

Livermore, George R. *An Historical Research Respecting the Opinions of the Founders of the Republic on Negroes as Slaves, as Citizens and as Soldiers* (1862)

Longfellow, Henry Wadsworth. *Poems* (1846)

———. "The Birds of Killingworth"

———. "The Building of the Ship"

———. "A Psalm of Life"

Lowe, A. T., comp. *The Columbian Class Book* (1824)

Lowell, James Russell. *The Biglow Papers* (1848)

Macaulay, Thomas B. *History of England from the Accession of James II* (1849)

Mackay, Charles. "The Inquiry" (1847)

Massett, Stephen C. *"Drifting About"; or, What "Jeems Pipes of Pipesville"
    Saw and Did* (1863)

McElligott, James N. *The American Debater* (1855)

Mill, John Stuart. *On Liberty* (1859)

———. *Principles of Political Economy* (1848)

Milton, John. "Lycidas" (1638)

Mollhausen, Baldwin. *Diary of a Journey from the Mississippi to the Coasts of the Pacific*
    (1858)

Moore, David A. *The Age of Progress; or, A Panorama of Time* (1856)

Moore, Thomas. *Lalla Rookh* (1817)

———. "The Legacy"

———, ed. *The Life, Letters and Journals of Lord Byron* (1830–31)

Murray, Lindley. *The English Grammar* (1795)

———. *The English Reader* (1799)

Neill, Edward D. *History of Minnesota* (1858)

Newell, R. H. (Orpheus C. Kerr). *Orpheus C. Kerr Papers*, 1st and 2nd series (1862, 1863)

Olmsted, Frederick L. *A Journey in the Seaboard Slave States* (1856)

Paine, Thomas. *The Age of Reason* (1794–95)

———. *Common Sense* (1776)

———. *Complete Political Works* (1856–59)

Paley, William. *Works* (1836)

Parker, Theodore. *Additional Speeches, Addresses, and Occasional Sermons* (1858)

———. "The Effect of Slavery on the American People" (1858)

Parkman, Francis. *The Oregon Trail* (1849)

Permanent Temperance Documents of the American Temperance Society (1835)

Peterson, Henry. *Poems* (1863)

Phillips, Wendell. [no information]

Pike, Nicholas. *Arithmetic* (1788)

Plutarch. *Lives* (1859)

Poe, Edgar Allan. *Poems* (1831)

———. "The Raven"

"The Pole-cat" (1846)

Pope, Alexander. *Essay on Man* (1733–34)

——. "The Temple of Fame" (1715)

——, trans. *Homer's Iliad and Odyssey* (1848)

Prentice, George Denison. *Life of Henry Clay* (1831)

Quin's Jests (1766)

Ramsay, David. *Life of George Washington* (1807)

Reed, Thomas B. *The Wagoner of the Alleghenies* (1862)

Riley, James. *An Authentic Narrative of the Loss of the American Brig Commerce* (1817)

Robertson, George. *Scrap Book on Law and Politics, Men and Times* (1855)

Roget, Peter M. *Thesaurus* (1852)

Rollin, Charles. *Ancient History* (1729)

Scott, Winfield. *Infantry Tactics* (c. 1852)

Scripps, John Locke. *Life of Lincoln* (1860)

Seward, William H. *Speeches* (1850–60)

Shakespeare, William. *Hamlet*

——. *Henry IV (1 & 2)*

——. *Henry V*

——. *Henry VIII*

——. *King John*

——. *King Lear*

——. *Macbeth*

——. *Merchant of Venice*

——. *Merry Wives of Windsor*

——. *Othello*

——. *Richard II*

——. *Richard III*

Smith, Seba. *Letters of Jack Downing* (1834, 1864)

Story, Joseph. *Commentaries on Equity Jurisprudence* (1836)

——. *Equity Pleadings* (1805)

Stowe, Harriet Beecher. *The Key to Uncle Tom's Cabin* (1853)

Tappan, Henry Philip. *Elements of Logic* (1846)

Thomson, James. *The Seasons* (1730)

Thomson, Mortimer N. (Doesticks). *Nothing to Say* (1857)

Thornton, J. Quinn. *Oregon and California in 1848* (1849)

Thucydides. *The Peloponnesian War* (1848)

Tucker, Nathaniel B. *George Balcombe* (1836)

Volney, Constantin. *The Ruins; or, Meditation on the Revolutions of Empires* (1791)

Voltaire (François-Marie Arouet). *An Important Examination of the Scriptures* (1819)

Wayland, Francis. *Elements of Political Economy* (1837)

Webster, Daniel. "Reply to Hayne" (1830)

——. *Speeches* (1830)

Webster, Noah. *An American Dictionary* (1828)

————. *The American Spelling Book* (1783)

————. *A Dictionary for Primary Schools* (1833)

Weems, Mason Locke. *Life of General Francis Marion* (1809)

————. *Life of George Washington* (1800, 1808)

Wells, David A. *Annual of Scientific Discovery* (1850–71)

Whiting, William. *The War Powers of the President* (1862)

Whittier, John G. *Poems* (1830, 1837, 1848)

Willis, Nathaniel P. "Parrhasius" (1835)

Wilson, John. *Elements of Punctuation* (1856)

Wise, Henry A. *Los Gringos* (1857)

Wolfe, Charles. *The Burial of Sir John Moore* (1825)

Worcester, J. E. *Elements of History, Ancient and Modern* (1826)

Young, Edward. *The Last Day* (1713)

Notes

1. The Sometime Schoolboy

1. Douglas L. Wilson and Rodney O. Davis, eds., *Herndon's Informants: Letters, Interviews, and Statements about Abraham Lincoln* (Urbana and Chicago: University of Illinois Press, 1998), 36 (hereafter cited as *Herndon's Informants*); Lowell H. Harrison, *Lincoln of Kentucky* (Lexington: University Press of Kentucky, 2000), 18; Louis A. Warren, *Lincoln's Youth: Indiana Years, Seven to Twenty-one, 1816–1830* (New York: Appleton, Century, Crofts, 1959), 10.
2. Harrison, *Lincoln of Kentucky*, 25.
3. *Herndon's Informants*, 28.
4. Ibid., 66.
5. Ibid., 28, 38.
6. Thomas Dilworth, *A New Guide to the English Tongue* (Delmar, N.Y.: Scholars' Facsimiles & Reprints, 1977), 85. For further discussion of the moralizing aphorisms and poetic sentiments Lincoln would have encountered in Dilworth, see Fred Kaplan, *Lincoln: Biography of a Writer* (New York: Harper Collins, 2008), 7–12.
7. Noah Webster, *The American Spelling Book* (Albany, N.Y.: Websters and Skinners, 1821), 4. Hereafter cited as *Webster's Speller*.
8. *Webster's Speller*, 43, 159.
9. Ibid., 159; Dilworth, *New Guide to the English Tongue*, 51.
10. Roy P. Basler, ed., *The Collected Works of Abraham Lincoln* (New Brunswick, N.J.: Rutgers University Press, 1953–55), 4:62. Hereafter cited as *Collected Works*.
11. *Herndon's Informants*, 93–94.
12. *Collected Works*, 3:511. "Ciphering to the rule of three" is a problem in elementary proportional mathematics: with three known quantities of a four-term ratio (e.g., 3/4 : 9/x), to solve for the fourth.
13. William E. Barton, *Abraham Lincoln and His Books* (Chicago: Marshall Field & Co., 1920), 9–11. Barton retells the story from Adlai E. Stevenson's *Something of Men I Have Known* (1909), who had it from Henderson. Henry C. Whitney, *Life on the Circuit with Lincoln* (Boston, 1892; Caldwell, Idaho: Caxton, 1940) offers an inferior variant of this story in the context of military contract-seekers pestering the president to adopt their invention (177–78).
14. Warren, *Lincoln's Youth*, 167.
15. List compiled from ibid., 290.
16. Charles Monaghan, "Lindley Murray and the Enlightenment," *Paradigm* 19 (May 1996), www.ed.uiuc.edu/faculty/westbury/Paradigm/monaghan2.html.
17. Warren, *Lincoln's Youth*, 103; Douglas L. Wilson and Rodney O. Davis, *Herndon's Lincoln* (Urbana: University of Illinois Press, 2006), 36.
18. Lindley Murray, *The English Reader* (Philadelphia: J. Ormrod, 1800), 3–4.
19. Hugh Blair, *Abridgment of Lectures on Rhetoric* (1832; Philadelphia: Kay and Troutman, 1849), 61.
20. Monaghan, "Lindley Murray," 11.
21. Murray, *The English Reader*, 86–87.
22. Ibid., 226–27.
23. The table of contents of *The English Reader* may be found on pp. 29–36.

24. William Cowper, *The Task* (London: John Sharpe, 1825), 31–33; Murray, *The English Reader.*

25. Murray, *The English Reader,* 7.

26. Murray acknowledges his debt to Blair for parts of his introduction (ibid.); he borrows freely from pp. 147–53 of the *Abridgment of Lectures on Rhetoric.*

27. *Collected Works,* 1:100.

28. Lincoln is decrying Adams's having procured affidavits from persons who are far from "disinterested" parties in the disagreement: his son and "some black or mulatto boy, from his being kept in the Kitchen" (ibid., 1:99–100).

29. Murray, *The English Reader,* 19.

30. *Herndon's Informants,* 146–47 and 147 n. 1.

31. *The American Speaker* (Philadelphia: Birch and Small, 1811), v–vi.

32. *Herndon's Informants,* 105 and 105 n. 8.

33. Frederick Douglass, *My Bondage and My Freedom* (1855; New York: Penguin, 2003), 116.

34. Caleb Bingham, *The Columbian Orator* (Boston, 1797), 242.

35. Abraham T. Lowe, ed., *The Columbian Class Book, Consisting of Geographical, Historical and Biographical Extracts . . .* (Worcester, Mass.: Dorr & Howland, 1824), 169–74.

36. Ibid., 351.

37. Preface, *The Kentucky Preceptor,* 3rd ed. (Lexington, Ky.: Maccoun, Til[ford], 1812), n.p. Louis Warren asserts that the Kentucky imprint is "primarily, a new edition of Caleb Bingham's *The American Preceptor* (1794), published in Boston" (*Lincoln's Youth,* 167). In this he is mistaken. *The American Preceptor* might have served as a *model* for *The Kentucky Preceptor* (both are designed as schoolbooks; both contain "select sentences" for stylistic emulation), but the two books have completely different contents (including their prefaces).

38. *Herndon's Lincoln,* 16. Scott's *Elocution* contains the stanza from the poem which includes the well-known line, but the entire text is printed in *The Kentucky Preceptor,* 216–18. See chap. 3 below for a fuller discussion of Gray's "Elegy."

39. Warren, *Lincoln's Youth,* 291.

40. Thomas Jefferson, *The Portable Thomas Jefferson,* ed. Merril D. Peterson (New York: Penguin Books, 1977), 294.

41. *The Kentucky Preceptor,* 7.

42. Ibid., 42–44.

43. Whitney, *Life on the Circuit with Lincoln,* 147.

44. *The Kentucky Preceptor,* 56–57.

45. Warren, *Lincoln's Youth,* 185, 261 n. 48. The report is at third hand from Allen Gentry's son, Absalom, as communicated to Bess V. Ehrmann.

46. Ibid., 184.

47. Albert J. Beveridge, *Abraham Lincoln, 1809–1858,* 2 vols. (Boston: Houghton Mifflin, 1928), 1:83.

48. Warren, *Lincoln's Youth,* 195; Wilson and Davis, *Herndon's Lincoln,* 80.

49. Beveridge, *Abraham Lincoln,* 1:83 n. 5.

50. Ibid., 1:83–84 and 83 n. 5; Warren, *Lincoln's Youth,* 195 and 263 n. 28. Beveridge explains the mutation of "King's Jester" into "Quinn's Jests" as the result "of that careless pronunciation which prevailed among the pioneers."

51. James Quin, *Quin's Jests; or, The Facetious Man's Pocket-Companion* (London: [S.

Bladon], 1766), 5–6, 20, 15, 83. Copy examined at the Huntington Library, San Marino, Calif.

52. *Joe Miller's Jests* (Philadelphia, 1817), title page.

53. Ibid., 119, 15.

54. P. M. Zall, *Abe Lincoln Laughing* (Knoxville: University of Tennessee Press, 1995); anecdote numbers 63, 87, 204, 232, 243.

55. Quoted in Daniel Kilham Dodge, *Abraham Lincoln: The Evolution of His Literary Style* (Urbana: University of Illinois Press, 1900), 16–17.

56. Zall, in his bibliography, lists fifteen jest books, published between the mid-seventeenth century and 1860, as sources for Lincoln stories (*Abe Lincoln Laughing*, 171–74). Though *Quin's Jests* is not among them, there are two related titles that suggest possible stand-ins for *Quin*, should this item with a rather shaky provenance be rejected as Lincoln reading: the *Court Jester* (London, n.d, [1790?]) and the *Royal Court Jester* (London, n.d. [1790?]).

57. *Herndon's Informants*, 114.

58. From Thomas Gray's "Elegy Written in a Country Churchyard," discussed below in chapter 2.

59. Wilson and Davis, *Herndon's Lincoln*, 40–41; Warren, *Lincoln's Youth*, 46 and 227 n. 12.

60. *Herndon's Informants*, 114.

61. Aesop, *The Complete Fables*, trans. Olivia and Robert Temple (New York: Penguin Books, 1998), 46; hereafter cited as *Aesop* (1998).

62. *Aesop* (1998), xi, xviii. A good example of a truly Greek fable, perfect for an uproarious symposium but one unlikely to pass muster in a modern *Aesop* designed for the edification of youth, is "Zeus and Shame:"

> When Zeus fashioned man he gave him certain inclinations, but he forgot about shame. Not knowing how to introduce her, he ordered her to enter through the rectum. Shame baulked at this and was highly indignant. Finally, she said to Zeus:
> "All right! I'll go in, but on the condition that Eros doesn't come in the same way; if he does,
> I will leave immediately."
> Ever since then, all homosexuals are without shame. (*Aesop* [1998], 91)

63. *Aesop and Others, Translated into English, with Instructive Applications, and a Print before Each Fable* (Philadelphia: R. Aitken, 1777); hereafter cited as *Aesop* (1777). The judgment that this was the version of *Aesop* Lincoln read is based on a comparison of American editions published between 1777 and 1820: only the Aitken *Aesop*, in its successive printings, contains the fable known as "The Blackamoor," accompanied by its woodblock print as described by Lincoln himself (see just below).

64. *Aesop* (1777), [viii].

65. *Collected Works*, 1:315; *Aesop* (1998), 68.

66. Anecdote 148, Zall, *Abe Lincoln Laughing*, 77–78.

67. Emmanuel Hertz, *Abraham Lincoln: A New Portrait*, 2 vols. (New York: Horace Liveright, 1931), 1:897–98; Zall, *Abe Lincoln Laughing*, 75.

68. *Aesop* (1777), 280–81. In *Aesop* (1998) the fable is called "The Ethiopian," and the editors note that in the earliest version the slave was Indian, only later an African (11).

69. *Aesop* (1777), 281.

70. Van Wyck Brooks, *The World of Washington Irving* (New York: E. P. Dutton, 1944), 1.
71. Ibid., 3; Mason Locke Weems, *The Life of George Washington*, ed. Marcus Cunliffe (Cambridge, Mass.: Harvard University Press, 1962), lix (hereafter cited as Weems's *Washington*).
72. Marcus Cunliffe, introd., Weems's *Washington*, xi.
73. Ibid., xiii, xvii.
74. *Collected Works*, 4:235–36.
75. Ibid., 4:190.
76. Weems's *Washington*, 131–34.
77. Ibid., 55–57.
78. *Collected Works*, 3:20.
79. Weems's *Washington*, 143–44, 148.
80. *Collected Works*, 1:111.
81. Weems's *Washington*, 157–58.
82. *Collected Works*, 1:115.
83. Quoted in Francis B. Carpenter, *Six Months at the White House with Abraham Lincoln* (1866; Lincoln: University of Nebraska Press, 1995), 115. The qualifier "generally" is used above because Lincoln *may* have read *Don Quixote* and Homer's *Iliad* and *Odyssey* (see chap. 3 below).
84. Robert Irwin, *The Arabian Nights: A Companion* (London: Allen Lane, Penguin Press, 1994), 15–16.
85. David Turnham, in *Herndon's Informants*, 129 and 129 n. 3; Warren, *Lincoln's Youth*, 70; quoting Eleanor Atkinson, *The Boyhood of Lincoln* (New York: McClure Co., 1908), 24–25.
86. *Herndon's Informants*, 773.
87. Warren, *Lincoln's Youth*, 69–70, 290.
88. *The Book of the Thousand Nights and a Night*, trans. Richard F. Burton, 6 vols. in 3 (New York: Heritage Press, 1934), 3:2015. Hereafter cited as *Arabian Nights*.
89. *Collected Works*, 2:467.
90. *The History of Sinbad the Sailor* (Boston, 1794), [iii]. Moreover, none of the three other early-nineteenth-century editions examined contain *Ecclesiastes* 9:4.
91. *Arabian Nights*, 3:2018–19; *Sindbad*, 7–8.
92. *Arabian Nights*, 3:2059.
93. Douglas Wilson, *Honor's Voice* (New York: Alfred A. Knopf, 1998), 55.
94. Warren, *Lincoln's Youth*, 109.
95. James Riley, *Sufferings in Africa*, intro. by G. H. Evans (New York: Lyons Press, 2000), vi. This is an abridged reprint of *Authentic Narrative of the Loss of the American Brig Commerce* (1817; Hartford: S. Andrus & Son, 1854).
96. Riley, *Sufferings in Africa*, 4–5.
97. Ibid., vii.
98. Riley, *Authentic Narrative*, 260–61.
99. *Herndon's Informants*, 41, 112, 121, 445, 752.
100. Warren, *Lincoln's Youth*, 66, 232. Fred Kaplan believes that Lincoln read the full *Robinson Crusoe* and even remembered some of the protagonist's language when composing the Second Inaugural Address (*Lincoln*, 20–21).
101. Daniel Defoe, *Travels of Robinson Crusoe* (Worcester, Mass.: Isaiah Thomas, 1786), 24–31; *The Most Surprising Adventures of Robinson Crusoe*, 3 vols. (Boston: I. Thomas and E. T. Andrews, 1794).

102. Defoe, *Travels of Robinson Crusoe*, 31.
103. Ibid., 23–24.
104. *Herndon's Informants*, 41, 112, 121, 455.
105. Warren, *Lincoln's Youth*, 48–49, 228. Warren is quoting from David D. Thompson, *Abraham Lincoln, the First American* (Cincinnati, 1894), 16. This is a young-adult hagiography of Lincoln, evidently fictionalized, and gives no source for the story of Lincoln's "delight" in having a copy of *Pilgrim's Progress*.
106. Mark Twain, *The Adventures of Huckleberry Finn* (New York: Charles L. Webster & Co., 1885), 137.
107. John Bunyan, *The Pilgrim's Progress* (London: A. Fullarton & Co., 1851), xlv.
108. Ibid., xlv–xlvi. Some editions give a title-page epigraph, Hosea 12:10: "I have used similitudes."
109. Bunyan, *Pilgrim's Progress*, xlviii.
110. Kaplan, *Lincoln*, 18–19.
111. Bunyan, *Pilgrim's Progress*, 10–15.

2. Young Citizen Lincoln

1. *Herndon's Informants*, 10, 10 n. 7, 80, 384, 426.
2. *Collected Works*, 4:62; Benjamin Thomas, *Lincoln's New Salem* (Springfield, Ill.: Abraham Lincoln Association, 1934), 48; William Dean Howells, *Life of Abraham Lincoln* (Springfield, Ill.: Abraham Lincoln Association, 1938), 29. This is a facsimile reprint of the 1860 edition, with Lincoln's penciled emendations in the margins. Douglas Wilson, *Honor's Voice*, 332–33 n. 59, identifies the source of the Greene story as an 1881 interview given to the *Weekly Inter-Ocean* (Chicago).
3. Charles Maltby, who along with William G. Greene clerked with Lincoln at Denton Offut's store, asserted that it was Murray's grammar Lincoln perused and mastered (*The Life and Public Services of Abraham Lincoln* [Stockton, Calif.: Daily Independent Steam Power Plant, 1884], 27). But whether it was Murray or Samuel Kirkham's *English Grammar in Familiar Lectures*, 11th ed. (New York: Robert B. Collins, 1829), 10, scarcely matters, as the latter is to an extent derived from the former.
4. *Herndon's Informants*, 10; Wilson, *Honor's Voice*, 63, 65.
5. Wilson, *Honor's Voice*, 66.
6. Quoted in ibid., 67, from an 1860 interview that Greene gave to reporter James Q. Howard (333 n. 61).
7. Kirkham, *English Grammar*, 21.
8. *Herndon's Informants*, 18. Although Greene remembered the year as "summer and fall of 1830," this is incorrect, as Lincoln was still in Coles County, Ill., at that time.
9. *Herndon's Informants*, 80, 10. Graham probably did assist Lincoln in his studies of grammar and surveying, but his assertion that Lincoln studied formally with him at his school for a period of six months or more in 1833 is dubious on its face and was directly challenged by William G. Greene (ibid., 26; Wilson, *Honor's Voice*, 64).
10. *Collected Works*, 1:5–9; the "Communication" is dated March 9, 1832. The assumption here is that Lincoln wrote the piece shortly before publishing it.
11. *Herndon's Informants*, 253; Kunigunde Duncan and D. F. Nickols, *Mentor Graham: The Man Who Taught Lincoln* (Chicago: University of Chicago Press, 1944), 132. This book is a novelized biography, scantily documented, which overstates the importance of Graham in Lincoln's education.

12. *Herndon's Informants*, 450.
13. Testimony of Nathaniel Grigsby, Dennis Hanks, Grigsby again, and Sarah Johnston Lincoln, ibid., 94, 104, 107.
14. Ibid., 123–24.
15. Beveridge, *Abraham Lincoln*, 1:73 and 1:73 n. 4.
16. John G. Nicolay and John Hay, *Abraham Lincoln: A History*, 10 vols. (New York: Century Co., 1890), 1:35.
17. *Herndon's Informants*, 42 and 42 n. 18.
18. Ibid., 11. Unfortunately, Greene's memory or writing is confused here: how could Lincoln at fourteen, living in Indiana, have written a story about a woman who spent her entire life in central Illinois?
19. *Collected Works*, 1:5.
20. See the discussion of "proves to a demonstration" later in this chapter.
21. Kirkham, *English Grammar*, 14.
22. Ibid., 219.
23. Ibid., 222.
24. Hugh Blair, *An Abridgment of Lectures on Rhetoric* (1832; Philadelphia: Kay and Troutman, 1849), [i].
25. M. L. Houser, *The Books That Lincoln Read* (Peoria, Ill.: Edward J. Jacob, 1929), 10, 29; Rufus Rockwell Wilson, *What Lincoln Read* (Washington, D.C.: Pioneer, 1932), cites Rankin's "statement to George P. Hambrecht" as the source for this assertion (43, 84).
26. James T. Hickey, "Three R's in Lincoln's Education: Rogers, Riggin and Rankin," *Journal of the Illinois State Historical Society* 52 (1959–60): 195–207.
27. Blair, *Abridgment of Lectures on Rhetoric*, 79.
28. Maltby, *Life and Public Services*, 31.
29. Kirkham, *English Grammar*, 13; italics added.
30. *Collected Works*, 1:8–9; italics added.
31. Nicolay and Hay, *Abraham Lincoln*, 1:106.
32. Douglas L. Wilson, *Lincoln's Sword: The Presidency and the Power of Words* (New York: Alfred A. Knopf, 2006), 21.
33. *Herndon's Informants*, 107.
34. Thomas, *Lincoln's New Salem*, 15.
35. Ibid., 6; Maltby, *Life and Public Services*, 27.
36. Beveridge, *Abraham Lincoln*, 1:138–39. This epithet, which Lincoln would carry with him throughout his life, was loosely used by nineteenth-century American Protestants as a synonym for *atheist*, though in fact it denoted only someone who disbelieved in the prevailing religion: as in *not a Christian*.
37. Thomas, *Lincoln's New Salem*, 29; Others in New Salem or its vicinity who had small personal libraries, mostly comprised of history and literature, and put them at Lincoln's disposal were Isaac Chrisman, Bowling Green, John McNamar, and Bennett Abell. *Herndon's Informants*, 91; Wilson, *Honor's Voice*, 61.
38. *Herndon's Informants*, 21.
39. Ibid., 91.
40. Michael Burlingame, *The Inner World of Abraham Lincoln* (Urbana: University of Illinois Press, 1994), 238; *Herndon's Informants*, 545–46.
41. Thomas, *Lincoln's New Salem*, 47.
42. *Herndon's Informants*, 384.
43. Ibid., 539; Wilson, *Honor's Voice*, 70–71.

44. Wilson, *Honor's Voice*, cites Fern Nance Pond's research into "literary clubs of the region" to indicate that their by-laws had one "'outstanding rule . . . no member should use the name of the Supreme Being in debate'" (70).

45. *Herndon's Informants*, 432, 472, 576–77.

46. Ibid., 576–77.

47. Beveridge, *Abraham Lincoln*, 1.130.

48. Let this example stand for the many American editions Lincoln could have read at that time: Edward Gibbon, *The History of the Decline and Fall of the Roman Empire*, 3rd American ed., 6 vols. (New York: E. Duyckinck, 1822). However, one must note that Lincoln, a little later, owned a personal copy of Gibbon, given to him by Ninian W. Edwards. Citations here will be from the Modern Library edition of *History of the Decline and Fall of the Roman Empire*, 3 vols. (New York: Random House, n.d.), hereafter cited as *Decline and Fall*.

49. For example, Stewart Winger, *Lincoln, Religion, and Romantic Cultural Politics* (DeKalb: Northern Illinois University Press, 2003), asserts that "Gibbon's entire historical vision blamed Christianity for the decline of Roman virtue" (174).

50. *Decline and Fall*, 3:863–65.

51. Likewise loaned to Lincoln by William G. Greene (*Herndon's Informants*, 21); Wilson and Davis, *Herndon's Lincoln*, 80; Thomas, *Lincoln's New Salem*, 63.

52. Charles Rollin, *The Ancient History of the Egyptians, Carthaginians, Assyrians, Babylonians, Medes and Persians, Macedonians and Grecians*, 4 vols. (New York: George Long, 1830), 1:13.

53. Ibid.

54. Ibid., 1:20–22.

55. *Decline and Fall*, 1:70.

56. *Collected Works*, 1:109.

57. Ibid., 1:112, 115.

58. Parke Godwin, *A Biography of William Cullen Bryant*, 2 vols. (New York: Russell & Russell, [1883]), 1:283; Henry Houston Peckham, *Gotham Yankee: A Biography of William Cullen Bryant* (New York: Russell & Russell, 1950), 144, 146.

59. Hay cited in William H. Townsend, *Lincoln and the Bluegrass* (1955; Lexington: University Press of Kentucky, 1989), 136; Michael Burlingame, *At Lincoln's Side: John Hay's Civil War Correspondence and Selected Writings* (Carbondale: Southern Illinois University Press, 2000), 138.

60. See Asher B. Durand's homage to the two, pictured *in* nature *discussing* nature, titled *Kindred Spirits* (1849).

61. William Cullen Bryant, "The Prairies," in *Poems* (Boston: Russell, Odiorne, and Metcalf, 1834), 39–43.

62. Charles Brown, *William Cullen Bryant* (New York: Charles Scribner's Sons, 1971), 410; *Collected Works*, 3:550.

63. *Decline and Fall*, 1:25–26.

64. Ibid., 1:64.

65. Ibid., 1:668.

66. *Collected Works*, 1:114.

67. *Decline and Fall*, 1:901.

68. Ibid., 3:790 n.

69. *Collected Works*, 1:8.

70. *Decline and Fall*, 3:726.

71. James Woodress, *A Yankee's Odyssey: The Life of Joel Barlow* (Philadelphia: J. B. Lippincott Co., 1958), 219–20; Constantin-François de Volney, *A New Translation of Volney's Ruins*, 2 vols. (Paris, 1902; New York: Garland, 1979), 1:viii. Hereafter page references to *The Ruins*, vol. 1, are cited in the text.

72. *Herndon's Informants*, 172, 210.

73. Beveridge, *Abraham Lincoln*, 1:138.

74. *Herndon's Informants*, 13.

75. Martin Bernal, *Black Athena: The Afroasiatic Roots of Classical Civilization*, 2 vols. (1987, 1991).

76. Burlingame, *Inner World*, 37.

77. *Collected Works*, 1:111.

78. *Herndon's Informants*, 441.

79. Ibid., 602.

80. Douglas Wilson, *Lincoln's Sword*, posits a redating of the "Meditation" to 1864 (255–56, 329–30 n. 255); Michael Burlingame, *Abraham Lincoln: A Life*, 2 vols. (Baltimore: Johns Hopkins University Press, 2008), 2:711, accepts Wilson's judgment. For reasons given in the text above, I have retained the 1862 dating.

81. *Collected Works*, 5:403–4.

82. Ibid., 2:123.

83. Robert Bray, *Peter Cartwright: Legendary Frontier Preacher* (Urbana: University of Illinois Press, 2005), 148–51; Douglas Wilson, *Lincoln before Washington* (Urbana: University of Illinois Press, 1997), 59–66.

84. Bray, *Peter Cartwright.*, 148–49.

85. *Herndon's Informants*, 61; Wilson and Davis, *Herndon's Lincoln,* 87; Beveridge, *Abraham Lincoln*, accepts Herndon on this matter (1:138).

86. Yet it forms part of the standard French edition. See Voltaire, *Examen Important de Milord Bolingbroke* in *Mélanges*, Pléiade Edition (Paris, 1961); and Kenneth W. Applegate, ed. and trans., *Voltaire on Religion: Selected Writings* (New York: Frederick Ungar, 1974), 93.

87. "Important Study," *Deist; or, Moral Philosopher* (London) 2 (1819), iii–62.

88. Found in the antichristian writings of Celsus (late second century C.E.): *Origen: Contra Celsum*, ed. and trans. Henry Chadwick (London: Cambridge University Press, 1980), xxviii.

89. "Important Examination," in *Voltaire on Religion*, 33.

90. Wilson and Davis, *Herndon's Lincoln*, 16.

91. *Herndon's Informants*, 637–39; Wilson and Davis, *Herndon's Lincoln*, 17.

92. *Herndon's Informants*, 172, 513.

93. Wilson and Davis, *Herndon's Lincoln*, 266; see also *Lincoln and New Salem* (Petersburg, Ill.: Old Salem Lincoln League, n.d.): "Among the books which Lincoln had picked up or borrowed about New Salem, were copies of Volneys Les Ruines and Paine's Age of Reasons. From these he had absorbed a taint of skepticism, which tended to lead him away from the simple faith learned at his mother's knee" (56).

94. David Freeman Hawke, *Paine* (New York: Harper & Row, 1974), 295–97.

95. Ibid., 300–302.

96. Beveridge, *Abraham Lincoln*, 1:139 n. 1, states that "it is said that 1,500,000 copies of the *Age of Reason* were sold in England alone."

97. Thomas Paine, *The Age of Reason; Being an Investigation of True and of Fabulous Theology*, in *Selections from the Works of Thomas Paine*, ed. Arthur Wallace Peach

(New York: Harcourt, Brace, 1928), 230–31. Hereafter page references for *The Age of Reason* are cited in text.

98. "Reply to Emancipation Memorial Presented by Chicago Christians of All Denominations," *Collected Works*, 5:419–20.

99. Nicolay and Hay held that the "Meditation" "was not written to be seen of men" (*Abraham Lincoln*, 6:341–42), but the similarity in logic and structure between the two quoted passages (see above, this chapter, for "Meditation") strongly suggests a public audience for Lincoln's private thoughts.

100. *Collected Works*, 2:437.

101. Ibid., 4:482.

102. Wilson, *Honor's Voice*, 81.

103. Winger, *Lincoln, Religion*, 175.

104. Wilson and Davis, *Herndon's Lincoln*, 266.

105. Hardin Bale and James H. Matheny, in *Herndon's Informants*, 12–13, 576–77.

106. Voltaire, *Important Study*, chap. 13, "On the Gospels"; *The Age of Reason*, 290–342.

107. *Herndon's Informants*, 429–30.

108. Ibid., 499.

109. Quoted in Wilson, *Lincoln before Washington*, 66.

110. *Herndon's Informants*, 167–68.

111. Ibid., 441.

112. Thomas, *Lincoln's New Salem*, 66–67.

113. *Herndon's Informants*, 21; Wilson, *Honor's Voice*, 117.

114. Two of the most popular novels to feature the Rutledge–Lincoln romance appeared in the same year, 1919: Bernie Babcock's *The Soul of Ann Rutledge* and Irving Bachellor's *A Man for the Ages*.

115. Wilson and Davis, *Herndon's Lincoln*, 266; *Herndon's Informants*, 62.

3. Tragicomic Melancholy

1. *American Poetry: The Nineteenth Century*, ed. John Hollander, 2 vols. (New York: Library of America, 1993), 1:552–55. See also *Collected Works*, 1:367–70.

2. *Collected Works*, 1:378.

3. Some of the poems of Robert Browning he may have known: Daniel Kilham Dodge quotes Egbert L. Viele's recollection of Lincoln reciting poetry during a river trip from Washington to Virginia, late in the Civil War: "[H]e would sit for hours . . . repeating . . . page after page of Browning" (*Abraham Lincoln*, 14–15).

4. *Collected Works*, 1:1; my lineation.

5. Thomas Gray, "Elegy Written in a Country Churchyard," *The Complete Poems of Thomas Gray*, ed. H. W. Starr and J. R. Hendrickson (Oxford: Clarendon Press, 1966), 37. See also *The Kentucky Preceptor*, 216–18.

6. *Herndon's Informants*, 57.

7. John Milton, "Lycidas," *The Complete Poetry of John Milton*, ed. John T. Shawcross, rev. ed. (New York: Doubleday/Anchor Books, 1971), 162 (lines 124–31).

8. Alexander Pope, "The Temple of Fame," *The Poems of Alexander Pope*, ed. John Butt. (New Haven, Conn.: Yale University Press, 1963), 174–88 (lines 25–28, 61–136).

9. Ibid., lines 288–93, 500, 523–24.

10. *Collected Works*, 1:8–9.

11. Maurice Lindsay, *Robert Burns: The Man, His Work, the Legend* (1954; London: Macgibbon & Kee, 1968), 29–30, 33–36, 38–39.

12. David J. Harkness and Gerald McMurtry, *Lincoln's Favorite Poets* (Knoxville: University of Tennessee Press, 1959), 2.

13. Ibid., 4 . The main dissenter is Daniel Kilham Dodge, *Abraham Lincoln*, 12.

14. *Herndon's Informants*, 421, 577.

15. Isaac Newton Arnold, *The Life of Abraham Lincoln* (1884; Lincoln: University of Nebraska Press, 1994), 444.

16. Wilson, *Honor's Voice*, 73; Maltby, *Life and Public Services*, 27.

17. Noah Brooks, *Abraham Lincoln: His Youth and Early Manhood* (New York: G. P. Putnam's Sons, 1888), 20.

18. Ferenc Morton Szasz, *Abraham Lincoln and Robert Burns: Connected Lives and Legends* (Carbondale: Southern Illinois University Press, 2008), 51.

19. Thomas, *Lincoln's New Salem*, 29.

20. Wilson, *Honor's Voice*, 72.

21. Edgar Lee Masters, *Jack Kelso* (New York: D. Appleton, 1928), 89–90.

22. *Herndon's Informants*, 577.

23. Allen Guelzo, *Abraham Lincoln: Redeemer President* (Grand Rapids, Mich.: Eerdmans, 1999), 50.

24. Szasz, *Abraham Lincoln and Robert Burns*, 52–55, emphasizes the importance of oral performance in American frontier communities.

25. Wilson and Davis, *Herndon's Lincoln*, 94.

26. *Collected Works*, 1:106.

27. Robert Burns, "Is There for Honest Poverty," in *The Poems and Songs of Robert Burns*, ed. James Kinsley, 3 vols. (Oxford: Clarendon Press, 1968), 2:762–63.

28. Burns, "Epistle to a Young Friend," in *Poems and Songs*, 1:248–51 (lines 7–8).

29. Harkness and McMurtry, *Lincoln's Favorite Poets*, 6.

30. Burns, "Epistle to a Young Friend," lines 21–24, 33–40, 51–56, 57–64.

31. Burns, "Address to the Unco Guid," in *Poems and Songs*, 1:52–54 (lines 24, 42–48, 57–58, 63–64).

32. Szasz, *Abraham Lincoln and Robert Burns*, 76.

33. *Collected Works*, 1:272–73.

34. Ibid., 1:272.

35. Ibid., 1:274–76.

36. Ibid., 1:276.

37. Ibid., 1:382.

38. Wilson and Davis, *Herndon's Lincoln*, 166.

39. Lindsay, *Robert Burns*, 77, 79.

40. Burns, "Holy Willie's Prayer," in *Poems and Songs*, 1:74–78 (lines 1–12, 43–48, 57–58, 61–66, 95–100).

41. Wilson and Davis, *Herndon's Lincoln*, 159–60; Lindsay, *Robert Burns*, 77, 83.

42. Burns, "Tam O'Shanter," in *Poems and Songs*, 2:558–64 (lines 59–67, 216–18).

43. Burns, "The Cotter's Saturday Night," in *Poems and Songs*, 1:148–51 (lines 73–74, 137, 163–66, 168).

44. Quoted in Wilson, *Honor's Voice*, 74.

45. John E. Hallwas, ed., *The Poems of H.* (Peoria, Ill.: Ellis Press, 1982), 75–80, 212.

46. Ibid., 6–7.

47. H., "The Small Beer Poets," in *Poems of H.*, 89, 212–14.

48. Ibid., 92.

49. *Herndon's Life of Lincoln, the history and personal recollections of . . .* , ed. Paul M. Angle (New York: A. and C. Boni, 1930), 74; Hallwas, *The Poems of H.*, 100.

50. For Kelso in Kentucky and New Salem, see Mary Turner, "Will the Real Jack Kelso Please Stand Up?," *For the People, a Newsletter of the Abraham Lincoln Association*, Winter 1999, 1.

51. *Collected Works*, 1:106.

52. Burns, "Address to the De'il," in *Poems and Songs*, 1:172 (lines 115–20).

53. *Herndon's Informants*, 21, 31, 471.

54. Fiona MacCarthy, *Byron: Life and Legend* (New York: Farrar, Straus and Giroux, 2002), 37, 40, 67.

55. Wilson, *Honor's Voice*, 275, 281–82, 292.

56. Joshua Wolf Shenk, *Lincoln's Melancholy* (Boston: Houghton Mifflin, 2005), 34.

57. In *Lincoln: Biography of a Writer*, Fred Kaplan asserts that Lincoln put on Byronic mourning weeds after Ann Rutledge's death, citing the early "On the Death of a Young Woman" as a poem Lincoln may have associated with this loss (72–74).

58. George Gordon, Lord Byron, "Nisus and Euryalus," in *The Complete Poetical Works of Byron*, ed. Paul E. More (Cambridge, Mass.: Houghton Mifflin, 1933), 107 (lines 3, 10), 110 (lines 375–84, 399–400).

59. Byron, *The Corsair*, in *Complete Poetical Works*, 340–65 (lines 227–30).

60. Michael Burlingame, e-mail communication to the author, citing an interview of Egbert L. Viele by William A. Crofutt, Sept. 23, 1885, clipping collection, Lincoln Museum, Fort Wayne, Ind.

61. Byron, *The Corsair*, stanzas 8–9.

62. Ibid., stanza 11.

63. Ibid., lines 632–35.

64. *Herndon's Informants*, 30–31, 470.

65. Whitney, *Life on the Circuit with Lincoln*, 148–49.

66. Byron, *The Bride of Abydos*, in *Complete Poetical Works*, 332–36, canto 2 (lines 363–75).

67. Ibid., lines 416–17.

68. Ibid., lines 574–82, 636–38.

69. Wilson, *Honor's Voice*, 125, 190; *Herndon's Informants*, 205.

70. Byron, *Childe Harold's Pilgrimage*, in *Complete Poetical Works*, 4 (canto 1, lines 64–72).

71. Wilson and Davis, *Herndon's Lincoln*, 42–44. However, see John Lair, *Songs Lincoln Loved* (New York: Duell, Sloane and Pearce, 1954), 24–25, for the case that "Adam and Eve's Wedding Song," both the tune and the words, were traditional in the northern Kentucky area early in the nineteenth century.

72. Wilson and Davis, *Herndon's Lincoln*, 48.

73. Thomas Moore, *The Life of Lord Byron; with His Letters and Journals*, 2 vols. (Philadelphia: Thomas Wardle, 1840), 1:129.

74. Jesse W. Weik, *The Real Lincoln* (Boston: Houghton Mifflin, 1922), 81.

75. The poem was rediscovered and attributed to Lincoln by Richard Lawrence Miller: "Lincoln's 'Suicide' Poem: Has It Been Found?" *For the People, a Newsletter of the Abraham Lincoln Association*, Spring 2004, 1 (all quotations from the poem are taken from Miller's transcription). For further commentary on the poem, see Shenk, *Lincoln's Melancholy*, 39–42.

76. Shenk, *Lincoln's Melancholy*, 41.

77. Byron, "Euthanasia," in *Complete Poetical Works*, 167 (lines 33–36).

78. Byron, "Darkness," in *Complete Poetical Works*, 189–90 (lines 66–67). See also Wilson, *Honor's Voice*, 190–91.

79. Byron, "Darkness," lines 66–67.

80. Wilson, *Honor's Voice*, 192–93; Byron, "The Dream," in *Complete Poetical Works*, 213–16.

81. Byron, "The Dream," lines 169–83, 190–201.

82. *Collected Works*, 1:367–70.

83. Byron, *Childe Harold's Pilgrimage*, in *Complete Poetical Works*, 19–42 (canto 3, lines 55–63).

84. Ibid., canto 1, lines 22–26, 82–88.

85. Ibid., canto 3, lines 397–405; Whitney, *Life on the Circuit with Lincoln*, 148.

86. *Collected Works*, 1:114; Wilson, *Honor's Voice*, 196–98.

87. Byron, *Don Juan*, in *Complete Poetical Works*, 745 (canto 1, lines 1–8).

88. *Herndon's Informants*, 589.

89. Wilson, *Honor's Voice*, 205; Byron, *Lara*, in *Complete Poetical Works*, 366 (canto 1, lines 13–16, 43–46).

90. Harkness and McMurtry, *Lincoln's Favorite Poets*, 41–42.

91. Burlingame, *Inner World*, 123. For a comprehensive and judicious examination of Lincoln's relationships with women in New Salem, see chap. 4 of Wilson, *Honor's Voice*.

92. Byron, *Don Juan*, 761 (canto 1, lines 929–36).

93. *Collected Works*, 1:118.

94. Wilson, *Honor's Voice*, 130–31.

95. Eliza Cook, *Poems* (London: George Routledge & Sons, [1848?]), 33–34.

96. Carpenter, *Six Months at the White House*, 115.

97. Nathaniel Parker Willis, *Poems* (New York: Hurst & Co., 1882), 228.

98. *Collected Works*, 4:48.

99. Fitz-Greene Halleck, *Alnwick Castle, with Other Poems* (New York: George Dearborn, 1835), 28.

100. *The Diary of Orville Hickman Browning*, ed. Theodore Calvin Pease and James G. Randall, Lincoln Series, 2 vols. (Springfield: Illinois State Historical Library, 1925), 1:554–55.

101. Fitz-Greene Halleck, "Fanny," in *The Poetical Writings of Fitz-Greene Halleck*, ed. James Grant Wilson (1869; New York: AMS Press, 1969), 151–57.

102. *Diary of Orville Hickman Browning*, 1:542.

103. Thomas Hood, "The Haunted House," in *Selected Poems of Thomas Hood*, ed. John Clubbe (Cambridge, Mass.: Harvard University Press, 1970), 179–84.

104. *Collected Works*, 1:367.

105. Hood, "The Haunted House," lines 117–24.

106. Hood, "The Lost Heir," in *Selected Poems*, 223–26 (lines 1–4, 25, 82, 89–90).

107. Michael Burlingame and John R. Turner Ettlinger, eds., *Inside Lincoln's White House: The Complete Civil War Diary of John Hay* (Carbondale: Southern Illinois University Press, 1997), 194.

108. Noah Brooks, "Personal Recollections of Abraham Lincoln," *Harper's Magazine* 31 (July 1865), 229.

109. Hood, "Miss Kilmansegg and Her Precious Leg," in *Selected Poems*, 599–600 (lines 2353–59, 2374–81).

110. Wilson and Davis, *Herndon's Lincoln*, 479.

111. William A. Butler, *Nothing to Wear* (New York: Rudd & Carleton, 1857), 23–24, 41–42.

112. Noah Brooks, "Personal Recollections of Abraham Lincoln," 229.

113. Michael Burlingame, ed., *At Lincoln's Side: John Hay's Civil War Correspondence and Selected Writings* (Carbondale: Southern Illinois University Press, 2000), 138.

114. Noah Brooks, "Personal Recollections of Abraham Lincoln," 229; Harkness and McMurtry, *Lincoln's Favorite Poets*, 56–57.

115. Henry Wadsworth Longfellow, "The Psalm of Life," in *The Complete Poetical Works* (Boston: Houghton Mifflin, 1922), 3–4.

116. Douglas L. Wilson, "Abraham Lincoln and the 'Spirit of Mortal,'" in *Lincoln before Washington*, 134–35; this section also follows Wilson's text of "Mortality."

117. William Cullen Bryant, "Thanatopsis," in *Poems*, 19–22.

118. William H. Townsend, *Lincoln and the Bluegrass* (1955; Lexington: University Press of Kentucky, 1989), 136.

119. Longfellow, "The Psalm of Life," 3.

120. Longfellow, "The Building of the Ship," in *Complete Poetical Works*, 100–103.

121. Quoted in Harkness and McMurtry, *Lincoln's Favorite Poets*, 77.

122. Oliver Wendell Holmes, "The Last Leaf," in *Complete Poetical Works* (Boston: Houghton Mifflin, 1923), 1.

123. Carpenter, *Six Months at the White House*, 58–59.

124. Henry B. Rankin, *Personal Recollections of Abraham Lincoln* (New York: G. P. Putnam's Sons, 1916), 125–27.

125. William E. Barton, *Abraham Lincoln and Walt Whitman* (Indianapolis: Bobbs Merrill, 1928), 92. Much more recently, Michael Burlingame, in the definitive analysis of Rankin's claims in an appendix to his edition of Jesse W. Weik's *The Real Lincoln* (Lincoln: University of Nebraska Press, 2002), has found them wanting to the extent that "historians should stop consulting his memoirs for information about Lincoln's time in Springfield" (397).

126. Daniel Mark Epstein, *Lincoln and Whitman: Parallel Lives in Civil War Washington* (New York: Ballantine Books, 2004), 6–8.

127. Ibid., 10.

128. Ibid., 11.

129. Ibid., 15.

130. *Collected Works*, 3:480. Kaplan also associates this section of the Wisconsin address, calling it "Lincoln's best poem" (*Lincoln*, 302–3).

131. *Herndon's Informants*, 519.

132. *Collected Works*, 1:377.

4. Necessity and Invention

1. *Collected Works*, 1:382–84. or a fuller analysis of the campaign and Lincoln's handbill, see also Bray, *Peter Cartwright*, 206–13; and Wilson, *Honor's Voice*, 311–12.

2. *Collected Works*, 1:382.

3. Allen C. Guelzo, "Abraham Lincoln and the Doctrine of Necessity," *Journal of the Abraham Lincoln Association* 18.1 (Winter 1997): 67.

4. Quoted in Warren, *Lincoln's Youth*, 113.

5. Winger, *Lincoln, Religion*, 180–81.

6. Guelzo, *Abraham Lincoln*, 106–7, 119–21.

7. David Hume, *Essays and Treatises on Several Subjects*, 2 vols. (Edinburgh: T. Cadell and W. Davies, 1809), 2:85.

8. Wilson and Davis, *Herndon's Lincoln*, 265.

9. Hume, *Inquiry concerning Human Understanding*, in *Essays and Treatises*, 2 :99.

10. Quoted in Ward Hill Lamon [Chauncey Black], *The Life of Abraham Lincoln* (1872; Lincoln: Bison Books/University of Nebraska Press, 1999), 494.
11. Wilson and Davis, *Herndon's Lincoln*, 263.
12. Hume, *Inquiry*, 9–10.
13. Ibid., 25–26, 31.
14. Winger, *Lincoln, Religion*, 98.
15. Wilson and Davis, *Herndon's Lincoln*, 356.
16. Hume, *Inquiry*, 147.
17. Ibid., 104.
18. Ibid., 107.
19. Hume, *A Dissertation on the Passions*, in *Essays and Treatises*, 2 :183.
20. Ibid., 186.
21. Dillard C. Donnohue, in *Herndon's Informants*, 602.
22. Hume, *A Dissertation*, 205.
23. Ibid., 206.
24. Ibid., 211.
25. But he was not "enrolled" by the clerk of the Illinois Supreme Court, a necessary step for full admission to the bar, until March 1, 1837. Mark E. Steiner, *An Honest Calling: The Law Practice of Abraham Lincoln* (DeKalb: Northern Illinois University Press, 2006), 37.
26. *Collected Works*, 4:65.
27. Mentor Graham, Lynn McNulty, J. Rowan Herndon, and Isaac Cogdal, in *Herndon's Informants*, 9, 81, 91, 441.
28. Frederick Trevor Hill, *Lincoln the Lawyer* (New York: Century, 1913), 50.
29. Jason Duncan and Charles Maltby, in *Herndon's Informants*, 540, 27.
30. Isaac Cogdal, in ibid., 440–41. A problem with understanding Cogdal's reminiscences is that he gave Herndon two interviews, both undated (but, according to the editors, probably during 1865–66). In the first he mentions Lincoln's having Blackstone in his possession in 1832; in the second, though he reiterates that he first knew Lincoln in 1832, his emphatic remark about Lincoln's studying "terribly hard" could by context be seen to refer to 1834–35, when Lincoln was courting Ann Rutledge. This is the interpretation that Douglas L. Wilson makes in *Honor's Voice* (107).
31. Mentor Graham told Herndon, "The Continued thought & study of the man Caused–with the death of one whom he dearly & sincerely loved, a momentary—only a partial & momentary derangement" (*Herndon's Informants*, 11). Wilson thinks that Graham was "soft-pedaling" what was a very serious "mental derangement following the death of Ann Rutledge" (*Honor's Voice*, 107).
32. First quotation in Steiner, *An Honest Calling*, 34, citing James M. Ogden, "Lincoln's Early Impressions of the Law in Indiana," *Notre Dame Law* 7 (1932): 325, 328; David C. Mearns, "Mr. Lincoln and the Books He Read," in Arthur Bestor, David C. Mearns, and Jonathan Daniels, *Three Presidents and Their Books: The Reading of Jefferson, Lincoln, and Franklin D. Roosevelt* (Urban : University of Illinois Press, 1955), 61, citing Allan Jasper Conant, "My Acquaintance with Abraham Lincoln," in *Liber Scriptorum: The First Book of the Authors Club* (New York, 1893), 172.
33. *Collected Works*, 3:344, 4:121. See bibliographic appendix for details of the other law texts named.
34. William Blackstone, *Commentaries on the Laws of England*, 4 vols. in 2 (New York: W. E. Dean, 1832). Hereafter page references to *Commentaries* are cited in text.

35. Wilson and Davis, *Herndon's Lincoln*, 78.

36. Ibid., 80.

37. Steiner, *An Honest Calling*, 44, lists John Bouvier's *Law Dictionary* (1839) as a reference Lincoln cited in an 1844 case; but nothing indicates that he knew of this work before entering law practice in Springfield in 1837.

38. *Collected Works*, 3.53/.

39. Steiner, *An Honest Calling*, 44, 46.

40. Russell Godbey, in *Herndon's Informants*, 450.

41. William E. Barton, *The Soul of Abraham Lincoln*, intro. Michael Nelson (1920; Urbana: University of Illinois Press, 2005).

42. Wayne C. Temple, *From Skeptic to Prophet* (Mahomet, Ill.: Mayhaven, 1995), 36–38.

43. Ibid., 39, 40.

44. Barton, *The Soul of Abraham Lincoln*, 160, 164, 359.

45. James Smith, *The Christian's Defence* (Cincinnati: J. A. James, 1843). Hereafter page references to *The Christian's Defence* are cited in text. In 1920 William E. Barton could locate but nine copies in the United States (including his own). *The Soul of Abraham Lincoln*, 165 n.

46. Temple, *From Skeptic to Prophet*, 39.

47. Barton, *The Soul of Abraham Lincoln*, 158.

48. Ibid. I examined the copy at the Rare Book and Manuscript Library, University of Illinois, Urbana-Champaign, June 2007.

49. Barton, *The Soul of Abraham Lincoln*, 359.

50. Sometime in 1836 or shortly thereafter, Lincoln was given a copy of Paley's *Works* by Ninian W. Edwards. Robert Bray, "What Abraham Lincoln Read: An Evaluative and Annotated List," *Journal of the Abraham Lincoln Association* 28.2 (Summer 2007): 68 n. 156.

51. Wilson and Davis, *Herndon's Lincoln*, 264–65.

52. For the history of *Vestiges*'s publication, see James A. Secord, ed., *Vestiges of the Natural History of Creation and Other Evolutionary Writings* (Chicago: University of Chicago Press, 1994), xxv–xxxv.

53. Robert Chambers, *Vestiges of the Natural History of Creation* , 10th ed. (London: John Churchill, 1853), 5–6. Hereafter page references to *Vestiges* are cited in text.

54. For Akers's "sermon on prophecies," see Robert Bray, "Abraham Lincoln and the Two Peters," *Journal of the Abraham Lincoln Association* 22.2 (Summer 2001): 27–48.

55. *Collected Works*, 3:16.

56. Francis Wayland, *Elements of Political Economy* (Boston: Gould and Lincoln, 1854), iv, 15–16. According to Gabor S. Boritt, Wayland's *Elements* "became the country's most popular text in its field" (*Abraham Lincoln and the Economics of the American Dream* [Memphis: Memphis State University Press, 1978], 123).

57. Emanuel Hertz, *The Hidden Lincoln* (New York: Viking Press, 1938), 117.

58. Ibid. Allen C. Guelzo, in *Abraham Lincoln: Redeemer President*, asserts that Henry C. Carey was one of "Lincoln's preferred authors" and names several of his books in addition to *Principles of Political Economy* as "Lincoln favorites" (107–8). Guelzo's source citation for this is *The Hidden Lincoln*, 116–17, but as noted above, Herndon says only that Lincoln "more or less peeped into" this title and does not mention any other Carey works. In this study, therefore, I do not examine anything by Carey closely. According to Stewart Winger, however, "Henry Carey was perhaps the chief economic theorist for the Whigs, and he therefore had great influence on

Lincoln's economic thinking" (*Lincoln, Religion*, 130). Yet Winger does not show that Lincoln got his sense of Carey's views from reading *Principles of Political Economy*. And David Herbert Donald, in *Lincoln* (New York: Simon and Schuster, 1995), 110, citing Boritt (*Abraham Lincoln and Economics*, 122), asserts that Lincoln "studied Herndon's copies of both Henry C. Carey's *Essay on the Rate of Wages* (1835) and Francis Wayland's *Elements of Political Economy*." But Boritt is hardly firm about this matter, carefully qualifying Lincoln's reading of this earlier work by Carey with an *if*—if he had happened to read it, he would have found, etc.

59. This defense of slavery as right for the slave, as for the South, was read and discussed by Herndon and Lincoln (Wilson and Davis, *Herndon's Lincoln*, 224).

60. *Collected Works*, 3:468.

61. Wayland, *Elements of Political Economy*, 18–19.

62. See ibid., section 6, 133–39.

63. Ibid., 106.

64. *Collected Works*, 3:541–42.

65. "Sixtieth thousand" appears on the title page of Hinton Rowan Helper, *The Impending Crisis of the South: How to Meet It* (1857; New York: A. B. Burdick, 1860) (hereafter cited as *Impending Crisis*). "Helper . . . produced an antislavery work the political and social significance of which was exceeded by no ante bellum publication with the possible exception of *Uncle Tom's Cabin*" (Hugh C. Bailey, *Hinton Rowan Helper: Abolitionist-Racist* [University: University of Alabama Press, 1965], 20).

66. *Washington Sunday Chronicle*, April 7, 1869.

67. Carl Sandburg, *Abraham Lincoln: The Prairie Years*, 2 vols. (New York: Harcourt, Brace, 1926), 1:118. Compare Beveridge, *Abraham Lincoln*, 2:550, which parallels and even may be based on Sandburg.

68. Sandburg, *Lincoln: Prairie Years*, 1:121–22.

69. David Brown, *Southern Outcast: Hinton Rowan Helper and "The Impending Crisis of the South"* (Baton Rouge: Louisiana State University Press, 2006), 177 n. 43.

70. *Collected Works*, 2:255.

71. Bailey, *Hinton Rowan Helper*, 53–54.

72. Hinton Rowan Helper, *Compendium of the Impending Crisis of the South* (New York: A. B. Burdick, 1860; facsimile reprint, Miami, Fla.: Mnemosyne, 1969]), 139 (hereafter cited as *Compendium*).

73. David Brown, *Southern Outcast*, 153.

74. Bailey, *Hinton Rowan Helper*, 51.

75. Ibid., 57; David Brown, *Southern Outcast*, 146–48.

76. *Impending Crisis*, 129.

77. Bailey, *Hinton Rowan Helper*, 55.

78. See ibid., chap. 4.

79. Wilson and Davis, *Herndon's Lincoln*, 224.

80. Quoted in Harvey Wish, ed., *Ante-Bellum: Writings of George Fitzhugh and Hinton Rowan Helper on Slavery* (New York: Capricorn Books, 1960), 13.

81. Ibid., 64.

82. Jesse Fell to Ward Hill Lamon, September 22, 1870, in *Herndon's Informants*, 579.

83. William E. Channing, *Works*, 6 vols. (Boston: American Unitarian Association, 1856).

84. Ibid., 1:v–vi.

85. Ibid., 1:x.

86. Ibid., 1:xviii.

87. Channing, "Remarks on the Character and Writings of John Milton," in *Works*, 1:27.
88. Channing, "The Union," in *Works*, 1:336–38.
89. Channing, *Slavery*, vol. 2 of *Works*, 7. Hereafter page references to *Slavery* are cited in text.
90. *Collected Works*, 1:348, 8:333.
91. Lincoln may have borrowed this famous phrase from Leonard Bacon, *Slavery Discussed in Occasional Essays* (1846).
92. *Collected Works*, 2:266.
93. Ibid., 3:16. Lincoln would employ the phrase again: three times in a speech at Carlinville, Illinois, August 31, 1858 (*Collected Works*, 3:77–81) and once in a speech at Columbus, Ohio, September 16, 1859 (ibid., 3:402, reiterating from the Ottawa debate).
94. Theodore Parker, "The Transient and Permanent in Christianity," in *Theodore Parker: An Anthology*, ed. Henry Steele Commager (Boston: Beacon Press, 1960), 49.
95. Ibid., 55.
96. Ibid., 73.
97. Theodore Parker, "The Effect of Slavery on the American People" (pamphlet; Boston, 1858), 5. Herndon's recollection here (Wilson and Davis, *Herndon's Lincoln*, 242) has caused lasting bibliographic confusion. The Parker volumes he appears to say he brought back from his eastern trip (early 1858) and gave to Lincoln were *Additional Speeches, Addresses, and Occasional Sermons*, 2 vols. (Boston: Horace B. Fuller, 1855). But the one sermon or essay title he mentions, "The Effect of Slavery on the American People," was delivered three years later.
98. Garry Wills, *Lincoln at Gettysburg: The Words That Remade America* (New York: Simon and Schuster, 1992), 107–8. More recently, Ronald C. White Jr., in *The Eloquent President* (New York: Random House, 2006), while accepting Parker as an influence, concludes that Lincoln "was more apt at Gettysburg to be building on his own words," adapted from the First Inaugural and the Message to Congress in Special Session, July 4, 1861 (252–53). Still more recently, however, another influence on the Gettysburg Address has received new attention. While Wills juxtaposed Lincoln's speech with the model of all Western "funeral orations," the *Logos Epitaphios* of Pericles, he stopped short of claiming that Lincoln had been even indirectly influenced by the latter. But in her senior B.A. thesis for Brown University, classicist Anne Wootton shows that Lincoln had access to Pericles's oration through Thucydides's *Peloponnesian War*—two volumes (22 and 23) in the Harper's Classical Library series, which was part of the White House Library when Lincoln was president ("The Classical Lincoln," Honors Thesis, Brown University Classics Department, 2009, 104–21, 127).
99. Quoted in Wills, *Lincoln at Gettysburg*, 198; *Herndon's Informants*, 580.
100. See Parker, "The Boston Kidnapping" (April 12, 1852) and "The New Crime against Humanity" (June 4, 1854), in *Additional Speeches*, vol. 2.
101. Parker, "Daniel Webster," in *Additional Speeches*, 1:234.
102. Ibid., 1:245–46.
103. Ibid., 1:278.
104. *Collected Works*, 2:383; Daniel Webster, "Reply to Hayne," in *The Great Speeches and Orations of Daniel Webster* (1879; Boston: Little, Brown, 1923), 269.
105. Wilson and Davis, *Herndon's Lincoln*, 245 n. See, for example, David Donald, *Lincoln*, 206.
106. Webster, "Reply to Hayne," 227.

107. *Collected Works*, 2:461. Historian Carl F. Wieck has come to the same conclusion; see *Lincoln's Quest for Equality* (DeKalb: Northern Illinois University Press, 2002), 91–123.

108. Webster, "Reply to Hayne," 257.

109. *Collected Works*, 2:132.

110. Ibid., 4:67.

111. As Parker noted at the beginning of "The New Crime against Humanity" (June 4, 1854): "I know well the responsibility of the place I occupy this morning. Tomorrow's sun shall carry my words to all America. They will be read on both sides of the continent. They will cross the ocean" (*Additional Speeches*, 85 n., 86).

112. Parker, "The Nebraska Question," in *Additional Speeches* , 1:300.

113. Ibid., 1:327.

114. Ibid., 1:366.

115. *Collected Works*, 2:116.

116. Ibid., 2:323.

117. Parker, "The Nebraska Question," 1:364.

118. Ibid., 1:366.

119. *Collected Works*, 2:465–66.

120. Parker, "Thoughts on America," in *Additional Speeches*, 2:69.

121. Parker, "The Dangers Which Threaten the Rights of Man in America," in *Additional Speeches,* 2:250. Wieck (chap. 4) points out that the correspondences discussed in the text above (and principally the figure of the divided house) make a compelling case for Lincoln's having assimilated Parker's "Dangers" sermon. I entirely agree (having read *Lincoln's Quest for Equality* after completing the above analysis). Wieck, however, seems to have been unaware that Herndon brought the two volumes of *Additional Speeches* back with him from Boston, believing rather that Lincoln read "Dangers" at some time between its first publication and early in 1858 (*Lincoln's Quest for Equality*, 91). My position is that Lincoln first encountered the sermon during or after March 1858 and that therefore Parker's influence on the conception and composition of the House Divided speech was fresh and immediate.

122. *Collected Works*, 1:315.

123. Moncure Daniel Conway Papers, ms. 0277, Columbia University.

124. Moncure Daniel Conway, *The Rejected Stone* (1861; Boston: Walker, Wise, & Co., 1862), and *Autobiography* (Boston: Houghton, Mifflin, 1904), 340–41. Hereafter page references to *The Rejected Stone* are cited in text.

125. "A company of gentlemen in Boston wished to distribute 'The Rejected Stone' among the soldiers, and I gladly relinquished my royalty for that large edition" (Conway, *Autobiography*, 343).

126. *Collected Works*, 5:296, 328, 336; Donald, *Lincoln*, 363, 364–66.

127. Conway, *Autobiography*, 345; Allen Guelzo, *Lincoln's Emancipation Proclamation: The End of Slavery in America* (New York: Simon and Schuster, 2004), 76. Guelzo misidentifies William Henry Channing as William Ellery Channing, who died in 1842.

128. Conway, *Autobiography*, 344–46; the rest of Lincoln's story may be found in Zall, *Abe Lincoln Laughing*, 51–52.

5. Nothing Equals Macbeth

1. For the "well-worn copy," see Wilson and Davis, *Herndon's Lincoln*, 199. The case in which Lincoln employed *Othello* (3.3.160–66) was heard in Tazewell County Court in 1847; George W. Minier, in *Herndon's Informants*, 707–8.

2. *Collected Works*, 2:384. All other references to Shakespeare occur in Lincoln's correspondence with the Shakespearean actor James H. Hackett, ibid., 6:392–93, 558–59.
3. Clarence Edward Macartney, *Lincoln and the Bible* (New York: Abingdon-Cokesbury, 1949), 7–8.
4. *Collected Works*, 2:437–42.
5. Macartney, *Lincoln and the Bible*, 6.
6. *Collected Works*, 1:108–9.
7. Though it must be admitted that Lincoln's resounding conclusion—"*the gates of hell shall not prevail against it*" {Matthew 16:18)—is an emphatic example of a political preacher preaching!
8. *Collected Works*, 2:461.
9. Ibid., 3:8–9.
10. Ibid. 3:17; Macartney, *Lincoln and the Bible*, [5].
11. Lincoln used the epithet "Saviour" six times, beginning with the December 1839 speech in the Illinois House on the Sub-Treasury and ending with thank-you remarks to a group of "loyal colored people of Baltimore" who had presented him with a Bible in September 1864 (*Collected Works*, 1:167, 7:542).
12. Ibid., 2:97.
13. Beveridge, *Abraham Lincoln*, 1:510; Thomas, *Abraham Lincoln*, 134; Donald, *Lincoln*, 153.
14. Quoted in Burlingame, *Abraham Lincoln*, 2:288.
15. Carpenter, *Six Months at the White House*, 230.
16. Whitney, *Life on the Circuit with Lincoln*, 126.
17. Henry C. Whitney, "Abraham Lincoln, a Study from Life," *Arena* 19 (January–June 1898), 474–75.
18. J. Max Patrick, *Francis Bacon* (London: Longmans, Green, 1961), 12–13.
19. Francis Bacon, "Of Truth," in *Essays* (Roslyn, N.Y.: Walter J. Black/Classics Club, 1942), 5.
20. Bacon, "Of Simulation and Dissimulation," in *Essays*, 21.
21. Bacon, "Of Counsel," in *Essays*, 86, 88.
22. Bacon, "Of Negotiating," in *Essays*, 200.
23. Bacon, "Of Great Place," in *Essays*, 42.
24. Bacon, "Of Empire," in *Essays*, 79, 83.
25. Bacon, "Of Cunning," in *Essays*, 94.
26. Ibid., 96–97.
27. Bacon, "Of Usury," in *Essays*, 171.
28. The verse in quotation or paraphrase occurs four times in the *Collected Works*, and the sentiment less directly on eight occasions.
29. *Collected Works*, 3:204–5.
30. Quoted in ibid., 2:286–87.
31. Bacon, "Of Revenge," in *Essays*, 17.
32. Ibid., 18.
33. Bacon, "Of Love," in *Essays*, 39–40.
34. Bacon, "Of Envy," in *Essays*, 35.
35. *Collected Works*, 2:383.
36. Ibid., 2:467.
37. Bacon, "Of Ambition," in *Essays*, 156.
38. Generations of biographers (and in the twentieth century "psycho-biographers") have speculated on the root cause of Lincoln's melancholy. Perhaps the two most balanced

and insightful accounts are Michael Burlingame, *The Inner World of Abraham Lincoln* (1994), chap. 5, "Lincoln's Depressions"; and Joshua Wolf Shenk, *Lincoln's Melancholy* (2005), a monograph on the subject that is excellent throughout.

39. Bacon, "Of Ambition," 158.

40. Bacon, "Of Deformity," in *Essays*, 182–83.

41. Quoted in Burlingame, *Abraham Lincoln: A Life*, 1:173.

42. Bacon, "Of Studies," in *Essays*, 207.

43. Ibid., 208–9.

44. *Collected Works*, 1:8.

45. Bacon, "Of Honor and Reputation," in *Essays*, 222.

46. Ibid., 223–24.

47. Ibid., 224.

48. Carl Sandburg, *Abraham Lincoln: The War Years*, 4 vols. (New York: Harcourt, Brace, 1939), 1:583.

49. *Lincoln Day-by-Day, 1861–1865*, ed. C. Percy Powell (Washington, D.C.: Lincoln Sesquicentennial Commission, 1960), 141; Burlingame, *Abraham Lincoln*, 2:407.

50. J. G. Holland, *The Life of Abraham Lincoln* (1865; Springfield, Mass.: Gurdon Bill, 1866), 393; Burlingame, *Abraham Lincoln*, 2:407.

51. Charles Farrar Browne, *Artemus Ward, His Book* (New York: Carleton, 1862), 34–35.

52. Quoted in Sandburg, *Lincoln: The War Years*, 4:117.

53. Browne, "The Shakers," in *Artemus Ward*, 22–35.

54. Sandburg, *Lincoln: The War Years*, 3:342.

55. Carpenter, *Six Months in the White House*, 151.

56. Sandburg, *Lincoln: The War Years*, 3:350.

57. Browne, "Interview with President Lincoln," in *Artemus Ward*, 180–81.

58. Ibid., 184–86.

59. *Lincoln Day-by-Day*, 326.

60. Browne, "Cruise of the Polly Ann," in *Artemus Ward*, 170.

61. Ibid., 172–73.

62. Ibid., 175.

63. Quoted in Burlingame, *Abraham Lincoln*, 2:720–21; the occasion (October 11, 1864) was an evening at the War Department, as Lincoln, Stanton, and others awaited election returns (*Lincoln Day-by-Day*, 288–89).

64. David Ross Locke, *The Nasby Letters* (Toledo, Ohio: Toledo Blade, 1893), 4. As had Browne/Ward, Locke/Nasby also fabricated an interview with Lincoln (ibid., 15–17).

65. Locke, "Negro Emigration," in *The Nasby Letters*, 5.

66. Ibid., 6.

67. Sandburg, *Lincoln: The War Years*, 3:354.

68. Locke, *The Nasby Letters* (Boston: I. N. Richardson, 1872), 7.

69. Ibid., 8. The pamphlet Sumner refers to comprised the gathering of Nasby letters published in 1864, from the earliest, "Wingert's Corners Secedes," through "Dreams," dated February 4, 1864.

70. Gideon Welles, *Diary of Gideon Welles*, ed. Howard K. Beale, 3 vols. (New York: W. W. Norton, 1960), 1:333.

71. Robert Henry Newell, *The Orpheus C. Kerr Papers*, 1st series (1862; New York: Blakeman & Mason, 1863), 285–86.

72. Ibid., 32, 201.

73. Ibid., 40.
74. *Collected Works*, 4:383.
75. Alexander Pope, *Selected Poems* (Oxford: Oxford University Press, 1963), 116.
76. Matthew Pinsker, *Lincoln's Sanctuary: Abraham Lincoln and the Soldiers' Home* (New York: Oxford University Press, 2003), 177–78.
77. Newell, *Orpheus C. Kerr Papers*, 1st series, 363.
78. Ibid., 36.
79. Ibid., 186–89.
80. William Scott, *Lessons in Elocution* (Philadelphia: W. Young, 1788), 354–56.
81. Warren, *Lincoln's Youth*, 76.
82. *Lincoln Day-by-Day*, 173, 227–28.
83. *Collected Works*, 6:393, n. 1. Hackett proved not to be a disinterested party in the correspondence. Not only did he release Lincoln's letter but also, like hundreds of others, tried to get a job out of the president—consul in London—which post he was denied (Burlingame, *Abraham Lincoln*, 2:744).
84. *Collected Works*, 6:392.
85. Ibid., 6:393 n. 1.
86. Ibid., 6:559.
87. *Hamlet* 3.3.53–55.
88. *Macbeth* 1.7.26–28.
89. Carpenter, *Six Months at the White House*, 49–51.
90. *Lincoln Day-by-Day*, 243.
91. Eleanor Ruggles, *Prince of Players: Edwin Booth* (New York: W. W. Norton & Co., 1953), 157; Noah Brooks, "Personal Reminiscences of Lincoln," *Scribner's Monthly* 15 (1877–78), 675.
92. Brooks, "Personal Reminiscences of Lincoln," 675.
93. "Spectacle is emotionally powerful but is the least integral part of all to the poet's art: for the potential of tragedy does not depend upon public performance and actors" (Aristotle, *Poetics*, ed. and trans. Stephen Halliwell [Chapel Hill: University of North Carolina Press, 1987], 38–39).
94. Kelso "drew Lincoln after him by his talk . . . they became exceedingly intimate . . . they loitered away whole days together, along the banks of the quiet streams . . . Lincoln learned to love inordinately our 'divine William' and 'Scotia's' bard, whom his friend mouthed in his cups, or expounded more soberly in the intervals of fixing bait and dropping line" (Lamon [Black], *The Life of Abraham Lincoln*, 144–45}.
95. Pinsker, *Lincoln's Sanctuary*, 10.
96. *Richard III* 1.1.1–4.
97. Carpenter, *Six Months at the White House*, 51–52.
98. *King John* 3.4.76–77, 93–98.
99. Burlingame, *Abraham Lincoln*, 2:297–300.
100. LeGrand B. Cannon, in *Herndon's Informants*, 679. Cannon published a similar version of this story in his *Personal Reminiscences of the Rebellion, 1861–66* (1895).
101. Carpenter, *Six Months at the White House*, 30; Sandburg, *Lincoln: The War Years*, 3:47.
102. *Macbeth* 5.5.18–27.
103. Ibid., 3.2.18–28; emphasis added.
104. Aldebert de Chambrun, *Impressions of Lincoln and the Civil War* (New York: Random House, 1952), 83.

105. Sandburg, *Abraham Lincoln: The War Years*, 4:195. According to Lincoln scholar Michael Burlingame, "Lamon's account of Lincoln's dream is highly suspect" (e-mail communication to the author, December 14, 2009). I have used it, nonetheless, as emblematic of Lincoln's tragic Shakespearean state during the last weeks of his life.
106. Ibid., 4:244–45.
107. *Richard II* 3.2.155–60.

Index

Robert Bray is the Colwell Professor of English at Illinois Wesleyan University, where he teaches nineteenth-century American literature, Caribbean literature, and Abraham Lincoln in fiction and biography. He is the author of *Rediscoveries: Literature and Place in Illinois* and *Peter Cartwright, Legendary Frontier Preacher.*